Partnership Education In Action

Edited by
Dierdre Bucciarelli
and
Sarah Pirtle

Center for Partnership Studies
Tucson, AZ 85751

We dedicate this book to our children and grandchildren, nieces and nephews, Alexander, Allie, Andrea, Benjamin, Bree-Olette, Brian, Cameron K, Cameron R, Dalia, Damon, Dana, Daniel, Dashiell, David, Emily, Emma, Eric, Eron, Eve, Geoffrey, Jackie, Jason, Jayden, Julia, Juno, Justin, Kelly Rose, Kristen, Kuri, Laura, Leora, Loren, Lucius, Mathew, Oliver, Robin B-T, Robin L-M , Ryan, Scott, Tommy, Wendy, and all the children of today and tomorrow.

TABLE OF CONTENTS

Acknowledgments

This book could not have come to fruition without the assistance and loving care of a great many people. Each contributed in her/his own way. But, no matter what their contributions were, they were all essential and are greatly appreciated.

We, first, want to thank the Center for Partnership Studies for engaging us to edit this book.

We are deeply indebted to the authors who worked in a partnership way with us to nurture and develop this book. Our sincere appreciation goes to Lethea Fay Erz, David Ketter, Jim Knight, Ron Miller, Bobbi Morrison, Elaine Packard, Ruthmary Powers, and Mara Sapon-Shevin.

Many thanks to Del Jones, Executive Director of Center for Partnership Studies and Director of the Partnership Education Program for her many wonderful qualities, including her unfailing personal support and leadership ability. It has been our great good fortune to work with Del.

We wish to express our heartfelt gratitude to the Center's president, Riane Eisler, the author of *Tomorrow's Children*, for her original work with partnership education, which stimulated us to publish this book. We are, moreover, indebted to her for her invaluable editorial assistance whose writing is an inspiration to us all.

Very special thanks to Ron Miller for his guidance and superb editorial skill, and steadfast commitment to this project. He never refused any request for help. We are, as well, grateful for his preface to this book and his Overview of *Tomorrow's Children*.

We extend our appreciation to all Partnership Education Institute participants who commented on and reviewed manuals that were used in the preparation of this book, including Jana Buck, Maureen Cain, Kathleen Cochrane, Teresa Cowan-Jones, Margret Crowdes, Scott Forbes, Marlin Foxworth, Christine Gomes, Lawrence Koss, Werner Krieglstein, Sonya Lanzen-Castellanos, David Loye, Nick Manolukas, Arlene Marks, Carol Massanari, Steve Motenko, Heidi Neale, Bruce Novak, Barclay Palmer, Belvie Rooks, Laurie Rubin, Hollis Stewart, Lynn Stoddard, Vivian Swearingen, Pam Hale Trachta, and anyone else inadvertently excluded. Much gratitude is owed to Louise Sample for a close reading and editing of an earlier version of Part Two of this book. And, thank you to Sheila Mannix for her help in the initial stages of this project.

Sincere thanks to the Center for Partnership Studies as well as to Riane Eisler, Karen Davis-Brown and Jim Knight for permission to use the graphics they designed for the August 1999 Weaving The Future workshop in West Chester, Pa.

We are grateful to John Mason for permission to use his curriculum loom and learning tapestry, originally created for use in *Tomorrow's Children*.

Earnest appreciation to DeNeill Phinney for essential formatting help, computer wizardry, and proofreading. Thanks go, also, to Merle Jones, proofreader, to publishing manager Charles Jakiela, and Norma Montaigne, book designer.

We, also, want to thank Leslie Trifilio of Design Concepts for her cover design. The cover photo is by Camille Tokerud; it is copyrighted by the photographer and by Tony Stone Images, Chicago, and we are grateful for permission to use it.

Thank you to Teachers College Press and editor, William Ayers, for permission to reprint Mara Sapon-Shevin's article, "Building a Safe Community for Learning," from *To Become a Teacher: Making a Difference in Children's Lives.*

Grateful acknowledgment to Educators for Social Responsibility for permission to reprint the song activities, "My Roots Go Down," and "The Colors of Earth," from *Linking Up! Using Music, Movement and Language Arts to Promote Caring, Cooperation, and Communication.* "What the Spirals Say "originally appeared in *Discovery Time for Cooperation and Conflict Resolution* (Nyack, NY: Children's Creative Response to Conflict, 1998).

We are especially grateful to the Foundation for Educational Renewal and the Threshold Foundation for their generous grants that made the writing and publication of this book possible.

Finally, we would be remiss not to express our gratitude for the support, encouragement, and sacrifices made by family members for the duration of this project. Our deepest and most loving appreciation goes to all of them.

D.B. & S.P.

Preface

When you first hear the expression "partnership education," it may sound like many other models and techniques that have been proposed over the years for improving schools. Many of these improvements are little more than gimmicks promising instant results in the classroom, and garnering healthy profits for their promoters; teachers and parents are wise to examine them with a critical eye. When you take a closer look at Partnership Education, I think you will agree that it is no gimmick. While Partnership Education offers a new, much needed model based on Riane Eisler's extensive research and its practical application to education, it also distills much of the best theory and practice developed by educational visionaries over the last hundred years. Eisler and her colleagues have successfully blended a thoughtful, insightful theory of education with an exceptionally useful and practical model of teaching and curriculum development.

A partnership-oriented curriculum, while very concrete and specific, is not a cookbook full of recipes to be slavishly followed. The teacher's wisdom and passions matter, and the students' goals and interests matter. Education is seen as a collaborative adventure, a true partnership in pursuit of understanding and meaning, and not—as the "Standardistos" would have it C a mechanical transfer of bits of information. Teachers need concrete ideas, and a partnership curriculum suggests many. Ultimately, however, Partnership Education is defined by its moral mission, not by the specific content of the curriculum. Education is never morally neutral, because it defines how we as a society or community understand the world and what we value. Reducing the pursuit of wisdom and meaning into standardized content, and relentlessly testing students to sort out academic winners from losers, is not merely a scientific or objective endeavor, but a moral vision of society—a vision that empowers technocrats and rewards fierce competition. Partnership Education is openly and frankly committed to a different vision of society, one that values the diverse abilities and potentials of all people, and tries to make a place for each of us. Partnership Education honors critical intelligence and scholastic achievement, but it is not merely a trick for raising students' test scores. It is a serious effort to help young people grow into responsible, kind, well-informed, capable adults and to make education an agency for cultural renewal and social justice.

Partnership Education as a coherent model is highly original, yet some of its core ideas are time tested. This is the kind of education that John Dewey wrote hundreds of densely-packed pages about during his long career, and many streams of progressive education find expression here. Although differing in details, it is also the kind of education that Maria Montessori, Paulo Freire, and other liberators of the human spirit described and practiced. It is remarkably similar to what many of us have been promoting in the emerging international movement known as "holistic" education. So, in taking seriously the theory and practices articulated in this book and in Eisler's inspiring book *Tomorrow's Children*, be assured that you are not joining some new educational fad that will quickly be replaced by yet another: You are being invited to share a moral vision of education and society that women and men from around the world have, for a century or more, believed to be an antidote to the cruelty, inhumanity and violence of the modern age. We believe that the creation of a more loving, compassionate, and just society is the genuine purpose of education.

Dr. Ron Miller
President, Foundation for Educational Renewal

Putting Partnership Education Into Practice: Using this Book

by Dierdre Bucciarelli

You hold in your hands a resource book that can help guide your efforts to use the inspiring way of thinking about education, called "Partnership Education," that was developed by Riane Eisler in her book, *Tomorrow's Children: A Blueprint for Partnership Education in the 21st Century*. This book is grounded on the partnership philosophy and values outlined by Eisler and is designed as a companion to her book. By providing you with guiding principles, tools, strategies, activities, and sample curricula, the authors of this book invite you to share this moral vision of education and society and translate it into concrete designs for action in your classroom and your school.

Partnership Education's educational perspective is timely because it speaks to our profound yearnings for "something more" and it responds to challenges that we confront at the dawn of the 21st century. Not only does it enable students to become all that they can be, helping them to develop their minds, hearts, spirits, and hands, it also gives students the tools to participate in the formation of a more equitable, just, and sustainable world. Few models of education are committed to both these important goals. But, in the worlds of today and tomorrow, such a plan is vital if we are to overcome both individual and institutional obstacles that stand in the way of creating both fuller selves and a more humane and caring world.

In this book we will explore the building blocks of Partnership Education and how it can be used in the classroom and the school to help us accomplish such worthy ends.

What is Partnership Education?

Partnership Education Explained

Partnership Education is a model of education that adopts a holistic or systemic approach rooted in a partnership worldview. In her earlier, ground-breaking study of cultural evolution, *The Chalice and the Blade: Our History, Our Future*, Riane Eisler identified both partnership and dominator worldviews or patterns of thinking that organize personal and social relations in cultures across time. A basic knowledge of these belief systems will help you to understand Partnership Education better. Both this book and Eisler's *Tomorrow's Children* explain the contrast between partnership and dominator patterns; for a more detailed elucidation of these patterns and an absorbing account of Eisler's historical investigation, you are urged to consult *The Chalice and the Blade*.

A *partnership* worldview refers to ways of thinking and acting in the world that embrace, as she explains, "a more democratic and egalitarian family and social structure, gender equity, a low level of institutionalized violence and abuse … and a system of beliefs, stories and values that supports and validates this kind of structure as normal and right" (*Tomorrow's Children*, p. 5). In short, a partnership perspective supports relations of reciprocity or "linking" rather than relations of control and "ranking." Partners also work in reciprocity with nature. Following is a visual representation of this model.

Partnership Model
Interactive CORE Configuration

Flexible hierachies of actualization and participatory decision-making	Violence and abuse are not institutionalized, and people and nature are respected
Neither half of humanity is ranked over the other, and women and stereotypically "feminine" values (wether these values reside in men or women) are included in governance	Belief systems are flexible, allowing exploration and awareness of both the partnership and dominator sides of the continuum

(Source: Riane Eisler with Karen Davis-Brown and Jim Knight)

A *dominator* perspective is at the opposite end of the continuum from a partnership viewpoint. It is characterized by an authoritarian family and social structure, gender inequality, a high level of institutionalized violence and abuse, and "a system of beliefs, stories, and values that make this kind of structure seem normal and right" (*Tommorow's Children*, p.4). A dominator view rests on relations of control and "ranking" where one person or group controls and "outranks" another. This worldview also leads to the "conquest of nature." Following is a visual representation of this model.

Dominator Model
Interactive CORE Configuration

Violence and abuse are
institutionalized, with little
respect for people or nature.

Rigid top-down hierarchies
of domination and
authoritarian rule

Belief systems present the
dominator model as
inevitable, normal, and right

Men and the stereotypically "masculine"
are ranked over women and the
stereotypically "feminine" — whether they
reside in women or men

(Source: Riane Eisler with Karen Davis-Brown and Jim Knight)

Partnership Education utilizes partnership ways of seeing and acting to help children acquire the tools, knowledge, skills, and dispositions they need to live their lives in democratic, caring, non-racist, and gender-balanced ways in concert with each other and with nature. When a school is a partnership school, partnership ways of thinking and acting permeate the whole school, including its content or curriculum, its process or teaching methods, and its structure or learning community. These three main interconnected elements form the core components of Partnership Education's integrated approach.

The Three Components Of Partnership Education

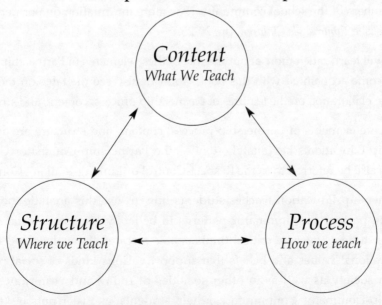

(Source: Riane Eisler with Karen Davis-Brown and Jim Knight)

While we have separated partnership process, content, and structure to make their meaning clearer and to help in the learning process, it is extremely important to realize that these three elements are not actually separate and distinct in the practice of a partnership school. In fact, one of the hallmarks of a partnership school is that partnership process, content, and structure are all thoroughly united.

• *Partnership process* is about *how* we learn and teach. It refers to what are commonly called teaching methods and techniques. In general, partnership process means that teachers work in a collaborative or partnership mode with their students, honoring their students' multiple intelligences, ways of knowing, and interests. (For more information on partnership process, see *Tomorrow's Children*, pp. 13-16.)

• *Partnership content* is about *what* we learn and teach. It refers to the curriculum. Partnership content fairly and accurately includes the accomplishments and knowledge of both women and men as well as many cultures and ethnicities. It also helps children to recognize partnership and dominator patterns throughout history and to understand that human possibilities can be expanded through partnership values and structures. (For more information on partnership content, see *Tomorrow's Children*, pp. 16-20, pp. 59-243, and Appendices A and C for sample curricula.)

• *Partnership structure* is about *where* learning and teaching take place. It refers to the kind of learning environment, culture or system of learning that we create. Partnership structure provides for a learning environment that models and fosters caring, respectful, and democratic interactions between and among all members of the school community. (For more information on partnership structure, see *Tomorrow's Children*, pp. 20-25.)

You will learn much more about the role of these elements in Partnership Education as you become acquainted with this book. You can also see the table on the following page for an elaboration on the features of partnership process, content, and structure.

The core elements of partnership process, content, and structure are anchored in Partnership Education's key analytic tool — the Partnership-Dominator Continuum, which can also be referred to as the Respect-Control or Linking-Ranking Continuum.

Partnership Education teaches students how to use this analytic tool to reveal underlying partnership-dominator patterns in belief systems and social structures. This helps students become critical thinkers able to carefully analyze and investigate the foundational values and beliefs that support various kinds of social relations in their own society as well as in other societies of today and yesterday. Using the Partnership-Dominator Continuum can help students, as Eisler puts it, "to think in holistic terms — that is in terms of relationships" (*Tomorrow's Children* p. 13).

Partnership Education Content, Process, and Structure

What We Teach (Content)

Women and girls featured equally with males

Multicultural education systemically integrated into the whole curriculum

Respect for, and partnership with, the natural environment

Models of social equity and personal responsibility

Emphasis on our highest human potentials

How We Teach (Process)

With understanding and respect for each child's multiple intelligences

Providing opportunities for both group and individual creativity and innovation with learning directed and initiated by the student

Defining the instructor's role as a resource and facilitator

Recognizing that learning is both a linear and non-linear process

Where We Teach (Structure)

All participants have a voice in planning, evaluation, and policy-making

Responsibility is shared among staff, students, parents, and the community

Relationships are viewed as links rather than ranks

Accountability flows in both directions, instead of from just the bottom up

The only hierarchies are those of actualization, providing structural support for nurturance and guidance

In a partnership approach, students learn that both dominator and partnership models are possibilities for human relations and organizations, but they learn that dominator ways are not inevitable. They learn that how one lives one's life can make a positive difference and they discover that by working together with others they can have a profound impact on changing structures of domination, structures that work against creating a more democratic, egalitarian, peaceful, caring, and environmentally sustainable world. In a partnership school, partnership process, content, and structure all harmonize to foster these goals. (See the following table for examples of this partnership unity as well as for examples of dominator values in process, content, and structure.)

Examples of The Partnership-Dominator Continuum In Educational Structure, Process and Content

The Partnership Model Values and Supports:	The Dominator Model Values and Supports:
Teacher and student knowledge and experience valued	Teacher is the sole source of information and knowledge
Learning and teaching are integrated and multi-disciplinary	Learning and teaching are artificially fragmented and compartmentalized
Gender-balance in curriculum, leadership, and decision-making	Male-centered curriculum: male-controlled leadership and decision-making
Multicultural reality of human experience valued and tapped as source of learning	One culture's world view is the measure with which others are analyzed and evaluated
Social and physical sciences emphasize our inter-connection with other people and nature	Social and physical sciences emphasize the conquest of people and nature
Mutual responsibility, empathy, and caring are highlighted and modeled	Relations based on control, manipulation, and one-upmanship highlighted and modeled

---

Partnership Education not only helps students to recognize barriers, it also opens up new horizons and assists them in actualizing, as expressed by Eisler, their "great human potentials for creativity and caring." Partnership Education gives students hope for the future as well as the tools for personal and social empowerment and transformation. By means of its integrated and holistic approach, Partnership Education helps children acquire what they need to live in partnership ways with each other and with nature.

How This Book Originated

This book had its origin at the first Partnership Education Institute, convened and sponsored by the Center for Partnership Studies, which took place in Tucson, Arizona, in late summer 2000. Most of the authors of this book met there for the first time. Here we got to know each other and learn of our mutual commitment to the kinds of holistic principles and practices that a model of education like Partnership Education advocates. We found that we were attracted to Partnership Education, in particular, because of its concern for developing the whole child and, at the same time, providing children with the tools that they can use to help make the world a more just, more caring place. In brief, we came together out of a general desire to foster partnership values in the world and in education. We had all been inspired by reading Riane Eisler's book, *Tomorrow's Children* and we wanted to work to put such ideas into practice. Riane, along with her husband, author David Loye, also participated with us at the Institute.

We spent several days together dialoguing about Partnership Education and engaging in exercises that could heighten our awareness of partnership educational issues. Some of us, whose work is represented in this book, were presenters at the Institute. We later invited Bobbi Morrison, Elaine Packard, and Mara Sapon-Shevin to join us as authors because of their unique perspectives and because we know they, too, are devoted to fostering partnership values.

We view this book as a collaborative effort not only with each other as authors but with like-minded people all over the world who also feel the obligation to try to make the world a more caring, loving, and just place, and who believe, with us, that Partnership Education holds the promise of helping us to create this world. We hope you will join us, as partners, in this endeavor.

Purpose of This Book and How It Can Be Used

We developed this book because we know it can be a daunting task to try to undertake any new pursuit alone, especially one as grand and inspiring as this. This book is designed to be a resource or reference book that can give teachers and other educators a general understanding of some aspects of the theory of Partnership Education, as well as a sense of the different approaches and content that can be utilized to achieve partnership goals.

This is also a practical manual or workbook that you can use to facilitate the implementation of partnership practices in your own educational setting. It contains many examples of activities, curricula, and processes that you can draw on to create exciting and caring classroom environments that are characteristic of Partnership Education. It also includes explanations and examples of partnership school culture and organizational structures that can be put into place in your school. You can feel confident knowing that many of the units, projects, and practices have been field and time-tested in actual schools and classrooms. We think you will find that you can easily use or adapt the ideas in this book.

Of course, this book does not represent all possible ways of practicing Partnership Education. Although there is much that is new with Partnership Education, there is also much that teachers will find familiar and so we encourage you to build on what you already know as you begin to explore the holistic perspective that Partnership Education offers.

It is important to point out that this book does not attempt to provide you with a packaged curriculum, a scope and sequence chart, or a set of prescribed methods to follow. In fact this would be contrary to the tenets of Partnership Education. By acquainting you with partnership theory, we hope to help you become more aware of the underlying values that are implicit in partnership educational practice. By providing you with practical tools, we hope to help you put a partnership perspective into practice in your classroom and school.

As a way to proceed, we suggest that, after you finish reading this introduction, you next read "An Overview of Riane Eisler's *Tomorrow's Children*" by Ron Miller, also in this volume. This overview will be especially helpful to those who have not yet read *Tomorrow's Children*. Those who have read and enjoyed Eisler's book will find it a useful refresher. But, neither the overview nor this book as a whole should be considered a replacement or substitute for reading *Tomorrow's Children*. *Tomorrow's Children* contains both the theoretical knowledge upon which Partnership Education is based and a wealth of ideas for activities and curricula, especially for the high school and college levels.

Next, we recommend that you glance through the three main parts of this book that correspond to the three main components of Partnership Education, partnership process, partnership content, and partnership structure, to determine what interests you the most and has the most relevance for your situation. You can use this book in any order as you become familiar with Partnership Education and as you work to put the elements of Partnership Education into practice — as long as you keep in mind that all of the segments of Partnership Education complement each other and operate together in an integrated fashion.

Once you have looked through the main chapters of the book, you will want to preview the last chapter, where you will find suggestions for the next steps you can take with Partnership Education and where you will see our open invitation to you to participate with us at the Center for Partnership Studies in this new undertaking. You will also want to consult the appendix, where you can become acquainted with self-assessment tools that you can use to begin a conversation about Partnership Education in your school and beyond.

You may find it helpful to keep a journal, a narrative account, or some other record of your experience and findings with Partnership Education. This record can serve as a way to evaluate and reflect on the success of your efforts with Partnership Education which, in turn, can be used to improve your practice and make you a better educator. It can also be used to get to know yourself and your students better as co-participants in Partnership Education ways of thinking and acting. And, if you share your reports with us (please see the last chapter), they can help us provide documentation for both the benefits and limitations of specific partnership practices so that we can make necessary changes and continue to move forward in our efforts.

Who Can Use This Book?

Partnership Education in Action was written to assist teachers and other educators in putting Partnership Education into practice in their classrooms and schools. But it can be used by anyone who has an interest in transforming educational practices into more partnership-oriented ones. It can be used by individual teachers, administrators, and support staff, as well as students and parents. It can also be put to use by groups of such individuals working together to implement a partnership educational approach. Home schooling families will also find much of worth here. In short, anyone concerned to bring partnership values into fruition in educational settings — whether the classroom, the school, or the home — will find much that is valuable and practical in this guidebook.

What Does this Book Contain?

Overview of Contents

This book is divided into three main parts, corresponding to the three main constituents of Partnership Education: partnership process or teaching methods, partnership content or curriculum, and partnership structure or school environment. In each section you will find concrete tools and tactics that you can use to help you put these components into practice. As you strive to implement a partnership model of education, it is important to remember that process, content, and structure are all tightly interwoven in the day-to-day operation of a partnership school.

In addition to acquainting you with practical strategies, you will find that various articles in this book also introduce you to partnership principles and facets of partnership theory. Although it is not necessary to have a deep understanding of the theory of Partnership Education in order to implement it, knowing the theoretical foundations can only help you do it better because you will have a more comprehensive and systematic understanding of what you, yourself, strive to accomplish. Ideally, theory should guide practice and practice should inform theory. This is why the practical applications in this book touch upon theoretical concerns.

Ron Miller's "An Overview of Riane Eisler's *Tomorrow's Children: A Blueprint for Partnership Education in the 21st Century*" helps to illuminate the importance of the connection between theory and practice. He not only summarizes Eisler's book, he also highlights the theoretical and philosophical underpinnings of a partnership model of education and discusses their special relevance to educational practice today. He shows how the Partnership-Dominator Continuum is used by Eisler as an analytic lens to examine both traditional disciplines and more contemporary subjects, such as media studies. He also discusses the necessary attention Eisler gives to domains of theory and practice that she calls, "Caring for Life" — domains that until now have been considered separate from the traditional disciplines but must be integrated into such study if our human world is to survive and flourish.

Partnership Process

Part One consists of chapters one through five. It also contains a brief introduction that restates the basic definition of partnership process. The articles in this part of the book present some of the principles upon which partnership process is based as well as many ways of implementing such processes.

In Chapter 1, "Practicing Linking," Sarah Pirtle presents a multitude of activities and strategies that can be used in the classroom to foster the partnership practice of "linking," whereby students learn to work together in a way that values everyone's contributions and creativity. She shows how to use cooperative activities, including morning greetings, to provide concrete ways for students to link. She also demonstrates how to use academic projects to increase interaction among students. Practicing patience and acceptance, learning to carefully listen and ask questions, and encouraging creativity are all essential "meta-skills" that she identifies in her classroom activities. Linking practices are important because, as she states, they "build the classroom community and help students feel safe as they take creative risks."

In Chapter 2, "Building A Safe Community for Learning," Mara Sapon-Shevin describes a number of educational scenarios and analyzes their implications for the

creation of classroom community. She wants us to understand that all decisions teachers make "have an impact on how students will learn, how they will treat one another,
and what the classroom atmosphere will feel like." She elaborates on her belief that
community building should "assume primary rather than secondary status in thinking
about teaching" and she asks us to consider what underlying values support community. Mara helps us to see that community is built and supported by values of friendship, trust, respect, and caring that help create an environment where students feel
safe. "Safety," she explains, "is the essence of community. A community is a safe space
to grow, a space that welcomes you fully, that sees you for who you are, that invites
your participation, and that holds you gently while you explore." She illustrates these
principles through her abundant and informative examples of readily usable classroom
community-building activities for every level of education.

In Chapter 3, "Learning: Bringing Conversation into the Heart of the Classroom,"
Jim Knight applies his well-researched findings on Teacher-Guided Professional
Development to practices within the classroom. Jim highlights partnership principles
such as equality, choice, dialogue, praxis, voice, and symbiosis. He describes six
Partnership Learning Processes: Thinking Devices, Question Recipes, Cooperative
Learning, Reflection Learning, Experiential Learning, and Stories. Continuing use of
these processes can help teachers become more skilled partnership educators. But they
are not methods to be followed in a mechanical way, rather, they are "tools to be used
to create an enriching learning community, a group-learning setting where everyone
grows and develops together."

In Chapter 4, "Transforming Violence: Peacebuilding, Anti-Bias Awareness, and
Conflict Resolution," Sarah Pirtle makes us aware of the need for schools to address the
overwhelming social climate of violence that children must confront every day. She
shows how Partnership Education "blows the whistle" on our implicit social acceptance
of the violence by allowing students to talk about the violence they see all around them
and helping them understand that they can make choices for peace and can collectively
work to create a safe, peaceful world. She offers guidelines for using partnership
processes in conversations about violence, and she provides activities that can be used
to heighten our awareness of the presence of violence in our society, as well as activities
that can help us resolve conflict and interrupt bias. Sarah encourages us to think of the
metaphor of violence as a "virus" and shares a poem called, "Don't Pass It On."

In Chapter 5, "Partnership Teaching: Our Own Growth," Sarah Pirtle encourages
us as educators to reflect on or attune ourselves to the cultures we create in our own
schools and classrooms. It is crucially important for us to do this since "partnership
schools are made of people who personally embody partnership values" and "hold the
pattern of partnership in the way they live, think, and interact." She provides tools that

can help teachers attune themselves to partnership values, as well as valuable exercises that school staff can use together to align themselves to a common partnership purpose. In addition she presents partnership processes that can be used by students and staff alike. Throughout, she invites us to draw on our own inner resources to nurture our own partnership voices and those of our students. She gives us the confidence to use partnership processes to approach teaching as an art.

Partnership Content

Part two is composed of eight chapters. In order to provide a thorough introduction to partnership content, we have presented several examples that can be used at all grade levels beginning in kindergarten. To give you a deeper understanding, the theoretical underpinnings of partnership content are also discussed in various chapters. Part two includes chapters six through thirteen as well as a short introduction that reiterates the meaning of partnership content and presents a sketch of this section.

Chapter 6, "Partnership Education: A Place to Begin — Seventeen Sample Activities," by Sarah Pirtle offers a wide variety of activities that you can incorporate into your curriculum. She also provides general guidelines for how to create a partnership activity. You will be able to use these activities *as is* in your classroom or you can modify them to suit your own purposes and particular circumstances. They can also act as springboards to design your own curriculum and activities. You will find that they are appropriate for many grade levels and cross many disciplinary lines. Sarah's activities culminate in a school celebration, a weekly partnership assembly that students help facilitate.

In Chapter 7, "Elements of Partnership Curriculum Planning based on the Curriculum Loom and Learning Tapestry," Dierdre Bucciarelli notes that, while there are no formulas to follow in planning a partnership curriculum, there are elements that must be included if the curriculum is to be considered a partnership one. She, thus, proposes a framework, which is based on the Curriculum Loom and Learning Tapestry outlined in *Tomorrow's Children*, that can be used to help with Partnership Curriculum planning. She also shows how to utilize the core elements of this framework in the initial curriculum planning stages as she begins to weave the horizontal and vertical threads of her sample curriculum tapestry on the Partnership Curriculum Loom.

In Chapter 8, "Foods and Plants — A Story: An example of a curriculum woven on the curriculum loom," Dierdre Bucciarelli continues the development of the sample curriculum, "Foods and Plants: A Story," that she began in the last chapter. In this chapter, she provides detailed lesson plans, activities, readings, and resources that can be used with kindergartners through third graders. This sample demonstrates the use of all of the elements of partnership curriculum planning.

In Chapter 9, "Music to Build Partnership," Sarah Pirtle notes how, since time immemorial, music has been "a primary force for experiencing community and connection." Yet, she points out, many of us have experienced music from within a dominator paradigm which ranks the best and the worst. She asserts that this is not necessary and offers five guidelines for how to "use music so that it takes place within a partnership paradigm." She also presents nine lesson plans (applicable to kindergarten through twelfth grade) that utilize these guidelines while introducing partnership content through the lyrics of songs. All of the music is written by Sarah and the lyrics draw on her talent as a songwriter.

In Chapter 10, "The Conscience of the Earth: Weaving the Theme of Evolution Using the Expressive Arts," Sarah Pirtle shows the many ways in which a diverse array of expressive arts — such as storytelling, creative dramatics, music, art, poetry, drawing, and movement activities — can both increase students' comprehension of the curriculum and provide direct participation in partnership relations. She helps us to understand that "when we participate in the arts in a partnership process, we are directly part of human evolution" since we are "encoded to create." She not only provides guidelines for developing expressive arts lesson plans, she also offers a month-long partnership curriculum unit on evolution with many science and social studies activities. This unit employs a variety of expressive arts forms while first through twelfth graders learn about their history and the history of the earth.

In Chapter 11, "The Connections Curriculum at Nova School," for grade levels nine through twelve, Bobbi Morrison reports on her curriculum on cosmology, myth, systems theory and cultural transformation that she developed as part of Nova's multi-disciplinary course called, "Connections." Her curriculum shows the link between the study of mythology and an understanding of partnership and dominator values. She shares four distinct curriculum units related to these themes, a "Cosmology and Creation Myth Unit" where students study the creation myths of seven different cultures; a "Myth and Symbols Unit" where students investigate symbols, especially female symbols, from various cultures and their relation to myth; a "Myth and Connections Unit" in which students use the lens of mythology to discover common threads that run through human existence; and "Systems Theory and Cultural Transformation," where students study how systems operate in order to understand systemic human behaviors that maintain partnership ways of being.

In Chapter 12, "Speaking Our Peace: Teaching the Language of Partnership," Lethea Fay Erz calls our attention to the many ways in which our language is riddled with dominator assumptions. She tells us that "if we hope to create a truly new paradigm based on partnership thinking, it's vital that we be aware of the underlying messages in the very words and metaphors we use to express our thoughts. If we don't, our good intentions may be undermined by the language we use to state them." Through activities and curriculum ideas, appropriate for grades six through twelve, she helps teachers and students examine the English language for both overt and hidden manifestations of sexism and other forms of "ranking." These activities also enable students to take a close look at the implications of language that we often use unconsciously on a daily basis. Other exercises help students figure out how we might we go about transforming language to reflect a partnership orientation.

In Chapter 13, "The Wisdom of the Elders: Curricular Resources for Unlearning Sexism," Sarah Pirtle provides a wealth of Internet resources (sponsored by both women's and men's organizations) that teachers can use to help their students unlearn sexism. She underscores the fact that "sexism is a matter of power and changing sexism means changing well-entrenched 'power-over' mechanisms." She shows that sexism makes it difficult for girls to develop a positive gender identity, but that boys are also hurt by it. Besides her astute theoretical discussion, she also presents sample activities that educators can use to help their students unlearn sexism. She closes her essay with visions of a new partnership curriculum that incorporate considerations about the shortcomings of typical disciplinary practices and she draws on the insights of our "wise elders," women and men, to help us "forge a new path."

Partnership Structure

In Part Three, experienced educators David Ketter, Bobbi Morrison, Elaine Packard, and Ruthmary Powers discuss the third element of Partnership Education. In the introduction and in chapters fourteen and fifteen, the authors help to clarify the concept of partnership structure and present examples of partnership-oriented school environments in action.

In Chapter 14, "Partnership Structure at Nova School," David Ketter, Bobbi Morrison, and Elaine Packard, all educators at this public high school of 250 students in Seattle, give us a real feel for the democratic decision-making and learning structures that have been in place at Nova since 1973 and that students and teachers participate in together. They explain in detail the workings of "the four C's" that Nova is guided by: committees, contracts, coordinating, and community, and they give plentiful examples of the built-in structures of the four C's that promote partnership values among students and staff. As they tell us, "Nova is a place where students don't just hear about values; they practice and live out democracy, responsibility, and choice."

Their vibrant descriptions draw us into the life of Nova School and help us understand how partnership structure is meant to work.

In Chapter 15. "Partnership Structure," Ruthmary Powers draws on her own experience as she raises critical questions about the calls for "restructuring" in education that have been mounted in recent years. Genuine restructuring of educational institutions, as she tell us, "must address the hierarchy of roles, the dynamics of power, and the maintenance of rules and procedures that determine the atmosphere in which teaching and learning take place." She notes how partnership education takes these issues seriously and makes use of the work of Riane Eisler, Peter Senge, and others to provide us with a conceptual understanding of the systemic "cultural" change that partnership restructuring requires. By means of her examples and practical advice, she also shows how we can actually begin to create school structures and cultures that help us engender and nurture partnership communities of learning.

Next Steps

We invite you to participate with us creating your own partnership content, exploring new partnership processes, and working in new partnership structures or environments. The last chapter, "Closing: Your Next Steps with Partnership Education," provides specific information on how you can get involved in becoming partners with us in developing this new vision of education through the Center for Partnership Studies' Partnership Education Program (PEP). The Appendix contains a variety of self-assessment tools, created by Sarah Pirtle and Dierdre Bucciarelli, that you can use in your own classroom or school to begin a dialogue about Partnership Education.

Meet The Authors

Now, please allow me to introduce our authors:

Coincidentally, I, Dierdre Bucciarelli, am alphabetically the first author. I was introduced to Riane Eisler's educational work by my Ph.D. advisor at Stanford University, Nel Noddings, who wrote the foreword to *Tomorrow's Children*. Part of my work in this book was prepared for the Partnership Education Institute, in which I participated. I was also involved in a "trial-run" Partnership Education Institute, held in West Chester, Pennsylvania.

Inspired by Nel Noddings's ethic of care and its application to education, I decided to return to school, after a hiatus raising young children. I have long been involved with educational issues as a parent, teacher, and social justice advocate. I have experience developing curriculum and teaching courses and workshops in various subjects, where I have given special attention to multicultural and gender issues and to uncovering the structural roots of racism and sexism. I have also worked as the coordinator of the Stanford Women's Center and have served on various community boards of directors in Princeton, NJ, including the educational equity organization, the Robeson Group, which I helped found. I currently serve on the Princeton High School site council, volunteer as the NJ state coordinator for the Fairtest/Alfie Kohn networks, and teach at Rutgers University.

Riane Eisler, of course, needs no introduction. She participated as an equal member, a partner, with us at the Partnership Education Institute. Riane Eisler is a cultural historian and systems scientist best known for her international bestseller *The Chalice and the Blade*. She is the author of many other books and articles, including the highly acclaimed *Tomorrow's Children: A Blueprint for Partnership Education in the 21st Century*. She is President of the Center for Partnership Studies and has taught at UCLA, Immaculate Heart College, and the California Institute for Integral Studies. She is also a consultant to schools and businesses, and keynotes conferences worldwide.

Lethea Erz took part in and presented her dissertation research at the Partnership Education Institute where many of us came to know her and her research on partnership language for the first time. It was a real treat for us to have her introduce her research with her own musical creation that she performed for us.

Lethea is completing her Ph.D. in Gylanic Studies at the Union Institute. Her dissertation is entitled, *Speaking Our Peace: Communicating Partnership in Deed and Word; a Curriculum for Teacher Education*. An educator (K-12, university), instructional designer, and workshop facilitator since 1974, she is also a professional storyteller, harp therapist, and reiki master. She has facilitated many partnership workshops in the US and New Zealand. Her CD, *Parables of Partnership*, combines transformative storytelling for adults with Celtic harp music. Lethea's work uses the power of re-mything to shift consciousness from domination toward partnership between women and men, among diverse human groups, and between humanity and the rest of Nature.

David Ketter also joined with us at the Partnership Education Institute and contributed his essential knowledge as a high school teacher, who has for a long time been involved in the creation of a partnership curriculum at Nova High School. David was also involved in a "trial-run" Partnership Education Institute, held in West Chester, Pennsylvania.

David is an avid naturalist, outdoorsman, and environmentalist who holds a masters degree in holistic/transformative education. He has been teaching for over 18 years in a wide variety of schools and education programs. Currently, he teaches at

Nova High School, a small democratically run public alternative school in Seattle, Washington. Last year, he and several other teachers — in consultation with Riane Eisler — developed and taught a partnership-oriented class called Connections. They are writing up the curriculum for this course for publication in the near future. David's contribution to the curriculum will be to create learning experiences that help students "link" with the earth and that facilitate students discovery of what it means to live in partnership with the earth.

Jim Knight was one of the main presenters at both the Partnership Education Institute in Tucson and the "trial-run" the year before. His dissertation research on partnership processes in teacher-guided professional development provided much of the knowledge base for the Institute.

Jim is an educational researcher at the Kansas University Center for Research on Learning. His primary research, on Partnership Learning and Teacher-Guided Professional Development, investigates how a partnership approach to school improvement can enable authentic and meaningful learning among educational professionals. Jim directs Pathways to Success, a comprehensive school reform model involving all middle schools and high schools in Topeka, Kansas, USD 501. He has presented his research across Canada, in more than 30 states, and in Japan.

Ron Miller also shared his knowledge at the Partnership Education Institute. He presented his dissertation research on the history of progressive educational movements, and his Foundation for Educational Renewal provided part of the funding for the Institute manuals. The Foundation is also assisting in the publication of this book.

Ron is currently the executive editor of the quarterly magazine *Paths of Learning*. Originally trained as a Montessori educator, he is a historian of education specializing in progressive, holistic, and alternative approaches. He co-founded both the Bellwether School near Burlington, Vermont and the John Dewey Project on Progressive Education at the University of Vermont. Ron received his Ph.D. in American Studies from Boston University. He has written or edited six books, including *What Are Schools For? Holistic Education in American Culture* and *Caring for New Life: Essays on Holistic Education*. He lives in Vermont with his family.

Bobbi Morrison was asked to join us as an author because of her long-standing expertise as a partnership educator in a high school setting. Educated in French and American universities, Bobbi wears many hats at the Nova Alternative High School in Seattle, Washington. She is the World History and Languages Teacher of French and Russian and, for the last 20 years, has fashioned the drama program. In keeping with a partnership approach to education, Bobbi's classes are noted for creating more student originated ensemble pieces on themes ranging from the Vietnam legacy, the Asian-

American immigration experience to dramatic tales of human rights abuses in Tibet, Guatemala, and East Timor. She has not only used drama as a vehicle to inhabit historical issues, but also as a means to seed cross-cultural experiences, organizing drama travel exchange programs between Russian and Nova students. Inspired by the interweaving of artistic expression with academic subjects, Bobbi's students have contributed their voices to partnering a more peaceful, creative, and sustainable future.

Elaine Packard was invited to join us as an author because of her abiding commitment to and extensive knowledge of partnership educational principles and practices. Born, raised, and educated on the East Coast, Elaine drove from Boston to Seattle in a 1963 VW van in the '60's to start a new life and a family. Her work with Nova High School began in 1971 as a volunteer facilitator in mathematics, music, and cooking. After two years of volunteering, she was hired as a mathematics teacher and became the school's director the following year. While her primary duties are administrative, she has continued to teach and serve as a coordinator for her own core group. She was a founding member and past president of the Washington Association for Learning Alternatives, a highly-recognized state organization advocating for and serving the needs of alternative education. She finds peace and quiet during her summer travels on road trips and in a tent. In addition to her passion for folkdancing, she loves being a grandmother.

Sarah Pirtle, my co-editor, was another one of the presenters at the Partnership Education Institute, where she brought her knowledge and skill of partnership educational processes into play. Without her hard work, unbounded energy, and editorial ability, this book would never have been completed.

Sarah's thirty year involvement in education has included working as a classroom teacher, graduate school teacher (The University of Vermont, Lesley University), staff development specialist, keynote speaker, and the first peace education coordinator at Traprock Peace Center. She is the author of four books including *An Outbreak of Peace*, a young adult novel which received the Olive Branch Award for outstanding book on world peace in 1988. Her books *Discovery Time for Cooperation* and *Conflict Resolution* (CCRC) and *Linking Up! Using Music, Movement and Language Arts to Promote Caring, Cooperation, and Communication* (ESR) were released in 1998.

She has recorded five CD's including *Two Hands Hold the Earth* and *The Wind is Telling Secrets* on A Gentle Wind label and has received five national awards for her original children's music. For eight years she's directed Journey Camp, a summer peace camp which is a laboratory for partnership education. Her sixteen-year-old son Ryan has been involved with her in the Children's Music Network, where she is a central founder and first editor of the journal, *Pass It On!* She has been active in feminism since 1969 and performed for seven years with the Big Mama Poetry Troupe.

Ruthmary Powers also gave a creative presentation at the Partnership Education Institute that dealt with issues of both partnership process and structure, and she took part in other sessions. For close to forty years, Ruthmary has been a Sister of the Humility of Mary, a Catholic order of religious women. Ruthmary's profound interests in people, education, culture, spirituality, and partnership have culminated in her working to create partnership communities of learning that move towards cultural transformation. As an educator, she has served as teacher, administrator, and superintendent. She has been able to use her great love of teaching on every educational level from pre-school through adult. Ruthmary's doctoral dissertation *Pathways to Partnership: Partnership Possibilities for Transforming the Educational Restructuring Movement* (1994), is based on Riane Eisler's work.

We are thrilled to have Mara Sapon-Shevin on board with us and we want to thank her and William Ayers for allowing us to reprint her article here, an article which originally appeared in his book, *To Become a Teacher: Making a Difference in Children's Lives*.

Mara is a long time peace and justice educator who is currently Professor of Education at Syracuse University in Syracuse, New York. Past co-president of the International Association for the Study of Cooperation in Education, she has led cooperative learning workshops and played cooperative games all around the world. The author of the book, *Because We Can Change the World: A Practical Guide to Building Cooperative, Inclusive Classrooms Communities*, she works actively with teachers and school districts to promote the full inclusion of all students in their neighborhood schools and to create genuine, caring communities in classrooms and schools. She is currently involved in developing and implementing anti-racism curriculum with high school and college students through a project called Eracism. Mara uses music extensively in her work, believing strongly that we need everyone's voice, and can ill-afford to silence anyone. Her two daughters, Dalia and Leora, of whom she is very proud, are also peace and justice activists.

An Overview of Riane Eisler's *Tomorrow's Children: A Blueprint for Partnership Education in the 21st Century*

by Ron Miller

Tomorrow's Children is an important book about education, because it addresses topics that normally concern teachers and administrators — curriculum, teaching/learning methods, and school culture — within a larger philosophical and historical context than educators normally consider. As its subtitle indicates, in *Tomorrow's Children* Riane Eisler proposes a new blueprint for education in the 21st century.

Much of modern educational practice still views children as impersonal components of an efficient social machine to be molded, tested, graded, and sorted like any other mechanical products or commodities. Eisler provides a stirring alternative vision for education. She argues that postindustrial society requires men and women who are flexible, creative, and independent thinkers, and that different educational practices are needed to cultivate these qualities. But the education Eisler proposes goes much further. Education, after all, does not simply involve a package of techniques practiced in school buildings: It is a cluster of beliefs, values, and assumptions representing a culture's explicit endeavor to define who we are as human beings and what our lives mean.

Tomorrow's Children builds on the research in archeology, biology, and psychology that Eisler presented in her earlier book, *The Chalice and the Blade*, published in 1987. After studying the evolution of numerous societies through history, Eisler developed a "cultural transformation theory" which identifies two basic structures that influence the character of any civilization, and in *Tomorrow's Children* she amply demonstrates how this way of understanding culture is extremely relevant to education.

These two structures represent opposite ends of a spectrum of cultural possibilities. At one end, societies can be rigid and authoritarian, where violence, abuse, and fear are used to maintain order and keep elites in power. Racial, linguistic or religious divisions are used to rank diverse human possibilities, and invariably such societies are male-dominated and highly value "masculine" qualities such as aggressiveness, competitiveness, and conquest of nature. Eisler calls this structure the *dominator model* of society. The opposite ideal structure is characterized by egalitarian and democratic values, gender equity, collaboration, caretaking, openness to diversity, environmental consciousness, and low levels of violence. Eisler terms this the *partnership model*.

Eisler has demonstrated that some cultures, including early civilizations largely forgotten by the Western world, have successfully practiced partnership values on a large scale. This fact alone, she argues, refutes philosophical and scientific claims that human beings are "naturally" violent, aggressive or selfish. These are biological possibilities of course, but so too are qualities of love, generosity, and compassion. The partnership model is a realizable moral ideal, so the perennial yet elusive dream of a truly humane, caring, nonviolent society can be achieved if we strive to develop social attitudes and practices that support partnership rather than dominator values. The primary argument of *Tomorrow's Children* is that education is an essential arena in which this must take place. "Partnership Education," then, is not merely a curriculum unit or instruction technique — it is an effort to nurture the full humanity of our young people for the purpose of creating a caring, peaceful, environmentally sustainable society.

A partnership approach addresses three major elements of education: Structure (the organization of decision-making and teaching roles), process (pedagogical relationships that invite the child to engage in learning in his or her wholeness), and content (a rich selection of thought-provoking experiences and narratives that enable young people to deeply understand their place in culture, history, and the natural world). *Tomorrow's Children* explains how an education for cultural transformation depends upon the integration of these elements, and Eisler uses the metaphor of a tapestry being woven on a loom with vertical and horizontal threads and cross-stitchings, to illustrate the complexity and interconnectedness of Partnership Education.

The particular techniques that Eisler recommends to give what she calls partnership process concrete form in classrooms are familiar to many educators — cooperative learning strategies, applications of multiple intelligence theory, integrated curriculum and experiential, project-based learning, to name a few. But Partnership Education goes much further. It grounds process, content, and structure in an integrated approach more than in any one specific method. It differs from many contemporary educational proposals in that it is not simply an add-on to the existing educational system.

Although *Tomorrow's Children* offers materials that can be immediately used by educators and students, it offers an approach that fully integrates gender-balance, multiculturalism, and environmental consciousness, as well as nonviolent conflict resolution, ethics, and caring into the entire educational fabric. Eisler states this orientation unequivocally, and expresses a clear preference for partnership over dominator values, yet she is careful not to present Partnership Education as a self-righteous moralistic approach; indeed, it would be self-defeating to promote partnership content by using conventional authoritarian, dominator-style processes. Instead, Eisler emphasizes the need for critical, reflective intelligence joined with the cultivation of empathy.

To this end, she proposes "the *partnership-dominator continuum* as an analytical lens to look at our present and our past." Students would be exposed to diverse cultural narratives — not only those that glorify conflict and conquest — and they would be encouraged to consider the wide range of cultural choices available to humanity, along with the consequences of these choices for human welfare and ecological sustainability. "A curriculum informed by the partnership model makes it possible to see that dominator relations are not inevitable, that there are viable partnership alternatives. It offers young people a larger perspective on both their day-to-day lives and on the world at large — showing that the tension between the partnership and dominator models as two basic human possibilities has punctuated all of human history."

Partnership Education essentially aims to empower young people to make thoughtful choices by offering them alternative experiences (partnership process), environments (partnership structure), and narratives (partnership content), rather than to forcibly inculcate certain forms of knowledge and values. It is also designed to cultivate what Eisler calls self-regulation (a term she prefers to self-discipline) so that young people learn to be ethical and caring primarily out of intrinsic positive motivations rather than extrinsic negative motivations, such as fear of punishment. One recurring theme in *Tomorrow's Children* is the belief that education in a democratic society must exhibit a deep sense of respect for human diversity and personal autonomy rather than seek to mold young people according to arbitrary standards: "We need to pay more attention to how children can develop their unique individual potentials rather than merely focusing on standardized test scores." Schools are seen as nurturing communities of learning.

There is a tendency in our society to assume that nurturing communities or schools based on caring are somehow contradictory to a focus on excellence in learning. *Tomorrow's Children* shows that this is a false assumption. Nurturing communities of learning also strive for student achievement and in reality create environments that support and enhance the quality of learning. Eisler recognizes that excellence in learning is more than the scores on standardized tests, which do not measure all that a student knows, but only sort students according to small portions of their understanding. True excellence in education can be established only when we use a variety of tools to assess and multiple formats to report what students really know. Doing so within a nurturing environment allows educators to better help students realize their individual potentials.

Partnership Education attempts not only to inform young people, but to inspire them. One stirring chapter of *Tomorrow's Children*, "Beginnings: From the Stars to Us," discusses humanity's place in the vast evolution of life in the cosmos. "What is the meaning of our journey on this Earth?" asks Eisler. "What about us connects us with, and distinguishes us from, the rest of nature?" Where conventional schooling often gives young people a fragmented batch of facts and curriculum "units," Partnership Education "offers young people a panoramic view of the creative sweep of evolution [that] reveals the general evolutionary movement toward ever greater variability, complexity of structure, integration of function, and flexibility of behavior." Evolution, and therefore human life, is creative, purposeful, and capable of unfathomable possibilities. Eisler provides an updated meta-narrative of evolution (from cosmic to cultural and personal) focusing on human possibilities rather than limitations. She explains that the uncritical application to human evolution of neo-Darwinian biology, with its emphasis on the purely selfish competitive struggle for survival, does not represent a neutral scientific finding, but is rather grounded in a theoretical position conditioned by the worldview of a dominator culture. In this chapter as well as another called "From Counting to Current Events: Making the Three R's Meaningful," *Tomorrow's Children* shows a different approach to science education, one that embraces a more balanced, holistic understanding of the world. Eisler describes extensive scientific literature that documents the importance of love, caring, and cooperation in the evolution of life, and she charges that most of the education young people receive about the natural world and biology neglects these significant and uncontestable findings. In these and other ways, Partnership Education integrates environmental education into the core curriculum.

Another provocative chapter, "Our Human Adventure," recaps Eisler's extensive research in archeology and mythology, explaining how dominator-oriented cultures have conquered or suppressed other forms of civilization. She argues that the earliest human societies were primarily partnership oriented, and that popular images of "primitive club-carrying Stone Age cavemen have no basis." Early human art expressed appreciation for "the life-giving and sustaining aspect of nature," and many ancient cultures appear to have been egalitarian and communal. But most modern narratives treat human history as the march of progress from "barbarian" to "civilized" humanity; they celebrate the conquerors who brought "civilization" (meaning, in U.S. textbooks, white, male-focused, Eurocentric culture), while they neglect other vital expressions of human experience. For example, most of our narratives either leave untold, misrepresent, or under-represent the stories of the lives of women in most cultures (to whom nonviolence and nurturance are relegated in dominator traditions.) A history of the experiences of both men and women in many supposedly "primitive" cultures, which have often been more partnership oriented, have also been either absent, distorted, or incomplete in our dominant narratives.

Eisler repeatedly shows that harmful messages are often embedded in the school curriculum. For example, even though children are told that nonviolence is good and violence is bad, they are at the same time required to memorize the dates of wars and battles as the historically significant events, with little attention given to nonviolently achieved social reforms. So again, children are taught what an established, dominator-oriented culture wants them to believe, and fail to receive a holistic understanding of human possibilities. *Tomorrow's Children* shows how this vital understanding can be cultivated through various academic disciplines, from mathematics to history to literature and art.

Another important topic in this book is critical media literacy. Young people in the modern world are educated by television, film, music, journalism, and other popular media at least as much as they are by parents and schools, and Eisler shows how many of the images and narratives promoted through mass media convey dominator rather than partnership values. "Children will learn that men are considered more important than women ... [and] that white people are more important than other people.... By the end of elementary school, the average child will have witnessed 8,000 murders and 100,000 other acts of violence on the TV screen" and will have been repeatedly exposed to violence being celebrated in movies and video games. The media also send strong messages — both overt and subliminal — about ideal body image, sexuality, and intimate relationships that in many ways can be psychologically damaging as well as harmful to positive, healthy relationships. An education for partnership values must help young people become conscious of harmful beliefs and behavior patterns that are taught mindlessly and insidiously by the mass media. Again, Eisler emphasizes that the point is not to moralize or censor but to "open channels of communication" and help young people think through the consequences of the behaviors and ideas that surround them.

Eisler passionately argues for a new educational system that can help young people face the unprecedented challenges of our time. She believes that modern civilization is at a crucial turning point, with two possible scenarios for future development. If recent trends continue unchallenged, we may well face societal and ecological *break-down* — a future of warfare, terrorism, ethnic violence, pollution and habitat destruction, and various forms of fundamentalism. The alternative is *breakthrough* or cultural transformation, the evolution of a partnership-oriented society "governed by standards of human rights and responsibilities.... a world where our human adventure unfolds in creative and caring ways, where the human spirit can flourish." *Tomorrow's Children* argues that substantive change in education is vital to achieving such a breakthrough, as young people who acquire a more holistic (multicultural, gender-balanced, environmentally sensitive, critically aware, and flexible) understanding of human possibilities, and who have opportunities to practice participating in democratic communities, will be much better prepared to join in building a more humane, caring, and environmentally sustainable society than those merely drilled in what are today considered academic basics and graded competitively. Eisler best sums up the goal of partnership education when she uses the phrase *Caring for Life*. That is exactly what we need to do, on a personal as well as cultural and ecological scale, if we are to avoid a violent disintegration of modern civilization.

In closing, Eisler challenges the reader of *Tomorrow's Children* to join an emerging cultural movement that is concerned with social equity, participatory democracy, environmental sustainability, and personal self-realization. While recognizing that the dominator culture strongly resists partnership values in education and other institutions, Eisler offers a positive vision, declaring that "fundamental change *is* possible" when people join together to work for values that truly serve human welfare. Eisler envisions a time in the near future when tomorrow's children "will be aware of the enormous range of their human potentials. They will be equipped to cultivate the positives within themselves and others. They will understand what makes for real political and economic democracy, and be equipped to help create and maintain it."

Tomorrow's Children: A Blueprint for Partnership Education in the 21st Century by Riane Eisler was published in 2000 by Westview Press (Boulder, Colorado), a member of the Perseus Books Group.

PART ONE

PARTNERSHIP PROCESS

Introduction to Part One, Partnership Process

Partnership process is about *how* we learn and teach. It means teaching with the whole student in mind through mutual respect and caring. It involves supporting individual feelings, gifts, abilities, and ways of knowing so that we are responsive to the unique way each person learns. It includes how what we do to build the classroom community.

Partnership process, along with partnership content and partnership structure, is one of the three key elements of Partnership Education. Although intertwined, in this section we study those particular practices that encourage positive interdependence, inclusiveness, and awareness of self and others while teaching content. Anti-bias awareness, conflict resolution skillbuilding, and character education are all in the purview of teachers attentive to partnership process.

Many teachers are already familiar with educational methods that are partnership oriented. These can include cooperative learning, multiple intelligences methods, project or inquiry-based learning, learning styles approaches, and apprenticeship learning designs. In the first three chapters of this section, authors Sarah Pirtle, Mara Sapon-Shevin, and Jim Knight give concrete examples of how partnership is fostered, being mindful of these and other practices that have been developed for decades. They discuss partnership principles and provide a treasure trove of classroom practices that can be readily used. Their goal is to assist in the daily decisions about how to teach and to reinforce why this is important.

Chapter Four deepens our understanding of what a partnership approach says about violence and oppression. Ten classroom activities help students encounter peace-building and non-violence from an anti-bias perspective. Chapter Five affirms each educator as a person expanding and developing innate partnership skills.

CHAPTER 1

Practicing Linking

by Sarah Pirtle

A truth about teachers that often gets lost in public debates is that most of us care deeply about our students and want to be the best teachers we can be. When we are greeting students, rethinking the day's lesson plans in the car on the way to work, or debriefing after school, we each look for that inner tuning fork, that standard that can act as our compass. We try to build this standard from all the best teaching we have seen or read about, as well as memories of our own teaching and our intentions for students.

During most of my three decades in education, this standard or tuning fork felt amorphous and un-nameable to me. Important practices like bias awareness, teaching with a multicultural perspective, cooperative learning, and teaching toward multiple intelligences all resonated and helped me develop a sense of whether or not I was staying on the mark. But I needed a way to hold them all together, a point of synthesis. The word "partnership" has become this synthesis for me, the touchstone I can use to decide whether I am on course or not.

In her germinal book, *The Chalice and The Blade*, Riane Eisler introduces what she calls the partnership model. She explains that any social situation can be structured to encourage "linking" and *power with others*, or structured to encourage "ranking" and *power over others*. When applied to education, linking can be described as becoming increasingly conscious of the whole group and the way we affect each other and, in turn, helping students to be increasingly conscious of the whole community. In *Tomorrow's Children*, Eisler shows how Partnership Education helps children develop their unique individual potentials by creating a culture where students are taught both parts of an essential dynamic — their individual integrity and their basic human interconnection. Partnership Education fosters excellence and achievement because it creates a culture based on the joy of learning rather than the fear of failure.

The three core elements of Partnership Education are partnership process, partnership content, and partnership structure. Partnership process consists of ways of learning and teaching based on mutual respect and caring. It pulls together what it is to be a respectful teacher of a whole person. For example, if I'm teaching a social studies lesson with partnership content, but unconsciously ignore the hands of some students who want to speak and favor others, or I use only a lecture format during the whole unit, I am not modeling partnership. My process would not be compatible with my content.

Through partnership process, the growth of each person is enhanced. There is an explicit understanding that one's personal development is not at the expense of, but rather is dynamically related to, the whole group. This chapter discusses how we as teachers can be more aware of linking as an inner tuning fork, and thereby generate the best teaching that we can. Whether we are studying math, language arts, social studies or science, as we help students develop their potential by interacting with others and valuing multiple ways of knowing, every type of learning increases. Partnership re-establishes a classroom community flowing as an open system. A hallmark of such a culture is that students are embedded within a caring community of learners.

These examples illustrate ways of making deliberate choices to encourage individual development through positive interdependence and connection among students. They provide some ideas about how you can apply partnership process in practice. I hope that they will be helpful to you as together we develop ways to articulate and explore the many dimensions of Partnership Education.

Academic Activities Can be Designed to Increase Interaction

Many teachers assign writing activities when students first arrive in the morning. One practice is to write a sentence on the board for children to copy, or to write a question on the board for students to answer in their journal. This variation encourages peer interaction.

<u>Activity:</u> Language Arts: Letter Exchange between Writing Buddies for 1st through 6th Grades

Each student writes a letter to another student during the writing time. A suggested topic is written on the board:

Suggested topics:
- Describe the look on the face of someone you know and how it tells you what they might be feeling.
- Describe a pet you have, or used to have, or a pet you wish you had.

These topics are posed only as suggestions; writers are welcome to use their own ideas. The writer can also comment on the content of the letter she or he received from their buddy the day before. Each week writing partners are randomly joined and continue for the entire week. If they are absent, accommodations are made. Letters may be shared right after the writing is done or the letters may be received the next morning.

Here's an example:

Julio and Katessa are writing buddies this week. Today the suggested topic is the recent snowfall. Julio writes:

> *Dear Katessa,*
>
> *I don't like the snow today. I had to wake up early and shovel the back steps. But I like the snow at recess because I want to slide. Yesterday you said that you never want to have a dog. I didn't understand your reason. You should see Jet. Jet's my neighbor's dog.*
>
> *Your buddy,*
>
> *Julio*

At the same time, Katessa, who has different skills, writes:

> *Dear Julio,*
> *I like the snow. I like your cat.*
> *Katessa*

The next day, they each respond to what they read. Julio writes, "Why do you like the snow?" At the same time Katessa is writing, "I like Jet," in response to his letter.

Partnership Skill Development:
Friendly Talking When You Don't Understand

Even though the two writers may express themselves differently, a whole series of interactions will still develop. Appreciating and working with differences is one of the areas of learning that occurs from this activity.

What if one writing buddy can't read the handwriting of the other buddy, or can't understand their spelling, or can't read their words? This is part of the process. The first weeks of using this writing method, it is important to take time to teach friendly ways of asking for help or asking for clarification.

A student's first impulse might be to say to their writing buddy, "Your spelling is lousy." Modeling ways to ask to have the words read and interpreted is part of the whole partnership experience. Practicing patience and acceptance toward partners who have different ways of writing, thinking, and expressing, is an important life skill. Respect needs to interlace the activity. Each week when the partners change, it's important to keep a firm agreement of no comments and no complaining when they receive the name of their new writing buddy.

Cooperative Activities Provide Concrete Ways For Students to Link

Some teachers start the day with activities with cooperation games to build social skills. These promote kinesthetic and interpersonal intelligence. A brief cooperative activity first thing in the morning tells students they are arriving in a classroom community held by partnership.

Activity: Name Toss for Kindergarten through 4th Grades

You will need a soft ball or rolled up sweatshirt for this activity.

As the ball is tossed lightly to a different person each time, the one who catches it is silent, but everyone else says their name. Part of the fun is remembering who has already received the ball.

Partnership Skill Development: Inclusion

One of the partnership skills embedded in this simple activity is inclusion. If the same three children are picked last every day, this won't feel like a cooperative experience. Those three children will dread the game. It would become a concrete way to mark them as outsiders. This means that the teacher needs to specifically teach inclusiveness along with the game, and it requires adding an additional step to the procedure. Ask students to choose to whom they will toss based on a specific invitation: "Toss to someone you haven't tossed to yet this week," "Toss to someone who has different color shoes than you," or "Toss first to the people who were last yesterday."

Activity: Spider Web Morning Greeting for Kindergarten through 6th Grade

You will need a ball of yarn for this activity.

Have everyone in the group sit in a circle. One person starts with a ball of yarn, holds the end of it, and tosses the rest of the ball lightly to another, creating the first strand in the web. As the ball of yarn proceeds around the circle, with each person still holding the strand, a shape like a spider web forms (Variations of this activity were created during the 1970's under many different names).

<u>Ecology variation:</u> Each person says the name of an element in nature. The person who catches the ball names an element in nature that interacts with it. For example, one person says "tiger," and the next says "grass," and the next says "bee," and the next says "flower," and the next says "wind."

<u>Community building variation:</u> This activity has been widely shared through *The Responsive Classroom* trainings led by the Northeast Foundation for Children.[1] Here's an important element that they add: Before tossing the yarn, the person the yarn will be thrown to is greeted. For example, Lenore looks across the circle and chooses to throw the yarn to Mario. She says, "Good morning, Mario." Mario then catches the yarn and returns the greeting, "Good morning, Lenore," before selecting the person to whom he will toss. The greeting comes before the toss and insures that everyone is welcomed that day.

Social Skills Instruction Helps Partnership Skills Be Part of Each Activity

In the sample activities above, we saw how the activity itself might not be a partnership experience if patterns of ranking interfered. We need to anticipate ways that the activity could break down and add specific instruction in skills of respectful interaction. How can we help students take greater responsibility when they work in a group, and learn thereby to be responsible to peers, as well as, responsible to the teacher in charge?

Dee Dishon, a leader in cooperative learning, emphasizes the importance of teaching social skills. Dishon and Pat Wilson O'Leary recommend six steps to implement when teaching social skills:

1. Define and provide rationale for the skill.
2. Describe how to perform the skill.
3. Practice the skill.
4. Receive feedback on performance of the skill.
5. Process learning about the skill.
6. Continue practice until the skill is automatic.[2]

In the letter exchange activity, students practice friendly ways of speaking to each other as they ask for help reading each other's writing. This practice occurs before they do the activity. Instruction on social skills and guidance in using them can take place during the whole span of the activity: pre-teaching, teachable moments, or processing afterward.

Beforehand: A Science Lesson

A teacher anticipates a part of the lesson which will involve interaction and helps students make deliberate plans.

Teacher: For our lesson on insects, I'm going to hand out magnifying glasses. There will be one lens for each pair of students. Each of you will examine two insects and draw pictures of their wings. Let's discuss how you'll share the magnifier. Who has an idea?

Sam: After we look at one insect, we could pass it before we look at the other one.

Flo: One person could hold the magnifying glass while the other one looks.

Del: We could figure out who went first the last time we were partners.

During: A Math Lesson

A teachable moment arises, and the teacher briefly addresses it. The teacher has been leading a lesson with the whole class. She sees a scuffle and an exchange of taunting and angry looks between Deena and Lee.

Teacher: I'd like to check in on what's going on, Deena and Lee.

Lee: Deena keeps kicking my chair.

Deena: That's because of what you said to me.

Teacher: Here are two choices. (The teacher can think of several options but chooses the two that fit this particular situation best.) You can set the timer for five minutes and go to the Conflict Corner and come up with a plan. Or, I'll set the timer for three minutes and you can talk it out right here.

Lee: Definitely not by ourselves.

Teacher: Deena, is it okay with you to talk it out publicly?

Deena: I guess so.

Teacher: Okay, I'll set the timer. (She looks as the Job Chart and sees that Robin is in charge of leading Problem Solving today.) Robin, will you read off each Problem Solving step on the chart as we come to it? Deena and Lee, please come up and Robin will guide you.

Robin leads both Deena and Lee through the stages of the process and turns to them to indicate when it is their turn to take part in each step.

Steps for Problem Solving

Take turns doing each step

Step One: Sharing Feelings
Please share your feelings with an "I" statement.

Step Two: Understand the problem
How would you describe the problem you're trying to solve?

Step Three: Brainstorm
What ways can you think of to solve it?

Step Four: Choose
Which solution do you want?

Step Five: Plan
Please restate the plan you have made

Robin: How do you feel right now? (She takes turns looking at the person who will answer the question first).

Deena: I felt really angry when you called me names, Lee.

Lee: Well, I felt upset that you were kicking my chair.

Robin: What's the problem you are trying to solve?

Lee: I want Deena to let me use her eraser on my math paper.

Deena: I don't want Lee to interrupt me because I have to concentrate.

Robin: So, what are the ways you could solve this?

Deena: When she needs an eraser she could ask someone else or she could go to the basket of supplies on the supply table.

Lee: The basket is empty now, so we have to make sure the basket of erasers is full in the morning.

Robin: What solution do you want?

Lee: I want the class to talk at meeting this afternoon about how to have more erasers around.

Deena: That's okay with me, but I also want us to say we won't do stuff like call names.

Robin: Please restate your plan.

Deena: We plan to not call names or kick chairs and we plan to bring up the eraser problem to the next class meeting.

Lee: And I want to plan to still eat lunch together.

Deena: Okay.

Robin: Thank you for talking it out.

<u>After:</u> A Social Studies Lesson

By allowing time for the experience to be discussed afterward, difficulties in interaction are processed and social learning increases.

Teacher: Now that everyone is back from the library, let's talk about how it went while you were looking up books with biographical information. I noticed that several times people wanted the same book. Since I was busy, I couldn't come over and help you figure it out. I saw different solutions. Let's talk about how you handled that situation. I think we can all learn from the different ways people dealt with it.

The teacher holds up the book *Herstory: Women Who Changed the World.*

Teacher: It turned out that a lot of people wanted to use this book. Do you remember the format we use called "Next Time?" Let's use it to figure out what to do tomorrow during library period when we're continuing the research. Who would like to work with the questions first?

Next Time

Use as many questions as you need to express yourself.

<u>Step One:</u> How do you feel right now?

Please share your feelings with an "I" statement.

<u>Step Two:</u> Look at all parts of the problem

What factors contributed to the difficulty you just had?

<u>Step Three:</u> Brainstorm

What would you like to see happen next time?

<u>Step Four:</u> Participation

How can you contribute to helping things work out next time?

<u>Step Five:</u> Help

What help do you need from others?

Ricardo: I feel upset because I only had a minute to use that book. The parts of the problem that I see are that four of us need the same book. But I think the people who have other books to use should use them first. There's a whole book on Marian Wright Edelman and a whole book on Rigoberta Menchu. But this is the only book that has Lakshmi Bai. So next time instead of one person grabbing the book we should sit down together and talk about how to divide the time up. I'd like you to help us plan before we start.

Teacher: Thanks, Ricardo. Who else would like to speak?

Kassie: Okay. I was the first person to use it, but I didn't know other people wanted it until everyone started screaming at me. I have this plan that I think would be really great. Everyone gets three slips of paper and we put our names on them. At the start of library, the librarian should spread out all the books on a table that are biographies. Also, she should put out a can for every computer that is open for us to use that day, so there would be four cans if all four computers are open. Then we walk around and put the slips in any book we are going to want, or in a can to use one of the computers. And we stand back and see who wants to use what.

Ricardo: Yeah, after we do all that, then anybody who wants the same book can divide up the time or use a different book first.

Teacher: So there'd be a planning period first before everyone starts research. Is there anyone who has any amendments to these ideas? (no hands go up). Then we'll use this new method tomorrow. Thanks for thinking about this. Would the person with the Supply Job get scrap paper ready for the slips of paper we'll need?

Social Responsibility Development

Teaching problem solving helps students be responsible members of a community. In Partnership Education, conflicts become an opportunity to explicitly teach social skills. When a conflict occurs, there are choices to keep in mind. Select the procedure that will most encourage students to learn how to link with each other.

Option A: Student-to-Student Communication

Encourage the students to handle the problem or make an intervention themselves. Teachers can coach students from the sidelines, or set aside time to train students themselves in how to interact and intervene. When a student reports a problem to the teacher, the teacher can respond with "What have you tried so far?" or "What are some things you could do right now?" In the classroom, a Peace Table or Conflict Corner can provide a neutral place to talk out a problem using procedures or timers placed there. Or, when a conflict erupts outside, students can work with each other on the spot.

Example: A student reports that others are name calling. The teacher helps the student think of words she or he can use to express their own discomfort, such as: "I don't like to hear someone called that name. Please stop."

Option B: Teacher-Facilitated Student Negotiation

The teacher negotiates while the students involved talk with each other. The teacher helps them calm down, helps acknowledge feelings, and sets up an opportunity to talk. Approaching calmly and saying "You look upset," helps students feel recognized. The teacher leads them through the same step-by-step process described on the chart Steps for Problem Solving above.

Example: As two students talk out a problem of name calling with teacher assistance, underlying factors can surface — such as jealousy of a new friendship — and the teacher can help address all that is contributing to the difficulty. In this case, students might make a two-part plan: "We won't call each other names when we're upset. We'll ask for help talking it out. And, all three of us will eat lunch together today."

Option C: Class Meeting — Bringing a Problem to the Larger Group

The teacher engages the whole community in addressing a problem by articulating what it is they want. First, the group identifies the facets of the problem, rather than singling out particular individuals. Second, brain-storming illuminates options. Lastly, a clear plan is made.

Example: Many times when students rush to sit in a circle, arguments begin: "I was here first," "I want to sit next to her," and "You pushed me," are some of the most common. The class identifies that they don't want assigned seats but they do want less bickering. They decide one person will place pillows in a circle. Another will call names in order. Each person takes a seat as their name is called and does not switch.

As teachers and students become increasingly adept at focusing upon a problem and inventing helpful solutions, they feel proud of their skill mastery. Each experience in a partnership group shows more methods which can be transposed to new settings. They become confident that "there is always *something* we can do."

Using Linking Instead of Ranking Helps
The Expressive Arts Belong to Everyone

When we integrate singing, drawing, and movement into our classrooms, unconscious baggage can come along if we're not aware of it. There is a tendency to rank artistic expression and set up standards, yet the expressive arts are one of our most poignant and direct ways to help students link. Here are ways to use linking practices.

Example: Science and Creative Drawing

Ranking: "Everyone take a look at Mark's drawing. Look how realistically he made that tree. It looks just like a tree."

Implication: The student who can draw the most realistically is the best artist.

Linking: "We've been studying trees in science. Now think of a favorite tree. It can be a tree you've seen before or a tree that you find in your imagination. Choose the kinds of materials that will help you express it — pastels, charcoal, pencil, markers, paint. Show the tree your own way to convey your feelings about it. It doesn't have to be done in the same colors our eyes see when we look at a tree. You can use any colors that will help your expression. Don't worry about making it realistic. Convey what this tree means to you."

Example: Social Studies and Movement

Ranking: "Now that we're studying Ghana, I'm going to play some lively music from Ghana. When you hear the music start on the CD, everybody dance. Let's have the best dancers out front to show us how it's done."

Implication: The way to enter an artistic experience is to follow a standard instead of trusting your own body to lead you in a felt response.

Linking: "Now that we're studying Ghana, I'm going to play some lively regional music. When you hear the music start on the CD, stand up and bring the beat of the music into your feet, then into your shoulders, and then find the way you want to move. You don't need to look like a dancer you've seen before. We won't even watch each other. We'll respond our own ways to the beat of the music."

Linking practices build the classroom community and help students feel safe as they take creative risks. We see a central dialectic operating: We develop our unique individuality while we participate in our community.

Partnership Processes Help Teach to All Intelligences

Example: Social Studies and Music

Ranking: "We'll be performing the Russian song Poost Siedga[3] in the assembly Friday. I notice that some of you are having a lot of trouble learning the song. Come on. If you just listen better and try harder, you can do it."

Implication: When children are having trouble, it's from a lack of effort. Yet perceptual differences and difficulties can be the root cause of impeded learning. In ranking, those who have strong linguistic intelligence are often ranked higher than those who learn best with other intelligences and children who learn best through kinesthetic or other intelligences can get left behind.

Linking: "We'll be sharing the Russian song Poost Siedga in the assembly Friday. The Russian words are unfamiliar, aren't they? I'm going to teach the song several different ways."

"First, I'll tell you the story of the song. Some people find it easiest to remember stories."

"Now, I'd like you to draw the story. Sometimes drawing helps a person remember."

"Next, we're going to act out the meaning of the words in motions. Movement helps others remember."

"Now I'm going to say each Russian word. Some people can catch the new words best with their ear."

"And finally, I'll show you the written words in Russian. Others learn new words easiest by looking at them."

Students can become more cognizant of their own unique mix of intelligences. Encourage them to reflect on how they learn and openly discuss different learning preferences and strengths. Help them link with, rather than rank, students who learn best in different modes. One way to say this is "You don't have to be smart the way I'm smart to be my friend."

Social Learning

Paradoxically, while there is more inclusion in Partnership Education, there is also more individualism because individuality is encouraged over rote conformity. Linking allows us to experience that fundamental dynamic between our human diversity and our human unity.

If I see hurtful exclusion among students, but remain a bystander, I am fostering ranking. Yet how do we as teachers intervene? For instance, how can we help a student if the peer group she depends upon is stuck in practices of exclusion? Whether she is "out" or "in" she is hurt by those practices of ranking. Erin Berard and I have had successful experiences assisting groups of children ages 8 to 12 become conscious of exclusion, and re-pattern themselves. Here is the language we use.

Activity: Ending the Spell of Exclusion for 3rd through 6th Grades

Create a letter that gives a broad context for the situation by framing hurtful behavior as a "spell" that needs to be broken out of. Give a copy of the letter to each person who is involved and then schedule a time to meet with each alone to talk about what specific help they need from adults.

Sample letter:

> We want school to be a place of growth. It's a time for learning about being yourself and learning about having friends. Here are some things that we believe are valuable to learn:
>
> ☺ I'll be appreciated here for all of who I am.
> ☺ I can be myself and at the same time I will have friends.
> ☺ I can be different from my friends.
> ☺ My friends will like more people than me and at the same time they will also still like me.
> ☺ I don't have to protect myself in ways that could hurt others.
> ☺ I can and will get help as I learn.

Getting Help With Spells

Sometimes people do things they don't want to do. It's as if a spell comes over them. Part of what we will learn is how to break out of this spell. Spells can look very different. Here are some things people might do that they don't want to do:

Four Spells

1. Saying negative things about others. ("Look what _____ is doing.") This is different from constructively disagreeing or asking for what you need.

2. Feeling afraid you'll be left out and instead leaving someone else out.

3. Abruptly leaving after someone else joins a group. ("If she's here, let's go away.")

4. Doing things that could lead to someone feeling ganged up on, like trying to get someone else to join you in disapproving of someone. ("Who does she think she is!")

Things get hard for people in different ways. Spells can also look like this:

☹ Accepting hurtful behavior and not standing up for yourself.
☹ Changing what you need or want because you feel afraid.
☹ Making excuses for the person doing it.
☹ Staying quiet and freezing up about a problem instead of getting help.
☹ Silencing yourself when you feel upset.

Which of these spells would you like help with?

Breaking Spells

These things can help break spells:

☺ Doing things that you know will help you hear your own feelings.

☺ Believing yourself when you feel upset, and talking to Sarah or Erin about it.

☺ Instead of talking with a friend about somebody who did something upsetting, coming to a staff person for help.

☺ When a person tells you their idea, checking that you understand what they are saying before you say you disagree.

Do you have other ideas about what helps you?

We are committed to helping people break out of spells. We will be firmly asking you not to do any of those four spells listed above. If ever you can't stop yourself or can't help yourself, we will assist and guide you. But we also see it as each person's responsibility to work on getting themselves out from under such spells. Please think about the kinds of help you would like from staff.

Interdependence Through Cooperative Learning

Learning structures can help break the "spells" of ranking by placing students in a positive social experience. One of the many benefits of using cooperative learning is that students have increased opportunity to mix with many others. Experiences in cooperative learning have been proven in research to be more productive and efficient ways to learn. They also have been shown to develop personal responsibility, promote friendships among diverse types of students, and help young people develop their skills in being part of a community.

Many teachers have received training in cooperative learning. It was advocated in the last three decades of the nineteenth century by the distinguished educator Francis Parker, and in the twentieth century first promoted by John Dewey. Research in the field of cooperative learning began in the early 1900's, but it is the key researchers and trainers of the last three decades who have refined it. While there is no common agreement about the central features of cooperative learning, here are key components:

• Interactive learning in small heterogeneous groups.

• Positive interdependence: both individual and group accountability.

• Explicit training in interpersonal skills.

• Reflection: Processing how well the groups are functioning.

• Distributed leadership.[4]

The following is an example of a cooperative learning lesson designed for students studying in the school library.

<u>Activity:</u> Science Report: Cooperative Study of Animals — For 2nd through 6th Grades

Groups of four students study a classification of animals — such as cetaceans (whales and dolphins) — and create a composite report covering categories of information such as what cetaceans eat, what they look like, how they communicate, and what struggles they face.

Pat McGiffin created and developed this activity working with third graders as a school media specialist in Amherst, Massachusetts. By teaching social skills, adding the expressive arts, and using cooperative learning structures she extended the activity into an effective month-long unit.[5]

Pat McGiffin incorporated these features in her cooperative learning design:

<u>Individual choice:</u> Each student picked one animal within the classification to study.

<u>Individual accountability:</u> Each student was responsible for researching the information about their selected animal.

<u>Distributed leadership:</u> Students shared their individual reports and looked for similar features within each category, such as "what does this animal eat." Together they recognized common qualities of each animal within their classification: "Oh, they all eat small fish."

<u>Social skills:</u> Students spent time practicing the skills of listening and asking good questions so that they could respond constructively to each other's reports.

The skills of listening and asking questions are critical to the success of the activity. One method that McGiffin employed to help them develop their listening skills was to provide a chart listing each category of information to be researched. Items included what the animal eats, where it lives, and how large it grows to be. As each member of a team reports on their animal — such as the Orca whale — the other team members know specifically what information they are listening for and fill it in on the chart in columns. This way a student is primed to listen for each type of information. If data on the length of the Orca isn't supplied, listeners request it: "I didn't hear you mention the length of your animal."

She also used the expressive arts to help students consolidate information. Together each group created animal biographies, made interconnected drawings with features of each animal, and ended with a creative dramatics presentation to the class. These segments of the unit also required guidance in social skills.

Partnership and Cooperation

Cooperative learning structures in and of themselves don't guarantee that the process is building partnership, however. Cooperative learning trainers, Liana Forest and Ted Graves, have said "Our most difficult task has been to get across to teachers and school staff the complete shift in perspective and attitude required for creating an environment supportive of cooperative learning."[6]

It is not just a matter of using a cooperative structure for one month or in one subject area. It requires looking at the mixture of messages throughout the whole school building. Nancy Schneidewind and Mara Sapon-Shevin raise questions that they feel teachers need to explore. These include:

- Do I see cooperative learning as a tool to better manage my class and retain my authority? Or is it a process through which my students can learn to take greater responsibility and in which power is increasingly shared with them?

- To what extent do I use cooperative learning without addressing the pervasive competition in schools and society? Do I help students connect their experience working collaboratively with heightened critical consciousness about effects of competition and cooperation on ourselves, others, and society?[7]

Experiences in cooperative learning take on significance, then, not only because they have proven in research to be more productive and efficient ways to learn, but because they develop friendships among diverse types of students and help young people develop their consciousness about being part of a community, and promote the very skills most needed for a flourishing world society.

We have an opportunity to complicate our thinking about cooperation and competition. Building partnership doesn't suggest that we "always structure cooperation and never use competition." It's more a matter of being attuned to how they are employed. Partnership education asks: Where is the learning going? What kind of classroom, school, community, and world are we training students to build together?

It's not cooperation in and of itself that is crucial, it's cooperation in caring for the whole. Adults can cooperate together to fix prices in the business world without being mindful of its broader effects. Students can cooperate together to exclude one person in the arena of a classroom. On the other hand, people can compete to develop more cogent language for a conflict resolution procedure, or race shoulder-to-shoulder with exhilaration, mutually urging each other on to surpass their previous limits. This kind of competition says "here's the best I can do; what can you do? What is possible? Can we go even further?"

Eisler poses these questions:

- How can we compete without being destructive in a society that fosters constant competition?

- Can we teach students to learn to strive for excellence rather than to beat their "opponents"?

What makes the difference is the context we keep: caring for the whole, sharing responsibility for the furtherance of pro-social group goals, and being partners in fostering the greatest good.

Closing

Partnership processes can help provide building blocks of health, experiences of nurturing respectful interactions. They function like cellular repair for an aching global family tree. Each experience of partnership registers and provides young people with an important model.

<u>Activity:</u> Our Cooperative World: A Study of How People Link Up — For Kindergarten through 12th Grades

Students are well aware of the amount of violence in the world. One method of introducing students to cooperative learning and other partnership processes learning is to talk together about the myriad of ways that people in the world cooperate.

Ask students to brainstorm all the examples of people cooperating that they see around them. Delineate different spheres to consider: Family, school, neighborhood, town or city, country, world. Ask students to make a list by themselves. Next, invite them to meet in small groups of 2-4 and merge their lists. When all lists in the class are put together, enjoy seeing that cooperation in making the lists allowed many more answers to come forward.

Our lives are built on a foundation of vast and complex interconnectedness. We depend upon other people to obey traffic laws, build bridges safely, sell unspoiled food, and manufacture safe medicine. Nations have established an international postal service and have agreements on uses of the ocean. Hospitals, airports, and schools function with complex teamwork. Most of the world's work is done cooperatively. When people are fired from a job, in 75 to 85 percent of the cases, it is because of the individual's inability to get along with co-workers, according to Dee Dishon.

Conformity, however, is not partnership. Getting along with others in a partnership setting involves not conformity but individualism, a true individualism that is based upon the development of each person's unique capacities rather than individualism measured on standardized scales. The more you are your own self in a group, sharing what you really think and feel, the more authentically you can connect with others, and this individuation builds a stronger group.

Since the late 1930's, competition has been in the forefront of public schools. Our culture holds up "toughing it out," "going it alone," and "rugged individualism" as qualities to admire and emulate. Yet, Albert Einstein wrote that the task of each human life is to become progressively aware of the unity of all life. He said, "Our task must be to free ourselves from this prison (of separate consciousness) by widening our circle of compassion to embrace all living creatures and the whole of nature in its beauty."[8]

Through Partnership Education, young people can encounter both their uniqueness and their belongingness. They make decisions, learn to take responsibility, and feel empowered as individuals and as a group. Moreover, they experience themselves to be valued members while they develop their separate selves. This makes for a dynamic relationship of mutual aid. A partnership classroom provides a learning ground for young people to learn the reciprocal action between furthering their own growth, and furthering the capacity of the whole community.

CHAPTER 2

Building a Safe Community for Learning

by Mara Sapon-Shevin

Visiting my students in the field, I have the opportunity to go into a lot of classrooms. I get to absorb little snatches of conversation, notice what hangs on the walls and how the room is arranged, observe a wide range of lessons and management strategies. And always, if I allow myself to notice, I have feelings about what I see and hear. I enter one classroom and am immediately struck by a feeling of gloom—tension, uneasiness, silence or bickering, a sense that all is not well in the world. The teacher is yelling, threatening, brow furrowed and intense, unhappy with this stance but somehow resigned to it. Entering another classroom, the easy joyfulness strikes me just as quickly— students talking, sharing, heads bent together over a shared project, the teacher talking, laughing, smiling, joking, the atmosphere light and alive with energy. How does one make sense of this contrast? Luck of the draw? Did one teacher just get all the "bad students" and another teacher the "good ones"? Explanations that center around "What can you expect from students who come from backgrounds like these?" or "When you teach in the city you have to yell to establish and maintain discipline" ring false when the two classrooms described above are in the same building, at the same grade level, drawing from the same population of students.

Teaching involves making an immense number of decisions, and all these decisions have an impact on how students will learn, how they will treat one another, and what the classroom atmosphere will feel like:

> Mr. Rimaldi passes back the math exams—in descending order of grades. By the time he gets to the bottom of the pile, many of the students are snickering. Jason, who receives his last, is trying to act casual, but he shifts in his chair and his discomfort is clear. Another student calls out, "Way to go, Jason."

> Ms. Herbert takes roll in the morning. After each absent child's name is noted, she comments that he or she will be missed and asks for volunteers to copy

assignments, take handouts, and call the student that evening. She points out that the classroom community is not complete and expresses her hope that it will be restored soon.

Ms. Boyle talks excitedly about the upcoming Christmas holiday. She describes, at length, her own plans and the Christmas activities that will take place in class—a play, a party, decorations, singing, and an assembly. Almost as an aside, she remembers and adds, "Of course, not everyone celebrates this holiday," and then continues detailing the schedule.

When Mr. Danvers returns to his class after recess, he finds that one of the students has called the class to the rug for an emergency meeting. There has been an incident of racial name calling on the playground and the students want to discuss it. Students share what happened and generate a plan for addressing the problem with the students involved. As a group, they agree to meet again in a week to follow up on what has happened.

Each of the scenarios described above reflects something about classroom community. The kinds of decisions these teachers have made—often decisions within other decisions—have implications for the ways in which students will interact within the classroom and beyond. Deciding to return papers by grade has an impact on how Jason sees himself and is seen by others. Ms. Herbert's style of roll taking and attention to absentees change the ways in which students will talk about and respond to returning students. Ms. Boyle's apparent disregard for cultural, economic, and religious differences in planning a Christmas curriculum will affect Marya's willingness to talk about Kwanzaa, Noah's comfort in talking about Chanukah, and Paul's openness in describing his family's hard times which will make Christmas difficult for them. Mr. Danvers's establishment of classroom meeting times and spaces and his comfort with student initiation and leadership provide opportunities for students to think together about important issues like racism.

Teacher education programs have courses called Math Methods and Curriculum Design, but rarely is there a course entitled Building Safe, Inclusive Classrooms or Creating Hospitable Communities. For the most part, little direct attention is paid to issues of classroom climate and student-student interaction; such concerns are sometimes subsumed under topics such as classroom management or curriculum planning, but rarely are teachers encouraged to explore and strategize about how community is created and nourished. And so I wish to share here some of my thinking about the importance of community building and the ways in which such concerns must assume primary rather than secondary status in thinking about teaching.

I begin all my classes and educational presentations with singing. I teach a song to the whole group, often one about community or connection, and encourage full participation. Hesitant voices and embarrassment generally abate as the collective of strong voices produces a powerful and pleasing sound. And then I ask, "Why did I begin with singing?" Generally, people answer, "Because it's fun"; "Because it is something we should be doing with children"; "Because it helps break the tension." And often, someone will comment, "Because it builds a sense of community—because we sound better together than we would individually." From that point of departure, we discuss what makes a community and explore times when the students or participants have experienced a sense of community. People share memories of hiking trips, school plays, church organizations, political rallies, and other times when they worked together toward a common goal. Words like "friendship," "trust," "respect," and "caring" become part of the discussion as people describe the ways in which the community transcended individual differences and difficulties.

My next question is harder: "Well, I just led the first song; which of you would feel comfortable coming up here to lead the next one?" A few brave hands are raised. "Well then," I continue, "which of you would rather die first?" There is always nervous laughter and a spate of hands. And then the final, most central question is posed: "For those of you who would rather die first, what would it take—what conditions would have to be met—for you to be comfortable coming up to lead a song?"

"I'd have to know a song." "I'd want someone to do it with me." "I'd want to know that everyone else would be doing it too." And then, the bottom line: "I'd want to be promised that no one would laugh. That no one would make fun of me or embar-

rass me." They want *Safety*: The safety to learn and to fail; the safety to show oneself fully and be appreciated or at least supported; the safety to succeed and the safety to be imperfect; the safety from humiliation, isolation, stigmatization, alienation from the group. This is the essence of community. A community is a safe space to grow, a space that welcomes you fully, that sees you for who you are, that invites your participation, and that holds you gently while you explore.

Can classrooms be made safe? In a time when keeping children from physical harm seems difficult enough, can we create classrooms that also feel psychologically safe? Emotionally safe? Can we create classrooms that welcome children for who they are, give them opportunities to know one another in a deep way, and encourage their interaction? This, to me, is the most important challenge to any teacher: Creating a space safe enough for students to be themselves, to stretch toward others, to learn, and to help one another.

In order to focus on community building as an essential component of teaching, one must accept the following premise: *Time spent building community is never wasted time.* Community building is not what you do if you have time, or only for the first 2 days of class. Building a solid, safe community must be a priority and an ongoing commitment. Many of the tasks that teachers wrestle with throughout the school year can be more easily negotiated if there is a good classroom community. Individualizing instruction is less likely to be met with complaints ("Why doesn't Michael have to do the same problems?") when students know and understand one another's individual differences. Cooperative group work, fast becoming an organizing principle in many classrooms, requires a firm foundation of positive interpersonal skills in order to be successful, and the everyday conflicts that occur in classroom settings can be resolved far more smoothly when students know and trust one another.

In a recent course called Cooperative Classrooms, Inclusive Communities, my coteacher, Sarah Pirtle, and I spent a full hour talking about class norms and agreements with the group. We discussed and agreed to norms of confidentiality so that people could share freely without fear that their words would come back to haunt them. The class agreed to work at implementing a standard of "no put-downs of self and others." The ensuing discussion—"What if I really am bad at something and want to say it?" and "What if someone else says something that I find offensive?"—led us to establish additional procedures for resolving conflicts in ways that felt honest and forthright. The time spent engaging in this discussion was not something we rushed through in order to get to the heart of the class—the "real content." Having this discussion together, modeling ways of speaking, asking questions and disagreeing respectfully, and acknowledging the importance of having such a discussion was the content of this class.

Later in the week, a discussion of racism in American schools produced considerable discomfort and even anger. One student's comment was difficult for the others to hear, and the temptation to marginalize that student was evident. But Sarah and I, as teachers, were able to remind the students of our agreements about "no side conversations" and "talking to people directly about what's bothering you" and to urge them, as they left for lunch, to remember that our class was committed to hanging together through adversity so that we all could learn and grow, to open and honest discussion, and to listening well to one another. What might have been a major disruption in the classroom and the occasion for the isolation of particular students became, instead, a real-life example of the importance of setting a tone, of making the goal of community explicit, of taking the time to notice and care how people are being treated by others.

Although we all might agree that having a community is important, how do we know when we have one? What are some of the markers of community, and how can teachers foster a genuine sense of connectedness and concern in the classroom? Student teachers returning from the field often share observations regarding the ways in which students interact, and these can be regarded as indications of the quality of the classroom community—a way of "taking the community's temperature" as an indication of its health:

> In one classroom, the students are assigned to read with a partner every day. They can go wherever they want in the classroom, and they take turns reading to each other. The teacher selects these partners by drawing two tongue depressors (with students' names on them) out of a can. It is noticeable that when the teacher announces the selection—Freda and Manolita, Jeremy and Shamira, Nicole and Danielle—there are no groans, no "Oh, yuck"s, or "I'm not reading with her." This is a healthy community.

> In the cafeteria, children are teasing one another about what is in their lunches. "You eat tofu—that's disgusting." "Why doesn't your mother pack you a real lunch?" "How come you don't eat meat—that's weird." One child is reduced to tears and dumps her lunch in the wastebasket. This is a community that needs work.

> In a school that includes students with disabilities as full members of regular classrooms, a boy is helping a classmate learn to navigate on a three-wheeler in the hallways. A visitor stops, addresses the boy, and asks, "What grade are you in?" "I'm in sixth grade," he replies, "and [indicating his friend] so is she." The message is clear: She may not talk, but she's part of our class. Don't leave her out, even in your question. This is an inclusive community.

What are the underlying values and priorities that support community building? How can classrooms be structured so that they move toward cohesion and support rather than toward fragmentation and distancing?

Communities Provide Opportunities To Show Ourselves Fully

A safe classroom community is one in which students are comfortable showing themselves, being themselves, and being honest about who and what they are. Think about your friends. Who are the friends who know you really well—and still like you? Aren't they the ones who have seen you at your best, but also at your worst? The ones to whom you respond with the truth when they ask how you are, and you're not doing well? The ones who listen well? How does one create that kind of safety in the classroom?

I often begin class with "News and Goods." We take turns going around the room with each student offering something good that has happened in his or her life recently. In the beginning, the offerings are often limited: "I saw a good movie last night"; "I got a new sweater yesterday." As the group members begin to know and trust one another, they share more fully: "I had a wonderful talk with my best friend last night and I feel really good about our relationship"; "I found out that my sister is pregnant and I'm going to be an aunt." And sometimes, "I have nothing good to share—my whole life is a mess," to which others may respond with sympathy and support; often a touch on the hand is offered by the person in the next seat.

Students are allowed to "pass" if they wish, and no one is forced to share. But there are also firm guidelines about how the group listens—no interruptions, no laughing, no snickering, no remarks. Each person's turn is sacred—his or her time for personal sharing— and the structure is not competitive. I explain repeatedly that we can figure out ways to be supportive of one another. One person's triumph in no way diminishes another's. Patty's delight at passing her math test is in no way minimized by the fact that Larry got a perfect score on his. We are, each of us, working on different things, struggling with different issues. We can support one another. It is possible for us to be proud of ourselves and of one another when the competitive element is removed.

Teachers working in classroom settings that include students with disabilities are especially conscious of the need to establish an atmosphere in which every person's accomplishments can be noted and appreciated. Karen's learning to tie her shoelaces is a major triumph for her, even though her classmate Morgan has been tying hers for years. Annabel's struggle (and victory) over spelling is worthy of celebration because she has worked hard and improved. It is not celebrated only if it is the "best" spelling paper or a "perfect" paper.

It is difficult for many people to accept compliments. They hem and haw and look the other way. "Thanks for saying I'm pretty, but actually I've gained weight and I'm fat"; "The report wasn't really as great as you think—I left out an important part and it should have been better." Accepting appreciation from others is problematic, particularly for women, because often we have not experienced the safety to be proud of ourselves. Feeling "too good" about yourself can feel dangerous, like looking for criticism. So we have learned to diminish our own accomplishments, to put ourselves down before someone else does. Creating a space in which people can be proud of themselves should be a central organizing principle of classrooms. Delighting in and sharing genuine accomplishments is distinguishable from "bragging" or "showing off" when it occurs within the context of community; arrogance, egotism, and self-absorption are fueled by competition, insensitivity, and real or perceived scarcity of success, all of which are antithetical to true community. Teachers must ask themselves: How can I create multiple opportunities for people to share and celebrate their triumphs and ensure that all people in the class are acknowledged? How can I make that opportunity safe for all class members? How can I remove the competitive orientation that often surrounds feeling good about oneself?

A classroom that feels safe to students allows them to be proud of their accomplishments, but it also allows opportunities to be honest about their needs and to ask for support. In a seventh-grade classroom, I heard a boy proclaim loudly, "I don't understand the math." Immediately, three students rushed over to help him. This student had the safety to share his frustration and to ask for help. The teacher in that classroom had provided a space in which such a request could be issued and had established classroom norms that allowed other students to offer support and assistance.

I was stunned when my older daughter came home from seventh grade one day and announced, "Today at lunch, I learned to tell time."

"What do you mean?" I asked. "You already knew how to tell time, didn't you?"

"No," she explained, "actually, I never understood it. I always had a digital watch so I never really learned the other way. But I told some kids at lunch and they showed me how it worked and now I understand."

I was awed that she had felt enough safety with her peers—other 12- and 13-year-olds—to let them in on what had been a well-maintained (even from her mother) secret. And I was further touched by the fact that they had responded to her not with scorn or derision but with support and teaching. This experience speaks volumes to children's abilities to learn quickly and painlessly when they feel supported and safe.

Communities Provide Opportunities To Know Others Well

Opportunities to show ourselves fully provide the possibility of knowing others well. When a safe community has been created and maintained, we can notice Rena's physical characteristics and the fact that she reads well, but we can also learn that she is struggling with her fear of the dark and her worry about nuclear war, that she is having a hard time with her older sister at home, and is hoping to be a carpenter when she grows up. We can learn enough about Rena, in her many facets, to enable us to find similarities and differences, spaces and ways to connect.

Many years ago, I gave workshops for teachers on how to teach students about differences and disabilities. One teacher approached me after such a workshop and said something that profoundly changed my orientation to the issue. "You know," she said, "my special education students are painfully aware of the ways in which they are different from other students. What they don't see are the ways in which they are similar."

Since that time, it has become even clearer to me that we must help students see both the ways in which they are different and the characteristics, needs, fears, and skills they share. Focusing exclusively on differences can result in the ultimate alienation: There is no one here like me, so I must be all alone. Focusing exclusively on similarities can result in making children's unique characteristics invisible, for example, not noting that Shamika is African American or that Nicole uses facilitated communication to talk. One teacher put up a grid in her classroom, with each child's name written across the top and down the side. During the course of the year, they were responsible for finding one similarity with every other person in the class. In the square that was the intersection of their own name, they were asked to share one thing that was unique about themselves.

I have my students engage in a diversity treasure hunt during class. They circulate with papers and pencils and are asked to find people who fit into different categories:

> Find someone who grew up with an older relative.
> Write his or her name here _____.
> What's one thing that person learned from the older relative?
> Find someone whose parents come from another country.
> Write his or her name here _____.
> What's one tradition or custom that person has learned from his or her parents?
> Find someone who has a family member with a disability.
> Write his or her name here _____.
> What's something that person has learned by interacting with the person with a disability?

The rules are that you can write someone's name down only once, that is, you must talk to 10 different people if there are 10 items on the list. Students are encouraged to seek out people they don't know. The room typically buzzes with stories, laughter, delight in finding someone who fits into a category. People often find themselves sharing and listening to stories that they don't typically tell: About a younger brother with cerebral palsy and how hard it is when people stare or make fun of him; about a grandmother from Italy who makes wonderful cakes. After people are finished, they are asked to share what they have learned. People listen attentively as Michael shares what he learned from Janet, as Carmen shares the funny story she heard from Dwayne. Students begin to realize connections that they can build on: Discovering a shared interest in turtles leads to an exchange of books; hearing about someone else's triumph in learning to swim after many years leads to an offer to go to the pool together.

The classroom conversation and interaction after this exercise are always deeper, richer. The safety of the community and the structure for sharing allow people to see one another and to be seen as well. Teachers have also used this activity to alter students' perceptions in specific ways. Juan, who has just moved from Mexico, has been isolated because of his language difference. The question that says "Find someone who was born in another country and can teach you a phrase in his or her language" makes Juan a necessary and valued part of the group activity; his differences are honored, not hidden, acknowledged, not ignored.

Just as learning to say nice things about oneself is challenging, learning to notice and appreciate others (and accept that appreciation) can be equally difficult. One teacher designates a "Child of the Week" (with each student getting a turn). That child brings in things to share (family artifacts and photographs, if they are available) and is interviewed by classroom reporters (with the right to pass on any question). The week ends for Tyler, the child in the spotlight this week, with every student contributing a page to a book whose theme is "what we like about Tyler." The teacher reports that she has had to do very little coaching about how to write "nice things" and that the students notice and appreciate many different qualities and characteristics of the child: "Tyler has a good sense of humor. He makes me laugh." "Tyler let me share his sandwich when I forgot my lunch money last week." "Tyler is really good at drawing pictures of dinosaurs."

Other opportunities abound for noticing others and appreciating them. My daughter Dalia developed a Thanksgiving ritual that I have translated for the classroom. She gives each person at the table enough little slips of paper for every other person and asks them to write one thing they like or appreciate about each person. Little people who cannot write are encouraged to draw or dictate their messages. All the slips of paper are put in a box, and the box is then passed around the table. Each person takes a turn drawing out a slip of paper and reading it: "I like Annegret's warmth and the way she reaches out to people"; "I like the way Lucy giggles when something is funny and makes everyone else giggle too." The slip of paper is then given to the person it is about. Although receiving compliments graciously is difficult for some people, I have never yet seen a person who did not take these little slips of paper home, tucked in a purse or a shirt pocket. Many people have reported, years later, that they still have these pasted on their mirrors or on their desks.

At the end of a class that had used cooperative learning family groups all semester, I gave each member a piece of paper that said:

My name:
My group says that I'm...
I want to remember that...

Each group member wrote affirmations and appreciations for every other group member: "I love the way you kept us going when we got discouraged"; "I appreciate how much you know about different topics and your willingness to share." Each person completed the last section individually. "I want to remember that I have friends in this class"; "I want to remember that other people think I'm smart and worth having around."

As the level of safety increases, we can encourage students to see and know one another at deeper levels. In Australia recently, I asked teachers to bring in and share objects that were important to them. People brought seashells, old photographs, a precious ring, a treasured poem, and an old doll. After they had shared these objects with the group, I asked not "What did Sharon share?" but "What did you learn about Sharon from what she shared?" People's responses were profound: "I learned that relationships are very important to Susan—she cares deeply about her friends." "I learned that Keith loves nature and that he really notices the beauty around him." And, perhaps most touchingly, about a woman whose outward reserve could have been perceived as standoffishness, "I learned that there's a lot more to Mary than meets the eye. She really has a deep, spiritual side to her." Several were quite moved during the sharing experience. The joy of being seen so clearly and so fully by relative strangers was overwhelmingly affirming.

Communities Provide Opportunities To Reach Out, Connect, and Help

The third component of community building is the chance for students to interact with one another positively, helping and supporting one another, teaching and sharing their skills and strengths. When an atmosphere has been created in which people freely share who they are and learn about others, the possibilities for connection are boundless. For example, I have students complete a classroom yellow pages in which they designate those areas in which they can give help or support:

HELP OFFERED:
Able to teach double Dutch jump roping
Know how to make friendship bracelets
Am good at remembering my assignments

Students can also ask for help or support in a range of areas:

> HELP WANTED:
>
> Want to learn to play four-square on the playground
>
> Need help figuring out what to do with someone
> on the playground who is bugging me
>
> Want support for not wasting time and getting
> my work done so I don't have to miss recess

Students are encouraged to find and support one another. The class is not divided into "those who need help" and "those who give help." Every child is both a teacher and a learner, a person who gives support and receives it.

In another classroom that included a child with challenging disabilities, the classroom teacher was eager to encourage support for her without stigmatizing her further. Rather than listing only Arden's goals on the board for the class to see, she invited each student to write a weekly goal and paste it on his or her desk. Students were invited to set their own goals (finishing my math, not getting into fights at lunch, reading more) and to figure out ways of supporting one another. Rather than marginalizing Arden as the only one with an educational goal in the classroom, the only person who needed help, the structure encouraged all students to see themselves as having goals and as being capable of giving support (including Arden).

The opportunities to promote positive social interactions and support emerge constantly during any school day. Classroom jobs can be completed by pairs of students rather than by individuals, students requesting help can be directed to other students for that support, and students can be explicitly taught how to help others. ("Don't give people the answer—help them figure it out themselves. Here are some ways to teach that.")

Learning to give help and solve problems can even be an explicit part of the curriculum. In one school, teachers have taught students to implement a collaborative problem-solving method in which they learn to use brainstorming and problem-solving skills that stress flexible thinking and creativity. Because the school district is committed to full inclusion (students with disabilities are full members of regular classrooms), the teachers and students have used these problem-solving skills to figure out how to ensure that students with disabilities are fully integrated. Students have brainstormed, for example, how to involve a young girl with cerebral palsy in a puppet show activity, how to allow a boy with limited body movement to play a dart game, and how to support a little girl on the playground so that she could use the equipment like other students. Learning to support others and include them is operationalized in the school's curriculum.

Other schools have implemented conflict-resolution training for students so that they can acquire the skills necessary to resolve fights on the playground and in the classroom. One teacher has a conflict-resolution corner set up as one of the learning centers in the room. Students who are experiencing difficulties can select another student to serve as a mediator, and the three students follow a step-by-step model for resolving differences. Teachers can model for students a commitment to working things out together, to developing the skills necessary for the classroom to function as a community.

Conclusion

Communities don't just happen. No teacher, no matter how skilled or well intentioned, can enter a new classroom and announce, "We are a community." Communities are built over time, through shared experience, and by providing multiple opportunities for students to be themselves, know one another, and interact in positive and supportive ways. Community building must be seen and felt as a process that we're all in together rather than as a task that is important only to the teacher.

Although the teacher is but one person in the community, the teacher's behavior must provide a model of acceptance, support, and honesty for the entire class. It is unreasonable to expect students to be loving and supportive of one another if the teacher puts down individual students or uses labeling or name calling. If teachers are working in settings in which they do not feel valued and supported, it can be difficult for them to provide that kind of support for students. If, as a teacher, you perceive a lack of community within the school or feel that teachers are not thought about or cared for, part of the task of community building for your students must include building a community for yourself.

It is essential to honor the fact that community building is neither automatic nor easy. Teachers must demonstrate a willingness to be honest with students about the conflicts that arise in forming and maintaining a community. Students may ask questions about issues related to other students: "Why does Michael go to the gifted program and not me?" or "Why doesn't Donnel talk?" Concerns and problems about working with others will be voiced as well: "Carolyn smells and I don't like to be around her"; "Shannon isn't doing her part when we work together." Some teachers feel that responding to such questions will make trouble or raise difficult issues. In reality, however, students are already aware of classmates' differences and differing needs, and failing to address such questions does not eliminate the concern; it simply drives it underground. The teacher must be willing to answer questions honestly and with integrity. The mystery of unexplained differences and the establishment of certain topics as classroom conversational taboos seriously impede the formation of a classroom community that feels safe for all students. In working toward the goal of an inclusive classroom community in which all children—regardless of race, disability, cultural or family background, or skill—are able to function as a cohesive group, teachers must engage students in forthright discussions of the joys and difficulties of building and maintaining a community. Such discussions may be hard and even painful, but the willingness to open up issues of exclusion, fairness, difference, prejudice, and discrimination, as well as the challenges of learning to work together can enrich the community as a whole and deepen teacher and student understanding of the many forces that keep people separate and isolated.

Taking on the task of building and maintaining a supportive classroom community can become a central organizing value. Teachers can examine every decision they make—about curriculum, about teaching, about grading, about management—and ask: How will this decision affect the classroom community? Will it bring students closer together, or will it push them further apart? Asking these questions and being willing to change our behavior can bring us closer to creating classroom communities in which all members—teachers and students—are nurtured.

CHAPTER 3

Partnership Learning: Bringing Conversation into the Heart of the Classroom

by Jim Knight

Did you feel like a partner in the classes you attended in school, college or university? Chances are that your education made you very aware of the fact that you were not a partner with your teacher. In truth, this may have been the number one lesson that your teacher may have taught, often with the best intentions. For most students, teachers deliver content and manage the classroom, while students learn whatever the teacher chooses to teach. Partnership Learning, the result of over nine years of research at the Kansas University Center for Research on Learning, proposes that students learn, enjoy, remember, and use more when they learn with teachers who see themselves as partners.[9]

> From the outset, the humanist educator's efforts must coincide with those of the student to engage in critical thinking and the quest for mutual humanization. The educator's efforts must be imbued with a profound trust in people and their creative power. To achieve this, the humanist educator must be a partner of the students in ... relations with them.
>
> —*Paulo Friere*

Our lives are enriched immeasurably by open and free conversation. In authentic dialogue we open ourselves to new ideas, new friends, new worlds. Through conversation we grow and learn, we express compassion, we touch others, and let others touch us. In conversation, we live the experiences of our lives, in spirited, moving talks around kitchen tables, beside fireplaces, at summer cottages, in winter lodges, in automobiles, and, we hope, in schools.

The Principles of Partnership

Partnership is coming to be regarded as an empowering alternative to more common patriarchal models of human interaction. Today, in disciplines as diverse as anthropology, organizational theory, philosophy of science, and educational theory, theorists are constructing a new partnership mindset as an alternative to the traditional patriarchy model. Running through the writing in numerous disciplines are principles representing the foundation of a partnership worldview. Those principles, described below, are also the foundation of the Partnership Learning approach to professional development and classroom use:

Equality

Partnership involves relationships between equals (Block, 1993; Eisler, 1987). Thus each person's thoughts and beliefs are held to be valuable, and, although each individual is different, no individual decides for another. All learners are recognized as equal partners, and consequently no one's view is more important or valuable than any one else's.

Choice

In a partnership, one individual does not make decisions for another (Block 1993; Senge, 1990). Because partners are equal, they make their own individual choices and make decisions collaboratively. Learner choice is implicit in every communication of content and, to the greatest extent possible, the process used to learn the content.

Dialogue

To arrive at mutually acceptable decisions, partners engage in dialogue (Bernstein, 1991; Ellinor & Gerard, 1998; Friere, 1970). In a partnership, one individual does not impose, dominate, or control. Partners engage in conversation, learning together as they explore ideas. When this principle is applied to classrooms, it means that teachers embrace dialogue rather than lecture. Avoiding manipulation, teachers engage students in conversation about content, and think and learn with learners as everyone moves through content being discussed.

Praxis

The purpose of partnership is to enable individuals to have more meaningful experiences. In partnership relationships, meaning arises when people reflect on ideas and then put those actions into practice (Friere, 1970; Gadamer, 1975; Senge, 1990). A requirement for partnership is that each individual is free to reconstruct and use content the way he or she considers it most useful. When this principle is applied to classrooms, teachers offer numerous opportunities for learners to reflect on the practical implications of new content being learned.

Voice

Partnership is multi-vocal rather than univocal, and all individuals in a partnership require opportunities to express their point of view (Argyris, 1990; Bohm, 1990; Isaacs, 1994; Vella, 1995). Indeed, a primary benefit of a partnership is that each individual has access to a multiplicity of perspectives rather than the singular perspective of the patriarch. When this principle is applied to classrooms, it means that all students have the freedom to express their opinions about content being covered. Since opinions will inevitably vary, conversation is encouraged that allows people the freedom to express a variety of opinions.

Symbiosis

In a partnership, all learners benefit from the success, learning, or experience of one learner (Friere, 1970; Senge, 1990; Vella, 1995). In other words, all members are rewarded by what one individual contributes to any group activity. When this principle is applied to classrooms, it has two major implications. First, one of the teacher's goals should be learning along with learners. Thus, the teacher learns about students' work contexts, the strengths and weaknesses of the content when seen as an application for that environment, multiple perspectives on the content being presented when seen through the eyes of learners, and so on. Second, it is important that teachers operating within the partnership paradigm should believe that learner knowledge and expertise are as valuable as their own. Then, it is important that they have faith in learners' abilities to invent useful new applications of the content they are exploring.

Group Partnership

Any sharing of knowledge is a deceptively complex power relation, and if it is to be a genuine partnership relationship, then ideas need to be presented provisionally. Partners allow and enable each other to make choices, and those choices include whether or not they agree with ideas. In partnership relations, ideas are shared through conversation, and learners decide on their own the merit of each new idea presented.

Six learning processes have been identified to help facilitate partnership learning. These are simple, easy-to-use, proven methods to increase the effectiveness of learning sessions with groups. In research studies of staff development presentations where these learning processes were used, measures of learner engagement, understanding, knowledge retention, and enjoyment showed that those processes described here are superior to traditional methods of training. They can be used separately but are likely more effective when used together. The partnership learning processes are: (a) Thinking Devices, (b) Question Recipes, (c) Cooperative Learning, (d) Reflection Learning, (e) Experiential Learning, and (f) Stories.

Thinking Devices

How can one learn the truth by thinking? As one learns to see a face better if one draws it.

Ludwig Wittgenstein

What Are Thinking Devices?

A Thinking Device is an object presented to a group of learners in a manner that allows the learners to critically analyze the work through dialogue. Any device that might prompt comments, ideas, or critical reflection (such as a film clip, photograph, case, vignette, painting, literary work, song) can function as a Thinking Device. What is essential is that the device is used in the class in a way that prompts open dialogue.

Why Use Thinking Devices?

Thinking Devices enable dialogue around content to occur. In other words, they provide a learning opportunity in which all learners feel free to reflect, voice their opinions, and think along with others in the group learning situation. Thinking Devices provide learners with an opportunity to critically analyze the content being covered, to discuss their prior knowledge of a subject, and openly explore the "real-world" positive and negative implications of the material being covered.

What Are the Elements of Effective Thinking Devices?

What counts with Thinking Devices is not the learners' immediate interaction with them, but rather the dialogue occurring after the device has been experienced. To provide opportunities for authentic dialogue, consider using the following strategies:

1. After learners have experienced a Thinking Device, begin by simply asking them to discuss what their experience of it was like, ask a generic Question Recipe (described in the next section of this chapter) such as, "What do you make of this?"

2. Consider suspending your views during dialogue sessions. When you enter into dialogue without suspending your point of view, you risk having your point of view dominate discussion, silencing learners in the session.

3. Accept each view as valid. Failing to encourage a multiplicity of views, is failing to provide opportunities for each individual to be a partner in the session. Thinking Devices are one way that you can communicate your commitment to partnership learning, to learning with learners as opposed to training learners.

What is an Example of a Thinking Device?

Thinking Devices take many forms: Simply writing the word respect on a white board and asking students to discuss respect is one basic use of a Thinking Device. Also, music or music videos can be used to surface conversation and dialogue about topics. Frequently, common texts can be used as Thinking Devices when the teacher encourages students to reflect and discuss their thoughts and feelings about a document. Some rich and meaningful conversations can be provoked by encouraging students to comment on the Bill of Rights or the Declaration of Independence.

In a course on non-verbal communication, film clips from popular movies, rock videos, and advertisements were used as Thinking Devices to heighten everyone's awareness of body language. After each clip was shown, students were asked what they read in the movements and gestures of the actors on film. Students were encouraged to look at the actors from a variety of perspectives and to really explore the many things that can be said without words. The result was a highly engaged, sensitive conversation about many complicated aspects of non-verbal communication.

What Are Some Do's and Don'ts?

Do:

1. Do use Question Recipes (described in the next section) to facilitate discussion of Thinking Devices.
2. Do use a variety of different media (art, music, literature, cartoons, vignettes and cases) for Thinking Devices.
3. Do encourage the voicing of a variety of perspectives on a Thinking Device.
4. Do validate all authentic responses to a Thinking Device.
5. Do delight in the learning you experience as learners respond to the Thinking Device.

<u>Don't:</u>

      1. Don't use Thinking Devices to elicit a predictable response.

      2. Don't judge responses to Thinking Devices as right or wrong.

      3. Don't be afraid to let the group dialogue move off track.

      4. Don't be afraid to bring the group dialogue back on track.

      5. Don't underestimate your learners' responses.

Question Recipes

always the beautiful answer who asks a more beautiful question
— *e.e. Cummings*

What Are Question Recipes?

Similar to recipes used in action science and dialogue sessions to promote organizational learning, Question Recipes are simple questions that teachers can use to open up conversation. Initially, Question Recipes may seem artificial and overly formulaic, but research suggests that effective use of recipes can enable teachers to create a context in which there is enriched dialogue. Remember, one principle of the partnership mindset is creating an environment that encourages open and equal dialogue. Question Recipes promote that dialogue.

Why Use Question Recipes?

Question Recipes are proven approaches for encouraging dialogue. Because Question Recipes are easy to remember and use, they are simple to practice. They help improve spontaneous questioning skills.

It's important to note that Question Recipes are not just Thinking Devices that teachers use with students. They are also for students to learn how to use to promote dialogue.

What Are the Elements of Effective Question Recipes?

Question Recipes promote the creation of an open environment in which all learners have an opportunity to voice their ideas and concerns, and where all learners feel that their points of view are equally valued.

Question Recipes have two essential elements: First, they are open-ended and as such they encourage detailed, broader responses. Second, Question Recipes are non-judgmental; they do not prompt responses that can be judged right or wrong. For example, if learners are asked how they feel about a film clip, they can respond without fear that they will be told they are wrong. Informal observations suggest that when learners are asked judgmental questions they are much less likely to respond and engage in spirited dialogue.

What Are Some Examples of Effective Question Recipes?

As you become more comfortable with this form of questioning, you will probably gather your own list of Question Recipes to use. Quite possibly you already have a repertoire of open-ended, non-judgmental questions that you use comfortably during the classes you teach. Here are some recipes you may wish to start with or add to your repertoire of Question Recipes:

- *Tell us more about that …*
  Use this recipe to encourage students to expand upon their comments.

- *How do you see this working …?*
  Use this recipe to push dialogue to a more realistic discussion.

- *What are some other ways of looking at this …?*
  Use this recipe to encourage multiple perspectives and to encourage students to voice their concerns and ideas with respect to whatever topic is being explored.
  Example: This is an effective Question Recipe at a Classroom meeting.

- *What questions do you have about …?*
  Use this recipe to encourage students to ask questions about the material that has been discussed.

- What leads you to believe …?
  Use this recipe to open discussion of the logic, rationales, or even prejudices that are used as justification for statement of fact.

- *How do you feel about …?*
  Use this recipe to open up dialogue around the emotional aspects of the issue being explored.

- *What do you make of …?*
  The most generic Question Recipe; use this to simply open up the conversation among learners.

What Are Some Do's and Don'ts?

<u>Do:</u>

1. Do use Question Recipes frequently to encourage dialogue.

2. Do listen empathically to each response.

3. Do encourage a variety of responses to Question Recipes.

4. Do recognize that each response is valuable.

5. Do be certain to have a genuine desire to learn what each person has to say in response to the Question Recipe.

<u>Don't:</u>

1. Don't allow your ideas and preconceptions to interfere with empathic listening.

2. Don't use Question Recipes in a manipulative way. If people feel manipulated, chances are they will respond negatively.

3. Don't allow each open-ended dialogue to continue longer than most want it to continue.

4. Don't allow one person's views to silence others.

5. Don't assume that Question Recipes are the only kind of question to use.

Cooperative Learning

The Master doesn't talk, the master acts.
When her work is done,
the people say, "Amazing:
we did it, all by ourselves!"

Lao-tzu, Tao Te Ching

What is Cooperative Learning?

Cooperative Learning is one of the most successful instructional strategies studied in the past three decades. Simply put, Cooperative Learning is learning mediated by the learners rather than the instructor. In cooperative learning, learners work in groups to teach themselves content being covered.

Why Use Cooperative Learning?

Cooperative Learning allows learners to take over the role of instructor. In many cases, Cooperative Learning, because it is by definition an interactive learning process which leads students to master material before they teach it to other learners, can be more engaging than outstanding lectures, and is consistently more engaging than less effective lectures. Cooperative Learning also promotes partnership in the learning session by allowing every learner to assume the role of instructor. Finally, Cooperative Learning provides an opportunity for learners who may not wish to speak out in a larger group, a more comfortable situation in which to voice their opinions.

What Are the Elements of Cooperative Learning?

Cooperative Learning can involve groups of any size, from two learners to very large groups, although triads are often considered the ideal size for a group. Cooperative Learning sessions can be used as a way for groups to cover material, problem solve, brainstorm, or invent new ideas.

What Are Some Examples of Processes Used in Cooperative Learning?

Turn-to-your-neighbor: Learners are grouped in pairs. Then, at various points throughout the class, the teacher asks the students to turn to their partners to discuss the material. For example, in a social studies class learning Cultural Transformation Theory, students might be asked to "turn-to-their-neighbor" and paraphrase the meaning of different concepts at different points during the discussion to ensure that they understand each idea being discussed.

Think-pair-share: Learners are grouped in pairs. The facilitator shares a Thinking Device with the learners, and asks them a Question Recipe. Then, they think about their individual answer to the question, perhaps writing down their response. Following this, they turn to their partner, and together they share and discuss their response to the Thinking Device. Finally, the facilitator asks learners to share with the larger group the insights they gained from their short conversation with their partner.

Jigsaw: Students form into groups with equal numbers of learners. Each group is given a portion of some larger text being covered during the session and works to learn its material so well that they will be able to teach it to others. After each group has achieved mastery of its portion of the material, the groups are reconfigured so that each new group has a member from each of the previous groups. Then each member teaches the others his or her version of the material until everyone has taught her or his material and all the content has been covered.

What Are Some Do's and Don'ts?

<u>Do:</u>

1. Do develop simple, clear instructions so that everyone is clear on how the Cooperative Learning activity will proceed.

2. Do plan ahead, and think through all aspects of the activity so that you can "de-bug" the process.

3. Do use Cooperative Learning as an alternative to lectures.

4. Do link Cooperative Learning to real-life concerns.

5. Do provide opportunities for learners to choose their topics and roles within each activity.

<u>Don't:</u>

1. Don't assume that Cooperative Learning "will just work out" without planning and structure.

2. Don't force learners into roles they'd rather not take on.

3. Don't ignore learners' personalities when setting up groups.

4. Don't ignore time lines.

5. Don't be oppressive about time.

Reflection Learning

It seems ... to be one of the paradoxes of creativity that in order to think originally, we must familiarize ourselves with the ideas of others.

George Kneller, The Art & Science of Creativity

What is Reflection Learning?

Reflection Learning involves carefully-structured team-learning tasks designed to enable learners to reflect on how they can apply content to their personal lives.

Why Use Reflection Learning?

Reflection Learning provides people with opportunities to explore, immediately, how content being covered can be generalized and implemented. Reflection Learning provides learners with an opportunity to explore realistically how content being covered might be translated into new behaviors or strategies, and to problem solve from new perspectives. Most importantly, perhaps, Reflection Learning enables praxis by providing concrete opportunities for learners to reflect, invent, and act on knowledge.

What Are the Elements of Reflection Learning?

Any learning activity that prompts learners to apply knowledge to their personal life can be considered Reflection Learning. Usually Reflection Learning involves posing a personal problem or issue, and then structuring a small group discussion in which group members explore how partnership education can help solve the proposed problem.

What is an Example of Reflection Learning?

A central task of partnership educators is the rewriting of curriculum to include partnership content. Thus, a common Reflection Learning activity is for teachers to explore how the partnership-dominator continuum can be used to inform instruction. For example, English teachers might explore how to incorporate into their classes more works by women from a variety of racial or cultural backgrounds, such as Toni Morrison, Alice Walker, Maya Angelou, Gloria Naylor, Sandra Cisernos, Leslie Marmon Silko, and Amy Tan. Humanities teachers could explore how curriculum could be adapted to a partnership perspective that is more multicultural, more gender-balanced, and more focused on issues of human rights and responsibilities.

What Are Some Do's and Don'ts?

Do:

1. Do tie the Reflection Learning activity to real-life challenges.

2. Do allow learners to choose their topic.

3. Do choose a facilitator from within the group to keep the group on track and positive.

4. Do write clear instructions and print handouts to guide learners through the exercise.

Don't:

1. Don't make instructions too complicated. Keep the task simple.

2. Don't ignore groups that seem to be off-track.

3. Don't lose track of time. Enable groups to maintain intensity and focus.

4. Don't give challenges to each group. Let them pick their own, and try to ensure that each group takes on a challenge that has real meaning for each member.

Experiential Learning

The best way to learn how to climb is to climb.
— *Alain*

What is Experiential Learning?

The term Experiential Learning refers to any learning activity that allows learners to experience the phenomenon they are exploring. In other words, Partnership educators employing Experiential Learning create activities that enable learners to act out the behaviors, strategies or other content being learned.

Why Include Experiential Learning?

Experiential Learning can provide an opportunity for learners to see how well they can use new concepts they are learning, remind learners of the concrete attributes of a partnership phenomena being studied, or allow learners to gain new insights into their thoughts, assumptions, and behaviors. Experiential Learning can be fun, challenging, engaging, and provocative — and at times uncomfortable.

What Are the Elements of Experiential Learning?

Effective Experiential Learning provides learners with a simulation of some elements of Partnership Education content being covered during the learning session. Thus, learners are provided with an experience that simulates reality. What matters in Experiential Learning is that learners experience content in a way that simulates the real-life cognitive, emotional, and sensual elements of the content being covered.

What is an Example of Experiential Learning?

In communication classes at Ryerson Polytechnic University, Susan Cody uses Experiential Learning to reinforce learning about cross-cultural communication. This activity can be used in secondary education as well.

In her classes, after covering content on cross-cultural communication, Susan divides her class into three teams, and explains that each team is now going to learn to embody a unique culture. The teams are directed to different break out rooms, with their cultural instructions in hand, and they then quickly learn the characteristics of a culture that they will role-play when the 3 teams are brought together. Of course the cultures are strikingly different: In one group personal space is 20 centimeters, in a second personal space is 60; one group has a sacred ritual it performs, another group is atheistic; one group believes in socializing, dining, and drinking, another group believes time is money and forbids some kinds of dining and drinking, and so on.

When Susan reunites the groups, she asks them to work together to resolve a business deal, but inevitably the teams have great difficulty dealing with their cultural differences. Often, the debriefing of this experience leads to learners gaining startling insights into their attitudes toward people from a variety of cultural backgrounds.

Another example, which is usually more emotionally laden, has been used in history classes where both ancient and modern societies are being studied using the partnership/dominator continuum as analytical lens. This is an exercise where learners are asked to close their eyes and imagine that they have just awakened to find that they are now of the opposite sex: that is, girls or women are now male and boys or men are now female. Learners are then asked to imagine what life would be like for them in this new identity. They are asked to imagine this, in detail, in the society of the United States today, and to pay attention to how they feel as they do so. Students usually find that what they felt and learned brings to life what they have been studying about the partnership and dominator social configurations. They are asked what they would feel like if they have to stay that way, what they would do to make their lives better, etc. Learners are then asked to come together and share their feelings and thoughts.

A variation of this exercise is to then also ask learners to imagine themselves in the Taliban's Afghanistan, in ancient Athens, and in Minoan Crete (all of which they have been studying). This exercise is a dramatic opportunity to experience how life is very different for both genders in partnership and dominator social settings, how, for example, because of the authoritarianism and constant warfare of dominator-oriented societies, despite their rank and privilege, males don't fare so well either, how hard it is for boys to take on the roles assigned to girls in dominator-oriented societies, what a huge difference it makes for girls' lives, etc.

Some Do's and Don'ts

Do:

1. Do use Question Recipes to debrief the session.

2. Do pay careful attention to learner's emotions during Experiential Learning and the debriefing.

3. Do encourage learners to respect the vulnerability of others following intense Experiential Learning activities.

4. Do enable learners to see the connection between the Experiential Learning activity and the content being covered.

5. Do encourage learners to reflect on the assumptions underlying their behavior.

Don'ts:

1. Don't ignore group dynamics during sessions.

2. Don't be overly obvious when highlighting links with content.

3. Don't allow groups to blame rather than reflect.

4. Don't underestimate the emotional intensity of Experiential Learning.

5. Don't force anyone to participate in Experiential Learning exercises.

Stories

> If stories come to you, care for them. And learn to give them away where they are needed. Sometimes a person needs a story more than food to stay alive. That is why we put these stories in each other's memory. This is how people care for themselves.
>
> *Barry Lopez*

What are Effective Stories?

In 1996, 80 university students were asked by the University of Kansas Center for Research on Learning researchers to describe the teaching strategies that most helped them learn. In those interviews, students repeatedly described stories as significant enhancements for learning. Stories are entertaining and engaging, and they give learners a concrete context in which to place abstract ideas. Stories make ideas real.

Why Include Stories?

Any presentation can be enhanced through the use of Stories that serve to illustrate important ideas being delivered. In fact, often Stories are the elements of a presentation that learners recall most vividly. For this reason, it is important to use Stories to illustrate content that is especially noteworthy, so that learners can carry away strong recollections of important material.

What are the Elements of an Effective Story?

The following comments are offered as suggestions, not hard and fast rules:

1. Often, the most effective Stories are on topics that are broad enough that most learners can relate to them. You may create successful Stories if they deal with topics such as family, school, sports, and so forth.

2. Effective Stories, although usually only 1 to 3 minutes in length, still need to have narrative unity. As Aristotle suggested, effective narrative requires a beginning, middle, and end, and all the parts should flow through that simple sequence. Parts of the story that do not contribute to the flow of the narrative are often parts that should be left out.

3. Finally, you may find it effective to include Stories that draw on basic human drives and emotions. Look for Stories that involve surprise, fear, desire, acceptance, love, reconciliation, spirit, and so on. As someone once said, there is no moving the mind before you move the emotions. Try to find Stories that speak directly to each person's heart.

What is an Example of a Story?

At a University of Kansas workshop on inclusive education for students with severe disabilities, teachers wrote moving Stories. One was about the friendship of two five-year- olds: Eric, who has cerebral palsy and utilizes a wheelchair, and Dena, a very chatty able-bodied five-year-old. At Christmas Dena wanted to give every child in her class a present. When her mother said she could only choose just one to receive a present, she chose Eric.

Here's a Section of the Teacher's Story:

Dena "thought it was a darn good idea if he had his own lap quilt, to keep him covered in the cold because of course he was bussed in and needed to be out in the air a lot, and he was a skinny little kid anyway, and he got cold quite easily. Dena and her Mom, who was a sewer, went out to pick the fabric, and, I think, Dena even asked what his favorite color was and made a quilt with a green border and little children's figures on it."

What Are Some Do's and Don'ts?

Do:

1. Do include several Stories in a presentation.

2. Do include sensual details that make your Stories come alive.

3. Do make note of delivery techniques (pauses, voice modulation, and so on) that render your Stories more engaging.

4. Do borrow any relevant, effective Stories you hear others tell.

<u>Don't:</u>

1. Don't include Stories that anyone might find offensive.

2. Don't tell Stories that are too long. You might be wise to always err on the side of too short rather than too long.

3. Don't include too many Stories.

4. Don't tell a Story unless it is relevant to the content being discussed.

Conclusion

The partnership learning processes described here are tools to be used to create an enriching learning community, a group-learning setting where everyone, grows, and develops together. In truth, the learning processes are tools that can be used to create something beautiful. And as with any other creation, the approach and spirit of the tool user is most important. Teachers with a genuine desire to learn, listen, grow, and develop, to be partners with all learners, hold an attitude and spirit that can make a difference. Their attitude begins to enable learning to be the intense, significant experience it should be.

CHAPTER FOUR

Transforming Violence: Peacebuilding, Anti-bias Awareness, and Conflict Resolution

by Sarah Pirtle

"My students arrive at school more and more upset," say many teachers. "Something is worse now. What is going on?" At this crossroads point in the story of humankind, the ache of our culture can be seen in the level of pain and confusion that many young people carry. They call out like the proverbial canaries in the coal mine, revealing their upset and feelings of fragmentation without being able to ask directly for help.

Despite our best intentions, our culture is not able to welcome its children into a secure circle of life. From a young age and on a scale so alarming that violence becomes commonplace and expected, they are initiated into the paradigm of violence and power-over others. The big story that they are truly part of is hidden from them, and they receive traumatic experiences which make it difficult to connect with others. Yet in the caring actions of ordinary people around them, they are able to meet the reality of another force, stronger than the force of violence, that insists upon fairness, connection, and healing.

We have gotten accustomed to the myriad manifestations of violence in the world, like the frog who is trapped in a pot of water that is heating up so slowly that it doesn't leap out of its surroundings. In the 1980's the US Surgeon General declared that violence reached epidemic proportions. Our children swim in a world where violence is accepted as normal and presented as something people have to adjust to. Partnership Education blows the whistle, not only by addressing the violence, but also by pointing to the resources we have to mend our schools, our communities, and ourselves.

Children routinely experience cognitive dissonance when on the one hand they learn that killing is wrong, and on the other hand focus in history lessons on the details of war and war heroes. Like the history books, the media portrays violence to the world as part of business as usual among world leaders entrusted with billions of lives. A newspaper cartoon illuminated this in a drawing depicting five male leaders of the world, usually at opposition, but here smiling, standing with their arms linked shoulder to shoulder, unified in the song they sang: "All we are saying is give bombs a chance." If we jump a paradigm from the political sphere to the evolutionary, the question arises: How do we as a species together turn around the killing, aggression, and multiple forms of violence in our world?

A key characteristic of Partnership Education is its ability to talk about the roots and tenacity of the epidemic of violence and describe why it is difficult to avert, while at the same time engaging us in the opportunity for change. Riane Eisler's books, *The Chalice and the Blade* and *Tomorrow's Children* direct us to a firm foundation to stand upon — our human encoding, our ability to redirect our intention, and our thousands of years as a species experiencing partnership.

Transforming Violence

With humanity at such a turning point, young people need to be included in facing this epidemic and included in making the choices that the crisis poses. During the 1980's peace educators searched for developmentally appropriate methods to use in talking with students about the threat of nuclear war. Silence was broken on the existence of weapons that could annihilate the world in minutes, but debates raged as to whether or not young people should be included in the conversations. It was compared to a family where family members are severely ill and the situation is hidden from the children. Psychologist Robert J. Lifton and members of organizations such as Interhelp and Educators for Social Responsibility helped teachers to see that it was more terrifying for children to be aware of danger and have adults not talk to them about it. They said that the silence of denial did not protect them. They showed how to raise the issues without asking young people to solve a problem that adults were responsible for solving — the task of creating a safe and just world that works for everyone. They also demonstrated the importance of giving students role models who engaged in addressing rather than avoiding the mammoth task.

Today talk about violence isn't hidden from young people; it abounds. It is not a distant problem; social violence, bullying, and prejudice are immediate problems that young people face. Young people can themselves participate directly in change; in the way they treat peers and siblings, students have a choice as to whether or not they throw their weight with the positive force for connection. Partnership Education looks at the character of these discussions.

Here are general guidelines:

• Students need to talk with the adults who matter to them about the forms of violence, domination, and prejudice that they see or experience. They need to have their experiences validated. They need to hear about and experience alternatives and encounter people who are working for change.

• It is important to recognize that all the manifestations of mistreatment are significant and hurtful whether they are physical, verbal, social, or the insidious interpersonal, cultural, and institutional violence of racism, sexism, and other kinds of bias. In fact, prejudice and oppression inject the violence of power-over into the whole social fabric. Facing and changing forms of oppression is crucial to blowing the whistle on violence.

• Young people — whether preschoolers or high schoolers — have a need to talk with teachers about forms of violence that are present for them. Be led by their needs. As events happen in the classroom, school, neighborhood that touch them, or as they are aware of regional, national, and world events, raise these and talk together. Let young people direct the conversations to what is on their minds.

• At the same time initiate conversations about bias rather than waiting for students to raise the topic, for bias breeds in silence and the insidious nature of power, prejudice, and privilege bears explaining.

• Keep in the forefront of the conversation a grounded sense of hope and possibility while, at the same time, allowing a range of emotions to be expressed. Point to all the nonviolent social changes that humans have made. Talk about the boundless creativity within human beings to face challenges and make breakthroughs.

• When talking about violence done by young people, make clear that these are examples of the influence of adult violence spreading to young people, rather than having it seem that the locus of the problem is within young people.

• Let young people know that every person has a choice for how they live, can make a choice whether they follow models of domination or models of partnership and alternatives to violence, and that every person's choice matters.

<u>Activity One:</u> What is Violence? What is the Opposite of Violence?

Grade level: 4th - 12th

Goals: To raise the topic of violence.
　　　　To present the force of active caring as ultimately stronger than violence.
　　　　To study the more subtle dynamics of violence.

Procedure:

1. Brainstorm examples of violence. If the list doesn't extend to many aspects, bring out examples that are far-reaching: Interpersonal violence in school, neighborhood or family; random violence, international violence.

2. Following the lead of students, decide whether this is an opportunity to share emotions. "How does violence personally affect you?" is a powerful question. It's not to be shared casually but, rather, with people who really care about the answers. Create a safe atmosphere for telling each other the kinds of violence that weigh heavily. Examples: A student says, "I get really upset when I hear the parents of the kid in the next apartment screaming at him. I bet he's being hit and that really gets to me." Or, "I can't stand the pictures in the newspaper with the dead bodies of people killed in war."

3. Also, brainstorm examples of caring and connection that they are aware of. Look for events around them that illustrate caring and community-building, and think of people who exemplify this. Examples: "Ms. Otis runs the Family Center in the school," "Mr. Kates at the News Store always jokes around with us," or "A high school club makes blankets for the homeless."

4. "As you look at all these examples, how would you describe what violence is?" Lead an exploration that will produce original thinking. If it's helpful, add that the dictionary definition of violence is "a use of force so as to injure or damage" or "unjust use of force or power." Another way to describe violence is "intent to harm." Help them get below the surface of the problem and describe what the crux of it is to them.

5. "What is the opposite of violence?" Encourage them to see that the opposite of violence is also a force, and both forces are present in the world. Sample descriptions: Connection, active caring, not just standing by, speaking up.

<u>Going further:</u>

6. One of the difficulties of addressing violence is that it can be used unjustly by a person in authority, a person with social status or political might. Another difficulty, as

scholars in the field of peace studies point out, is that unjust force can be not only physical, but also economic, or social.

For instance, the song "Seed Savers" in Chapter 9, "Music to Build Partnership" illustrates economic violence which results from companies with economic clout patenting seeds. When impoverished farmers are forced to purchase seeds, rather than reusing seeds as they always have, this can lead to physical harm — to hunger and entrenched poverty.

As appropriate for your group, explore these other dimensions of violence. Structure this as a discussion so that students are encouraged to explore their own thoughts. Frame questions. Example: Is it harder to see an act as violent if it is done by a person who is admired? Include racism, sexism, and other oppressions as examples of violence and intent to harm. Clarify what emotional violence means and how abuse, discrimination, and constant humiliation and subjugation of a person or a group of people has very similar traumatic effects as physical violence.

7. Emphasize that we are looking not only at one force — violence — but we are looking at two forces. The force of positive connection, caring, and partnership is also an active force. Gandhi, Martin Luther King, Barbara Deming, and other people who have dedicated their lives to nonviolence, in fact, describe it as the strongest force. In Partnership Education, we describe this active caring force as fundamental to humans and available at every moment.

Extension: Art Activity: Two Forces in Our World

Draw or make a collage that expresses the presence of violence. Then react to it: Tear it, scribble over it, express your feelings about this violence. Next, draw or create a collage that expresses the opposite of violence. Paste or place these two in relationship to each other.

8. For older students, examine the mindset of domination. The military defines war as "imposing your will on your adversary." Talk about two adversaries pitted against each other with these positions: "You must do what I say" and "I refuse to do what you say." Partnership offers a whole different mindset. It says: "I want to think together about the common good and find what is in the highest and best interest of all."

Activity Two: How Violence is Like a Virus

Grades: 5th - 12th

Overview: The following four concepts can be used for several class discussions in social studies. Present the information in the best way to encourage dialogue and allow students to grapple with the concepts.

Procedure: Pick and choose the sections that are relevant for your own class.

1. Violence and trauma have ongoing effects.

Violence doesn't glance off people: It sticks to them.

Talk about cartoons which portray that it is easy to experience violence and then get up and walk away as if nothing had happened. In reality, the influence of violence lasts after the physical pain has gone away. Discuss examples of people they know who have experienced forms of violence. How does violence linger after the deeds or threats are over? Collect stories from local, national, and international news which present the feelings and experiences of survivors of violence. For instance, look for stories of people in Bosnia and Northern Ireland, as well as, local people. Be sure to define violence and trauma broadly so that the effects of racism, sexism, poverty, child abuse are also seen.

2. Violence has been operating like a virus.

Violence has created a world-wide social illness from which the world is reeling. In medicine a virus isn't removed; to heal the body the virus becomes inactive as the body's own protective mechanisms are strengthened so that the virus no longer governs and balance is restored.

As you examine the metaphor of violence as a virus, list these parts of the analogy and encourage discussion and debate: (a) Violence debilitates a person's normal functioning and robs energy, (b) It brings focus to itself and distracts from the usual tasks needed to continue life, (c) It replicates; it can cause victims to pass on the violence and continue repeating it through some form of mistreatment of others, (d) Violence tries to subdue and destroy efforts to stop itself.

3. <u>Why is peace a dirty word?</u>

Encourage a candid discussion of negative associations with the word — "peace." Examples: Peace is wimpy, peace is promoted by people who aren't cool, peace is impossible.

Then examine: If violence can be characterized as a sneaky virus, why would violence want peace to be denigrated?

What words would the class prefer to use for the force that ultimately helps all people by restoring our communities to a state of connection? Note: In the sections that follow, the word "peace" is used. Replace and translate it as necessary so that the positive force can be seen without an overlay of stereotypes.

4. <u>Violence is a Distortion.</u>

Partnership is one way to describe a social body where the virus of violence has been rendered inactive. But partnership doesn't mean lack of conflict. Conflict is basic to the dynamic nature of life. Violence is an aberration. A place of partnership where violence doesn't hold sway wouldn't be a place without conflict. What would it be like?

Example: There would still be daily conflicts, disagreements, and differences to resolve. The difference is that there would also be a multitude of creative and constructive ways of addressing these. People would handle the underlying issues, needs, and emotions nonviolently using constructive communication.

Activity Three: **"Don't Pass It On"**

Grades: 5th - 12th

Overview: Song lyrics and discussion get across this human problem: How do we make a conscious choice not to repeat unfair things that happened to us?

Procedure:

1. Discuss the phrase: "Pass it on" and how it applies to social mistreatment. Can you remember a time someone did something to you that you didn't like — putting you down, or picking on you because you are younger or smaller? Did you notice at the time that you didn't like it? Did you conclude from that experience that you wouldn't put someone else down or wouldn't pick on someone else because they are younger or smaller, or did you conclude that you would be sure to treat someone else the same way? Why or why not?

What happens inside us when we are mistreated?

Now apply this to violence. When someone has experienced or faced violence, how do they choose not to repeat it and pass it on? This imagery relates to the metaphor above: Violence acts as a virus that by invasive action is wanting to be continued.

2. Share this story to seed discussion. Students at a high school in Springfield, MA were discussing nonviolence with Sarah Pirtle. Two students reported an important decision made by their mothers; their mothers had told them that when they were little they were hit by their parents (the students' grandparents) but they made the decision never to hit their own children. As a result, the class created these song lyrics. Share these words as a poem or create a tune for the words.

> There are secrets in some families,
> nobody wants to say.
> A slap in the face, a scream in the night.
> A life of fright, push the troubles away.
> Don't pass it on, don't pass it on.
>
> Don't pass it on, don't pass it on.
> But I won't do that to my child.
> Even though it was done to me.
> Take my hand and take a stand.
> We won't pass on what should not be.
> Don't pass it on, don't pass it on.
> Don't pass it on, don't pass it on.
>
> Keeping secrets in the back of my mind
> I start to find that I don't want to hide.
> It's no shame. I can't change the past,
> but I can walk in the truth I have at last.
> Don't pass it on, don't pass it on.
> Don't pass it on, don't pass it on.

3. Discussion questions: Is the decision to repeat violence that is done to you conscious or unconscious? Can you think of an example of someone experiencing mistreatment but not passing it on? Also, discuss how this happens during interactions in sports when a player must decide how to respond if they feel a member of the other team has purposefully hurt them. Talk about the process of "breaking the chain."

See also the song, "Courage," by Bob Blue in Activity Five.

4. Study this quote from Dr. Paula Green, director of the Karuna Center for Peacebuilding: "Self-awareness or consciousness involves recognizing and monitor-

ing the flow of thoughts and emotions in the mind so that one's behavior is ethical, principled, and clear rather than dictated by negative thought-forms or conditioned feelings." Discuss how hard it is the heat of a conflict to notice that we have a choice, yet how important it is.

Activity Four: Passing Along Violence — An Historical Perspective

Grade level: 4th - 12th

Goals: To look at human efforts to maintain partnership behavior.
      to look at nonviolent social change.

Procedure:

1. Some archeologists posit that for most years of human history people lived more peacefully, and that this was how the majority of people lived during the long span of time scholars call the Paleolithic and Neolithic, or Old and New Stone Ages, and in some places such as Minoan Crete well into the Bronze Age. It may be that intraspecies warfare for those people was unthinkable, that weapons were used to kill animals for food, not to kill other humans, and when strangers arrived they were not considered potential threats or enemies, but potential resources for trading or new skills.

   Recorded history gives the predominant image that societies have primarily been organized around domination, yet archeological information reveals thousands of years of partnership societies that pre-date them and were systematically hidden through the destruction of books, the twisting of myths, and the appropriation of key symbols.

   Use the information in the activity, "What the Spirals Say" found in Chapter Six, "Partnership Education: A Place to Begin" to introduce this research, or refer to *The Chalice and the Blade.* You may also want to use the timeline activity in Chapter Six, "Sample Activity Ten: The Lost History of Peace."

2. According to this scholarship, towns living in partnership in Neolithic times were introduced to violence. They were attacked by invaders intent on destroying the town, killing all the men, and capturing the women. This led to a major cultural shift, toward a system where warfare, both offensive and defensive, spread like a virus. Ask students to imagine what choices the inhabitants of these towns faced. What happened when violence was introduced? Why was it so difficult to reverse? How did warfare then spread like a virus? How have the effects of violence passed down through history?

Resources:

- *The Chalice and the Blade* by Riane Eisler (Harper&Row, 1987). See Chapter Five, "Memories of a Lost Age."

- *The Year the Horses Came* by Mary Mackey (Onyx, 1993) is an adult historical novel based upon extensive research. It depicts such events and portions could be used with students.

3. Talk with students about events in history where a peaceful society, unaccustomed to people hurting other people, meet humans who are intent on dominating them. Example: The Tianos encounter with Columbus. What happens when we look at these historic events through the partnership/dominator lens?

4. Study the importance of social reforms achieved nonviolently. These include:

- the prohibition of physical punishment which was once common in schools

- less violent and more humane treatment of the mentally ill

- the end of slavery

- African Americans' right to vote

- women's right to vote

- prohibiting the violence of toxins such as DDT poisoning our natural environment.

Cornerstones: Here is a summary of key information about violence.

- Violence is not pre-determined by biology. Aggression, dominance, and violence are not hallmarks of homo sapiens. The fundamental force in human history is partnership.

- Human beings are encoded for cooperation. The brains of young children grow and develop through caring interactions.

- Children learn by modeling, by imitation. Children become aggressive when their central models use aggressive solutions to solve problems. Children seek enduring models of partnership.

- Violence is not normal, and we don't have to adjust to it. By acclimating to violence, it is perpetuated.

- Violence is traumatizing. Because violence hurts us, we need help from others to heal from this hurt.

- It is not inevitable that people will be violent.

- Some people who have been mistreated or hurt by violence try to get rid of their hurt by doing to others what was done to them. Every person can unlearn violence if they have sufficient support and the intention to change.

- The majority of people want to make a world free from violence, a just world that works for everyone.

Violence in all its forms takes a tremendous toll. Rudderlessness, addiction, and disconnection are some of the symptoms of widespread social trauma. We're in a culture organized around domination, and that means there is an inherent insecurity. "We are living in an epidemic of depression.… Every indication suggests that more people are depressed, more of the time, more severely, and starting earlier in their lives, than ever before," according to Richard O'Connor, author of *Undoing Depression* (1997). He adds that, depression is not just a biochemical process, "but the individual has been made susceptible to depression through life experiences." Yet we don't talk enough about the number of people in society who are showing symptoms of trauma, and we don't talk about the social causes.

Contemporary theory on trauma recovery provides insights. In her book, *Trauma and Recovery: The Aftermath of Violence — From Domestic Abuse to Political Terror* (NY: Basic Books, 1992), Dr. Judith Herman describes common stages that war veterans and other violence survivors go through. "The fundamental stages of recovery are establishing safety, reconstructing the trauma story, and restoring the connection between survivors and their community" (Herman, 1992, p. 3). She explains that in the safety of a healing relationship a person travels from remembrance and mourning, to reconnection, and then a feeling of commonality. It could be said that just as individuals make this courageous transition from denial to healing from violence, step by step our whole society has the opportunity to embark upon a similar journey in dealing with the long-term effects of domination. We are trying to create places for young people and adults alike to be able to speak about what has been denied, and help students face the history of war not as a history of glory, but a history of trauma.

Herman explains that the study of psychological trauma "provokes such intense controversy that it periodically becomes anathema" (Herman, p. 9). Orienting students to the critical need to transform violence is also controversial. And, the activities presented in this chapter may be hard to implement due to the very upset in students that we are wanting to address. But at least, as educators we can discuss where we would like to bring them. I believe that we need to let young people know that interconnection and interdependence describe the fundamental relationship of human to human, and that this fundamental relationship is now eroded. Interlocking spells of sexism,

racism, glorification of violence, and visionless materialism urge young people to perpetuate this erosion. We need to reveal to them that interconnection — described in a
myriad of ways as unity, co-creation, mutually-enhancing respect and empowerment,
or simply brotherly sisterly love — is not sappy or idealistic. It is real and it is in danger. This is serious and we are not powerless. We can shift this in our every interaction.

Transforming Conflict

We turn now to the work in schools that is analogous to the strengthening of the
immune system: Conflict resolution skillbuilding, peer mediation training, character
education, bias reduction, diversity awareness, and other ways of developing positive
social skills. Partnership Education encompasses practices that have been in development by many people over many decades. For this reason, in looking at conflict resolution, it is important to provide an historical context.

History

Peace education and specifically the movement to help children communicate and
handle conflict constructively began visibly after World War II. Quakers and others
who actively hold a religious peace tradition were part of this initial movement, as
well as members of the Women's International League for Peace and Freedom
(WILPF); these groups articulated that a fundamental part of preventing war is teaching children peace.

Starting in 1973 the Children's Creative Response to Conflict Program (CCRC)
affiliated with the Fellowship of Reconciliation began training teachers in New York
City schools and discovered that unless foundational skills in community building,
affirmation, and cooperation were developed, children could not fully integrate conflict resolution procedures and make them their own. Educators for Social
Responsibility (ESR) and the Community Board in San Francisco were developed in
the late 1970's and through a multiplicity of avenues teachers all over the country
began to awaken to the importance of the social curriculum. Over the past fifty years
this work has grown exponentially through many avenues including peer mediation
training for 5th-12th graders and social skills trainings both for staff and for young
people three years old and up.

Core Elements of Conflict Resolution

Surveying conflict resolution programs and approaches nationwide, here are the
features that they have in common.

1. They provide perspectives on the nature of conflict:
   • Conflicts are an opportunity for communication.

- Conflicts can have a positive outcome.
- Conflicts are part of human experience; what matters is how we handle them.

2. The goal of the methods is to support students in learning communication skills, and educating students rather than punishing them for mis-behavior. Some groups call this creating a peaceable classroom or creating a democratic classroom.

3. The program helps students realize that they have options and choices when a conflict occurs.

4. Programs help students recognize what will make a problem worse; they learn that blame or attack words, threats, and verbal or physical violence will escalate a problem.
- They help students understand how disrespect of differences is unfair and inflammatory.
- They help students take responsibility for solving the problem constructively.

5. They help students expand their communication skills:
- They learn how to actively listen and paraphrase.
- They learn how to make "I statements" which express needs in a way that invites collaboration on solving the problem.

6. They recommend a sequence of steps which will allow all disputants to hear each other, identify the problem, brainstorm solutions, and work towards choosing a plan together.

7. They help students learn component skills which will strengthen their ability to resolve conflicts constructively:
- Students learn to seek out win/win solutions.
- Students learn about the nature of prejudice, bias, and oppression.
- Students learn how to affirm themselves as they learn new skills.

Seven Contributions of the Partnership Perspective

Partnership Education points to the extensive work that has been developed in nonviolent conflict resolution and anti-bias. Our goal is to make the resources created by organizations and individual educators even more widely valued and utilized, and at the same time help integrate a nonviolent, respectful, and caring approach into the entire learning tapestry, both in the curriculum and day-to-day interactions. It helps to see transformative processes through a partnership lens

1) Providing an Historical Perspective of Partnership

Conflict resolution training can be enhanced when we provide students with the information outlined in *Tomorrow's Children* about their past and their future. It is urged that social skills trainings explicitly share partnership content:

- Archeological investigation points to the possibility that our species lived together for thousands of years in peace and partnership. Perhaps the preponderance of human history has been spent interacting in partnership. This has tremendous implications for our understanding of what it means to be a human being.

- Archeology interpretations show that warfare, violence, and weaponry were introduced later rather than as an outgrowth of our nature. Fortification and armament were in response to domination rather than initiated as part of normal social human functioning.

- Looking at the present through the lens of partnership we see violence in school, town/city, and the world as a problem to be solved instead of an inevitability that we must adjust to.

Such information can help young people understand why partnership skills may feel hard or unfamiliar or dissonant. We can then invite them to think of themselves as partners in human evolution. Together we are discovering how we can shift from domination to partnership. It enhances their understanding of the importance of learning how to include others, communicate non-violently, and work cooperatively. It also gives a new perspective on diversity education when we see domination as inherently fostering racism, sexism, ableism, and other divisions.

2) Professional Partnership

In the 1980's the National Association for Mediation in Education (NAME) formed to further collaboration and professional communication. In the 1990's NAME became CREnet, the Conflict Resolution Education Network which is "dedicated to making conflict resolution education an integral part of the educational process in every school. CREnet has been the professional umbrella organization uniting teachers, trainers, and students. In 2000 CREnet merged with the Academy of Family Mediators and the Society of Professionals in Dispute Resolution, creating an organization of 8000 members that is now called the Association for Conflict Resolution (ACR).

At the CREnet web site, further information for educators can be obtained: www.crenet.org. A fact sheet on peer mediation is available as well as a research and evaluation report, "Conflict Resolution Education Research and Evaluation Synopsis and Bibliography" by Marsha Blakeway and Daniel Kmitta.

3) An Integrated Approach to Addressing all Forms of Domination

Work on conflict resolution skills is incomplete without recognizing prejudice, bias, and oppression. Work on non-violent communication and work on anti-bias and respect for diversity are essential components of the same fabric. Today as conflict resolution and mediation methods are formulated, trainers inform teachers that the methods need to be culturally relevant to all their students. The role that racism, sexism, and other forms of oppression play in conflicts is articulated. In fact, at CREnet conferences and now, following their merger, at the Joint International Conference of the Association for Conflict Resolution, every presentation must include an anti-bias perspective. Three activities in anti-bias awareness will be presented later in the chapter.

4) Commitment to the Long-Term Work of Partnership

Within a generation, enormous changes have been felt in education. Today the majority of teachers in the United States have attended at least an introductory workshop on helping their students develop positive social skills such as character education, conflict resolution, wholistic education or as part of cooperative learning training. It may have been led by the school guidance counselor or by an author of one of the thousands of volumes of social skills curriculum that now exist. Today most school libraries have at least one of these books or curriculum modules, many guidance counselors train students in social skills, and on many elementary school playgrounds peer mediators from the upper grades come forward to mediate disputes.

This is difficult work, and it's helpful to take a long-view. We are currently doing partnership work within a dominator culture. When statistics tell us that students are viewing enormous doses of violence, a one-week training on using "I Statements" is going to be working against the messages of domination. Diane Levin writes, "By the end of elementary school the average child will have witnessed 8,000 murders and 100,000 other acts of violence on the TV screen," (*Remote Control Childhood*, p. 9)

We can explain to teachers why they may feel like giving up on teaching social skills and why they shouldn't give up. We can help these efforts not become marginalized. The history we have just reviewed reveals that we are the first generation that has created a concerted national effort in schools on behalf of partnership. We can help teachers resist undervaluing these efforts — "We tried conflict resolution last year and it didn't work." We can help them not see partnership work through the judging eyes of domination that demand quick visible change or threaten if it's not produced to wipe out the opportunities. Teachers may feel that their conflict resolution lessons are not sticking as well as they hoped, and we can help them see that this is a life-long effort.

5) The Evolutionary Force of Partnership

On the other hand, given the incredible weight of domination indoctrination that children receive, its very significant how even brief exposure to partnership processes can immediately be taken in and used by students.

Social skills training try to provide true nourishment, and try to avoid feeling wooden, unrealistic or irrelevant to students. I bet each conflict resolution trainer has their own favorite stories of times the training really sunk in. Here are two of mine.

Anecdote One:

At a New England Association for the Education of Young Children workshop, I shared with early childhood educators a finger-play song I use with 3 to 7 year-olds to give a concrete experience of cooperative communication during a conflict. "Two in the Fight" is sung to the tune of "There were Two in the Bed." Children hold up two fingers and pretend they are two children summoning the courage to talk out a problem instead of fighting it out. The first verse of the story says:

> There were two in the fight and the little one said, "I'm angry, I'm angry."
> The other one started to run away. "Come back and hear what I have to say.
> Keep talking, keep talking.
> Come on back, come on back.
> We can figure this out."
> "Two in the Fight"
> (from *Linking Up!* by Sarah Pirtle)

I demonstrated the song and suggested that it might be a useful model. I said that I'd found that children sometimes imitated it. One teacher reported later that as I was speaking she thought to herself, "Yeah, right." But she decided to try it anyway. After teaching the song once in her class of three and four year-olds, she later saw two girls that same day putting their fingers up to talk to each other when they had a conflict. When we work with young children and say to them in effect, here's a way to be partners together, they believe us.

Anecdote Two:

At an elementary school in Dalton, MA, I was providing 45 minute conflict resolution introductory workshops. In a second grade I was emphasizing giving a friendly but firm message like "stop" when someone is doing something that goes against your own boundaries, and also emphasizing the importance of listening to the messages of others. Later that day a teacher reported that during a chronic conflict — two children sharing a work table, one child shaking the table teasingly so that the other was not able to write — today the second child spoke up for herself. She asked the other to stop. When he didn't she said, referring to the training, "That lady said that when I say stop you have to stop."

I believe that the ability we see in children to understand and incorporate partnership processes after even a brief exposure underscores that indoctrination toward aggression goes against the grain of human encoding. We're encoded for partnership.

6) Teaching Partnership Processes with Partnership Process

Even conflict resolution could be taught in a dominator way. We could impose a format for conflict resolution on our students rather than involve them in discussing, digesting, and adopting it. We could leave out the child in the class who is hearing impaired while we're talking. We could ask only the boys to do the role plays. We could focus only upon the students who are waving their hands wildly. Enough said.

7) A Partnership Model for Conflict Resolution Training

A basic principle of Partnership Education — to link rather than rank — applies also to how professionals deal with the panoply of social skills resources. From a partnership perspective each teacher and each school can select the type of social skills methods, trainings or curriculum that works best for them rather than debating, or even denegrating other approaches. Methods do not need to compete with each other, and approaches can be individualized to fit each school.

When entering a school to help with training in social skills, it is important that outside consultants work as partners with all school staff, aiding in individualization instead of imposing one approach. Here is a model for this style of assistance:

Step One: Dialogue about needs and goals

The social skills consultant meets first with a sub-set of the staff: The principal, guidance counselors, representative teachers, and specialists. The consultant listens to concerns about school climate, hears their needs and asks the group to express their wishes. Rather than imposing a particular curriculum or set of new vocabulary, methods are presented as possible options.

Example: A sub-set of the staff of Sheffield Elementary School in Turners Falls, Massachusetts met for an hour to talk about school climate. Their principal, Laurie Farkas, provided these focus questions:

- How can we bring about more positive change through the student body and staff?
- Is there a way to do this without buying into and training in a specific curriculum?
- How can we integrate this into daily classroom and recess life without straining resources and adding stress?
- How can we involve and empower as many students as possible in this process?

Step Two: Input from the whole staff

Next, the key ideas from the smaller meeting are shared with the whole staff and they work together to reach consensus selecting one or two doable changes.

Example: A busy staff found time during lunch shifts to discuss what they wanted to do to improve school climate and increase social skills. To collect opinions, each person wrote a response to two brief questions using one word answers. This allowed for a productive, quick meeting where people could think for themselves without pressure.

Step Three: Look for agreement on one or two action steps while at the same time remaining flexible and responding to individual needs.

Example: A staff wanted to increase social interaction and communication among students as well as return more of the fun to their classrooms which they felt they had lost due to new state mandated testing. They decided to institute a daily time where students could connect, share, and do cooperative activities, but they had different ideas of how this would happen. Many teachers suggested that they lead morning meetings using the model of Responsive Classroom Morning Meeting (see Chapter One for information about Responsive Classroom). Teachers in the building had used the model several years ago, were excited about its success, and wanted to return to that practice, but not everyone had the training. Some teachers wanted to lead a community-building experience at a different time of day like right after lunch and recess. Others wanted to expand upon the types of activities they had tried previously and learn other ways of facilitating social interaction. Also, the guidance counselors offered to help lead training during this time on social skills. The staff decided to create an umbrella term, "Connection Time," and allow each teacher to define the time of day and the content of the activities during that period. This also opened the door for guidance counselors to schedule time with classes during the "Connection Time" slot.

Interrupting Bias: Affirmation Plus Information

The tenacity of racism, sexism, classism, homophobia, and all other forms of oppression is that they involve not just personal prejudice, but are kept in place by prejudice plus power, the power of cultural and structural forces. Partnership Education involves being alert to how these oppressions operate and it involves intervening deliberately at every level to restructure and realign. Violation and the threat of or presence of violence is at the foundation of these forms of domination. Deliberate awareness and intervention is needed so that they aren't replicated. Each learning community needs to progress in consciousness about these issues so that the cultures and identities of all individuals are respected and so that girls and women are equals in every aspect of the community.

Ageism also needs to be addressed and children's ways of knowing honored. Young people have their own versions of partnership. Young people need private times with peers to create their own culture of jokes and games. This culture is different from what adult imposed media culture depicts as "kid culture." Adults can learn from what young people find significant so that together we are co-creators of partnership curriculum and students, as well as teachers, are heard and take leadership.

Activity Five: Courage

> Overview: This song is one of the most effective ways to help student think about exclusion and mistreatment.
>
> Ages: 4th - 12th
>
> Source: "Courage" by Bob Blue.
>
> Procedure:

1. Play a recording of "Courage" by Bob Blue or show it performed on the video, "What Matters." To learn how to order these resources, contact the Children's Music Network at P.O. Box 1341, Evanston, IL 60204-1341, or Catharine Haver, 34 Bay Road, Belchertown, MA 01007. Another method is to use the lyrics as a poem.

Courage

A small thing once happened at school that brought up a question for me.
And somehow it forced me to see the price that I pay to be cool.
Diane is a girl that I know. She's strange like she doesn't belong.
I don't mean to say that it's wrong, we don't like to be with her though.

And so when we all made a plan to have a big party at Sue's.
Most kids in the school got the news, but no one invited Diane.

The thing about Taft Junior High is secrets don't last very long.
I acted like nothing was wrong when I saw Diane start to cry.

I know you may think that I'm cruel, it doesn't make me very proud.
I just went along with the crowd, it's sad, but you have to in school.

You can't pick the friends you prefer. You fit in as well as you can.
I couldn't be friends with Diane, or soon they would treat me like her.

In one class at Taft Junior High we study what people have done
With gas chambers, bombers, and guns in Auschwitz, Japan and Mei Lai.
I don't understand all I learn. Sometimes I just sit there and cry.
The whole world stood idly by to watch as the innocents burned.

Like robots obeying some rule. Atrocities done by the mob.
All innocents doing their job, and what was it for, was it cool?

The world was aware of this hell, but how many cried out in shame?
What heroes and who was to blame, a story that no one dared tell.
I promise to do what I can to not let it happen again.
To care for all women and men... I'll start by inviting Diane.

(words and music by Bob Blue)

2. Create discussion questions that fit your students. Focus upon how Diane felt, what support she would have wanted, as well as memories, feelings, and realizations evoked by this story. This can be a poignant lead-in to the next activity.

Activity Six: Being an Ally — Making New Choices

Grade level: 2nd - 12th

Goals: to address put-downs, bias, and exclusion that is occurring for students.
       to teach how to intervene and help change social unfairness.
       to set a new social norm for inclusion and fair treatment of all students.

Procedure:

1. Over a period of weeks ask students to write down examples of situations they see or experience of put-downs, mistreatment, or exclusion. Instead of using names, write, "someone … " and tell the action without telling who was involved.

2. Collect and review the slips of paper. Take the situations and use these as a basis for role plays.

Examples of situations:

• In our science class someone was assigned to our lab group who speaks very little English, and people in the group made faces to show they didn't want him there.

• When someone struck out at baseball, lots of people called him names and someone said to him, "you're such a girl."

As you review the possibilities, pick the situation that is the least charged and use it for the first role play. Ask for volunteers to act it out and create fictitious names for the characters. To help the role play experience feel safe for all participants, establish that any actor can exit at any point by saying "cut" or putting up a T hand-signal to call a time-out. Make a clear framework, by saying "curtain up" at the beginning of the role play, and "curtain down" at the end.

Discuss the word "ally." This is a person who witnesses something unfair happening and steps in to intervene. One person in the role play will be struggling with whether or not to be an ally and will be trying to figure out what to do to help.

New Choices Role Play

After the actors depict the problem, they freeze. Pick one character in the drama to focus upon as a person who can make a new choice, the ally. Engage the audience in verbalizing what is going on inside her/his brain. Show the person thinking about what they could do.

While the actors are frozen, the audience expresses the range of thoughts they guess that character has, illustrating the struggle between conflicting feelings. Have people call out different thoughts:

- "It's not okay that he's being called names."
- "But if I speak up, maybe they'll call me names."
- "Somebody should do something. This isn't okay."

The audience also verbalizes all the options the person has for what to do:

"I think I'll just forget it and pretend I didn't hear it."

"I'm going to say something."

The actors unfreeze and continue the action, showing the decision that this character makes.

3. Speaking Up: Before doing another role play, teach what is involved in being an ally.

When something unfair is happening or you witness mistreatment, there is something you can do. I like to call this method of intervention: Affirmation + information.

Sample situation: A kickball game is progressing, ignoring Jacob on the sidelines. Jacob is in a wheelchair. He wants to play, but he feels bad about being left out and doesn't want to say anything. What could a person do who is in the game and is witnessing this problem?

   a. The first stage is stepping forward and intervening.
      Examples: "This isn't okay."
            "Let's talk about what's happening."
            "I don't feel comfortable with ... "

   b. The second stage is supplying your information about the issue:
      Example: "It looks like our team is leaving out Jacob because he's in a wheelchair. Jacob, I know you can kick and go around the bases. Do you want to play?"

   c. The third aspect involves the whole way you talk — and that is affirmation. You are helping bring back partnership, and that means respecting all participants. You are helping to connect and link each person once again. Example: "I'd really like everyone to be part of the team."

4. Work with another role play situation and decide which character will make the new choice. Again have characters freeze and ask the audience to explore all the thoughts the main character has as she or he reviews what to do. Encourage them to be realistic rather than depicting ideal behavior. It helps to examine the real inner struggle.

Other situations to use for a role play:

• Members of a sports team are picking a night for their fall dinner. Once again it has been scheduled for Rosh Hashanah and people are unmindful that it is an important Jewish holiday. Once again Jewish members of the team will be left out. How do you intervene?

• A new family who are Tibetan moves into your community. The young people who come to school know very little English. You watch as one European American student makes faces and mocks after one of the new students tries to communicate. How do you intervene?

Develop role play situations that fit your own school. Don't begin with whatever would be the most charged situation, but don't omit it. Start with an event where students already have the skills to speak up, and then progress to the harder situations.

Be sure to allow time for processing each role play at its conclusion.

<u>Activity Seven:</u> Diversity Dialogue

Grade level: 6th - 12th

Overview: These activities were developed by Tim Wernette in partnership with other diversity educators. To contact him by email: crystalmist@peoplepc.com, or write Tim Wernette 7217 E. Crystal Mist Drive, Tucson, AZ 85750.

Procedure:

1. Dimensions of Diversity

As a class brainstorm a list of all the many ways that people are different.
Examples: Economic class, learning styles, spiritual or religious beliefs, type of family, heritage, height, physical health. It is possible to have a list of 30 - 40 differences. Introduce the concept that these are all "dimensions" of diversity. Ethnicity or gender are but a few of many dimensions of diversity. The word "dimension" helps us understand that we all have diversity. Otherwise, conversations about diversity falsely imply that some aspects are "normal" while others "create diversity."
Variation: Tim comments, "Unless it's a very small group of five people or less, I prefer to have participants do this in small groups of three to five people. This gives people more opportunity to contribute ideas and is especially helpful for introverts who may not feel comfortable contributing in a large group setting. Then I go around and get one diversity dimension from each group, and continue adding one from each, until the list is complete. If the class/entire group has not mentioned an important diversity dimension (such as sexual orientation), the facilitator may want to list this and ask the group why they think it wasn't mentioned."

2. Self Description

Pick several of these dimensions and describe yourself in respect to them. Write down notes. What is your identity in respect to each dimension you chose? Each person decides whether to keep this list private.

3. Personal Reflection

Look at the dimensions again, and ask yourself, which 3-4 dimensions are the most significant or powerful in my life now? Write about or tell a partner about what makes them important or how they have influence on you. Being with a partner or in a small group not larger than three or four students can be a safe arena for sharing important diversity dimensions and discussing experiences with privilege and prejudice. Tim adds, "Next I ask for a couple of volunteers to share what they discussed with the larger group."

4. Group Reflection:

Complicate thinking about diversity. Discuss factors that affect the importance of any diversity dimension.

Environment — Does having this diversity dimension mean I'm in the minority or the majority in a particular setting? The setting influences how this dimension is experienced at that moment.

Consciousness — Are others aware of this identity?

Privilege — Does this identity give me privilege?

Oppression — Will this identity mean I will be targeted by the dominant culture generally?

Might I be targeted in the particular setting I'm in? Is my identity in respect to this dimension something that is designated for targeting?

Forcefulness of the oppression — If I am targeted, will this prejudice be less expressed and more hidden or will the targeting be more direct or forceful?

5. Pick dimensions and discuss power, privilege, prejudice, and oppression as they relate.

E.g., The dimension of age: At what ages do people generally receive more regard and respect in the culture? Have there been ways that ageism has personally affected you, that you have received more or less respect because of your age?

6. At our school, how can you tell if a certain dimension of diversity is disapproved of or targeted? What behaviors tell you this? Which dimensions of diversity are the basis for the most put-down's, disapproval or ostricism? Make a hierarchy about which dimensions matter the most at school. Frame this in terms of social support. Which dimensions have the least social support for contradicting oppression? In other words, where is the oppression forceful? Where is their social support for contradicting privilege in favor of fairness? Ask students for examples from their personal lives which illustrate how this operates.

Here are some insights that Tim Wernette adds to discussions about diversity dimensions:

- Each one of us is a unique mosaic of diversity dimensions. Diversity impacts all of us, not just target or oppressed groups. White, middle class, heterosexual males are as impacted by diversity as anyone else. Because each of us is made up of many different dimensions of diversity, someone may simultaneously be in a powerful group (male, white, middle class) and also in a disempowered group (gay, disabled).

- Which diversity dimension(s) is/are salient or powerful at any one time is constantly changing. If I'm in a group with people who are similar to me in race or gender, I may not notice those dimensions of diversity. Being in a "minority" status in a particular setting often highlights or makes more powerful a diversity dimension. Changes in our lives often influence which diversity dimensions are most important or powerful for us (marriage, divorce, birth, death). Sometimes a diversity dimension will change over time. For instance, during youth getting older is generally considered positive, then beginning in the 20's/30's aging takes on a more negative connotation, and finally in old age (80+) people often become proud of their age as an accomplishment of living a long life.

•Diversity dimensions are intimately linked with issues of power, privilege, and oppression. This is often the most difficult aspect of diversity to deal with because of people's strong feelings about this, feelings of anger, hurt, guilt, shame, or defensiveness. Instead of lecturing to students about which groups are more powerful or less powerful, I think it's better to have people discuss this. Again, have the discussion in small groups first and then summarize in the large group.

•It's important to acknowledge that people may have very different experiences and perceptions of the power aspects of diversity. It's helpful to share these concepts:

   a) Privilege is not something that is taken, but rather something that is given. Thus as a white, middle class, heterosexual male I do not need to feel guilty about the many privileges I experience, just as people of color, women, or gays/lesbians do not need to feel responsible for their oppression. But each of us is constantly making choices in our lives about whether to oppose privilege and oppression or to support it. Doing nothing supports the status quo, which favors some people and groups and disenfranchises other people and groups. There's a whole continuum of how people respond to privilege and oppression, from active support of the status quo, to tacit support for the status quo (doing nothing), to active support for change.

   b) Generally, people who are in privileged groups are less aware of oppression than people who are in oppressed groups. This is because privileged people/groups do not constantly experience the oppression than disenfranchised groups experience. One of the biggest privileges is not having to notice or acknowledge that one has privilege. People of privilege can become more aware of issues of power/privilege/oppression by talking with people in disenfranchised groups, reading, attending diversity workshops, placing themselves in situations/groups where they are the "minority."

   c) People in disenfranchised groups struggle with a similar but different issue: internalized oppression. Part of the effectiveness of oppression is convincing the disenfranchised people/groups that they deserve their oppression, that if they worked harder, or were nicer, then they wouldn't experience their oppression. So both privileged and disenfranchised people/groups may be in denial about diversity power issues.

d) There's a hierarchy of social acceptability to prejudice/ stereotyping/ oppression regarding diversity dimensions.

Extension Activity: Envisioning a School Without Bias

1. Say that we are going to "paint a picture" of five types of schools based on five different attitudes towards diversity: A school that actively rejects diversity, a school that discriminates, a school that tolerates diversity, a school that accepts diversity, a school that welcomes diversity. Put the five stages as a continuum on the board or on a large piece of paper. Add these concepts to the continuum — on the one end there is active support of the status quo and rejection of diversity, in the middle there is tacit support for the status quo and mere tolerance of diversity, and on the other side of the continuum there is active support for change and active welcoming of diversity. Ask for any questions about the meaning of these five stages.

2. Divide into five small groups. Assign one of the five stages along the continuum to each group and have them write examples of behaviors at school which would "paint the picture" of that state. Examples: What does the lunchroom look like, what does recess look like, what does the bus ride look like, who is on staff, how are parents treated, what is on the bulletin board, what students socialize with which, which staff people socialize with which other staff. Remember to include many dimensions of diversity and not just ethnicity and gender.

Studying Transformation Through the Expressive Arts

Activity Eight: Envisioning Partnership

Overview: This is a language arts activity that involves creative writing.

Grade level: 2nd - 12th

Procedure:

1. Ask students to visualize living in a time where violence and bias are no longer actively dominant, a time when conflicts are solved with constructive communication, and when diversity is welcomed. Provide a vantage point for them to look at this world. Imagine you are walking down the street. Or, imagine you are opening up a newspaper. Or, imagine you are going to a movie. What is different? How do you feel? What do you see? What tells you that this is now a world of fairness and interconnection?

> Imagine that you live in your same town or city but stretching in all directions, in every building, in every dwelling, there is no one being deliberately hurt or mistreated, there is no violence.

2. Another way to approach this is to take a location that they have already described as containing violence, prejudice/oppression, or violent solutions to conflict. It might be their neighborhood or the playground or the television. Now, ask them to imagine that same location without violence, prejudice, and oppression. What would be happening instead? Keep emphasizing that we are looking not so much at an absence of one force but the presence of an active, positive, nurturing, inclusive force.

3. Ask the class to draw, write a story, write a poem, or describe what they perceive.

   Resources: For more details, see the activity, "Picturing the Future: Social Studies Unit" in "Discovery Time for Cooperation and Conflict Resolution" by Sarah Pirtle, (*Children's Creative Response to Conflict*, 1998, pp. 46-49.)

   Dr. Elise Boulding, Warren Zeigler and Mary Link led programs in "Imagining a World Without Weapons" starting in 1980; to contact Future-Invention Associates and Warren Zeigler, his email is warren.fia@worldnet.att.net. Here in this partnership activity the concept of "without weapons" is not the key pivot point, but rather the emphasis is on transformation through nonviolent communication and the welcoming of diversity.

Activity Nine: Can the Dominator Be Transformed?

Grade level: 2nd - 12th

Overview: Creative dramatics explore the dynamic tension between domination and partnership. Short role plays or longer drama projects are developed from this activity.

Procedure:

1. Ask students to think about books that they have read with characters who are dominators. In these books, do the characters change at the end? If so, what brings about this change? What specifically makes a "good character" good and an "evil character" evil?

2. Use creative dramatics to investigate the hold of domination. The main point of the activity is to feel the contrasting positions between wanting partnership for all of us, and promoting domination for self or for narrow interests. This is different in kind from the usual formulation: Good versus evil.

3. One method is to set up a role play between a group of people who are in collaboration and one dominator. Establish in the beginning that words rather than physical contact will be used to portray the dominator and his/her interactions. Repeat the role play so that several people, both female and male can try the role. Create charac-

ter names and a setting that work for the students to help them have a context for entering the role play.

Example: Grade Three - Wizard and villagers.

This dialogue can start the scene:

Wizard: I have almost taken over the world, but you — you people oppose me.
Villager: We don't oppose you. We want to include you. Partnership will be for all of us.
Wizard: Partnership will destroy me!
Ask, what happens next? Try several short scenes, using "curtain up" and "curtain down" to delineate beginning and ending. Allow any participant to stop the role play at any time.

Snapshot: Pageants at Journey Camp

The activity, "Can the dominator be transformed?" has held great power for groups of young people ages 7 to 12 at Journey Camp in Deerfield, Massachusetts each summer. Campers collaborate to develop characters, and write the story and dialogue for a one-hour pageant themselves. Journey Camp is a laboratory for Partnership Education directed by Sarah Pirtle since 1994.

One year a boy decided to be a character he named, "Wario." Wario was the arch-dominator. Other campers portrayed cronies that he brought into his fold. He used them to help carry out his plots against a group of villagers, but always he stayed on top. To write the ending collectively, people grappled with whether or not Wario would or could change at the end. As they examined this, campers raised the point: Do the "evil" characters ever change in the books we read? After heated discussions, they agreed they wanted Wario "to become good" but they wanted to come up with a reason that made sense to them. Finally they reached consensus that at the end of the pageant, Wario would fall down and hit his head. When he woke up, other characters would show him a picture of himself as a young boy and that would restore him to what he was like at that age.

Each year the story for the camp pageant is made from the campers' suggestions, and year after year it can essentially be described as, "How Partnership is Restored." Here is another example of the intricate plots that have been developed at Journey Camp. During the summer of 2000, campers chose this theme: "How do we end the spell that has been cast on the earth?"

This first step in pageant-making is to allow each person to say who they want to be. Two girls said, "We want to be the evil ones in the pageant this year," evil being their translation of what it means to be the interfering force in the story, "but this time we refuse to change at the end." They named themselves, "The Quintox." They said the Quintox had opened a door between the earth and the rest of the universe, and now the only way to stop them would be to drive them off the earth and close the door again.

One camper wanted to build a dragon because it was the Year of the Dragon, celebrated by her family, and she saw the dragon as a partnership force. Another girl asked to be the Karate Peace Master of the Wind; she said there should be a series of Peace Masters that the audience meets. All these ideas were woven together. They decided that the Peace Masters were hidden all over the earth, awaiting discovery. In fact, the children who were the central characters don't know that their own mother is secretly a Peace Master. When a dragon appears to them to get their help driving out the Quintox, they are afraid to tell their mother. When, after much debate, they introduce her to the dragon, she reveals that she "is deeply associated" with the dragon already because she is a part of the world-wide group of Peace Masters who work with the dragon as part of the fundamental healing force of the earth.

This pageant, described from an adult perspective, is about the unblocking of human evolution. The force that the campers dubbed the Quintox is interfering and stopping humans from connecting with each other and mutually engaging in the tasks of life. During the creation of the earth, the door to the universe needed to be wide open, but this allowed the Quintox to get in. Now the children, the dragon, and the Peace Masters work together to build a special hoop which will block the door.

Characters who the campers called "the Ancient Ladies" deliver to the mother a Sacred Hoop that had been faithfully protected and passed along from generation to generation since paleolithic times. This hoop has the power of the earth, but it needs to be constructed with the other elements — air, fire, and water — before it can be placed in the door. The dragon leads the children to the realms of each of these elements. Campers added their own humor: The dragon translator wore a pilot's helmet and carried a parachute as she made a crash landing at the site of the Peace Masters of the Wind. She wore a fire fighter's helmet while visiting the Realm of Fire, and donned goggles and flippers meeting the Water Peace Masters.

The campers decided that the Quintox were completely selfish, but pretended to be polite and sickeningly sweet. By casting spells on people, the Quintox attempt to turn humans against their own best interests. In the Realm of Water, after a spell cast by Quintox, people at a beach get obsessed with showing off muscles, wearing fashionable outfits, and not breaking painted fingernails. But their effort to convince people to focus on trivialities fails when their lies are washed out by the Peace Masters of the Water. In the fire scene, the Mighty Sisters teach the children, "There's a time to be nice and a time not to. Now's the time to say No to the Quintox." They unmask the Quintox and lead a fiery chant of "No."

After a comic scene where the Quintox try to wheedle the Sacred Hoop from the audience by bribing them and promising them candy, they are driven out of the door to the universe and the door is permanently closed with the Hoop. From now on this screen will be more selective in inviting in elements from the furthermost reaches of the universe. This is the chorus of the song that campers wrote which closes the pageant:

"We all have the power. Now we know it's true.

We keep getting stronger with everything we do."

Peacebuilding: Human Potential and Inspiration

As educators our work is to restore connection and give students information and perspective about the struggle and journey we humans are engaged in. We invite them to join with us in choosing and developing partnership culture by actively placing themselves as part of that positive force. In the next activity, students study the people involved in this work.

Activity Ten: Social Studies Research: Building Peace and Transforming Violence

Grade level: 4-12

Overview: Students study a few of the multitude of organizations who are working on aspects of peacebuilding. These groups themselves exist in partnership because there are many ways of creating positive change, and each is important and complementary.

Procedure:

1. Divide the class into small groups of 2-4 students. Provide a list of organizations to study. Use the eight listed below and add local organizations in your area that work on issues such as community mediation, domestic violence, child abuse, unlearning racism, and social justice. Option: Incorporate into your list those organizations that work to transform sexism which are listed in Chapter Thirteen, "The Wisdom of the Elders: Curriculum Resources for Unlearning Sexism."

2. Describe each organization briefly and ask small groups to pick one they would be interested in studying. Coordinate the decision so that each group in the class will focus upon a different organization. Once assignments are clear, the small groups research their organization by using the Internet, assembling flyers or articles from the organization, or conducting telephone interviews with staff.

3. Every group of students prepares an oral report covering: (a) What social problem does their organization address? (b) How do they do their work? How do they see themselves as a positive force for change? (c) How can other people be a part of their work? (d) Would you like to be part of an organization such as this? If so, in what way? Ask students to divide up the questions so that they each provide part of the information.

4. An alternative method is to select four organizations and study all four as a class, using the same questions above. Examine their diverse approaches and discuss how together they are complementary.

Eight Different Kinds of Peacebuilding Organizations

■ The Anti-Defamation League, founded in 1913.
Web site: www.adl.org
 The work of ADL is to fight anti-Semitism, bigotry, and extremism. Through thirty regional centers in the United States and three overseas offices, they provide a place where people can report encounters with bigotry, hatred, or discrimination where they work, live, or study. Their extensive web site includes updates on other web-sites which pedal hatred.

■ Center for Nonviolent Communication, founded by Dr. Marshall Rosenberg.
Web site: www.cnvc.org Email: cnvc@compuserve.com
Address: Box 2662 Sherman, Texas 75091-2662
 This organization trains people in nonviolent communication "to strengthen our ability to inspire compassion from others and to respond compassionately to others and to ourselves. Nonviolent communication guides us to reframe how we express ourselves and hear others by focusing our consciousness on what we are observing, feeling, needing, and requesting." Books on nonviolent communication are available from the center.

■ The Children's Defense Fund, founded by Marian Wright Edelman.
Web site: www.childrensdefense.org
Address: The Children's Defense Fund, 25 E Street NW
Washington, DC 20001 Phone: (202) 628-8787
 The mission of the Children's Defense Fund is to Leave No Child Behind and to ensure every child a Healthy Start, a Head Start, a Fair Start, a Safe Start, and a Moral Start as well as a safe and secure passage to adulthood with the help of caring families and communities. It exists to provide a strong and effective voice for all the children of America, who cannot vote, lobby, or speak for themselves. By clicking the "Get Involved" section of their web site, students can learn about projects such as these:

The Student Leadership Network for Children (SLNC) is a national network of servant-leaders, age 18 to 30, committed to improving the lives of children.

The Student Health Outreach Project, SHOUT, is an opportunity for college and high school students to participate in the national effort to reach and enroll America's uninsured, eligible children for free or low-cost health insurance.

■ The Karuna Center for Peacebuilding, founded and directed by Dr. Paula Green.
Web site: www.karuna.center.org
Address: Karuna Center for Peacebuilding, 49 Ritchardson Road,
N. Leverett, MA 01054

Karuna leads cross-cultural dialogues globally and has trained peacebuilders in numerous locations including Bosnia, Rwanda, Israel, and Oklahoma City. By promoting dialogue between people from "opposite sides" of a struggle, strategies for healing and transformational change can develop. See the web site www.sit.edu/conflict for information about the combined work of Karuna and the School for International Training. Their Summer Institute and Graduate Certificate Program is called Contact: Cultural Transformation Across Cultures. Download the article, "Training a New Generation of Peacebuilders," from Karuna's web site, or request by mail the article, "Peacebuilding Perspectives."

■ The National Priorities Project, founded by Greg Speeter.
Web site: www.natprior.org/
Address: 17 New South Street, Suite 302, Northampton, MA 01060
E-mail: infor@natprior.org

The National Priorities Project (NPP) is a non-profit research and education organization providing citizens, community groups, and elected officials with the tools they need to shape federal budget and policy priorities. At their web site, students can take interactive quizzes and learn about where tax money from their congressional district goes. A variety of facts are available including child poverty rates, data on federal spending for education, and information on the condition of public schools.

■ The Southern Poverty Law Center and *Teaching Tolerance* magazine
Web site: www.teachingtolerance.org
Address: 400 Washington Avenue, Montgomery, AL 36104

In response to an alarming increase in hate crimes among youth, the Southern Poverty Law Center started *Teaching Tolerance* magazine in 1991. It is sent twice a year for free to half a million educators across the country. The web site provides activities for teachers, and a list called, "101 Tools for Tolerance." Videos and other curricular materials are available.

■ Wilmington College Peace Resource Center

Web site: www.wilmington.edu/PEACERC.HTM

Email: pre@wilmington.edu

Address: Peace Resource Center, Wilmington College, Pyle Center Box 1183, Wilmington, OH 45177.

Since 1975 it has taken an active role in providing peace education materials throughout the United States through a book purchase service, audio-visual rentals, and a research collection on the effects of the 1945 atomic bombings of Hiroshima and Nagasaki.

■ Youth M-Power

Web site: www.youthmpower.org

Contact Youth M-Power: Youth Making Peaceful Options with Effective Results.

1527 New Hampshire Avenue, NW, Third Floor, Washington, DC 20036.

Youth M-Power is described as "an evolving partnership that seeks to empower youth to develop a culture of respect, constructive conflict resolution, and peace. It has an Information Center of resources for and about youth in conflict resolution, networking opportunities to connect youth and adult dispute resolvers, and does public education to support a stronger youth voice and presence in the conflict resolution field and the larger public." The web site has a youth webboard and a copy of their newsletter. This organization was initiated by the Association for Conflict Resolution (ACR).

Extension Activity: Meeting Peacemakers in Our Community

Design a method for students to meet people in your community who are working for positive social change, or obtain a copy of the curriculum, "Making Peace Where I Live," by Elise Boulding, Cynthia Cohen, Gail Jacobson, Lyn Haas, and Mary Lee Morrison. Intended for 10-12 year olds, this curriculum can be used to help young people meet peacemakers and peacebuilders in their own communities. It teaches the skills of oral history and interviewing, and is designed as a practical contribution to the United Nations' and UNESCO's Decade for a Culture of Peace and Nonviolence for the Children of the World. Write Mary Lee Morrison, 129 Penn Dr., West Hartford, CT, 06119. (860) 232-2966.

In addition, browse the web using phrases such as, "Anti-Racist Groups" to learn more about other national and regional efforts for peace and social justice.

Closing

As we focus together on what makes us whole, this brings us to the spiritual dimension, a dimension that is non-sectarian and not applying to any one religion. Each person has their own understanding of the mystery that undergirds our lives. The more we attune to and consciously draw upon our own connection to universal sources, as we understand them, the more we are able to embody and enact partnership.

Thomas Berry and Brian Swimme write:

"We can ask, then, 'For what sort of work do humans experience an abundance of energy?' Is there any work that all by itself sustains our interest? In such work lies the future of the Earth; for it is just that form of work that the universe provides an ever-renewing energy — just as it did in the work of bringing forth the galaxies.… Out of such confidence in the universe, a great power is born. For suddenly, one is not an isolated individual or community working against impossible odds. Rather, one is participating in an energy that suffuses each sentient center with the time's creativity."

—"Cosmic Creativity and Human Culture," *Breakthrough Magazine* of Global Education Associates, winter/spring 1990.

From our hearts, what does our generation wish for the next? We wish more than mastering the tests and assignments we've constructed for them. When we awaken to our deepest responsibility, we have a large goal — to help them align with human evolution as active participants. We are bringing young people into nothing less than the awareness of the common mystery that we share. We do so with assurance that each one of us has a place, that each one of us is necessary. We help them look at how human society isn't working, and we address the "nightmare" together so that we may awaken from it and break free to a place of greater consciousness and responsibility. In so doing, we create a classroom that mirrors the inclusive world we want. Together we sit down at the welcome table.

CHAPTER 5

Partnership Teaching: Our Own Growth

by Sarah Pirtle

We have the opportunity to participate directly in cultural transformation within the very culture we create in our own classrooms and in all the places we encourage the growth of children. Partnership Education involves self-reflection. Partnership skills are not acquired by learning someone else's approach; they are inherently located inside, available to be developed.

Attuning Ourselves to Partnership

Partnership classrooms and schools are created by people who want to embody partnership values in themselves. As we become more conscious of the values we want to transmit to our students, as we become more self-reflective about our classrooms and ourselves, every one of us can help develop partnership learning communities.

Like a seed holding the pattern of an evolving plant, communities need people who hold the pattern of partnership in the way they live, think, and interact. The phrase, "holding environment," gives an apt image; it is a phrase from D. W. Winnicott that is articulated by Robert Kegan in his book *The Evolving Self*. Kegan says, "Your own sense of wholeness or lack of it, is in large part a function of how your own current embeddedness culture is holding you." (Harvard University Press, 1982, p. 116) The adults who set up the "holding environment" in a classroom can hold young people in partnership and embody a commitment to partnership.

Commitment is the key word here. None of us will be perfect. None of us will act in a partnership mode all the time. But we can all become more attuned to partnership, and the capacity for partnership skills in inherently located inside of us, available to be tapped and developed.

Here are three tools of attuning ourselves to partnership.

Tool One: Encourage your own independent thinking about partnership

Partnership is a force that we observe, describe, and participate in. It's not a new method that could later become dated. It's fundamental. If we approached partnership in a dominator mindset, we might get into arguments about the best words to use to describe it, or the best methods to teach it, or who is more of a partner than whom. To approach partnership within a partnership paradigm, we have to deal with dynamic knowledge.

We have different ways of describing this fundamental force of partnership and the lack of that force. What words and phrases best describe for you the concept of partnership? What words or phrases best describe domination? How do you glean what is meant by these concepts? Which of your intelligences help you experience what they mean — is it a kinesthetic sense? Is it linguistic? Is it pictoral? And, how do your senses inform you that what is going on around you feels like partnership or feels like domination?

All educators will not use the same words for these phenomenon. It is important to hear each other's way of expressing the partnership/dominator lenses and feel the dynamic interplay of this variety.

Tool Two: Take up the challenge of partnership growth

By inviting yourself to become more knowledgeable about partnership, you are inviting personal change. Thinking about partnership is like shining a spotlight that helps us better see old territory, as well as, new vistas we did not see before.

The places where domination occur become more visible — this might be in your school building, or in family relationships, or your own ways of teaching and interacting. You walk into the school library and notice that most of the covers of a well-respected social studies magazine for children feature wars, making it seem as if these are the most important and noteworthy events in history. You walk into the staff room and hear put-down's embedded in jokes. You remind your own children about chores and feel that your voice sounds like a drill sergeant's bark.

A minor earthquake can result as what was unseen becomes seen, but this awareness of imbalance is the seed for positive change. We're trying to walk our talk. We're trying to declare an outbreak of peace inside us and in our classrooms. The impediments and difficulties will surface as part of this intention for growth. It doesn't mean we are hypocrites or insincere in our intentions. It's part of the process of increasing consciousness. It's helpful to find friends or colleagues who can talk with you about your perceptions and efforts.

New vistas are also visible. The encouraging words of a family member ring with greater resonance. We watch a friend skillfully assert boundaries and mentally file away her phrases and her attitude of "being yes while saying no." We find ourselves valuing the commitment of staff members in our building with deeper appreciation. In these and other ways we see the moments of dedication and caring more clearly as well.

Tool Three: Ask Questions

We can develop an inner tuning fork of what domination and partnership feel like, look like, sound like. Learning how to live inside partnership is a dynamic process. The crux of locating the inner tuning fork of partnership is through asking questions.

Partnership process:

When am I dominating when I could instead be holding, developing, or guiding?

How can I hold this group in partnership values?

How can I structure this activity so that many voices can contribute?

How can I provide examples and then move back and allow the child's unique creativity to come forward?

How can I coordinate the rhythms of many people in a manner that is mutually enhancing?

What other questions would you ask?

The Oops Method

A simple partnership process to introduce is to say the phrase, "oops," when a social mistake occurs. "Oops" takes off the onus of blame and shame, takes responsibility, and encourages social learning. It mixes the key ingredients of compassion and accountability.

I learned the phrase "mistaken behavior" from Daniel Gartrell, author of *A Guidance Approach for the Encouraging Classroom* (New York, Delmar, 1998). He suggests we look at children's unsuccessful attempts at negotiating social situations as mistakes rather than as "misbehavior." Here's how I described it for early childhood educators:

"Misbehavior assumes that children are willful and want to do something wrong. If instead we see children as active learners, we assist them in developing social skills, just as they learn new speaking or writing skills, without being punished as wrongdoers when they have difficulty." (*Linking Up!*, Educators for Social Responsibility: 1998, p. 22)

The "oops" method works in Junior High and High School and with adults, too. When our dominator training comes to the fore, the use of the word "oops" can diffuse the situation and direct attention to change.

The Dalai Lama says that peace develops one person at a time through the internal transformation of individuals. Teachers encourage this transformation when they use guidance rather than punishment in the classroom. This helps students build self-control and take self-responsibility.

Teaching The Oops Method: Grades K-6th

There are many ways to implement a plan of social agreements which accents self-responsibility and awareness of others. You are invited to make revisions in this wording so that you have words that best express how you want to hold students in agreements of mutual respect. After having revised models for teaching social skills for different settings over many years, here is a framework I devised recently as a K-6th grade music teacher at the New Hingham School in Massachusetts.

This is a Safe Zone

1. Every person here is a good person.
2. Our job in this room is to work together.
3. We are part of a group. We think about what the whole group needs.
4. If we make a mistake in our behavior, we fix it. Our job is to realize what the mistake is and learn how to change.
5. If someone else makes a mistake, it helps if we don't laugh.

We respect: each other's space
               each person's feelings
               ourselves
               everyone in the room
               the materials we use

The students provided the name, the "Oops" method. The way it worked is that when someone made a social mistake — such as yelling, hitting, pushing, throwing — I as teacher or another student would say, "Oops." It acknowledged the situation and clarified that they had to change it. As needed, I might add — "How can you fix this?" If the mistaken behavior continued without effort at self-responsibility, I handed the student an "Oops" form where they reflected in writing. The form asked questions, including "What was the mistake?" and "What will you do differently next time?" so that they could identify not only what they did that was a mistake but also how they could change or fix it.

Snapshot:

A fourth grader who had difficulty controlling her impulses was part of a group quietly listing to storytelling after lunch. Each person was able to use a piece of modeling clay during the story as a way to focus. When she felt finished with the clay, instead of waiting until the story was complete and placing it back in the container in the center of the circle as was the usual procedure, suddenly she threw it from a distance. The simple word, "Oops," gave her a clear message reinforcing the expectations for the group without placing shame. She walked forward, picked up the clay, and placed it carefully. Ten days later, after hearing the phrase used many times both by adults guiding children and adults owning their own mistakes, the phrase became internalized for her. The same girl caught herself racing around while the rest were gathering to focus at a meeting, noticed, and said, "Oops."

Discovering Nonviolence:
Discussing Partnership Process

Grade level: 5th - 12th

> "Undreamt of and seemingly impossible discoveries will be made in the field of nonviolence."
> —*Gandhi*

1. Explain to student, in your own words that there is a dynamic relationship between caring for ourselves and caring for others. It can happen at the same time. It's both/and rather than either/or. We practice self-respect within a context of community-respect. These aren't dialectically opposed — caring for ourselves and caring for the whole — because as humans we are encoded for mutual respect. Part of what we teach in our classrooms is how to listen to oneself while at the same time being responsible for the effects on others of our behavior and our choices.

2. Talk about the reality of the unseen by reflecting upon the action of gravity. Ask students either to imagine or actually to hold something in one hand and drop it into the other. Discuss: Is gravity real if we can't see it? Establish an understanding that there are forces we can't see which, even though they are invisible forces, are essential. These forces help all life on earth.

3. One of the other unseen forces was articulated by the peacemaker Gandhi in India. He named it Satyagraha (pronounced saht-yah-grah-ha). This means truthforce, but a combination of truth and love, or truthful love.

Gandhi believed that the strongest thing in the world, in the universe even, is this truthful love. Tell students about nonviolence, Gandhi's way of communicating to the British colonial government when it did things that hurt the people of India. Gandhi was insisting on mutual respect. Explain that he believed that people are held in a bond of mutual caring and love.

4. Engage in creating classroom agreements as an experiment in truthforce. Talk together: When someone forgets or uses means that hurt others, by speaking truthfully we insist that they return to this common bond of caring. In our classroom we are doing experiments using truthforce. We will set up our classroom agreements using this truthforce to hold us as a caring community."

Professional Partnership: Nonviolent Communication

Teachers will inevitably be different from each other, and we can use these differences as a basis for linking with each other or as a basis for ranking, judgment, and separation. We may hold different assumptions about how children learn, we value different parts of the curriculum, we have different personal styles. To teach effectively, we have to begin from our own strengths. However, since our our culture is imbued with dominator social structures, many schools are places that aren't fed by colleagial respect and partrnership. This is not rooted in an intent to harm so much as inexperience with partnership or habitual entrainment to domination. Just as when one child in a classroom is mistreated by others, no child can truly feel safe, each staff person isn't socially safe to be themselves and teach at their best in an atmosphere where differences are a source of social stratification rather than appreciated and expected.

A key component of any work in becoming a partnership staff, is learning how to disagree and communicate constructively. Having not grown up in schools ourselves where we learned how to disagree in a friendly way, where we felt safe to go directly to the person we disagree with rather than talk behind their back, it's hard for us to create a new climate. One contribution that Partnership Education can make is to lead trainings for principals in how to set up partnership norms and processes in their building among all staff members.

In some schools teachers overtly or covertly speak disparagingly of others and the culture of that particular staff is to accept or even expect put-down's. As a school examines its culture, the pattern of using humor can be revealing. When we use humor to indirectly raise problems and conflicts, does it help lead into constructive communication or just vent emotions without communication? Do the jokes increase a feeling of community or are indirect messages of conflict or censure delivered through jokes and innuendoes? Do some jokes carry the punch of zingers rather than the fun of friendly joking banter?

Humor can also be a healing force. In a university class for teachers working on their Master's degree, participants used levity when anyone spoke from a "ranking" mindset. Humorously, the teachers called out the reminder, "linking, linking," when a joke felt too sharp.

Anecdote: Nonviolent Communication

Partnership Process Skills: Address conflicts directly.
                                 Look for common ground.

Trainers within a peace education organization had a disagreement. The organization had a standard procedure for teaching conflict resolution in elementary schools. A book was about to be published for early childhood. Early childhood trainers within the organization had independently discovered that the standard wording didn't work as well in younger settings and weren't finding it developmentally appropriate. What method would be presented in the new book?

Dominator choices abounded: Challenging each other argumentatively at staff meetings. Covertly speaking behind people's backs. Accessively praise methods publicly while privately denegrating them. Personalizing: Attacking the person instead of the problem — "he/she always goes off on his/her own," "never listens to me."

Instead, the organization took a partnership direction: Two early childhood educators requested that people involved meet together and collaboratively create a framework that made sense for the early childhood age group. They decided that they liked the purpose of each step in the elementary model but wanted to redo the wording to be more useable by younger children. The educators who worked with younger children reported on the wording that they actually used. Each set of words were listed, compared, and then revised by everyone. The framework was published under the names of all people present at the meeting.

Partnership Questions

Here are questions that a staff can use to examine current school climate and build partnership. A comfortable method for staff reflection needs to avoid putting people on the spot. A several stage process includes these steps: (a) empower a small group to amend and add to this list, (b) hand out the questions for everyone to look at individually in advance, and (c) set up a time to take suggestions for new agreements and new methods of operating that will be mutually respectful.

- When we disagree with someone on the staff, what do we do now? What do we want to do? What might make it difficult to talk directly? How can we help direct constructive communication to happen?

- How do we use humor to communicate? Do we use jokes that stereotype each other? Do we use humor to indirectly communicate what we feel we can't say directly?

- Are all staff members included in social functions? Do people hear about social functions through the same methods? Are dates, locations, and activities selected with input from everyone?

- Are there more ways that the valuing of custodial, clerical, and cafeteria staff can be communicated?

- Are staff differently regarded due to ethnicity, gender, or sexual orientation?

Interventions can be made by individuals. They can speak up when put-downs occur, just as one would intervene in a racist or sexist remark modeling partnership, or step in to help relations with all members of the staff. Intervention will be strongest when a whole school staff can articulate together that they are committed to functioning together as partners — and use the "oops" method when they make a mistake.

Co-Creators of Knowledge

In Partnership Education all people — students, staff, other educators — are recognized as contributors to the growth and learning. We are invited to value and share with each other our struggles, our experiments, our "oops," and our realizations. As we nurture our own partnership voices, we use the parts of ourselves that are fluid, receptive, and creative. We are invited into ever-deepening self-knowledge. People of every age, young people and teachers alike, are important seeds holding the essence of partnership. As we approach teaching itself as an art, we become participants in evolving growth.

PART TWO

PARTNERSHIP CONTENT

Introduction to Part II, Partnership Content

Partnership content is about what we learn and teach. Traditional curriculum is included and expanded as the themes of ecological awareness, gender equity, cultural inclusiveness, and non-violence are interwoven throughout the curriculum. Students not only learn important information; they gain the skills of critical thinking and the tools to participate in the formation of a more equitable, just, and sustainable world.

Partnership content involves helping students learn to recognize partnership and domination patterns. Chapter 6 provides methods to introduce these concepts and shows applications for the development of social responsibility. In seventeen varied activities, Sarah Pirtle shows how to give students an understanding of partnership; how to bring partnership to recess, school bus rides, and assemblies; and how to lead social studies and science activities which teach relevant content.

In Chapters 7 and 8, Dierdre Bucciarelli uses an analytic approach to develop a framework for partnership curriculum planning and for designing curriculum. She makes explicit use of the Partnership Loom and Learning Tapestry, proposed by Riane Eisler in *Tomorrow's Children* and introduced here in Chapter 7. Bucciarelli illuminates how to use the vertical and horizontal threads of the Partnership Loom to expand curriculum and tell a story by presenting in her curriculum for K-3rd graders the human story of foods and plants.

Students are introduced to partnership content in social studies and science using the expressive arts through Sarah Pirtle's work in Chapters 9 and 10. Chapter 9, "Music to Build Partnership," shows how to use song lyrics to introduce meaningful concepts. Chapter 10 proposes that humans are becoming the conscience of the earth. We see how curriculum can introduce students to the "big questions" of how the earth began, how human culture developed, and what our human potential is for helping to create the future.

Bobbi Morrison in Chapter 11 shares curriculum units she teaches at Nova School on mythology as one way to help students, in Eisler's words, "see the underlying tension between the partnership and dominator models that can be traced throughout recorded history."

The last two articles in the section speak to topics not often addressed in the curriculum. In the many language arts activities she presents, Lethea Fay Erz offers ways to examine the dominator messages embedded in our language and to develop language that has a partnership orientation. In the final chapter of the section, Sarah Pirtle heightens our awareness about unlearning sexism, providing useful resources, discussion questions, and exercises.

Throughout this section, authors help students value the accomplishments and experiences of both women and men, a crucial intent since women's concerns and experiences have been systematically ignored, downplayed or distorted in most textbooks and curriculum. Partnership content restores imbalances of gender and ethnicity and gives students the understanding that we all help create knowledge.

CHAPTER SIX

Partnership Education: A Place to Begin

by Sarah Pirtle

If we were meeting around a table, peer to peer, these questions might be raised:

How can I picture what a forty-five minute lesson with partnership content is like?

What elements can I add to what I already teach in my classroom?

Is there a short activity that I could try as an experiment to see if I find it effective?

Are there more extensive activities that develop a sense of partnership across the whole building?

This chapter aims at answering these questions and others by helping you to picture partnership activities that span many grade levels. They are offered as a palette to show what is possible. I hope they can be springboards in designing your own activities, and that you will find helpful pieces that you can use immediately.

Every teacher has important insights to share. The closing section of the book tells how you can relay your own experiences with teaching partnership content. We hope you will share methods that you have developed during your own years of teaching. We also hope that you will test out activities from this book, modify them, and invent more of your own. These four topics are covered:

- Introductory Partnership Lessons: Activities 1 - 5

- Methods of Increasing Social Responsibility: Activities 6 - 9

- Social Studies Lessons on New Views of Ancient History: Activities 10 - 14

- Teaching Science and Social Studies Partnership Content with Movement and Creative Dramatics: Activities 15-17.

"The Lost History of Peace" uses a yarn timeline to give students a visual sense of how long humans may have lived without constant warfare. It is a short activity that can also be used as an effective introduction. See Sample Activity 10.

Introductory Partnership Lessons

Activity One: Personal Stories of Partnership

Grade level: 7th-12th

Goals: To develop a personal reference for the meaning of partnership
To gain new insights by hearing other's memories of partnership.

Overview: This is an excellent activity for staff training as well as with students.

Optional equipment: A basket, a piece of pottery, and stones that can be held in the palm.

Procedure:

1. Sit in a circle. If you are using stones, provide one for each person to hold. Participants report that this tactile experience helps evoke their memories. Point to the basket and the pottery and explain that objects like these have been made throughout the world for thousands of years. Pause to discuss this together.

2. Ask, "Think of a memory from when you were younger of a time that you experienced partnership." Use a popcorn approach instead of going around the circle, so that whoever has a memory can speak first. Often, hearing others' experiences, sparks recall. Make sure everyone has a chance to talk, but also allow people to pass. Encourage an expansive definition of partnership. In fact, if a student says, "I'm not sure that this is really an example of partnership," encourage them to share it and clarify that what you are interested in is their personal definition; all examples are welcome. Option: Pass a talking object around, such as the basket, for people to hold while they are speaking.

   Example: "My family moved a lot. I remember being new in a school in second grade. Everyone was waiting in line outside the school building the first day. Some girls came over to me and said, 'Come on, join us,' and introduced me to other kids. This made a big difference in how I felt."

3. Reflect upon the different facets of the stories. You may notice qualities such as feeling trusted, having creativity encouraged, experiencing freedom, feeling welcomed into the adult world as well as elements of cooperation and collaboration in the sto-

ries. Rather than trying to apply a narrow standard of what partnership means, we are trying to study it in all its forms.

4. If you have a basket and a piece of pottery, reflect as well upon ways people have passed on skills from generation to generation. Ask: How long ago do you think the first baskets were made? Think about the partnership that exists between one generation and the next.

<u>Activity Two:</u> Our Nurturesphere — Drawing Our Circle of Caring

Grade level: 1st-12th

Goals: To become aware of our interconnection with others who nurture us.
     To notice concrete examples of caring in our lives.
     To notice that caring involves a flow of giving and receiving.

Overview: As in other affirmation drawings, students are asked to draw pictures of people, places, and events that matter to them. In this variation it is our interconnections that is stressed. The intention is to help students grasp the centrality of caring in our lives. Instead of using individual pieces of paper, students draw on a shared sheet of paper.

Equipment: Prepare large sheets of paper ringed with circles around the edges. Each student will need a circle about 8 inches in diameter to draw inside. You can use an aluminum pie plate for tracing. Depending upon the number of people in your group, place the circles on one long piece of butcher paper with circles on either side and the edges, or on several large pieces of paper that have circles for four to eight students all around. Provide cups of magic markers so that everyone has access to many different colors.

Procedure:

1. Provide eight-inch circles in front of each student on a shared sheet of paper. Select a name for these circles, such as the Caring Circle, the Circle of Life, the nuturesphere, or simply "your circle." Ask students to use a favorite color to represent themselves in the very center of their circle, and do this by coloring a smaller circle the size of their thumbnail to stand for themselves.

2. Clarify how we are using art. Think of it as an inner conversation using the language of art for exploring. Throughout the activity, encourage people to draw symbolically rather than endeavor to be realistic. A line or splotch of color can represent

something adequately. It is only for you to know what it means. By drawing privately for yourself, the art experience becomes a way of dialoguing and learning differently than through verbalization. Note: At times students may need to draw dots or quick dashes that are active or noisy. As long as they are purposeful, try not to curtail their expression.

3. Tell them, "Look at the shared space on the paper between the individual circles. We are going to use art to explore all the different ways caring comes to us and all the different ways we reach out. You can draw inside your circle and in the space around. Think about the people near you. We'll agree at the start not to draw in anyone else's circle. We also won't draw in the space directly around their circle unless we ask them first."

4. Give examples of things they may want to include in their Circle of Caring. Reflect upon what guidance they will need. Ponder how much to provide explicit directions and how much to leave open to each student. Sample directions:

- Think about the people you know who care about you. Inside your circle, around this small circle that represents yourself, you can place other circles or shapes or lines to represent friends, family members, and other people in your life who are important to you.

- I'm going to name certain common sources that we all share, such as music. Show how this source affects you or gives to you. If you like you can extend a line from the common space into your own circle or add a drawing inside your circle.

- Name the source of "Sunshine," and invite them to draw in their nurturesphere something they love to do outside under the sun.

- Name, "Food," and invite them to draw favorite foods. If they like, they can draw in the shared space where they come from.

- Name, "Animals" and invite them to represent a pet they've had or wish they had, an animal that they like, or an animal they conveys qualities that they want to receive.

- Name, "Library," and invite them to represent people they have read about in books who matter to them — either invented characters or people in history.

- Name, "Family" and invite them to show an activity they do with people they are close to, whether blood family or family of the heart.

- Name, "Friends" and invite them to draw or list an activity they do with friends.

- Name, "Music" and invite them to include experiences with music they find nourishing.

Also, suggest they invent ways of connecting to other circles and adding their own elements. Discuss the fact that we both give and receive. Elements from their circle can also travel outward.

Example: A person who plays guitar draws it in their nurturesphere and then draws the music traveling to the circles of other students.

5. Let students know that they can keep their drawings completely private. If they are interested in doing some sharing, decide whether to share drawings in pairs or as a whole class.

6. Reflect upon what they have discovered about care by doing the drawings. Discuss and consider how much care goes into the making of each one of us, and how much care we bestow on one another in the course of our daily lives.

7. With secondary level students, present this background information:

The term, "nurturesphere," was coined by partnership educator Bruce Novak of the University of Chicago. He believes that what is truly evolutionarily new about human beings is not so much that we are *sapiens*, that is, "knowing" beings, but that we are primarily caring, nurturant, teaching beings. "Nurturesphere" is related to theologian Teilhard de Chardin's term, "noosphere." Novak writes:

> "Our world grows, not as we know more, but as we broaden our circle of care. Most scientists and philosophers have thought that what makes us human is our ability to know, hence the term 'homo sapiens' or 'knowing man.' Teilhard de Chardin translated this notion of 'man the knower' into terms of cosmic evolution, saying that with human life a new sphere of evolution is opened: On top of the biosphere and the zoosphere is the noosphere, where consciousness — not just genes and behavior — evolves. Partnership science and philosophy, though, sees knowing as truly evolutionary only when it refrains from dominating nature and other human beings. In this light, what is truly new about humans is our ability to nurture nature and one another, to elicit new life forms through our behavior in our families, our communities, and the world around us by giving the best of ourselves in caring relationships. David Loye, in *Darwin's Lost Theory of Love*, has shown how this was actually Darwin's original theory of human evolution."

Novak continues that by reframing ourselves as nurturing, teaching beings, we are "more insistent than many scientists and philosophers often are, that in order to be fully human, we need to be committed not just to knowing 'what is' but helping 'what should be' become reality, carefully nurturing in partnership what is best in ourselves, in others, and in the world in which we dwell."

Discuss his concepts as well as these statements: Our life in the nurturesphere is crucial for our individual as well as our collective life support system. We can either advance or impede the development of ourselves, our community, and the earth itself, depending upon our respect for the growth of our nurturesphere.

Activity Three: Partnership and Domination in Diagram

Grade level: 2nd - 12th

Overview: Any of the next three activities work well in combination. For instance, second graders can comprehend diagrams when combined with the dialogue activity. These can be used as an introduction before any activity where students will be cooperating.

Goal: To introduce the concept of partnership and domination symbolically.

Procedure:

1. Show students a diagram of people interacting with domination or ask them to suggest a diagram of such a relationship. Discuss the meaning.

   Examples:
   - a seesaw with one dot high and one dot low.
   - billiard balls colliding.
   - a pyramid with dots at many levels and only one dot at the top.
   - a circle where all the dots relate only to one dot.

2. Show students a diagram that represent the relationship among people when there is partnership, or ask them to suggest one. Discuss the meaning.

   Examples:
   - Draw a circle and place dots all around the circumference.
   - Connect the dots around a circle with many crisscrossing lines to show each dot relating to many others.
   - Show the inter-relationship between neurons in a neural net, connected through their synapses.

Activity Four: Partnership Movement Game

Grade level: 1st - 12th

Overview: Once a basic description of partnership has been introduced, use movement to make it concrete. This activity provides a movement break for a class or within a staff training.

Goal: To physically experience patterns of partnership.

1. Explore the physicalization of partnership. One person suggests a framework and others try it out. Start with this format: Place all hands in a circle like spokes of a wheel.

> As you try a shape, clarify when the group stops holding that position. For instance, say, "Hold 1, 2, 3, and release." Try several suggestions as a whole group, inventing what forms represent partnership to you.

2. Form groups of 4-8 people. Next try: Make a pretzel shape connecting to as many people as possible with your hands, elbows, or head. Hold and release. Ask for other suggestions for shapes.

3. Curl hands together in a spiral shape. The way to do this is for everyone to put the same hand — such as the left one — into the center, and each hand nests together like flower petals. After everyone has linked up in this manner, try repeating the shape by building it gradually. Start with just three people each nesting one hand in the curled spiral, then add a fourth, a fifth, until everyone in the small group of 4-8 people is now connected.

4. Study the way we respond to and are influenced by each others' movements. Make a large circle, standing spread-out. Each person only faces the person to their right so that they can't see the person who is in turn looking at them. Once the direction is established, close your eyes and experiment with movement while staying in your spot. Find a movement that feels comfortable to you, like swinging your arms, or a swimming motion. When you are ready, open your eyes and look at the designated person ahead of you. Be aware of their movement, and imitate parts of it if you choose. Keep a balance of attention on what movements feel right to you, as well as what suggestions you want to try from the person you are watching. You'll have a sense of movements travelling around the circle.

These activities were co-created during a Partnership Education training sponsored by Traprock Peace Center in Deerfield, Massachusetts. Sally Ahearn, Sarah Ahearn, Mavis Gruver, Sunny Miller, Susan Pelis, and Sarah Pirtle all contributed to the idea.

Activity Five: Dominator Dialogue and Diversity

Grade level: K - 3rd

Overview: Before the class does a cooperative activity, this dialogue sets the stage. It models how to link across differences. This can also be a helpful intervention when certain class members dominate discussions verbally.

Goal: To introduce what it looks like and sounds like to be partners.

    To spell out what dominator behavior is like.

    To provide information on unlearning bias.

Equipment: A puppet or a doll.

Procedure:

1. For an early childhood group, after having introduced the meaning of partnership and domination through verbal descriptions, diagrams, or movements, illustrate the meaning by the way you talk to a puppet or doll. Hold up the figure to pretend you are addressing it. Shake its hand, look at it, and greet it. Explain to the class: When you meet a person, you can connect with them and be partners, or you can say messages like, "someone is better than the other," or, "someone is going to take over and be boss."

Illustrate how domination uses differences not for linking but for ranking, and structures domination around them. Choose dimensions of diversity which will be most informative to your students. Use a format to make clear that the domination isn't recommended:

e.g., Teacher speaks: "What if I said _____, would that be fair?"
Teacher or the class supplies a response that contradicts the unfair statement.

The concept here is by the teacher playing a role and articulating bias, the group has a chance to consciously unpack what is going on and reverse the bias.

Sample dialogue:

• Dimension of diversity: <u>Height</u>

Illustration of dominator attitude:

(Said by teacher talking to the puppet or doll) "I'm much taller than you, and short people are less important. Only I can be line leader because I'm taller."

Contradiction response: "That's not fair and that's not true. You can guide our line just as well as I can. It's not height that makes a good line leader. What's important is that no one pushes."

• Dimension of diversity: <u>Age</u>

Use a puppet or doll that represents someone younger than yourself.

Illustration of dominator attitude: If I said to this new person I'm meeting — "I'm a woman, and you're younger than me. You're a girl. I'm better than you because I'm older so I should talk more because I have more important things to say — would that be fair?"

Contradiction: People of every age have important thoughts and feelings to share. Being older doesn't mean that you're more important.

• Dimension of diversity: <u>Skillfulness and experience in nonviolent communication.</u>

Illustration of dominator attitude - part one: "I bet I can threaten you and get you to do what I want."

Contradiction: (pretend the puppet or doll is responding) "Then I don't know if we can be friends because I like to choose friends who can talk things out rather than bully."

Illustration of dominator attitude - part two: (using a shark or lion puppet who illustrates growling or threatening) "We could be fighting friends who both like to fight and we could gang up together on other kids. What do you think?"

Contradiction: "If we think its fun to gang up on other people, then we're being really unfair."

• Dimension of Diversity: <u>Ability at talking, ability at sharing thoughts verbally</u>.

Illustration of domination: "I want to do most of the talking in class meeting because I've already thought of what I want to say. I'm going to wave my hand wildly and call out and insist that the teacher call on me. (speaking to puppet or doll) You don't talk as much as me. I guess you don't have as many thoughts as I do. Well, I don't really care what you have to say."

Contradiction: (imagine the puppet or doll has spoken and the dominating person has learned from them). "Oh, so you're telling me that you have a lot of thoughts but it's hard to speak and have a turn when I'm insisting on doing a lot of talking. You say that you prefer talking to a few people at a time more than talking to a whole group." Ask the class, "How could I be more of a partner to my friend?"

Use as many examples as you need to help your class examine domination.

Focusing on oppression issues:

There are limitations to this activity. The oppression of racism is so insidious and lethal that using a doll to talk about it in the way shown above means the core issues could get compromised. Racism is referenced through skin color but actually involves much more. The unconscious ways that white people are taught to be white and ingest attitudes, behaviors, and privileges is a crucial part of how racism continues. Here's another way to do the activity. Model how to identify the bias we have ingested in order to explicitly eject it. Share your thought processes with your students.

Example: Articulating the process of unlearning racism.

As each teacher works on unlearning racism, we can share more of our new under-standings with our students. As a white teacher, I feel it is particularly important that white teachers model this for white students and let students of color know what white allies are doing. Working with a second grade class where every student in the school was European American, here is what I said as a European American to intro-duce concepts and make explicit the thought process of unlearning racism. This dia-logue is not meant to be complete. It shows one step. It illustrates my own style of talk-ing, but each person will find their own words:

> "I've been finding out that when I was growing up, I heard lies told about the differences between people and believed them without even knowing what was happening. I grew up white. I was taught not only to notice skin color, but also to treat people differently because of it. I didn't want to do that. My heritage is that my parents' parents came from England, France, Ireland, and Germany. My heritage is called European American. My skin color which you see is light brownish pinkish. I didn't realize that it wasn't really about skin color. It was about separation and unfairness to group one group of people with lighter skin into one category and rank them higher. I was definitely taught that if you were white you were better."

> "One thing that helped me was to learn scientific facts about skin color. I have light skin because my ancestors lived in a cold country. Their skin was light because they didn't need much of the coloration chemical called melanin in their skin so they could take in lots of sun. My friend Jody, who is African American, has ancestors who lived in a hot country where they need-ed more melanin in their skin to protect them from the hot sun. We are both part of one human race. We're not from different races. The idea of different races was made up to keep the lie going."

> "But when Jody and I do things together I've watched ways that some peo-ple who are white treat her differently than they treat me. She is a professor and teaches at a university. I've also thought a lot about the fact that all the Presidents have been white men, and most of the lawyers and doctors and professors I've known are white. It's not because white people are smarter. I realized that some white people want me to keep accepting the unfairness, and I made a decision that I wouldn't. I want to help end this horrible prob-lem that is called racism."

With older students I address the charge — "you're trying to be politically cor-rect." I explain that I have a lot of passion for unlearning racism and it's not because I want to be correct or accepted. It's because I fervently want racism and all forms of oppression to change. The new vocabulary I've learned as an adult — words like oppression, ally, and targeting — has given me language to talk and think about something I didn't have words for, and that's why I'm passing those new words on to them as well.

3. Discuss: What does dominating mean? Can you explain in your own words the difference between (a) being respectful partners and (b) being dominating or being bossy or biased or unfair?

4. Tell the group, "In this class, there are many ways we are different, and we're all important. When we do (name the cooperative activity you are about to do) today, we'll show in the way that we treat each other that everyone is important. Make sure to make room for everyone to talk in the group."

Methods of Increasing Social Responsibility

Activity Six: Looking at Recess Through the Dominator/Partnership Lenses

Grade Level: K-6th

Goal: To help students discern which recess activities further partnership and which activities are unproductive or hurtful.

Overview: Recess is a unique time of day where young people can develop their own culture. Adults are general supervisors, yet many games and events are not led by adults. Many conversations and exchanges happen out of the earshot of adults. It can be a time where creative play flourishes. It can also be a time where exclusion, racist or sexist remarks, and other put-downs occur without anyone intervening.

Procedure:

1. Look over these two contrasting states and find words and phrases that will introduce them most effectively to your students. Start two columns with one or two phrases heading up each so that the basic idea is clear.

   a. "partnership," "everyone counts," "working together," "fun for everyone," "peace," or "connecting."

   b. "domination," "not fair for everyone," "fighting," "putting people down," or "hurting."

2. Now, more fully flesh out these concepts. Under the headings you've selected, brainstorm as a class as many words and phrases as you can that help describe that par-

ticular state. For example, on the partnership side, students might suggest "taking turns," or "keeping things fair." On the domination side, students might say "bullying" or "getting too rough." Notice the nuances, like the difference between "cooperating for connecting" and "cooperating to exclude someone." Choose two phrases that they can use to represent the two states.

3. Identify that these are two ways of looking. Let's imagine the class has chosen the phrases, "working together," and "hurting and harming." Ask them to watch what happens at recess from these two ways of looking. How did you see people working together at recess? Did you see any hurting or harming at recess? As you collect observations it's important to make an agreement to list situations but not give people's names.

Example: Hurting or harming: "Someone shoved going out the door," instead of "Lee was shoving people."

Example: Working together: "Someone helped push people on the swing," instead of "George gave us pushes on the swing."

You can use different times during the day to collect observations. Responses may be different if you do the activity before recess has occurred, recalling experiences from that week or from any time during the year, and if you do the activity right after recess when memories are fresh and more details can emerge. Both can be valuable.

Examples of Partnership: Someone taught a game, people talked about how to share a ball, people got help from a peer mediator, the teams for kickball were made fairly because we let new people pick teams today.

Examples of Domination/Not Helping: Someone hit, a group chased kids who didn't want to be chased, someone was told it was too late to join a game but then the players let someone else in later.

Also, give students a piece of paper where they can write down anything that has happened to them or other students which they felt was unfair or hurtful. They can sign the paper or they can leave it anonymous. Here is a chance for a hidden harmful event to be shared with a caring adult.

Extension: Partnership Glasses That You Can Wear

Work with students to cut out paper glasses of oak tag for each person. Cut eyeholes and show them how to bend the sides of the glasses and put them on. Ask them to decorate the outside surface of their glasses with dynamic colors to represent partnership/respect. Instruct them to select their favorite phrases from that side of the list and write them on the inside of the paper glasses.

While reflecting on a situation, put on your glasses. As you look through the lenses, imagine it is easier to tell the difference between partnership/respectful behavior and hurtful/dominator behavior. When you see or think about problems and conflicts, imagine that wearing these glasses you are able to picture how the situation can be transformed.

Variation: Partnership and Domination Lenses

Make a drawing of the frame of a pair of glasses. In one eyehole draw a recess problem. In the other eyehole show a partnership solution to the problem.

4. Partnership Process Ideas:

- Student Leadership: Repeat step 3 of the activity another day, this time with one or two students facilitating as the lists are made.

- School Sharing: Create a skit to share at a school assembly that shows the glasses being worn and depicts partnership and domination events at recess.

- Partnership Report: During assemblies, classes report on new ideas for increasing partnership at recess.

<u>Making Partnership Interventions</u>: How to Work with the Information You Gather:

Use the lists that you have brainstormed. Select a situation where there is hurting or harming. "Now we are going to use the partnership side of thinking. Let's imagine ways that this unfair situation could change." Here are ways to work with the list the group has created.

(a) Partnership contributions: Think of activities and interactions that could happen which would increase partnership at recess. Pick one to try and brainstorm how to do it.

Example: <u>Older Students Teach Games:</u> By looking at recess, the class notices that a group of younger students gets habitually involved in chase games which often lead to fights. They deduce that one of the problems is that this group can't think of other activities they would enjoy. The class decides they will become partners to the younger students and teach them some new games.

(b) Intentions which aren't working: Think of ways to reduce the dominator events. Pick one to try to change and get very specific about where communication is breaking down. Emphasize what is the intention of each participant and learn how to assist them.

Example: <u>Kickball communication:</u> The class notices that their kickball games frequently end in name-calling and hard feelings. They dissect what contributes to the problems and how to turn these around. One child reveals that they feel criticized and pressured, and when they feel under pressure they lash out. The others examine what things they are doing that may feel like pressure and look for other ways to talk to each other during the game.

Example: <u>Turn taking:</u> The class watches younger children argue each day over the same valued game or item (such as swings, balls). They realize that the children need a way to ask for turns and keep track of who will be first the next day. They come up with the solution of writing the names of the children who usually want the item on clothespins and suggest that all the labeled clothespins be kept in a can. They introduce a method of attaching the clothesppins to a piece of cloth or felt to represent the order in which they will take turns.

(c) Gender: Discuss the ways that gender issues come into play at recess.

Example: <u>Examine Chase Games:</u> At many schools small groups of girls and of boys chase each other. Look at this. Do the boys chase girls in a manner where the girls don't feel they have the power to stop them or put limits on the game? Address the specific events and also talk about the larger picture. As appropriate to your age group, engage them in being part of a world-wide effort to make sure that boys and men don't dominate women and girls.

(d) Expressing personal boundaries: Make sure that students have a chance to set their own boundaries and speak up for their needs during recess. Talk more specifically about what domination means.

Example: <u>Don't Just Put Up With It:</u> There may be instances of domination which students have become inured to so that they now accept them. Spell out what kind of fair treatment each person deserves.

(e) Frame goals for recess in partnership language, such as, "we want everyone to feel nurtured and safe at recess." Then when students are called to line up after recess, take a moment before going inside to name one of these goals and ask if it was met.

Example: <u>Check-in on Rules During Line Up:</u> Address the line, "It matters to me that everyone felt safe today at recess. If anything happened to you that didn't feel safe, be sure to mention it to me and I'll help with the situation."

Extension:

• Ask your students to help identify other times during the day when they wish there could be more partnership interactions, such as waiting in line for the bus, the lunch room, or during the bus ride. Use the same procedure to diagnose what is and what is not working and plan interventions which can help.

<u>Activity Seven:</u> Bus Monitors

Grade level: 3rd - 12th

Overview: Students and staff analyze what problems are occurring boarding and riding buses. A bus monitor job is formulated. The counseling staff of the school trains students to be able to intervene when unfair things happen during the bus ride.

Goals: To give students responsibility in maintaining bus rides that are fun social experiences rather than times that hurtful behavior can flourish unchecked.

To show students that a school community can address a problem using a partnership approach.

Procedure:

1. Start by reviewing as a school staff what the expectations are for behavior on buses.

2. Next, gather information. What do students think the bus rules are? In each classroom, engage students in listing types of problems that have occurred on buses. What kind of unwanted events (fights, name-calling, exclusion) are happening? Are there situations of saving seats or choosing seats that are feeling unfair to some? Are there problems waiting in line, or getting on the buses? Learn more about the dynamics on the buses: How do people choose seats?

Example of a bus-related problem: First graders and sixth graders both approach the same bus from different directions and when they get to the bus the sixth graders push in front of the first graders' line.

Tell them the school community will develop a method of changing the problems. Get their ideas about what role bus monitors could play. What do they think that students could do to help keep things fair as bus monitors?

3. Decide which problems to address.

• Look for problems that the staff themselves can address, e.g., decide whether the first graders or sixth graders go on the bus first or how they take turns.

• List ways that more policies or practices could be established.

• Discuss and define together the role of bus monitor: How could students help set a positive tone? In what ways could they speak up and intervene from where they are seated when inappropriate behavior occurs?

4. Using this information about what bus monitors could potentially do, the principal talks with bus drivers to negotiate perimeters. Create a plan.

Sample Plan for an Elementary School

For each bus, a team including one person from grades 3, 4, 5, and 6, will be designated as the bus monitor committee on that bus. We will rotate the position so that many students can be in a position of leadership. Ideally, most every student would have a chance to take the role of bus monitor at some time during the year. The school counselor will train a new group for each month, and hold weekly meetings with bus committees for a half hour on Friday to provide help.

Questions to consider:

- What are the expectations of the bus monitors?
- Where do the monitors sit?
- How long do they remain monitors before rotating?
- How many monitors will you need to have to allow for people being absent?
- What grades will be included?
- Will you include everyone in the class in the rotation? If not, on what basis?
- How will you check in on how its going?

4. Engage the school in a social experiment. This means that changes and adaptations are expected. The proposed plan is introduced to the school at a school assembly. Describe the role of monitor not like a policeman, but as a guide or guardian. (See the next activity for a more thorough explanation of social guidance in a systems model).

5. Each classroom discusses a "working draft" of the plan. Circulate a one sheet summary of the ideas. Make sure it tells what is expected on the buses and also how monitors will help maintain this. Students are invited to give feedback on the plan and offer any amendments. Use questions like, "How would that work?" to help students envision the consequences of their ideas.

Students or teachers take notes on the feedback. Ask for a representative from each classroom to come to a meeting to report on the opinions of their class. Avoid unhelpful entrenched positions of "our class wants it this way and your class wants it that way." Do this by focusing on the issues and problems to be solved. From this planning, draw up a final summary that takes into account the concerns and makes use of new insights. Whatever plan is made, clarify that it will be tried, and can then be modified. Emphasize that we can develop improvements as we participate in the social experiment.

6. School counselors train the first group of bus monitors and set up a method to check in with them as to how it's working. Post the schedule of monitors in each classroom. Give the summary of what the monitors will do to each bus driver and to each parent. Use this letter to parents as an opportunity to talk about how the school teaches social responsibility.

<u>Activity Eight:</u> Partnership School Council

Grade level: 1st - 12th

Overview: Involve students in helping to govern the school using a systems view of human social interaction. Teach students a partnership structure for helping to coordinate the community. Empower classes to discuss important social issues, to give feedback on areas where change is needed, to notice unconstructive behavior, and to help make plans for changes.

Goals: To formalize a structure whereby students give input and set a tone for the whole community.
To understand a systems view of community functioning.

Procedure:

1. Talk as a staff about what a partnership method of governance is and how it is modeled on life systems:

Myth: Partnership means anything goes, laissez-faire, a tyranny of structurelessness.

Actual definition: Partnership means order. Just as the pattern of a healthy plant is established by a seed, the shared goals and purposes of the school community are the seed around which an orderly structure is based. The human organism operates through complex coordination of cells and organs. Each cell has its own vitality and clear boundaries while at the same time it works in partnership within the community of all the cells of the body. Likewise, each person in a partnership structure is responsible for maintaining their own behavior and integrity as well as being responsible for helping to maintain the integrity of the whole.

Learning: Teachers are well aware of the number of students for whom it is difficult to be in charge of themselves or to perceive themselves as part of a group. Nonetheless, using this systems model is an effective way (a) to diagnose how to help with the problem areas in a community, (b) to set up training in responsibility, and (c) to structure governance.

2. Within this model, the way to maintain a healthy system is to have a coordinated method for receiving feedback and responding to feedback so that the whole community can flourish. Establish a School Council as a mechanism for student feedback and as an avenue for developing student responsibility. However, instead of electing certain students as representatives who are already considered the positive leaders, include all students in rotation, working in pairs, so that they get practice in being accountable. Two members of each classroom attend a weekly student meeting with the principal or counselor. If the group will be too large, work with half the school at

a time. Every student at some point in the school year gets to represent their classroom at the School Council meeting.

Suggested format: On Monday the principal sends each classroom one or two questions to discuss. These are on the agenda of the meeting. Every class has four days to make time to discuss these issues. Sample question — "What can we do about the problem of people throwing our metal silverware into the trash can at lunch?" Although the discussion may generate many different ideas, each classroom must pare down their feedback to 1-3 statements.

Each classroom on their job chart rotation includes the jobs "representative" and "assistant representative." These students attend together. The representative is responsible for reading out loud the feedback that their classroom is giving, and also brings back any announcements from the meeting and reads them to the class. The assistant watches, and the next week they become the representative and fulfill those same duties. On Thursday afternoon, representatives attend the School Council meeting for half an hour. On Friday they report back to their class what happened at the meeting. Each class makes their own plan of what they will do if reps are absent for illness.

Some issues will be simple reports, such as, "Does your class want to make a presentation at the holiday assembly, and if so, how many minutes do you need?" Such a matter could be handled at a staff meeting, but by using it as a School Council issue, student understanding of community is increased. Other issues may be on the agenda for several weeks, each time getting closer to a school consensus on what changes to try.

Example: Bus-related issues. Each week the classrooms discuss a portion of the problem.

Week 1 — What problems are occurring when people in your class board buses? Tell actions without using specific names of students.

Week 2 — Does your class like the current method for choosing seats on the bus? If not, can you think of other ways that seats could be chosen?

Week 3 — What problems during the bus ride have people encountered?

Week 4 — What are your suggestions for changing problems during the bus ride?

Week 5 — Here is the suggested bus monitor plan we have developed. Are there any changes you would like to make?

3. Staff Involvement:

a. Agenda: Staff will be more involved and included if they are able to have input on what will be part of the School Council agenda. The principal could propose the next week's agenda to the staff the week before students address it.

b. Uniform policies: Make sure that staff agree that no student will be excluded from the rotation. This means that no matter what a student's behavior has been like on a given week, if the job chart says they are the representative that week, they are responsible for carrying out their duties as class representative. This way each student has a chance to develop their skills in leadership, responsibility, and communication.

c. Staff Inclusion: Talk about a way for staff themselves to be representatives on the School Council. Staff who aren't classroom teachers — custodians, cafeteria workers, guidance counselors, librarian, special education teachers — can figure out a method for attending during agenda items germane to them or as part of a regular rotation.

4. Use a bulletin board to share information from School Council. One image is that each classroom is one circle all linked to a central hub. Spokespeople who represent each class go into the center circle, like spokes of a wheel. Show this graphically to reinforce the idea that we are like cells in one body.

5. Apply this basic method — a few people are delegated to discuss a problem that affects the larger group — to other situations. Set up ways for people to give feedback when there is a problem, and establish avenues for this feedback to be regarded and taken into account.

Examples:

• All the classes who have recess together can address a chronic problem at kickball by having representives meet at the start of recess to compare plans from their classrooms.

• Small groups within a classroom can discuss a problem on behalf of the whole. For instance, if there are problems that occur during music class, randomly draw three names and ask those students to meet with you to discuss ideas for how to improve the situation.

6. Continue to become more informed on the systems model of developing social responsibility. The belief in operation here is that to maintain order and strengthen healthy behavior we need to engage students in practicing it. The goal is to return healthy functioning to the system of the school by showing how to give appropriate feedback, by raising awareness of community, and by actually practicing responsibility.

Some teachers may express concern that empowering students means encouraging them to push for whatever they wish without respect for others. Clarify that we aren't empowering them for them to dominate, we are requiring them to be part of an orderly community where they are empowered to be part of democracy. Empowerment in a systems model means empowering to contribute to the healthy functioning of the whole. In fact, we are telling students: You are part of this group, and what you do impacts all of us.

In every school, systems of accountability are strained by students who chronically exhibit mistaken behavior. A partnership model also holds them accountable. They are seen as having strong unmet needs. The goal is to engage these students in perceiving and owning: What is it you really need right now? What is the best way to get those needs met? Including them rather than excluding them from participation in School Council is part of entraining them into being responsible for their actions.

Activity Nine: School Celebration — A Weekly Partnership Event

Grade level: K-8th

Overview: Students help facilitate an assembly of 30-40 minutes. This activity helps to build social responsibility because students develop a stronger sense of community, share responsibility for conducting the assembly, and have an avenue for being recognized.

Goals: To develop a sense of community.
To give opportunities for the work done in individual classes to be shared.
To highlight creative work by individuals — poems, artwork, instrumental performances.
To share important events in the life of the school.
To encourage partnership throughout the building.

Procedure:

1. Think about the activities you want to include in your School Celebration and set up a sequence. Here is an example:

- Listening music while walking in.
- Greeting Song.
- Announcements by the principal or school counselor.
- Birthdays of the week — All students with birthdays come forward and the school sings to them.
- Sharing Time — Students sign up in advance to share a poem, dance, artwork, or a performance on an instrument. Time is given for 1-3 students each week.
- New ideas — Classes share curricular activities, or a song with a theme or message is presented.

- Spotlight — Time is given to a special concern or event that week, or something else currently relevant to the life of the school.
- Closing Song.

If you like, these categories can be shifted around to use whatever order fits best for that day.

2. Students in the oldest grades (3rd-6th in elementary school, 7th-8th in middle school) sign up in advance to be announcers. Two students — usually one girl and one boy — take turns reading an adult-prepared script to introduce each presentor.

3. One staff member, such as the music teacher, coordinates the student sign-up process and holds the overview of what each assembly will look like. At least one or two hours weekly are needed for planning and rehearsal. To make sure that roles are shared, lists need to be kept of who has had a turn doing the various parts — being announcer, sharing a poem, showing artwork, setting up chairs — and which classes have had turns giving presentations.

4. Begin the event with listening music as students walk in. This helps maintain calm and focus. Announce the name of the music that was played. This practice introduces students to a variety of styles of music.

5. Choose a familiar tune for the greeting song, such as "This Land is Your Land." Every class takes a turn writing the verse of the week which shares their news or comments upon the weather, seasonal changes, holidays, or other events in the life of the school. Each week repeat the verse from the week before, and add the new verse written by the featured class. Establish that the verse doesn't need to rhyme. It's more like a list. Sample verse by a fifth grade class:

> We went to the art museum.
>
> We saw the Impressionists.
>
> Some liked Monet's Water Lilies.
>
> Some liked Van Gogh's paintings.
>
> The bus broke down.
>
> We sat and ate our snack.
>
> This school was made for you and me.

6. Two older students can be stage managers each week and help set up. To extend the number of roles for students who want to help, have one person be a chart holder who holds the schedule for the assembly and points to what is next, such as, "Birthdays of the Week."

7. Using a microphone increases the enjoyment and sense of pride for students.

Snapshot

I facilitated a School Celebration each week for the New Hingham Regional School, a rural public elementary school in Massachusetts, during the 1999-2000 school year. We used a friendly relaxed tone and supported people when they felt nervous. If someone spoke too softly, we simply asked them to repeat their words. The whole staff kept their eye out for students who they'd like to highlight; for example, three girls shared a skit they had memorized in their special education class. All older students were urged to take a turn as announcers. We looked for ways to increase student leadership, like having the fifth grade lead the birthday song that week, or asking the sixth graders to choose and lead a closing song.

The art teacher frequently selected a class assignment to be featured — like animal masks or shadow puppets. We also included examples of art created by parents. The Spotlight Time was diverse. At various times it included safety advice from firefighters about Halloween, scientific information about clouds, and reports on a class trip to a museum. During the Sharing Time, we valued all levels of performance; students who could play a simple song one-handed on the keyboard were as welcome as students who knew a more complex two-handed song from their piano lessons. Students were spurred to write poems or songs because they knew they could be heard in the School Celebration. These factors combined to make the weekly assembly a time of fun, appreciation, and warmth.

Social Studies Lession on New Views of Ancient History

<u>Activity Ten:</u> The Lost History of Peace

Grade level: 2nd - adult

Goals: To use a timeline representing 230,000 years of human history.
To gain prespective on how long humans may have lived without widespread warfare.

Overview: According to this interpretation, for only about 1/37th of our history is there documentation for the presence of inter-group warfare.

Equipment: yarn 69 inches long

Background: "Do you think there has to be war?" "Do you think there have been periods of time without constant warfare?" "Is warfare inevitable?" These are poignant questions, and the basis of lively debate. This activity makes use of the research done by anthropologist Marija Gimbutas about societies of

Old Europe in prehistory, which is described in *The Chalice and the Blade* and *Tomorrow's Children*, as well as the work of other researchers.

Procedure:

1. Make a timeline by cutting a piece of yarn 69 inches long. The length will represent 230,000 years ago. Explain to students that this shows when the oldest piece of art identified to date was found. *Tomorrow's Children* describes the discovery as, "a carved object excavated in Israel at the site of Berekhat Ram in the Golan Heights: A grooved pebble that 'bore some characteristics of a female body,' with incised grooves delimiting the head and arms.'" (*Tomorrow's Children*, p. 95) Recent microscopic analysis of this find adds evidence that this is indeed an artifact and not a natural phenomenon.

Each inch of the timeline represents 3333 years. In preparing your timeline, mark two dots:

Place a dot 3.89 inches from the end. This represents 11,000 BC in the Near East/West Asia, and shortly thereafter in Europe. This marks the transition from hunting and gathering to agriculture. Many researchers believe that the change in means of subsistence is the most fundamental fact in the change in human behavior.

Also place a dot 1.88 inches from the end. This represents 6,300 years ago, which is roughly the time that the first wave of invasions began to over-run the villages in Old Europe, according to Dr. Marija Gimbutas, as described in *The Chalice and the Blade*.

2. Showing this timeline, ask: "Do you think warfare has been a continual part of human history? Please make a guess by pointing to a place on the timeline when you think that widespread warfare began in the area that is now called Europe." Very often students guess close to 230,000 years ago.

3. After they have guessed, show the two dots.

  • the dot at 3.89 inches represents 13,000 years ago. This marks the change from the peacefulness that characterized the hunter-gatherer way of life.

  • the dot at 1.88 inches from the end marks the time when some archeologists believe that early "warfare" began in that area of the world.

Dr. Marija Gimbutas's research indicated that between 4300 and 2800 B.C.E., three waves of invasions from southern Russia drastically altered the societies she had excavated. Before the invasions of the Indo-Europeans, called the Kurgans by Gimbutas, signs of destruction through warfare were not in evidence in those Neolithic villages. This timeline makes use of her interpretation of archeology. She postulates that for the years before these invasions, trading relationships, not warfare, took place between Neolithic societies. Make it clear that this timeline refers to Old Europe. In other areas, widespread warfare and inter-society aggression may have developed at other times in other parts of the world.

4. Help students drink in the information that for all those years — represented by 67.1 inches — evidence indicates that people in Old Europe may have lived without the widespread violence and warfare that characterizes modern times. Discuss this revelation as a lost history of peace. Ask, "How does this change your perceptions to entertain such a possibility?"

5. Acknowledge the complexity of these issues. Historians, anthropologists, and archeologists delineate a full spectrum of human behavior in history. We know that throughout the world there have been cultures — such as the Maya, the Incas, the Aztecs — that acted aggressively toward other groups. Moreover, Gimbutas' work in particular is controversial among archeologists, and her finds have been interpreted other ways.

6. Look at the full expanse of this timeline and think together about what kinds of behaviors humans would have needed to advance and develop. Robert Slavin, a researcher at John Hopkins University in the field of cooperative learning, writes:

> "Why have humans beings been so successful as a species? … We're intelligent — but an intelligent man or woman alone in the jungle or forest would not survive long. What has really made humans such successful animals is our ability to apply our intelligence to cooperation with others to accomplish group goals."

(Robert E. Slavin, *Synthesis of Research on Cooperative Learning*. Alexandria, Va.: Research Information Service, ASCD, 1981, 655)

Professor Jiao Tianlong, speaking of the Paleolithic period, says that "there must have been equality and mutual aid between the members, who struggled together against immense odds in order to subsist." (As quoted in *Tomorrow's Children*, p. 95 in reference to early hominid finds in Asia.)

It is on this basis that partnership educators feel it is important to teach students new views of the human story.

Variation: If the use of a timeline is new for students, use an extended lesson plan — "Activity Thirteen: Timelines and Human Partnership" — which shows other timelines and leads up to this activity.

<u>Activity Eleven:</u> Social Studies Activity
What the Spirals Say: Art and Archaeology

Grade level: 3rd - 12th

Source: *Discovery Time for Cooperation and Conflict Resolution* by Sarah Pirtle, (Nyack,
      NY: Children's Creative Response to Conflict, 1998).

Goal: To reveal Old European history of great significance today using art from a site
      in Bosnia.

Equipment: paper and pencils, map of Europe

Overview: Joseph Campbell helped to make the broader public aware of historical
      information about Old European culture from 7000 – 3500 B.C. that has a
      tremendous impact on how we think of ourselves today. Extensive evidence
      reveals this to be a period without warfare and suggests a time of partner-
      ship, not patriarchy, between women and men. Campbell points to the
      twenty volumes of research by Marija Gimbutas, professor of European
      archaeology at UCLA. He comments, "The message here is of an actual age
      of harmony and peace in accord with the creative energies of nature which
      for a spell of some four thousand years anteceded the five thousand of what
      James Joyce has termed the 'nightmare' (of contending tribal and national
      interests) from which it is now certainly time for this planet to wake." (San
      Francisco: HarperCollins, 1991, p. xiv.) This information is important for
      European-American students because it help them gain a more detailed and
      accurate picture of their heritage. It is important for all students to know of
      thousands of years of history when women were not subservient to men,
      and to perceive that the human story is not an unbroken line of aggression.
      Here the language of art becomes a means for the past to speak to the pre-
      sent. The pieces of pottery that are the focus of this lesson were excavated
      from the region that is present-day Bosnia.

Teacher's Note: The unfamiliar can be uncomfortable when it is so different from the
      picture of history one has carried. Campbell felt that this information
      was a crucial part of reclaiming human interconnection and transform-
      ing human warfare. It will feel new, unusual, and perhaps unsettling
      for many of us, both children and adults. The term "Goddess" is key to
      describing this historical era, and is not the teaching of religion, but an
      imparting of an historical period that has insights for us in our time.

Orientation: Tell students: "Today we are going to step back in time 7000 years ago in
      Southeastern Europe and find out what life was like. We will use art to
      help us understand the people."

Understanding the Historical Period

Procedure:

1. On a map, locate north of Sarajevo, Bosnia and tell students: "We will be talking about evidence from archaeologists at a site named Butmir. This settlement was excavated near Sarajevo from 1893 to 1896 and then in 1967 and 1968."

2. Describe the work of archaeologists. "They carefully unearth objects from the past, including tools, skeletal remains, and pottery. They date the material using a radio-carbon technique involving the radioactive decay of carbon 14, and then they double-check the date by counting tree rings. Then, based on all the information about that site and other sites nearby, the archaeologist reaches careful conclusions about the life of the people at that time in that location."

3. "Let's look at what our stereotypes are about life back then and compare our guesses to the archaeological evidence. The objects we will be talking about were dated to be 7000 years old; that is, from about 5000 B.C." Ask students these four questions to help them describe that they think life was like at that time at this spot in Europe:

   a. "What kinds of dwellings did people live in?"

   b. "What did they eat and how did they get their food?"

   c. "Did they live in peace or fight with other people and have wars?"

   d. "What kind of art did they do?"

4. Write the name of the archaeologist — Marija Gimbutas (pronounced *Maria Gim-boo-tus*) — on the board. Tell students that she wrote twenty books about her work as an archaeologist studying Old Europe. She excavated the Butmir site with Alojz Benac in 1967–1968, and it is her book that describes the life of the people and that gives us pictures of the art found at Butmir and throughout Old Europe.

Source: *Civilization of the Goddess: The World of Old Europe* by Marija Gimbutas (San Francisco: HarperCollins, 1991, pages 56–62.) Compare these conclusions from her work with the guesses made by the class.

   a. People lived in houses made of wood with stone wall foundations. The walls of the house were coated with clay. The roof was made of wood and straw. Two-room homes contained a round bread oven and had deep storage pits for refrigeration of food. Grinding stones and spindle-whorls for spinning were also in the homes, and ash was used as a detergent to wash linen. They had stools, tables, and lamps.

b. People hunted wild bull, wild swine, red deer, and roe deer, and they caught fish such as carp and sturgeon with fishhooks made of bone and antler. In the forests they collected acorns, hazelnuts, strawberries, gooseberries, crab apples and cornelian cherries. They grew wheat and barley to make bread, and they raised cattle and pigs.

c. The archaeologists have concluded that for thousands of years there was no warfare. Here is the evidence — no lethal weapons were found, the villages had no fortifications, and the houses were built near rivers or streams. The people at Butmir lived in open villages in valleys and built ditches around their villages, not as moats but to drain off rainwater. If they had chosen steep hills for their houses, which are more difficult to live on, they would have known that the people were protecting themselves against an invader. A thousand years later than the time we're talking about, in about 4000 B.C., invaders on horseback entered this area from southern Russia, introduced the idea of war for the first time, and eventually destroyed the Old European culture. Knowledge of this civilization has been lost to us until recently.

d. The people made magnificent pottery vases. They decorated them with intricate designs and painted bands of red above a black background. They mined copper, and they traded with other people for obsidian, shells, and painted pottery.

5. Butmir was called "the cradle of the spiral art" in Europe. We will be drawing the same spiral shapes that people back then drew onto their pottery. This will help us find out more about how the people thought. When they drew spirals on their pottery, they were expressing the thoughts most important to them. They also had a written language and the spiral S was one of the symbols.

Language of Spiral Art

Procedure:

Photocopy these spiral designs or draw them on the board.

1. Give each student drawing paper and a pen, pencil, or marker. Ask students to practice drawing simple spiral shapes. "Let your hand be guided by the momentum of the spiral. Can you draw without crossing over any lines?"

    First, have them draw small spirals in both directions.

* *Outside to in.* Make a big circle and spiral farther and farther into the center.

* *Inside to out.* Start with a tiny circle and spiral farther out to about two inches.

    Help students pay attention to the sensation of drawing. Say, "Notice how it feels to draw spirals. Do you like the feeling of going in one direction more than the other, or are they both enjoyable to you?"

2. Now work with an S curve to connect two spirals. Start on the left inside one spiral, let it get bigger, and then curve across to begin another spiral going farther into its center.

Sketch to sense the general feeling.

Then work carefully to make continuous spirals of equal size.

3. Tell students: "Professor Gimbutas discovered that the decorations people drew on their pottery all had a meaning. The people drew these spirals to give a message. What do you think they were saying as they drew spirals?"

After students have guessed, add the meaning that Professor Marija Gimbutas learned, not to contradict their guesses but to amplify what they were discovering. She said that spirals describe the force of life, such as the force inside the stem of a plant or the trunk of a tree to help them grow. Energy inside the human body moves in spirals. She also said that spirals have the forward motion of growing and becoming. She wrote, "The pulse of life demands an unending stream of vital energy to keep it going." (Gimbutas, *The Language of the Goddess,* San Francisco: HarperCollins, 1991. p. 277.) This means they are saying through their spirals, "We are part of nature, and we change and grow like every other part of nature."

4. Tell students: "Now we will work with more difficult forms. Try a simple S again, but give a thickness to it, like a coil of clay. Go from left to right and then double back, tracing from right to left without crossing over the lines. Who will discover how to leave space between the lines of the curves?"

5. Continue: "How do you make an ongoing run of spirals? As you go out on the S curve, you have to double-back. The design below is one that appears frequently in the pottery. Decorations with runs of spirals were found on vases from Butmir dated 5100–4900 B.C. (Gimbutas, *The Civilization of the Goddess*, San Francisco: Harper Collins, 1991, p. 59.) Here the secret is to curve once around, twice around, and then curve back the other way. This is a metaphor for conflicts; when you are in a tight snarl, go back the other way and this gives dynamic energy to move forward."

6. Have the students examine how the spiral shape relates to two things they have learned about this culture.

   • How does this meaning of the spiral reflect the fact that they had no warfare?

   • How does it reflect the fact that women and men were equally regarded and lived in partnership? Have the class look, for example, at the dynamic interrelationship of opposites in the form of spirals.

To help get this idea across, approach it from another direction. If a person were sending a different message, he or she would use a different kind of line. Ask students: "What line could you draw to say this message "I feel like a machine. I try to do everything the same and not make a mistake.""

7. Lastly, try the complex shape which appears below. A spiral-decorated Butmir vase from the 49th–48th century had a design just like it. Tell students—one way to experience the intelligence of the people is to draw what they drew.

Source: Figure 3-7, Vase 2 in *The Civilization of the Goddess* (San Francisco: Harper Collins, 1991, p. 57).

Hint: The secret of this shape is to draw the top curve first like a wave and then add the bottom line to nest in it.

Extensions

Language arts: "Create a story about a child living in these times. Decide whether he or she will learn to make pottery, spin, catch fish, hunt, or build houses. How do they feel to live in a time when there is no violence?"

Songwriting: Write a song as if it were written by a person living at this time in Old Europe.

Movement

1. Stand in place. Roll your hands in a decreasing inward spiral shape until you are curled up, then expand as you roll your hands with an increasing outward spiral.

2. Walk a spiral shape. Holding hands, the line leader takes the line spiralling into the center, then turning to double-back out again.

Background

The term *Old Europe* applies to the civilization of 7000–3500 B.C. from the Atlantic to the Dnieper. Evidence of this culture is just reaching us because it was systematically destroyed by authorities of the cultures that supplanted it. The Indo-

European tribes from southern Russia overran these people from the fourth millennium B.C. in three waves and ended Old European culture between 4300 and 2800 B.C. They brought cattle-herding, they introduced and imposed the practice of male domination, and they brought their language, which became the basis for English. They buried important males and their weapons in round barrows, called *kurgans* in Russian, and Professor Gimbutas refers to them as the Kurgan Culture. She writes, "We are still living under the sway of that aggressive male invastion and only beginning to discover our long alienation from our authentic European heritage — gylanic, nonviolent, earth-centered culture." (Gimbutas, *The Language of the Goddess*, San Francisco: HarperCollins, 1991. p. xxi).

The Old Europe people had other symbols in common besides spirals: eggs, zigzags, streams, chevrons, rams, deers, bears, and snakes, all of which were life-giving symbols. They also invented a written language and had a common script of symbols 2000 years earlier than the Sumerians, previously thought to have been the creators of the first complex written communications. Joseph Campbell compares Professor Gimbutas' extensive study of pictoral motifs that undergird Western civilization to the discovery of the Rosetta Stone that unlocked the meaning of Egyptian hierogylphics.

Source

The 500-page *Civilization of the Goddess: The World of Old Europe*, San Francisco: HarperCollins, 1991, by Marija Gimbutas, is out of print, but you can use Interlibrary Loan or an out-of-print book search service (like www.amazon.com) to find a copy. The book shows drawings of the excavated houses and extensive illustrations of pottery. Students can create designs using other motifs in the illustrations, and learn the basic signs of Old European script on page 308.

Activity Twelve: Entering a Partnership Village in Neolithic Times

Grade level: 2nd - 5th

Overview: This is a social studies creative dramatics activity. Using a method of simultaneous role-play, build a story together where each child acts out actual activities of a village. Share historically accurate information to incorporate in the drama.

Goals: To hear information about societies based on partnership in ancient history as places where everyone is involved in enhancing and protecting life.
To experience living in partnership.
To grasp what it means that we all help each other.

Preparation: Clear a section in the room where the drama can take place. Collect props
　　　　　　　such as stones, baskets, twigs or grape vine, cloth, pottery, grinding stones.

Snapshot:

I led these activities January 2001 at New Hingham School. "We traveled back in time 7000 years ago," a second grader named Allyson wrote after the lesson. "I was a girl who fed the animals. We did a play and here's what I learned. They did not have war at those times." Max wrote about his choice in the play, "I shot a deer, then I thanked it, then I ate it."

Children learned archeological information about a particular site, Butmir, excavated by Marija Gimbutas and Alojz Benac. Then they enacted daily life in that village based on the information. They used a method named "story-building" by the students. In keeping with partnership processes, they each chose their role. Baskets, grinding stones, pottery decorated with spirals, colorful cloths, rocks, and sticks were all supplied as props. The students knew that they were portraying not fantasy but history. One explained, "We copied a story from a long time ago." The group didn't want the activity to end and some called out, "Let's play this at recess."

At the end of the activity, each student told how they contributed to their village: "I went to find the calf that escaped from the fence," "I picked berries and made jam," "I built the house." After each person spoke, the students responded, "Thank you for helping our village." Their teacher, Ingrid Gliniak, commented, "This is a lesson that they will remember all their lives."

Procedure:

1. Ask for predictions about what life was like in Old Europe 7000 years ago. This section uses information detailed in the previous activity "What the Spirals Say." Ask students to make guesses about a specific area that is near Sarajevo in the former Yugoslavia. Archeologists Marija Gimbutas and Alojz Benac excavated that site which is called Butmir. What do you think that people ate? What kind of dwelling did they live in? What kind of art did they do?

Sample predictions: They lived in caves. They hunted bison. They made fires and they made wheels.

2. Now reveal this information. List it on a chart called, "7000 years ago."

> Houses: They had wood houses built on top of stone walls.
> There were two rooms. One had a round bread oven.
> The walls were of wood coated with clay. Roof of wood and straw.
> Deep storage pits to keep food cold.

Grinding stones. Spindles for spinning yarn.
Stools, tables, and lamps.

Activities: Made pottery vases..
Painted complicated spirals on their pottery.
Washed linen clothes with ash from the fire.
Hunted wild bull, wild swine, and deer.
Carved fish hooks from bone and antler.
Fished for carp and sturgeon.
Collected acorns, hazelnuts in the forest.
Picked strawberries, gooseberries, crabapples, cherries.
Raised cattle and pigs.
Made bread from the wheat and barley they grew.
Mined copper.
Traded with visitors for their pottery and shells.

If possible also show examples of script from this period. See Marija Gimbutas, *The Language of the Goddess* (San Francisco: HarperCollins, 1991).

3. Say, "We're going to play act that we're in this time. What are different things you could do in the village? Look at the sample activities on the list — carving fish hooks and fishing, building a house, making pottery, grinding grain." Students think of one activity which particularly interests them. Clarify that in the village people do activities that gave life and protected life. Tell them at the end they will each say out loud how they helped their village.

4. Give students a few minutes to talk to each other and plan in reference to what others want to be. Now, ask each person to state out loud their choice. Plan a way to share props. Designate sections of the room for a house or houses, fenced-in area for domesticated animals, forest.

5. Supervise the role play. Students may want to portray hunters. How can this take place in a way that is safe, productive, and instructive? Hunting can become a volatile part of the role-play unless there is clear guidance, yet it is a part that students like to pick. When depicting hunting:

• Talk about the mystery of the hunt. The hunters in a sense remained as partners with the animals. They didn't kill the young ones, and they didn't get carried away with hunting. They deeply respected the animals and stayed in tune with them. They thanked them for their gift of life. I said to the students, "When the hunters come back with food for the village, they are giving food that will make it possible for the people to live. But if they come back and they are so shocked from killing that they start to hurt people, then a terrible thing will happen to the village. When matters even more than the food they bring back to feed the people, is that they return still able to care for people. The hunters can help the village or hurt the village depending on how they connect with the animals who give their lives." The second graders put this in their own words, "Don't kill too many animals and don't go crazy over hunting."

- Set up a group of 1-4 elders (girls and boys) to whom the hunters report to before they leave on the hunt. Ask the elders to remind them to thank the animals and specify how many animals they are allowed to kill.

- When the hunters encounter animals, ask them to move in slow motion. They agree to only kill an older animal who is ready to give its life as a gift to the village. You can use a a blanket to represent that animal.

- Ask hunters to pause and thank the animal.

- When the hunters bring the animal back, have them again check-in with the elders. At this point, the elders ask them, what will you do now to help the village? This helps them make a transition. Ask the hunters, do you want to skin the animals (pantomime)? Do you want to fish? Do you want to make pottery?

In the example of the second grade class at New Hingham, one boy who had been building a house was in tears when the hunters returned and it appeared they had killed twenty animals. The girl who had chosen to be an elder talked with them afterward about the hunt. They had conflicting stories about how many they had killed, but one had shot his pantomime bow so many times that it appeared he'd killed twenty. It was necessary to process this event for many minutes until all feelings and concerns were heard. It was instructive to see how deeply the children were affected by this.

5. Sometimes students want to be animals. As students choose what role they want, if some are intent upon being animals, have them be domesticated animals inside a fence rather than the animals who are hunted. They can can add adventure to this role by escaping and needing to be found again.

6. Narration: Use a device such as putting on a cape or waving a cloth to signal that you are entering the time of the story. Narrate the action at first to keep track of what is occurring. Be ready to help make a transition when the hunters return. Assist each actor to stay integrated into the story.

Students particularly enjoy working with props. Provide lots of stones the size of a hand or smaller. Some like to create outlines of homes with these. Also, have pottery available that they can pretend to paint, as well as baskets. Offer paper and pastels for drawing.

7. Closure: End by sitting in a circle. Ask each person to tell what they did. Since the role play is simultaneous, they won't have been able to see all that occurred.Now they can hear about it. After each person speaks, the others reply, "Thank you for helping our village." This reinforces that each member of the village has their own way to care for the welfare of the whole.

Activity Thirteen: Timelines and Human Partnership

Grade level: 2nd - 5th

Overview: Math and social studies are integrated with the social curriculum. The lessons convey (a) that warfare is not inevitable, that there have been times without constant warfare, (b) that people can change, and (c) that mistakes in social behavior can be altered with group effort for the common good.

Goals: To learn how to use a time-line.
    To conceptualize how long people lived without constant warfare.

Equipment: Yarn timeline 22.8 inches long.
    Book on an important historical event with yarn timeline to match.
    Yarn timeline 69 inches long as described in Activity Ten.
    Cardboard representation of figure 4.1 in *Tomorrow's Children* p. 96.
    Book with a picture of the Paleolithic drawings in Lascaux, France.

Procedure:

1. Work with four different timelines. In each case, clarify what scale is used. First make a timeline of hands. Each hand equals one year. Several students stand shoulder to shoulder, each placing their hands alongside each other's.

    Example: To show eight years old, four people stretch their hands next to each other, knuckle to knuckle. Students tell changes that they experienced. Let several students have a chance to say one change they have experienced: Learning to ride a bike, moving to a new place, a new sibling born. Ask, "How old were you when that happened?" Next, ask them to come up to the hands, count the years, and find the spot on the timeline (the hand) that represents the year that it happened.

2. Now show a yarn timeline with reference to something familiar. To make a timeline of the school year, prepare in advance a yarn time-lines using 1/16 of an inch to represent a day. Create a length of yarn 22.8 inches long to represent a year. Ask students to estimate where today is along the timeline. Again, clarify what scale is used.

3. Now use a timeline of the recent past. Select a book about an historic event that represents an important social change relating to social justice such as overcoming racism or sexism. Make a yarn timeline to show when it happened.

   Example: *Teammates* by Peter Golenboch (Harcourt Brace Jovanovich, 1990) depicts a moment from 1947 when Jackie Robinson and PeeWee Reese played baseball with the Brooklyn Dodgers. When Robinson stood on the field amid racist taunts in a Cincinnati stadium, Reese (who was from nearby Louisville, Kentucky) walked over to him and put his hand on his shoulder to say, "This is my friend and teammate." To create a yarn timeline for this event, use the scale of 1 inch equals one year. Measure one inch for each year since 1947.

4. Next, take out the yarn timeline of 69 inches long. Lead the activity described in Activity Ten.

5. What was it like to live in a time when people mainly used stones and sticks for carving, hunting, digging, and not for hurting other humans? Show pictures of the cave paintings in Lascaux, France which are from 24,000 - 17,000 years ago according to different estimates. Find the spot for 20,000 years ago on the yarn timeline by measuring 6 inches from the present.

   Sources for pictures: (a) *Talking Walls* by Margy Burns Knight, illustrated by Anne Sibley O'Brien (Tilbury House, Gloucester ME, 1992) (b) *Sanctuaries of the Goddess* by Peg Streep, Little, Brown and Company, 1994. Help them imagine being in the cave by providing details: One central chamber has a nineteen foot tall ceiling. In the flicker of the candles you would see black and red animals painted on the white walls. Some were eighteen feet long. Then you would walk along a winding corridor that would get narrow then wider for twenty feet with stags, bulls, and horses painted along it.

6. Archeologists can arrive at different interpretations as they put together clues. Show the example of figures carved on a piece of bone from 200,000 BCE either by photocopying page 96 in *Tomorrow's Children* with our permission, or by sketching an enlarged version of the same picture on cardboard. Ask, "What do you see?" After they have shared their interpretations, point to the plant shapes which were thought to be "wrong-way arrows," and talk about the mistaken supposition that these were arrows.

7. Option: Now do the activity above that studies how people lived in Old Europe 7000 years ago. Engage students quickly in demonstrating 100 by stretching out all ten fingers ten times. Explain that 7000 would mean doing that 70 times. Find the spot for 7000 years ago by measuring 2.1 inches from the present.

<u>Activity Fourteen:</u> The Paleolithic Period of Human Life

Grade level: 5th - 10th grade.

Overview: Creative dramatics helps older students devise skits about the period 400,000 to 10,000 years ago, the culture of Homo erectus to Homo sapiens. Drawing and writing also help students uncover the interactions of partnership which were the foundation of our evolution.

Goals: To realize that caring and creativity are key themes of evolution, as described on page 81 of *Tomorrow's Children*.
To bond imaginatively with the people in the paleolithic period.

Procedure:

Day One — Creative Dramatics
Space requirements: Arrange the room so that each group has space for movement.

1. Preparation for pantomime:

"Slowly move your hand and watch as it moves, but watch as if you are a visitor from another planet who will be reporting on how special and unique is the wonder of the human hand. Look at flexibility, and also vulnerability." Discuss observations. Also, explain that what made humans strong was not size or muscle-power but our ability to work in partnership toward group goals; we used our hands to interact with others in nurturing ways. As a warm-up, ask the whole group to experiment with pantomime. Establish the feeling of privately creating a scene — ask them to enter their own space bubble. Each student simultaneously pantomimes the crafting of a large bowl out of clay; tell them, "imagine that you can feel the clay as you are working."

2. Pantomime of Paleolithic Developments: Write these three words on the board: change, create, care. "I'll be asking you to devise a silent skit where you will use your hands in pantomime. You will be exploring how groups of humans made discoveries that were important for human life. You will show how you changed something together, what you created, and how you cared for each other while you were doing it."

3. Divide students into small groups of 3-4. Give each group one of these topics. Clarify that as they develop their skit, students can talk together while they are planning, but they will need to show the skit silently. The audience will guess what they are demonstrating.

Topics for Pantomime Scenarios:

a. You discover lightning has caught grass on fire. You find a way of keeping this fire burning in a special location so that you can have fire whenever you wish. You use the fire for heating food and for warmth. You take turns watching the fire so that it doesn't go out.

b. You find stones that you can carve in the outcroppings of the hills. You fashion stone fish hooks of flint and use them to catch fish to eat.

c. You carve sewing needles and use the needles to make warm clothes with animal skins and blankets for each other and for a baby. When someone is shivering and ill, you cover them up and provide them with soothing broth to drink.

d. You attach skins to sticks and bones to create houses. Your shelters have a place for keeping food cool, a place for cooking, and a place for sleeping. Your house is very lightweight. When you need to move to a new location, you take down the walls and carry it to a new location.

e. You discover clay by a riverbank. You make pots from the clay, and find a way to bake the clay with fire to make it hard. You carve decorations in them with shapes that have meaning for you. You have a celebration where everyone passes around the bowls you made.

f. You collect plants that you want to eat but they are too hard to chew. You cut them, discover a way of grinding them with stone to make them easier to eat, and cook them.

e. You collect plants and examine them to learn what are their healing properties. You discover plants that help stop bleeding and will heal wounds. While you are out walking, leg injuries happen. You use the plants to heal the injuries.

f. You track bison together. You fan out and signal each other as you hunt in a group, and then thank the animal before you eat it.

g. You live by a rushing river that you can't swim across. You select a tree that can be carved into a boat. Before you cut it down, you put your hands on the tree to tell it what you are about to do and thank it. Together you carve it into a boat. You get inside the boat and travel together.

h. You find ways of drumming by striking logs. You experiment with different sounds until you find your favorites. Together keep the beat with everyone in your group and create a dance.

i. Dogs circle around your hunting camp each night. You leave food for them, and as they come closer, you pat them, and teach them they can trust you. As your group prepares to leave and move to a new location, you persuade the dogs to come with you.

4. Use these cooperative learning structures to facilitate the activity.

(a) Place students in heterogeneous groups based on two factors: Partnership skills, and familiarity with pantomime, creative dramatics, and using imagination.

(b) Before beginning the work on the pantomime, ask each topic group to restate the directions and the topic to make sure that everyone understands the assignment.

(c) Shared roles: Ask students to divide up these roles.

• Time keeper — You help us get the job done keeping in mind
    how much time we have.
  • Introducer — You say "curtain up" when the role play is about to begin
      and "curtain down" to tell us we are ending.
  • Discussion leader — You make sure each person gets a chance
        to contribute their ideas.
  • Sequence Maker — You help us keep in mind the beginning, middle,
        and end of the story.

If a group has three members, either one person will take two roles or the whole group will be mindful of the function of the fourth role.

(d) Cooperation agreement: We are going to use a method where each person is able to pick the role they want to take in the scene. Each person gets their first choice — if two people want to do the same thing, they both do it. For example, in the group who is pretending that someone has a hurt leg, if everybody wants this role, they all pretend they have a leg injury rather than debating and arguing. Organically, if this isn't working, they will shift and adjust. Allowing for one's own choice reinforces the principles of partnership.

(e) Individual accountability: Help each person prepare to make a contribution.

Method One: Ask everyone in the room for silence. Have each person stand so that once again they are in their own space bubble. "Now, before you put your ideas together as a group, place yourself in the scene on your own. Without looking at anyone else, imagine yourself doing something that is part of that scene. Pantomime what you imagine it would be like to do this, just as before you pantomimed what it would be like to make a bowl out of clay." Work with simultaneous role play for just a minute or two.

Method Two: Each person draws the scene they've been assigned first by themselves to help them imaginatively enter the situation.

(f) Time keeping: Write on the board two time markers —

Ending time for the discussion. (An end point helps the planning not get bogged down.)

Ending time for all the preparation.

(g) Group discussion: Each person take turns telling what they want to do in the scene. Discuss how to put the ideas together in combination. The discussion leader assists.

(h) Blocking out the action: Remind the group to think about the sequence as they prepare. The person in charge of sequence is asked to remind them to spell out where everyone will be at the beginning of the scene. Spell out what you want to have happen in the middle. Spell out how it will end. Keep it simple.

(i) Practice the scene. Use the help of the introducer to provide the structure of "curtain up" and "curtain down."

5. Presentation of scenarios: Each group takes a turn showing their scene. Encourage the student taking the role of introducer to say, "curtain up," and encourage the sequence maker to help keep the sequence on track. The actors pick an audience member to answer one of these questions:

  a. What did we do together?
  b. How did we show we cared about each other?

Day Two — Drawing

1. Explain that we have few drawings on rock or bone to tell us what human life was like in this time. On the board, copy figure 4.1 on page 96 of *Tomorrow's Children* by Riane Eisler. Ask students to guess how old the drawing is before telling them it is 22,000 years old. Using the explanation on page 95, discuss the "wrong way arrows." Explain that many of the pictures in books that illustrate the Paleolithic period of life show a caveman.

They depict him with a club that he uses as a weapon against other people, and women are either not shown or are doing something less important than the men. These pictures are as mistaken as the misinterpretation of drawings of plants as 'wrong-way arrows.' "Today we are going to make new pictures of what we can now imagine early life was like."

2. Invite the class to make drawings to show what they imagine. Add this agreement: "So that we don't make assumptions like the 'wrong-way arrows,' I'm going to add this invitation. Please show in your picture an equal number of women and men and have all of them doing something important to care for their whole community." The

time period we are looking at — 230,000 to 10,000 years ago — is very vast and covers lots of developments.

To build your drawing, start off by picturing a place. What is the land like? What is their source of water? What is the weather like there? Where do people live — caves, stick houses, houses from mammoth bones? Once you can imagine the place, now show the people there, each doing something to help their group.

Notice that developments happened because many human beings together held a question they were trying to answer — like, how do we make fire? It wasn't one inventor alone, but a cooperative inquiry. Many many people all over the planet made similar discoveries.

3. Gather in a circle with the drawings. Provide time for each person to present their drawing and answer any questions about it.

Day Three — Writing

1. Share this historical information. As you read each item, ask the class to think of a skit or a drawing from the previous days work that demonstrated it.

Here are our best current guesses about this part of the human journey.

Community:
   • People lived in small groups and helped everyone in their group.

Tools:
   • Sticks and stones were used primarily for group goals such as to dig up roots and to soften foods to make it easier to eat, not to hurt or threaten other people.
   • Vegetables were fashioned into slings and baskets to carry food.
   • People discovered how to make fire and keep the fire going.
   • People discovered how to fashion and make use of a wheel.

In direct contradiction to the usual assumptions, it is postulated that women invented fire and the wheel because of the role of women as the first potters.

Relationship to the whole of life:

   • People paid close attention to the predictable changes in the moon.
   • People developed a close bond to animals and thanked the animals who they killed and ate.
   • Children were usually closely cared for and affectionately treated with a lot of physical contact and comfort.
   • People felt themselves directly part of nature, and not separate.

- People engaged in intense observation of plants and learned how they grew and how humans could relate to them. They learned which were nourishing, and which had various healing properties, and they passed on this knowledge from generation to generation.

2. Invite students to make other guesses.

3. Imagine what it would be like to be alive at that time. What skills would you most want to explore? What would feel mysterious to you? Imagine yourself making a discovery. What is it? Share your thoughts in writing.

Option: read this quote to help them prepare.

> "Can you imagine you remember? We feel pretty vulnerable; we
> haven't the speed of the other creatures, or their claws or fangs or natur-
> al armor. But we have our remarkable hands, opposable thumbs to help
> shape tools.... And we have in our throats and the frontal lobes (of our
> brains) the capacity for speech. Grunts and shouts turn into language as
> we collaborate in strategies and rituals. Those days and nights on the
> verge of the forests, as we weave baskets and stories around our fires,
> represent the biggest (longest) hunk of our human experience."
>
> by Joanna Macy, from *Thinking Like A Mountain*
> (New Society Publishers, p. 62)

Teaching Science and
Social Studies Partnership Content
With Movement and Creative Dramatics

<u>Lesson Fifteen:</u> Animals in Partnership

Grade level: PreK - 2nd

Goal: To explore animal partnership experientially.

Requirements: Room to move.

Equipment: Sound signals for the teacher to use like a bell or drum.

Procedure:

1. Talk about what it means to be partners. What can animal partners do together?

   Examples: They could bring each other food, they could find a place to sleep, they could show each other a path, they could build a house together.

2. Establish ground rules together so that all children playing the part of animals are partners with each other during the activity. This means none will engage in fighting each other during this game, or in making threatening noises or movements. Set up two signals: One for zero noise — like a drum, a bell, or blinking the lights — which will ask for immediate quiet, and one which means the story is ending, and says, in effect, "curtain down."

3. Discuss: Have you ever seen animals helping each other?

   Set up small groups of three or four students. Give each group one of these real-life situations to depict. Help them visualize it and understand what it means. Each group works with one of these sentences and creates a pantomime:

   We are geese supporting a wounded one.
   We are bats sharing food with the old ones.
   We are whales travelling together in a pod.
   We are cats rescuing drowning kittens.
   We are elephants in a circle protecting our young.
   We are marmosets mashing food for the babies.
   We are wolves rescuing a cub trapped in rocks.
   We are elephants freeing a calf stuck in the mud.

   These specific partnership actions are described on pages 73 - 74 in *Tomorrow's Children*.

Add information about animals that you have studied — such as the way beavers engage together to build a lodge — and engage children in enacting what they have learned about animal behavior.

4. Now ask students to pick their own scenario of animal partnership. Again work in groups of three or four children. This time each child picks the animal they want to be and the situation they are in like, "I'm going to be a baby lamb who can't walk," or "I'm a hungry dog who is lost." They make individual choices and don't have to pick the same animal. In other words, the whole group doesn't have to pick only wolves or only beavers. The stipulation is they can't tell someone else what to be or do. Students can, however, make invitations like, "What if I'm the father wolf and somebody is a baby?" But you can't pressure anyone else if they don't want to follow up on your invitation. After planning is complete, call the group back to attention with the zero noise signal.

5. Provides a sample scene that can apply to many types of animals: "Start off sleeping. Then as you wake up, you feel very hungry and you're going to look for food." Or, "On the next day there was a strong storm and one of the animals got lost." Each group will simultaneously act out their own story, not as performers for an audience, but for the joy of being inside the game.

6. Provide narration for transition: "And so the sun was going down and the animals who sleep at night started back to their homes." With the sound maker, establish a clear sound that means the story is over and its time for quiet. Now, groups circle up and get ready for the next "chapter" of their story. As the procedure gets more familiar, each group can do more and more of their own planning for the story scenario.

7. Children who have chronic upset or problems working in groups will need guidance and support. For example, despite the ground rule, a child might begin growling. Speak to the child within the story framework and provide guidance: "I hear the cat growling. I'm going to go over and find out what that cat is feeling. Cat, are you afraid of something? Are you giving someone a signal with your growl? Tell me more. That growl might scare the other animals."

8. Closure: When it's time to end, ask all animals to sit together and create some kind of motion, or handshake or hug to thank each other for being partners. If there is time, come together in a circle as a whole class and give a chance to tell ways that they worked as partners.

Option: This game can be used in conjunction with the song, "My Roots Go Down." See Chapter Nine, "Music to Build Partnership," to learn this song.

Extension: The Storybuilding Game

At New Hingham Regional School in western Massachusetts the first grade did an even more complex version of the animal partners activity, and it proved to be their favorite activity. The whole class engaged in one story.

Step One: Individual Planning. They took three minutes to choose the part they wanted. They could talk to anyone, mill around, and plan the part they wanted.

Step Two: Unification. The students took turns telling the whole class who they chose to be. They chose any character: whale, fairy, mermaid, jaguar, wolf, dragon, waffle, grape. They then found a location in the room which would be their home. As groups clustered together, they planned out details of the story — "let's have you get lost and we'll go look for you," "let's pretend we're thirsty and have to find water," or "how about if I'm the daughter and you're the mother."

Step Three: Adult Narration Guides Simultaneous Acting. They go to a spot in the room — ocean, woods, whatever they need for their character — and pretend to go to sleep. The drama is structured around — "On the first day … this and this and this happened … and then everyone went to sleep. And on the second day … this and this … happened and then everyone went to sleep." Students take turns providing ideas for what they want to occur. Write these down and introduce them into the narration.

Step Four: Closing. Children need a transition to help them leave their story characters. They can take turns quickly going across the room and show one last movement as their character. Then they get into line at the door. Or, stand in a circle and have each person wave goodbye as their character. If you have no time to do this kind of closing, simply ask students to do a quick procedure for turning themselves back to themselves; they enjoy pulling on their own ear lobes and saying their name, such as, "I'm back to being Colleen."

Lesson Sixteen: Dominator and Partnership Role Plays

Grade level: 4th - 12th

Goals: To anchor understanding of partnership and domination through creative dramatics.

Requirements: Prior teaching of these concepts and of prehistory.

Procedure:

Select a scene for improvisation. Present it to the class, and ask for volunteers to enact it. Use the framework of "curtain up" and "curtain down" to provide a boundary. Allow any character to say "time out" if they feel stuck and want to ask someone in the audience to provide a line for them to say.

Here are possibilities for situations, time periods, and characters.

People from 7000 years ago:

- Depict people living in a Neolithic society structured for partnership. Show that when villagers have a visitor from another village, they expect to trade goods. Pantomime or use baskets, jewelry, or seeds for trade and barter.

- Add a character from a warring nomadic band that is engaged in invading villages. This person was a prisoner, but has escaped. They try to warn the villagers about the dangers of invaders, but they aren't believed because the villagers can't imagine humans killing and hurting others.

Contemporary people on a talk show:

- Two people who work for the United Nations are interviewed on a talk show. Others ask them questions about how they got interested in working for partnership. They invent stories of events in their lives that made them want to work to establish a world that works for everyone.

- Students think of people who've lived in the last hundred years or who are still alive today who examplify partnership or examplify a dominator approach. Set up a TV interview with one person from each approach. Try this same scene more than once, making sure that both male and female characters of each type are used.

People of the future who live in a world without widespread warfare: Year 2100:

- Two of your great-great-great-grandchildren are speaking in the future about the choices made in the last century whether to go towards partnership or domination and are looking back on what occurred.

- Year 3000: You are taking a school class on a tour of a museum of nuclear weapons which are now extinct. You tell them about how things used to be.

Activity Seventeen: A Pantomime of How the Ear Hears

Grade Level: 3rd - 12th

Overview: In this lesson, students act out the way that the human ear operates using movement and creative dramatics.

Goals: To underscore the partnership interactions within our bodies.
  To compliment science units on hearing.
  To use cooperative movement to build partnership skills.

Preparation: Diagram on the board or photocopy pictures of how the ear works.

Procedure:

1. Divide the class into five groups and explain that each group will act out one portion of the sequence of hearing. For older students, provide a sheet of paper with the assignments for all five groups. Since the groups don't have to be of equal size, it's most effective to allow students to choose which part of the process of hearing they will represent.

> Review the process of hearing:
> The outer ear channels the sound.
> Sound waves travel down the ear canal.
> The eardrum vibrates.
> The three bones in the inner ear vibrate.
> Waves travel through the fluid in the spiral-shaped cochlea.
> These vibrations make the tiny hairs in the cochlea move.
> The hairs create electrical messages.
> These messages pass along the auditory nerve to the brain.
> The brain interprets what the source of the sound is.
> Unless the body chooses no response, a verbal or physical response
> is made to the sound.

2. In this activity, we will imagine the listener is asleep. We will represent, one at a time, three sounds that the person is hearing. Act out the sequence three times, each time reacting differently depending upon the loudness and intensity of the sound.

Give groups a description of their role.

GROUP ONE: Someone from your group will be the sound itself, and will initiate each of the three sounds; make the sound out loud or use an instrument or other sound maker. Together the group shows the sound collected in the outer ear, then funneled to the eardrum. Show how the sound travels down the canal and makes the eardrum vibrate.

GROUP TWO: You will be affected by the movement of the eardrum. You will show the sound moving in turn each of the three bones in the inner ear — the malleus, the incus, and then the stapes. These bones in reality are about the size of the pencil lead at the point of a sharp pencil.

GROUP THREE: You will be the cochlea, the spiral shaped tube filled with fluid, which has little tiny hairs that vibrate. The sound vibrations travel through the fluid and stimulate these hairs. The louder the sound, the more hairs react.

GROUP FOUR: You will show the electrical messages that are created by the movement of the hairs and how these messages travel along the auditory nerve to the hearing center of the brain. The auditory association center identifies what sound it is from the memories of the sound. It is okay to use words to show this identification.

GROUP FIVE: You will show the next step of processing the information as other centers of the brain get involved. The person whose brain you are representing speaks words in reaction to the information. First, identify out loud what the sound is. Then show what the person says in response to each sound. What are they thinking or feeling once they know what it is?

3. Explain what the three sounds will be:
   a) A cat on your pillow purring right by your ear.
   b) A radio alarm clock.
   c) The sharp sound of a tea kettle boiling in the kitchen which
      someone else in your family has put on to make breakfast.

Together the five groups are helping to tell a story of a person asleep who hears first their cat, then their alarm, and then the kettle. The sound is made, the groups show how it travels, and then the fifth group adds the verbal reaction to the sound.

4. Plan the space of the room. Designate where the sound comes in and have group one stand there. Place group two next to them, then group three, and so on, until all are positioned in a logical order.

5. Each group meets by itself for about ten minutes to plan their own pantomime. This is when the pictures of the ear are important to see the shape of the cochlea, and the shape of the three bones in the inner ear, which are the smallest bones in the human body.

Give them guidance in their planning. Lead them through these steps:

   a. Talk about all the different things your group needs to convey.

   b. Decide how many people will need to do each part.

   c. Divide up the tasks so that it is clear who is doing what.

   d. Try them out.

   e. Add any sounds to accompany your movement.

6. Use a signal to get everyone's attention. Before trying the whole story, do a practice run to see the movements each group has planned. Supervise as one group passes to the next, the eardrum from group one signalling the start of group two's movements, and so forth. When the sequence is coordinated, begin the story. Narrate the situation: A sleeping person is awakened by a sound. Help them portray the process of hearing purring, then the radio alarm, and finally the kettle.

7. Part of the enjoyment is seeing that every single person in the pantomime is important in the sequence. Process the experience of working together. If you like, solve any problem areas and try the story again.

General Guidelines for Creating a Partnership Activity

Identify partnership content that you want to convey and partnership skills that you want to foster.

- Look at times in the life of the school where partnership could be increased.
  Example: Activity Six: Looking at Recess Through the Dominator/ Partnership Lenses
  Goal: To increase partnership behavior at recess.

- Find sections in *Tomorrow's Children* that are meaningful for you and for your students.
  Example: Activity Fourteen: The Paleolithic Period of Human Life (5th - 12th)
  Goal: To help students learn about the thousands of years humans worked in
      partnership with each other to create the foundation for our species.

- Use expressive arts activities to give students the opportunity to experience partnership.
  Example: Activity One: Drawing Our Nurturesphere (1st-12th)
  Goal: To help students think about who they are in partnership with in their own life.

- Activity Sixteen: Dominator and Partnership Role Plays (4th - 12th)
  Goal: To engage students in partnership dramatic play.

- Develop structures which can provide education about partnership.
  Example: Activity Nine: School Celebration: A Weekly Partnership Assembly (K-8th)
  Goal: To build school community and value each person.

- Look for ways to take subject matter and see it from a partnership perspective.
  Example: Activity Seventeen: A Pantomime of How the Ear Hears
  Goal: To perceive how hearing is coordinated in the body.

- Structure in methods of partnership process.
  Questions to ask:
  Does the lesson plan ensure that all learners will be regarded and included?
  Is cooperation built into the design?
  Will students have a chance to make their own discoveries? Do students have the opportunity to add their own thoughts and creativity?

In summary, these are the underpinnings of partnership content. We discover knowledge directly and personally. We experience learning as an ever-expanding journey. We connect with our vast potential for growth.

CHAPTER 7

Elements of Partnership Curriculum Planning

Based on the Curriculum Loom and Learning Tapestry

by Dierdre Bucciarelli

What is the content of a Partnership Education curriculum? In *Tomorrow's Children*, Riane Eisler uses the symbolism of a tapestry to depict the content of a partnership-oriented education. Of course, actual tapestries have both vertical and horizontal threads, and so does a partnership curriculum tapestry. The vertical curriculum threads help to tell a story of what it means to be human and how our universe, our species, and other species evolved. The horizontal threads connect to student and teacher interests and provide the tools to engage in disciplinary thinking and caring actions.

Now, as both vertical and horizontal threads of a real tapestry are woven on a loom, so too are the threads of our partnership curriculum. A partnership curriculum makes use of the loom or theoretical frame of the Partnership-Dominator Continuum. This Continuum is a key analytic tool of Partnership Education. It helps students reveal underlying partnership-dominator patterns in belief systems and social structures. Partnership patterns, as we've learned, refer to ways of seeing and acting in the world that embrace a democratic, egalitarian, growth-oriented, and caring system of beliefs, values, and institutional structures. A dominator perspective is at the opposite end of the continuum from a partnership viewpoint. It rests on beliefs and structures that are grounded in fear, violence, inequitable or hierarchical relations, control and domination.

The metaphor of the loom and curriculum tapestry are very appealing and vivid. But, you are no doubt wondering how they can be employed in partnership curriculum planning. Although there are no formulas to follow in developing partnership curriculum, in this chapter I have provided a framework for one systematic way to use the loom and curriculum tapestry that you may find helpful.

First, I have outlined essential Elements for Partnership Curriculum Planning. Included in the loom and tapestry are the partnership loom and curriculum tapestry. Next, I have shown how to use the loom and tapestry to prepare a preliminary outline for a curriculum for kindergartners through third graders that I have entitled "Foods and Plants: A Story." This outline can be considered a prelude or preliminary step to the development of curricular units. In Chapter 8, the preliminary outline is put to use to develop a full-scale curriculum with detailed lesson plans, activities, readings, and resources.

Elements of Partnership Curriculum Planning Based on The Partnership Curriculum Loom and Learning Tapestry

- Weave the vertical and horizontal threads of your Learning Tapestry on the Partnership Curriculum Framework or Loom

- Utilize the vertical threads of the Learning Tapestry to develop a partnership story that will be meaningful and motivating to students

- Weave the horizontal threads of the Learning Tapestry into the vertical threads

- Develop life-long learning goals

- Select compatible learning activities

- Undertake evaluation in harmony with a partnership educational philosophy

Riane Eisler's description of the Partnership Curriculum Loom and Learning Tapestry can be found on pp. 45-56 in *Tomorrow's Children: A Blueprint for Partnership Education in the 21st Century*. All quotations below are taken from this book.

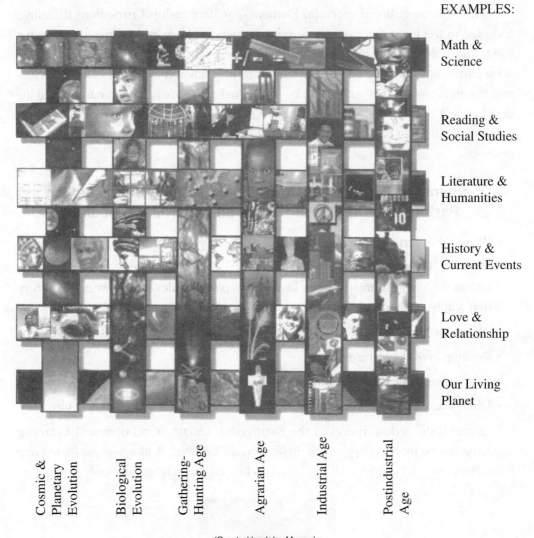

Math &
Science

Reading &
Social Studies

Literature &
Humanities

History &
Current Events

Love &
Relationship

Our Living
Planet

Cosmic &
Planetary
Evolution

Biological
Evolution

Gathering-
Hunting Age

Agrarian Age

Industrial Age

Postindustrial
Age

(Created by John Mason)

The Curriculum Loom

The whole curriculum (i.e., the vertical and horizontal threads) rests on the loom or framework of the **Partnership-Dominator Continuum**, the worldview elucidated by **cultural transformation theory** "which identifies the partnership and dominator models as two underlying possibilities for social organization" (p. 45). Design your curriculum so that it helps students learn to use the **Partnership-Dominator Analytic Lens** to reveal underlying partnership-dominator patterns in belief systems and social structures. Also plan your curriculum to emphasize "our human possibilities rather than our limitations, showing that it is possible...to structure relations in ways that help us actualize, rather than inhibit, our great human potentials for creativity and caring" (p. 45).

EXAMPLES:

Ethics

Computer Literacy

Physical Education

Current Events

Social Sciences

Art and Music

History

Life Sciences

Math

Reading and Writing

Cosmic and Planetary Evolution

Biological Evolution

Cultural Evolution

Prehistory Gathering/ Hunting

Agrarian Revolution

History Industrial Revolution

Nuclear, Electronic, and Biochemical Revolution

The partnership of Dominator Future

(Created by John Mason)

Content of a Partnership Curriculum

Vertical Threads of the Curriculum Tapestry

A partnership curriculum utilizes a **narrative approach**. This means that the curriculum *tells a story*. It tells a story of what it means to be human and how our universe, our species, and other species evolved. The curriculum you plan will tell parts of this story as you weave this story together with the horizontal elements while situating the curriculum in the curriculum loom (noted above). The vertical threads give your curriculum an historical and a sociological perspective.

Horizontal Threads of the Curriculum Tapestry

Student interests, purposes, learning styles, and multiple intelligences are integrated into the curriculum. This allows the curriculum to be personally motivating, fulfilling, and meaningful for each student. When appropriate, students can co-design curriculum with teachers; students and teachers can also engage in joint brainstorming sessions to help elicit the topics or themes that interest them.

Teacher interests, too, are taken into account in the planning of curriculum. Teachers will then, more likely, be enthusiastic, even passionate, about what they are teaching; and they will be excited about working as partners with their students. A teacher (as Paulo Freire expresses it) is an "educator-educatee" and a student is an "educatee-educator." In the language of Partnership Education, they are educational partners engaging in continual dialogue to foster the student's growth.

The curriculum draws on the traditional disciplines but it does so by incorporating **multicultural & gender-balanced perspectives**.

Emotional, parenting, scientific, environmental, and spiritual competencies are integrated throughout the curriculum. Included in these competencies are the experiential teaching and learning of caring and caregiving, known in Partnership Education as **"caring for life."**

Life-Long Learning Goals

Curriculum preparation is guided by the **life-long learning goals** of Partnership Education. Life-long learning goals are different from the "behavioral objectives" that many teachers are familiar with. When using narrowly-focused behavioral objectives, teachers list specific and discrete skills that every student should achieve for each lesson. Life-long learning goals, on the other hand, are broader, more complex goals that allow room for student initiative, interest, and creativity as well as for students' varying capacities and developmental needs. They also allow room for students to learn specific skills as the need arises in the context of more engaging work. Life-long learning goals for each curricular lesson or unit are always oriented to the overarching purpose of Partnership Education, which is to help students acquire the tools that will enable them to move towards a more partnership-oriented world. Curricular goals are designed to help students develop a positive understanding of what it means to be human, to critically analyze more negative conceptions of "human nature," and to learn to put their new understanding into practice.

For example, in a curricular unit on the environment, life-long learning goals might be to help students understand the importance of living in harmony with nature; to understand that human beings have done so successfully and do not need to dominate and control nature; and to learn how to actually live in an environmentally sustainable way, i.e., to undertake activities that demonstrate caring for the environment.

Partnership Learning Activities and Experiences

Learning activities and experiences that are used with the curriculum need to be compatible with a partnership approach to education as well as the life-long learning goals of the curriculum. It is possible to plan various activities, some of which may be cooperative ventures and others may be occasions for independent study. Many activities can be planned in conjunction with students. Many experiences will simply arise in the course of exploring the curricular content, taking one in a direction that was not at first anticipated, but that the students find stimulating and meaningful. It is fine (and even encouraged) to follow the students' lead since there are multiple ways to achieve partnership goals. Truly caring for students means that we come to know our students and their communities well in order to help students undertake activities that fulfill their quest for meaning and to help them make connections with their prior knowledge and future experience.

Partnership Evaluation

If we are true to Partnership Education, we will not expect all children to learn the same things as a result of our educational program. We realize that different children will learn many different things, all of which can be congruent with the life-long learning goals and a partnership world view. This means that we will work with individual students to see what they, in particular, have accomplished instead of focusing our sights on pre-established outcomes and evaluating all student work in relationship to these outcomes. This means that in trying to ascertain students' individual achievements, instead of asking the traditional educational evaluation question, "Did Suzy or

Johnny accomplish x?," teachers are instead guided by the evaluative question, "What did Suzy or Johnny accomplish?" Various types of "authentic" assessment, planned jointly with students, can be used to evaluate student work in a partnership way.

Using the Elements of Partnership Curriculum Planning To Prepare a Preliminary Curriculum Outline

In this section, you will find suggestions for how to use the first three elements of partnership curriculum planning: the vertical threads, the horizontal threads and the curriculum loom. We will use these to prepare an outline that will eventually lead to the development of curricular units and activities. To illustrate, I have made use of a sample partnership curriculum that I find appealing. This sample will be called, "Foods and Plants: A Story." In the next chapter, we will employ the life-long learning goals, partnership learning activities and experiences, and partnership evaluation to complete our curriculum plan.

As you weave together the vertical and horizontal threads of your curriculum tapestry, you may find it helpful to proceed as follows:

First, become familiar with your students and their interests, abilities, multiple intelligences, learning styles, and backgrounds. These student factors represent one part of the horizontal threads that you will weave into your curriculum. Make sure that you discuss with your students what they want to learn and be on the lookout for things that seem to fascinate them. I prepared the preliminary outline for the curriculum below because my students and I had been working with plants and their (and my) curiosity was piqued. They wanted to learn more, and so did I.

Then, use your knowledge of your students and your own interests and intelligences to develop an appealing story that you consider important and interesting. A partnership curriculum is planned as a story where one section or unit leads naturally into the next. This will be the beginning of your vertical storyline. Because of my students' and my interests, I decided I would tell a story about "foods and plants."

Next, besides incorporating your own and your students' concerns and curiosities, your story will draw on your disciplinary knowledge (a horizontal thread) to weave your curriculum tapestry.

The following curriculum outline tells a story (the vertical curriculum thread) while weaving student and teacher interests into interdisciplinary studies and caring practices (horizontal curriculum threads). At this point, I have labeled each part of the story that I will eventually develop into a curricular unit with a capital letter and I have given each unit a name.

(A) The Human Need for Food

This curriculum unit begins with the story of the human need for food. Children discuss and share some of their favorite foods; they learn about nutrition and plan and, if possible, cook a meal together. This section draws on the disciplines of human biology, nutrition, and diet.

(B) Women as Gatherers & Creation Myths with Mother Earth

This module discusses women as gatherers of fruits and berries and possibly inventors of the first tools, such as sticks to dig for roots and tubers, mortars to soften babies' food, and leaf slings for baskets to carry babies and food back to camp. Children hear stories including creation myths with mother earth; dictate or write their own stories; draw pictures; paint; create a play which they perform, etc. This section makes use of knowledge from the disciplines of pre-history, mythology, and anthropology.

(C) How Plants Grow: Planting & Gardening

The unit then proceeds to farming and planting of foods and how plants grow, starting from seeds. Children learn about plants' need for sun, water, air, soil nutrients. Children plant different seeds and take care of plants as they grow, planting a garden if possible. They also plant squash/gourd seeds to be used in the next curricular unit. Children also learn about women's role in the history of agriculture. This section relies primarily on the disciplines of botany and social studies.

(D) Harvest and Planting Festivals: A Celebration

Children next read about harvest and planting festivals and music and dance that accompany such festivals, and create their own festivals, instruments, music, and dance. Children learn that some cultures create instruments using plants. They can also learn to hollow out the gourds they have planted to make their own gourd rattles. This section calls on the disciplines of mythology, anthropology, music, and dance.

(E) Vegetarian Cuisine Around the World

Children now learn about various cultures by reading stories about and tasting the different kinds of foods people eat in different cultures, with a close look at the plant-based foods cultures around the world use in their cuisine. They take a trip to a local market or health food store; they get acquainted with cookbooks; cook, if possible, with foods from their harvest; and share meals. This section makes use of the disciplines of botany, geography, sociology, and culinary arts.

(F) Popcorn: Let it Pop!

As part of the above, children take a close look at "popcorn," the cultivated food of indigenous peoples of the Americas. They do a series of activities related to popcorn. They learn that originally certain foods were only available in the places in which they grew or were cultivated. This section draws on the disciplines of botany, anthropology, and cooking.

(G) The Continuing Story of Plants and Our Basic Human Needs

There is now more dialogue about plants and what they give to the earth and to us: Why we need plants for other reasons than for food. This brings us back to basic human needs: Plants provide shelter/housing (many houses are made from wood from trees); plants provide clothing (using cotton, flax, linen); plants supply medicine to heal our bodies, fuel to heat and cool our homes, paper to write on; plants provide shade (especially appreciated on a hot day); the roots of plants prevent erosion of valuable topsoil; etc. Although the various ways in which plants contribute to our welfare are discussed, the focus is on how plants provide oxygen for us to breathe and plants' partnership role with us and other animals in the cycle of life. This section draws on many different disciplines in the sciences and social sciences, including the discipline of ecology.

(H) Why We Need Clean Air

This leads to a conversation about why we need clean air and includes activities related to human respiration. This, in turn, leads to activities related to pollution with a focus on air pollution. This section weaves in knowledge from various scientific disciplines, including the discipline of human biology.

(I) Rain Forests: Lungs of the Earth

This leads to discussion on the rain forest, "the lungs of the earth" and to activities centered on "caring for the environment." This section relies on many different scientific and social scientific disciplines.

(J) Caring for Others

The theme of caring leads to activities associated with "caring for others." This section relies on domains of human caring. For a discussion of "domains of caring," see page 341 in Chapter 13 of this book, "The Wisdom of the Elders: Curriculum Resources for Unlearning Sexism," and also pages 219-241 in Eisler's *Tomorrow's Children*.

Next, the vertical and horizontal threads of this curriculum are woven on the loom of the Partnership-Dominator Continuum. This means that the Partnership-Dominator Continuum is used as an analytic tool or lens throughout this unit on foods and plants to enable students to become critical thinkers, to help them understand underlying partnership-dominator patterns in the belief systems and social structures that are associated with eating habits, approaches to growing and acquiring food, ways of caring for each other and for the natural environment, and our relationship to the cycle of nature. Partnership values are emphasized to reveal our human possibilities rather than our limitations, to show that we can work together with each other and with nature in a cooperative, caring way, and to demonstrate that we can build social structures that provide for an environmentally sound and sustainable future.

Since this curriculum is for K-3rd graders, "partnership" is defined at an elementary level as caring about oneself, others, nature, and the world. It means learning that how one lives one's life can make a positive difference. It means learning that by working together with others one can have a profound impact on changing structures of domination, structures that work against creating a more democratic, egalitarian, peaceful, caring, and environmentally sustainable world. Since this curriculum is for such young children, we must not scare them about the horrors of dominator ways. We must help them to feel empowered to act in partnership ways.

Now, let's take a look at how my curriculum outline might be situated on the loom of the Partnership-Dominator Continuum.

Weaving on the Curriculum Loom

(A) The Human Need for Food

The partnership-dominator lens is used here to analyze premises about good and bad ways to take care of oneself through the different kinds of foods one eats. Partnership values help students focus on the need for healthy, nutritional food as well as the need to share in the planning, cooking, and eating of a meal.

(B) Women as Gatherers and Creation Myths with Mother Earth

The partnership-dominator lens is used here to confront assumptions about women's "natural" role as well as to help children develop an appreciation for the contributions of women and respect for domains of human caring.

(C) How Plants Grow: Planting and Gardening

The partnership-dominator lens is employed to examine assumptions about women's role in the development of agriculture in various cultures. Partnership values are used to help children develop respect for nature through their care of plants and gardens.

(D) Harvest and Planting Festivals: A Celebration

The partnership-dominator lens is used here to examine assumptions about the quality and skill involved in the music, instrument-making, and dance of non-dominant cultures and to help students appreciate these contributions to culture.

(E) Vegetarian Diets Around the World

The partnership-dominator lens is used here to expose erroneous assumptions about a plant-based diet being unhealthy or unbalanced. Partnership values are used to help students appreciate the many vegetarian foods they eat on a daily basis and to value the various vegetarian cuisines from around the world, as well as the people who have created them. The purpose is not to condemn other diets but to increase awareness about the importance of plants and the sophistication of cultures with plant-based diets.

(F) Popcorn: Let it Pop!

The partnership-dominator lens is used here to confront presumptions about the impact of the contributions of indigenous peoples of the Americas on the world diet. Partnership values help children understand and appreciate the gifts that indigenous peoples have given to all the people of the world. These values help children develop respect and tolerance for all people.

(G) The Continuing Story of Plants and Our Basic Human Needs

The partnership-dominator lens is used here to begin to reveal assumptions about dominant beliefs regarding our relationship to nature, and to confront the view that human beings can use all of nature's resources to their heart's delight without ever having to consider the consequences on nature. Partnership values are used to help children develop an appreciation and respect for all that nature, and in particular plant life, offers us and to learn to understand that their actions do matter.

(H) Why We Need Clean Air

The partnership-dominator lens is used here to continue to uncover assumptions about dominant beliefs regarding our relationship to nature. Partnership values help children learn that pollution is not inevitable and that through human efforts, including theirs, the environment can be cleaned up. Furthermore, partnership values teach them that by acting together we can work to prevent future pollution.

(I) Rain Forests: Lungs of the Earth

The partnership-dominator lens is used here to continue to challenge assumptions about dominant beliefs regarding our relationship to nature. Partnership values are used to help children learn to understand that it is not right for human beings to try to dominate and control nature; instead they need to learn to work with nature in a partnership way and become stewards of nature. As they participate in actions to save the rainforest, they acquire the skills, dispositions, and intellectual and emotional tools to "care for life."

(J) Caring for Others

The partnership-dominator lens is used here to examine dominant assumptions which state that caring for others is of less value than the disciplines in the context of school, and of less worth than career and work in the context of adult life. Partnership values help children understand the importance of caring for others in our human community; help them acquire the dispositions, skills, and attitudes to learn to care for others; and provide them with the opportunity to learn how good it feels to give and to share with others.

Our preparatory curriculum planning steps are now complete. We are ready to develop the actual units of the curriculum, which we turn to next.

CHAPTER 8

Foods and Plants — A Story:
An Example of a Curriculum Woven on the Curriculum Loom For Grades K - 3

by Dierdre Bucciarelli

Please note: I am grateful to the many individuals and organizations who shared their resources in the public domain, resources that I used to build this curriculum. My use of their materials does not constitute an endorsement for my curriculum by any of them. I have credited all sources using standard referencing methods.

The following curriculum, entitled "Foods and Plants: A Story," is developed for kindergartners through third graders. The first section of this curriculum is an overview and the sections that follow contain more detailed lesson plans, activities, readings, and resources. This curriculum builds on the preliminary outline that was prepared in the last chapter. It also makes use of the elements of partnership curriculum planning that were detailed there. As the units of the curriculum are constructed in this chapter, I incorporate life-long learning goals that I consider important for each unit. I also design partnership learning activities and experiences that I believe would appeal to my students and help achieve the goals.

This curriculum, "Foods and Plants — A Story," is presented as an example of the kind of curriculum that can be designed by weaving the vertical and horizontal threads of the curriculum tapestry on the partnership curriculum loom and by making use of the other elements of partnership curriculum planning. The curriculum offered here is not meant to be exhaustive. In fact, it is far from all-inclusive; it is only intended to give you some sense of what is possible. In developing partnership curriculum units, there are many different threads that one can pursue. Ordinarily, teachers will try to follow the lead of students and go in a direction that interests them since almost any path can lead to partnership goals.

To evaluate your success with the unit and your students' learning, you will use various "authentic assessment" measures that are in keeping with the overall purposes of partnership evaluation. It is important to reiterate that partnership evaluation is different from traditional evaluation. The goals of a partnership curriculum are always to have students understand how to uncover partnership-dominator patterns in beliefs and social structures and to know how to engage in and promote partnership ways of thinking and acting, both individually and collectively. Beyond this, since we want our students to fulfill their individual potentials and to accomplish as much as their potentials allow, what your students achieve depends on their own goals and interests. Because evaluation is dependent upon the students and the circumstances of each teacher, you will notice that the format for evaluation, repeated throughout the following curriculum, provides only principles for evaluation; it does not detail specific evaluative strategies. With Partnership Education, how students are evaluated cannot be determined prior to knowing the particular students a teacher will work with.

Overview of Curriculum Units

(A) The Human Need for Food

(B) Women as Gatherers and Creation Myths about Mother Earth

(C) How Plants Grow: Planting and Gardening

(D) Harvest & Planting Festivals: A Celebration

(E) Vegetarian Diets Around the World

(F) Popcorn: Let it Pop!

(G) The Continuing Story of Plants and Our Basic Human Needs

(H) Why We Need Clean Air

(I) Rain Forests: Lungs of the Earth

(J) Caring for Others

(A) The human need for food

This curriculum unit begins with the story of the human need for food. Children discuss and share some of their favorite foods; they learn about nutrition and plan and cook a meal together. This section draws on the disciplines of human biology, nutrition, and diet.

Life-Long Learning Goals

- To know that everybody needs certain kinds of foods to be healthy since food contains substances or nutrients that are needed for growth and to provide energy;
- To understand the importance of eating a variety of foods in a well-balanced diet;
- To learn how to care for and be in harmony with one's body by attending to the foods one eats;
- To appreciate the benefit of sharing food and cooperating to make a meal that everyone enjoys and that is made from food that was grown in a healthy and enviromentally sustainable way.

Introducing the Unit: Setting the Stage

Before focusing on the need for food, this unit begins with an introductory story that provides an overview of general human needs.

Activity One

The teacher begins the unit by reading the children's book, *All Kinds of Children* by Norma Simon, Illus. by Diane Paterson. (Ill.: Morton Grove Publ., 1999). This book discusses the needs that children throughout the world have in common, including "their need for food, clothing, a home, people to love them, and the opportunity to play." This children's story is used to connect with students' prior knowledge, to arouse students' curiosity, and to draw them into the developing story of the curriculum.

Note: For older students, the teacher might begin this lesson by stating that all people have certain needs. Ask students, "What do all people need to live?" The teacher can lead a brainstorming session and a discussion with the students about the basic human needs that everyone has. Then, the teacher can read students the book noted above. After the story, continue the discussion.

Communication-Dialogue Connection
Children and teacher together discuss their needs and they come to realize that all children have the same basic needs. Children learn to listen as others speak; they learn

to take turns expressing their opinions; they learn to value others' views. The teacher helps them to understand that another basic human need that everyone has is to be listened to and taken seriously.

Moving on

Since the emphasis of this unit is on foods and plants, the teacher moves the discussion in that direction.

Activity Two

The teacher tells the students, "We're now going to look closely at one of the needs we have discussed, the human need for food." Since everyone has experience with eating and everyone has favorite foods, begin this unit by asking students, "What do you like to eat? What are some of your favorite foods?" The teacher facilitates a discussion and points to food preferences related to cultural backgrounds.

Research Connection

Students go to the school library to search for pictures of their favorite foods as well as books related to cooking, nutrition, and diet.

Art Connection

Students draw, paint pictures, and/or make clay, play dough or construction paper models of their favorite foods.

Reading Connection

The teacher can read books to students which they then discuss.

One book the teacher can read includes: *Bread and Jam for Frances* by Russell Hoban; Pictures by Lillian Hoban (New York, Harper & Row, 1964).

This book is also available in Spanish as *Pan y Mermelada para Francisca*, traducido por Tomas Gonzalez (New York : Harper Arco Iris, 1995).

Jam on toast is Frances' favorite food until she has it for the sixth meal in two days.

Students who read can also look in the library for storybooks about food that they can read to other students.

Writing Connection

Students can dictate or write stories about their favorite foods and experiences they have had eating them. They can also record their feelings about these foods in their journals. Students can also dictate or write other stories related to food, such as stories about dinnertime at home or lunch in the cafeteria. They can also write fantasy stories about food and eating.

Caring for Others Connection

If possible, the students either bring to class or, with help from the teacher, acquire from the cafeteria, some of their favorite foods, which they will share with their fellow classmates.[*]

Moving on

Children learn about the nutritive value of food and the importance of eating a healthy diet by planning a meal together. This project is the primary motivator for this lesson on nutrition and learning about different classes of foods. The meal, as noted later, can also be an imaginary one.

ActivityThree

Students can either plan a nutritious meal for themselves or a larger group; they can also pose as restaurateurs and plan meals for restaurant goers. Students can shop for foods, planning a shopping list in accordance with the healthy foods they want to cook and serve. Students also cook and serve the meal together as well as clean up after the meal is over. Even if students are not able to actually share a real meal, they can still plan a meal and, with the aid of their own drawings, clay, play dough or paper models, they can pretend that they are serving and sharing a meal. Students especially seem to enjoy pretending to be restaurateurs.

Science Connection: Nutrition

Experimenting

To connect with students' prior knowledge, you can contrast nutritious with junk foods. Ask students, "What do we call foods that aren't good for you?" Most students are familiar with the label, "junk foods." Some students know that junk foods contain too much sugar, fat or salt.

For a host of activities and experiments related to food and nutrition, see *Foodworks: Over 100 Science Activities and Fascinating Facts That Explore the Magic of Food* from the Ontario Science Centre, illust. by Linda Hendry (Reading, Mass.: Addison-Wesley Pub. Co., 1987).

---

[*]With all of the eating activities in this section, the teacher must take special care to be sensitive to cultural and economic differences of the students. In some communities, children will not be able to provide food to share with other students. In this case, instead of foregoing an activity that the children would find enjoyable, meaningful and intellectually stimulating, the teacher might either try to access foods from community resources or work with the school cafeteria personnel. Another option might be for a teacher to use some of her/his classroom budget (if she/he has one) to purchase some food items. Still another option is to apply for educational grant money to fund such activities. If none of these options are viable, students could share luncheon items from the school cafeteria. Cafeteria foods could be supplemented with whatever additional foods are available. Finally, since students will be growing foods later in this unit) again, if this is possible), a meal could be planned around the harvest.

Reading

Read and discuss *The Berenstain Bears and Too Much Junk Food* by Stan and Jan Berenstain (Random House, 1985).

This book can help students begin to become aware of the value of eating a healthy, well-balanced diet and of not overeating.

Classifying

Note: Many teachers use the USDA Food Pyramid when teaching nutrition and the classification of food. However, since there is controversy about the diet recommendations included in the pyramid, you may choose not to use it with this age group - since it is not essential. Certainly, high school students, and perhaps middle school students as well, can be introduced to the debate itself. For more on the controversy, see the article entitled, "Food Pyramid Scheme" by Salim Muwakkil in"In these Times.com" August 7, 2000 which claims that the guideline that all Americans consume two to three servings of dairy products each day "despite the fact that most non-white Americans are lactose intolerant" represents institutional racism.

You want students to understand that food contains certain substances or nutrients that give them energy and help them grow and be healthy. Students can learn this without the aid of the USDA pyramid. Foods can also be classified according to their nutrients, as well as according to their source, e.g., carbohydrates come mainly from plants; protein comes from both animal and plant foods; fats of different types come from animal foods and plants; and minerals and vitamins come from plant and animal sources. Although the pyramid tells us how many average daily servings of each type of food we should eat, whereas these other classification systems do not, the general advice given in the pyramid (and by other sources) is that we should eat a variety of foods with a diet that is heavily plant-based. This is what students need to learn. Later, they will learn that such a diet is not only nutritionally sound, it is also an environmentally compatible one.

(For more on the history, the politics and the development of the USDA pyramid, see 1991 issues of Nutrition Action Healthletter *from the Center for Science in the Public Interest. Their web site is located at:* www.cspinet.org. *The Center for Science in the Public Interest is a great resource for current information on the history and politics of food in the United States as well as for information on diet, nutrition, and healthy eating. They do a great job of interpreting scientific research for a lay audience. They also have a small selection of wonderful resources available for children. Related to this section, see their book,* Creative Food Experiences for Children *by Mary Goodwin. And educators and parents will want to see their book,* Eating Better at School: An Organizer's Guide.*)*

Students can sort the food they bring to class to share and/or the fake food or drawings that they have made according to where the food comes from. Does it come from an animal, a plant or is it a food that animals make (this is the dairy category)?

Students can keep a list of foods they eat over the course of a week or more in a food log for analysis in the classroom.

Students can classify as well as analyze the foods in school cafeteria or in the school lunch program for their nutritional value and make suggestions for change, if necessary.

Older students can analyze ingredient labels and newspaper grocery ads.

Social Studies Connection

Students can analyze TV & radio ads about food that are directed to children. This helps students to not only be aware of nutritional issues, but also issues related to marketing, selling, and media manipulation.

Math Connection

Children figure out how many people they will be serving and, with the aid of the teacher, calculate how much food they will need. They will not be using cookbooks in this section, although they will be later on; they will be drawing on common knowledge to make calculations, e.g., if we serve each person one apple and there are thirty people, how many do we need altogether?

The children's book, *The Lunch Line* (New York : Scholastic Inc., 1996) by Karen Berman Nagel (Illust. by Jerry Zimmerman) containing math activities by Marilyn Burns can be used as a supplement to this activity. In this book a child tries to calculate which appealing foods in her school cafeteria she can purchase with her dollar.

Art and Music Connection

Students can work at creating an ambiance in the classroom or school lunchroom that is conducive to pleasant dining by decorating the room in an attractive way, making centerpieces and placemats for their tables, choosing enjoyable music to listen to, etc. They learn that these things also nourish their spirits.

Art and Writing Connection

Pretending to be restaurateurs, children can create attractive menus that describe their favorite foods or the foods they will be serving in appetizing ways.

Caring for Self and Others

Children learn how to care for themselves and others by preparing and eating proper foods which nourish and sustain them.

Caring for Others Connection

Students learn how good it feels to work with and get along with others. They learn the importance of kitchen safety, especially when so many cooks are in the kitchen. They learn they must take special care to be safe and not to hurt anyone. Students learn that planning, cooking, sharing a meal, and cleaning up can be a way to express caring for another person.

Students can also show their appreciation to the school lunchroom personnel for serving them their meals. Students can send them notes of thanks or have a thank-you celebration.

Evaluation

This depends on your individual students' purposes as related to the curriculum. If we are true to Partnership Education, we will not expect all children to learn the same things as a result of our educational program. We realize that different children will learn many different things, all of which can be congruent with the life-long learning goals. This means that we will work with individual students to see what they, in particular, have accomplished instead of focusing our sights on pre-established outcomes and evaluating all student work in relationship to these outcomes. Various types of "authentic" assessment, planned jointly with students, can be used to evaluate student work in a partnership way.

Alternate and/or Additional Storylines

- Chemistry of Taste and Smell
- Food Preservation Methods
- Junk Food/Healthy Snack Food
- In-depth study of Nutrition
- Study of Digestion and the Digestive System
- And whatever else interests students and teachers

(B) Women as Gatherers and Creation Myths About Mother Earth

This section discusses women as gatherers of fruits and berries and possibly inventors of the first tools, such as sticks to dig for roots and tubers, mortars to soften babies' food, and leaf slings for baskets to carry babies and food back to camp. Children hear stories including creation myths with Mother Earth as the creator; dictate or write their own stories; draw pictures, paint, create a play which they perform, etc. This section makes use of knowledge from the disciplines of pre-history, mythology, and anthropology.

Life-long Learning Goals:

- To know that women, as well as men were, and are, a vital force in the evolution of culture and history throughout the world;

- To realize that at one time women were revered for their ability to bring forth life and that such reverence for women was expressed through the creation myths or stories of various cultures;

- To develop an appreciation for the contributions of women and to value domains of human caring;

- To understand that through the gathering of fruits, berries, nuts, etc., women provided the bulk of the food for their families.

- To appreciate that all people, like the venerable women represented in pre-historic accounts, can work cooperatively with nature in a partnership way to acquire the food

Introducing the Unit: Setting the Stage
We've learned that the need for food is a basic human need. We'll see more clearly that it is a need that all human beings have in all times and places. Now we'll go on an adventure to learn about the different kinds of foods that people gathered and ate throughout history and time, people like your great, great, great, great, great, great. great, great, great, great, great, great grandparents (we're talking about a long, long time ago, aren't we?). We'll also learn how people in the past thought of and worshipped the earth like a mother because the earth provided food for everyone to eat. Today we still call the earth, "Mother Earth" and we speak of "Mother Nature."

Activity One

Students hear and discuss stories that the teacher will tell them based on his/her readings of various pre-historic accounts about the role of women in providing food for the family and possibly inventing the first tools, tools that were related to digging for roots and tubers, food processing, and food transport. Students also listen to and share their musings about different creation myths from various cultures about Mother Earth. Students also observe pictures of both mythological stories and pre-historic portrayals.

For more information on the role of women in pre-history:

See *The Chalice and the Blade: Our History, our Future*, especially pp. 1-42 and *Tomorrow's Children: A Blueprint for Partnership Education in the 21st Century*, pp. 77-115. Both by Riane Eisler. You will find many additional resources on this topic in both books.

See Marija Gimbutas' *The Goddesses and Gods of Old Europe, 6500-3500 B.C.: Myths and Cult Images* (Berkeley: Univ of Calif. Press, 1990) for many wonderful pictures of pre-historic archeological goddess figures.

Also, see the web-site of Kathleen Jenks, Ph.D., www.mythinglinks.com, for a comprehensive, well-documented, and fully researched list of references on various mythologies from around the world and across time, including sacred narratives of creation from the pre-historic period.

Reading Connection

The teacher can read books to students which they then discuss. Some examples of worthwhile books follow:

Books that teachers can read to children which re-tell tales from around the world of strong, adventurous women and (sometimes) of gentle, caring men include: *Tatterhood and Other Tales* edited by Ethel Johnston Phelps, Ilust. by Pamela Baldwin Ford (New York: The Feminist Press, 1978) and *The Maid of the North: Feminist Folk Tales from Around the World* also by Ethel Johnston Phelps, Ilust. by Lloyd Bloom (New York: Holt, Rinehart & Winston, 1981).

Although not specifically partnership-oriented, see *Beginnings: Creation Myths of the World* compiled and edited by Penelope Farmer, Woodcuts by Antonio Frasconi (New York: Atheneum, 1979) and *In the Beginning: Creation Stories From Around the World* told by Virginia Hamilton, Illust. (beautifully) by Barry Moser (San Diego: Harcourt Brace Jovanovich, 1988). The last book includes the Huron Confederacy story "The Woman who fell from the sky: Divine woman the creator."

A lovely book on indigenous North American folktales that feature legends that celebrate the passage from girlhood to womanhood is *The Girl Who Married the*

Moon: Tales from Native North America told by Joseph Bruchac and Gayle Ross (BridgeWater Books, 1994). From the Introduction: "In the teachings of Native peoples, to speak of becoming a woman is to remember the Earth who is the mother of us all" (p. 9)

Also see *Corn is Maize: The Gift of the Indians,* written and illust. by Aliki (New York: Crowell, 1976). As well as presenting the history of corn and foods made from corn, this is the only children's picture book that I could find that shows women gathering food from the wild (p. 14). It also shows women (and men) planting and tending cultivated corn crops in the fields.

And see the historical novel written for children, *The Basket Maker and the Spinner* by Beatrice Siegel, Illust. by W.S. Bock (New York: Walker, 1987). As described by the publisher, this book "looks back to the quiet time when Indian women made baskets and colonial women spent long hours at the spinning wheel." This book also contains lovely drawings of women and girls involved in basketry and spinning; it also has pictures of different kinds of baskets made with natural materials.

A children's storybook that tells a contemporary story that involves a girl and her grandmother weaving in Guatemala is *Abuela's Weave* by Omar S. Castaneda, Illust. by Enrique O. Sanchez (New York: Lee & Low Books, 1993). This book also contains lovely pictures of the girl transporting her tapestry to market in a large basket she carries on her head.

Art Connection

Students can draw or paint pictures which tell their own creation story and/or are a rendering of a story they've read or heard.

Students can tell a creation story with finger puppets or paper bag puppets they have made.

With help from older students, parents, and teachers, students can make their own costumes, stage decorations and props for a play they write and produce (noted below under "Drama Connection").

Students can make simple baskets that they weave together from grasses, pine cone needles, construction paper strips, etc.

For references for teachers on how to make baskets see:

Willow Spokes and Wickerwork; the Nature Book of Weaving with Wild-growing Things by C.M. Stephens. (Stackpole Books, 1975);

Indian Basketry, and How to Make Indian and Other Baskets by George Warton James (RioGrande Press, 1970);

Basketry Today with Materials from Nature: Weaving, Twining, Pine Needles, Plaiting, Coiling, Free Form by D. Z. Meilach & D. Menagh (New York : Crown Publishers, 1979).

Writing Connection

Students can write their own creation myths or they can write stories or poems about Mother Earth.

Students can also imagine what it would have been like to be a child in pre-historic times. What did children do for fun? Did they have chores to do? Did they have toys? What were their toys made of? What games did they play?

Movement Connection

Children can play the games that they imagine children in pre-historic times played.

Drama Connection

Students act out a play they've written or dictated to the teacher or to older students imagining, with their partnership consciousness, what it would have been like to have lived in pre-historic times.

Science and Geography Connection

If students live near woods or open fields, they can take guided walks in these environments to forage for edible fruits, berries, and/or weeds. Both prior to and after their walks, students can learn that certain foods grow naturally in certain environments and certain regions of the world. While on their nature walks, students can look for signs of the partnership between plants and animals. Students can keep science exploration journals as they venture into nature.

Of course, children and teachers should NOT eat any wild plants they are not absolutely knowledgeable about. For information on edible wild plants, see books by Euell Gibbons. See for example *Stalking the Good Life; My Love Affair With Nature* by Euell Gibbons, Illust. by Freda Gibbons (New York, D. McKay Co., 1971). But no one should rely on this book to determine whether something is edible!

Evaluation

The same principles of evaluation discussed for the first unit, "The Human Need for Food," apply to every unit in this curriculum. Please review the discussion on pages 153 and 160.

Alternate and/or Additional Storylines

• Study of Astronomy and Scientific Stories of the Birth of Our Universe. A children's storybook which succinctly tells the story of the universe, from the birth of the sun through the appearance of people on the earth to modern farming and the change of seasons is *Life Story: The Story of Life on our Earth From its Beginnings up to Now* by Virginia Lee Burton (Boston, Mass.: Houghton Mifflin & Co., 1962). This is a unique and clever book with interesting illustrations that is worth a look, although it does contain some sexist assumptions which teachers will have to address.

• Stories of Scientists (particularly women of all races and ethnicities and nonwhite men) involved in Cosmological Research (For references, see *Tomorrow's Children: A Blueprint for Partnership Education in the 21st Century*, pp. 63-67.)

• Indigenous North American women of yesterday and today (See *Women in American Indian Society* by Rayna Green (New York: Chelsea House Publ., 1992).

• Preserving and Storing of Food

• And whatever else interests students and teachers

(C) How Plants Grow: Planting and Gardening

This section investigates the farming and planting of foods and how plants grow, starting from seeds. Children learn about plants' need for sun, water, air, soil nutrients; they become acquainted with the benefits of organic growing. Children plant different seeds and take care of plants as they grow, planting a garden if possible. They also plant squash/gourd seeds to be used in the next curricular unit. Children also learn about women's role in the history of agriculture. This section primarily relies on the disciplines of botany and social studies.

Life-long Learning Goals

- To understand how plants grow, starting from seeds;

- To learn about the needs of plants and how to care for them;

- To begin to develop a first-hand appreciation for the miracle of nature by watching seeds that have been planted and cared for blossom into full-grown plants;

- To realize the importance of treating plants and nature with care.

Partnership values teach children the importance of treating plants and nature with care. Partnership values allow them the opportunity to experience the gift of life as they watch the seeds that they have planted and cared for blossom into full-grown plants that they will be able to eat.

Introducing the unit

So far we have learned about the kinds of foods that are good for us to eat. We also know that ancient people got most of their food by gathering it from nature and we are aware that they revered "Mother Earth." Now we will learn where much of the food that we eat today comes from and how it grows and we will see why we, too, must respect the bounty of nature. Now we will be learning about the magic of seeds and plants.

Activity One

Students grow plants from seeds in containers and/or gardens. They plant both vegetables and flowers, including gourds and pumpkins which they will use in later sections of this curriculum. In the process they learn what plants need to live and how to care for plants, including how to garden organically.

See the Center for Science in the Public Interest's book, *Ladybugs & Lettuce Leaves* by Project Inside/Outside and the companion volume, *Ladybugs & Lettuce Leaves*

— *Teacher's Manual.* Although these books are intended for the 4th through 8th grades, teachers will find them very useful. Also see the web site of the Center for Science in the Public Interest at www.cspinet.org for more resources for teachers.

Rodale Press in Emmaus, Pa. is also a fabulous, perhaps the pre-eminent resource for information on organic gardening. They publish the magazine, *Organic Gardening* (formerly *Organic Gardening and Farming* started in 1941). See their website: www.OrganicGardening.com.

Gardening Together With Children: Roots, Shoots, Buckets and Boots by Sharon Lovejoy (New York: Workman Publ., 1999) is a lovely book that gives simple instructions on how to garden both in the ground and in containers.

An eclectic and very appealing book that contains, as its title suggests, *Down to Earth: Garden Secrets! Garden Stories! Gardener Projects You Can Do!* is created by Michael J. Rosen and 41 Children's Book Authors and Illustrators. (San Diego, Calif.: Harcourt, Brace & Co., 1998.)

Science Connection
What's inside a seed? Students can look inside a seed (lima beans are good for this) to reveal a tiny stem, leaves, and stored food. Students can draw a picture of what they see.

How do plants grow? If students use a transparent container, they can plant a seed and watch it grow. A glass or plastic jar works fine. Help students plant the seed close to the side of the glass so they can watch how it develops. (This idea comes from the book noted directly below.)

A good science resource book that is intended for children is *The Hidden Magic of Seeds* by Dorothy E. Shuttlesworth (Emmaus, Pa.: Rodale Press Inc., 1976). This book does not contain many activities that children can do, but it does have wonderful pictures and clear scientific explanations.

Do plants need sun? To show that plants need sun: Place a board outside on a plot of grass and keep it covered. After several days, lift it up to reveal grass that is starting to turn brown. Students predict what will happen and record their observations through pictures and/or writing in a science journal/log.

There are many more experiments that can be found in science books for children which they can perform to show that plants need sun, water, and soil to grow. The above experiments are only intended to give you some indication of what you can do with plants and science; they are not fully developed here.

Math Connection

Students can collect a variety of seeds from the meals they eat. Then they put them into categories.

Students can measure how much plants grow each day and record their growth. They can also do experiments to measure how much plants grow under different conditions.

Students can keep a record calculating the total amount of water needed until seeds sprout. Do different kinds of seeds require different amounts of water?

Students can design and measure a garden plot. They can calculate how many seeds to plant in the space allotted.

Art Connection

Students can make a seed collage with seeds that they collect.
Students can decorate the pots that they plant in.

Writing Connection

Students record their observations and the results of their experiments in science journals.

Students tell stories about the magic and wonder of plants.

Students can write letters to relatives like the ones found in *The Gardener*, noted below.

Reading Connection

The teacher can read books to students which they then discuss. Some examples of worthwhile books follow:

> One of many stories that could be read to the children is the beautifully written and illustrated storybook, *Bringing the Rain to Kapiti Plain* by Verna Aardema, Illust. by Beatriz Vidal (New York: Dial Books for Young Readers, 1981). This book tells an African folktale which emphasizes the necessity of water and rain for all living things.

> Other children's storybooks of interest include: *The Gardener* by Sarah Stewart, Illust. by David Small (New York: Farrar, Straus, Giroux). This book tells the story, through a series of letters, of a young heroine with a passion for gardening who uses containers to raise various plants which transform her uncle's bakery in the city into an enchanted place. (Sound and video recordings of this book are also available from Live Oak Media, Pine Plains, NY.)

Eric Carle's *The Tiny Seed* (New York: Crowell, 1970) has become a classic. It tells the story of the journey of a seed and a plant's life cycle through the seasons.

Another book, similar to Eric Carle's is *The Dandelion Seed* by Joseph Anthony, Illust. by Cris Arbo (Nevada City, Calif.: Dawn Publ., 1997).

Caring for Self and Movement Connection

Children can learn the Yoga asana or exercise, "Soorya Namaskar," translated as "Salute or Greeting to the Sun."

> This series of yoga asanas can be found in almost any book depicting yoga pos-
> tures. Also see the children's book on yoga, *A Child's Garden of Yoga* by Baba Hari
> Dass (Santa Cruz, Calif.: Sri Rama Publ., Inc., 1980).

Caring for Others Connection

Children can get involved in a community garden project.

> "Official" community gardens were started by "Share Our Strength," one of the
> nation's leading anti-hunger organizations. (For more information see *Garden
> Secrets! Garden Stories! Gardener Projects You Can Do!* by Michael J. Rosen and 41
> Children's Book Authors and Illustrators (San Diego, Calif.: Harcourt, Brace &
> Co., 1998), pp. 62-3.

Caring for Others and Social Studies Connection

Children can save seeds that are collected from their plants. They can learn to preserve them for future planting as well as for sharing with others in their community. Older students also begin to learn about the social, economic, geographic, and political need to preserve local seed and plant varieties.

> For information on the world-wide need to preserve indigenous plants, see chap-
> ter entitled, "Music to build partnership" (Song Activity Seven: Seed Savers). This
> information can be adapted for younger students' use.

Activity Two

Children visit a farm or a large garden, if one is nearby. Children can also visit a lawn and garden center, a nursery, and/or a florist. They learn about and observe women and men involved in contemporary occupations related to caring for plants. They also learn about women's historical role in the development of agriculture and they become informed about the important place that agriculture plays in their communities and the world.

For more information on women as the first farmers, see *The Chalice and the Blade*, pp. 63-73 and *Tomorrow's Children: A Blueprint for Partnership Education in the 21st Century*, pp. 96-108, both by Riane Eisler.

Also see *With These Hands: Women Working the Land* edited by Joan M. Jensen. (New York: The Feminist Press). This book "traces the history of farm women of all races in the United States, beginning with the Native Americans who were working the land when the first Europeans arrived in North America."

There are not very many books for children depicting women as farmers but there are a few. A beautiful story of a woman as a sheep farmer is *The Sheep Book* by Carmen Goodyear (Chapel Hill, NC: Lollipop Power, 1972). This book tells the story of a woman who raises sheep for their wool, caring for them from their birth as spring lambs through their summer shearing. In winter she spins their wool into yarn and knits a sweater, and she continues to care for her sheep through the seasons.

Another book directed to older children is *What Can She Be?: A Farmer* by Gloria and Esther Goldreich (New York: Lothrop, Lee & Shepard, 1976). This book is about women as dairy farmers.

Activity Three

Children who live in farming communities can consult farmers about issues of fairness and economic markets in their communities. Children who are permanent residents can also work with children of migrant farmers to plan a campaign to advocate for better funding for migrant education programs. For children who do not live in farming communities, some of this work can occur through the internet.

The idea for this activity comes from Patrick Shannon's paper, "Promises made, Promises broken," pp. 17-18, where he describes the "Towns/Farms Together Project intended for first and second graders in a farming community in Pennsylvania." His paper was delivered at the International Education Summit for a Democratic Society, June 27, 2000, co-sponsored by the Whole Language Umbrella, Whole Schooling Consortium and the Rouge Forum. It can be found on the internet at http://www.coe.wayne.edu/communitybuilding/wsc.htm/

Evaluation

See the discussion of partnership evaluation principles on pages 153 and 160.

Alternate and/or Additional Storylines

- Processing food: A visit to a mill to see the processing of grains.
- Food Distribution (See the "Reading Rainbow" book, *Night Markets: Bringing Food to a City* by Joshua Horwitz (New York: Harper & Row, 1984).
- Learning which parts of plants are edible: Which parts of a plant can we eat? Do we eat seeds? Which foods that we eat regularly come from seeds?
- Study and planting of herbs and spices.
- Study and planting of ornamental flowers to be used for vegetarian table in a subsequent section.
- And whatever else interests students and teachers

(D) Harvest and Planting Festivals: A Celebration

Children read about harvest and planting festivals and music and dance that accompany such festivals, and create their own festivals, instruments, music, and dance. Children learn that some cultures create instruments using plants. They learn about making gourd rattles. Children can also learn to hollow out the gourds they have planted to make instruments. This section relies on the disciplines of mythology, anthropology, music, and dance.

Life-Long Learning Goals

- To know that many different cultures expressed their gratitude for a successful planting and harvesting of crops through festivals that they created and celebrated together;
- To be aware that some contemporary holidays were originally related to planting and harvesting;
- To appreciate the music and instruments created by various cultures around the world;
- To delight in the joy of making music and dancing together;
- To understand the importance of giving thanks to others.

Introducing the Unit: Setting the Stage

Now is the time to celebrate our harvest and to make music and dance together, as well as to learn about the music, instruments, and dance of different cultures throughout the world and throughout time. We will also learn how much music and dance evolved from planting and harvest festivals.

Activity One

Students hear and discuss accounts of ancient and contemporary harvest and planting festivals from cultures around the world.

Good references include *Celebrating Nature: Rites and Ceremonies Around the World* by Elizabeth S. Helfman, Illust. by Carolyn Cather (New York: The Seabury Press, 1969). The rites and ceremonies in this book, both past and present, are related to the seasons and planting and harvesting. In Part 1, "In Earliest Times," the author recognizes that "at first it was the women who sowed the seeds in the earth, and the earth itself was considered the Great Mother of all life." The book also traces the roots of our holiday traditions, noting that they originated in these ancient ceremonial traditions.

Also see picture books for children on specific myths related to planting and harvesting such as *The Dancing Granny,* retold and Illust. by Ashley Bryan (New York: Macmillan Publ., 1977). Granny Anika danced and sang all day long as she planted her fields and she even dances with the trickster spider Ananse. This is a retelling of one of many African folktales involving spider Ananse. "The seeds stirred in the earth to the vibrations of Granny's song and dance."

Activity Two

A celebration! And planning for it.

Reading Connection

The teacher can read books to students which they then discuss. Some examples of worthwhile books follow:

See the storybook, *Dancing With the Indians* by Angela Shelf Medearis, Illust., by Samuel Byrd (New York: Holiday House, 1991). This book tells the story of a young African-American girl, who with her family, dances at a powwow with the Seminoles whose ancestors rescued her grandpa from slavery. She dances the Ribbon Dance, the Rattlesnake Dance, and the Stomp Dance.

See the storybook, *Wood-Hoopoe Willie* by Virginia Kroll, Illust. by Katherine Roundtree (Watertown, Mass.: Charlesbridge Publ., 1992). This book tells the story of Willie who's always tapping out a rhythm wherever he goes. Interwoven into the story is information about various African rhythm instruments. The story ends with a Kwanzaa festival. There are lovely pictures of the instruments throughout.

Music and Math Connection

Students hollow out their gourds under adult or older student guidance, let them dry out, and then make a shaker or gourd rattle.

> See *American Indian Music and Musical Instruments: With Instructions for Making the Instruments* by George S. Fichter (New York: David McKay, Co., 1978) for information on how to make a gourd rattle (pp. 58-62) and other instruments.

Students learn basic music and dance rhythms and learn to count out beats.

Dance and Music Connection

Students do circle dances that they and the teacher have created to celebrate their harvest. Some students play instruments to accompany the dancers to folk music that the teacher, parents or students supply.

> For Resources for folk music and dance videos, check your local or school library for records and tapes from the Smithsonian Institution.

> Some Smithsonian resources include:

> *The JVC Smithsonian Folkways Video Anthology of Music And Dance of Europe*
> JVC, Victor Company of Japan; Barre, VT: Distributed by Multicultural Media, 1996.
> *The JVC Smithsonian Folkways Video Anthology of Music and Dance of the Americas*
> JVC, Victor Company of Japan; Montpelier, VT: Distributed by Multicultural Media, 1995.
> *The JVC Smithsonian Folkways Video Anthology of Music and Dance of Africa*
> JVC, Victor Company of Japan; distributed by Multicultural Media, 1996.

The web-site www.folkthings.com has folk dance videos, CDs, and many other products and resources, including information on folk dance festivals, academic programs, performance companies, museums, archives, periodicals, books, organizations, costumes, ethnic artifacts, master teachers, internet links to other web-sites, etc.

Try your local music store or one of the bookstores available through the internet for more resources.

Students and teacher invite local folk dancers into the classroom and join them in dance.

To find out if there are folk dancers and/or teachers in your area consult, the web-site www.folkthings.com, click on "The Directory."

Evaluation

See the discussion of partnership evaluation principles on pages 153 and 160.

Alternate and/or Additional Storylines

The sky's the limit! Use your imagination! Find out what students are most interested in. Draw on students' imaginations!

(E) Vegetarian Diets Around the World

Children learn about various cultures by reading stories about and tasting the different kinds of foods people eat in different cultures, with a close look at vegetarian diets and the plant-based foods people eat around the world. Children also explore the eating and cooking customs of different cultures. They take a trip to a health food store or local market; they get acquainted with cookbooks; cook, if possible with foods from their harvest; share meals. This section incorporates knowledge from the disciplines of botany, geography, sociology, and culinary arts.

Life-Long Learning Goals

- To know that a vegetarian diet is one of the most healthy diets in the world;
- To understand that many people all over the world depend heavily on this kind of diet to maintain their health and their lives.
- To appreciate the many vegetarian foods everyone eats on a daily basis;
- To value the various vegetarian cuisines from around the world as well as the people who have created them.

Introducing the Unit

We planted lots of vegetables and flowers. And we've learned that our ancestors ate lots of fruits and vegetables that they, at first, gathered and later planted. But did you know that most people around the world today eat mainly a vegetarian diet? We'll learn what that means for different cultures, exploring different cuisine and the cultures themselves as we take an imaginary trip around the world, a world food tour. We'll also try some new foods as we travel on our wold food tour and we'll use our harvest to share some vegetarian meals.

Activity One

Students take an imaginary trip around the world experiencing new and unusual plant foods, learning about vegetarianism as they travel, collecting information on foods and the role foods play in various cultures, and learn to cook and/or prepare a vegetarian meal using cookbooks as well as their new knowledge.

References for teachers on plant-based foods include:

Vegetables: An Illustrated History With Recipes by Elizabeth Burton Brown, Illust. by Marisabina Russo (Englewood Cliffs, NJ: Prentice-Hall, 1981).

Grains: An Illustrated History With Recipes by Elizabeth Burton Brown, (Englewood Cliffs, NJ: Prentice-Hall, 1977).
Rice by Pam Robson. (Danbury, Conn.: Children's Press, 1998).

This book "follows rice from its source on farm or plantation right through to the table, discussing how rice is grown, processed, and produced."

Corn by Pam Robson (Danbury, Conn.: Children's Press, 1998).

Potatoes by Claire Llewellyn (Danbury, Conn.: Children's Press, 1998).

Also see other books in the *What's For Lunch?* series by Children's Press. Included are books on potatoes, peanuts, chocolate, honey, the banana, and milk.

And see the VHS video recording for children, *How to Make an Apple Pie and See the World* produced by Lancit Media Productions, Ltd., a production of WNED-TV & GPN; produced by J. Gluckson, written by A. Gutelle, directed by L. Lancit & K. Lombard, hosted by LeVar Burton (Lincoln, Neb.: GPN, 1995).

And, for a fantastic resource that teachers will not want to miss, see, *The Cambridge World History of Food* edited by Kenneth F. Kiple & Kriemhild Conee Ornelas (Cambridge: Cambridge Univ. Press, 2000). This resource consists of a monumental two-volume set which, as its publisher states, "encapsulates much of what is known of food and nutrition throughout the span of human life on earth … [it is] a unique guide to every food that we eat — its origins, nutritional makeup and cultural impact." Although not focused on plant foods, there are several chapters that discuss plants and it "concludes with a historical dictionary which contains concise histories of the world's plant foods."

Science and Nutrition Connection

Teachers can provide examples or specimens of various vegetarian foods in both dried and cooked forms that they show to students. A variety of dried beans and grains can be displayed in labeled glass jars; cooked beans can also be displayed this way. Students can try to determine which dried and cooked samples belong together. Teachers can also show students posters or pictures from books of some of these plants growing in the ground, or better yet, take a trip to a nearby farm that grows some of them and/or have students plant them. Students can also sample some of these specimens.

Students play "guess which food?" as they try to guess which plants certain foods come from. Teachers can relate this game to the foods that students normally eat. For example, teachers can ask, What is bread made of? What about tortillas? Bagels? Cake? What about cereal? Where does ketchup come from? Where does rice come from? What about peanut butter and jelly? The cocoa in hot chocolate or chocolate ice cream? Marshmallows? Oatmeal? Pancakes? (They are all made from or come from plants.) In the process, students will also find that they eat many more plant-based foods than they would have originally thought.

Students taste a select sample of vegetarian foods that are new to them, such as sunflower or pumpkin seeds or more exotic foods like kelp and, again, learn about their source. Students learn that many vegetarian foods are healthy snack foods.

Students keep a list of foods they eat over the course of a week or more to analyze how much of their diet is plant-based. Children can compare, classify, chart, and discuss lists in class. This could also lead to some interesting discussions about cultural differences.

Students analyze the foods in school lunch program to see how many of them are plant-based.

Students analyze ingredient labels for the same purpose.

Music Connection
As students learn about the foods of different cultures, they can continue their explorations of music from those cultures.

See the "World Music Store" at www.worldmusicstore.com.

Students can also choose music that would be appropriate for their vegetarian meals together.

Math Connection
Students learn to do calculations based on recipes, using measuring cups and spoons to aid them.
There is a wide selection of cookbooks for children. One such reference is
What's Cooking? Favorite Recipes From Around the World by Margaret Brink Warner and Ruth Ann Hayward. (Little, Brown, 1981).

Also see *The Kid's No-cook Cookbook* by Beth Goodman (New York: Scholastic, 1990).

Students can shop for some pre-packaged vegetarian foods, comparing prices of different brands or different products. They can also compare prices of fresh produce.

Art Connection
Students can make posters that include the foods, as well as, other aspects of the different countries they visit in their culinary travels around the world.

As students learn about the foods of different cultures, they can become acquainted with the variety of art forms from those cultures. Students make their own artistic creations that emulate the art from different cultures (they can focus on themes of peace and caring). They then create their own "museum" in which they exhibit their art work. They can also design invitations for the "opening" of their art show which they send to invited guests.

Students can create an ambiance in the classroom or school lunchroom that is conducive to pleasant dining and learn about aspects of the culinary arts that make dining more enjoyable, e.g., they learn how to select foods for their colors and textures, as well as for their nutritive value (fruits and vegetables are, of course, wonderful for all these purposes). Students can also learn how to set an appealing table; they can pick wildflowers, grow their own flowers or make paper or clay creations. They can also make other kinds of centerpieces for the table and create placemats. Students learn that cooking can be an artistic expression of oneself and a way to express one's caring for another person.

Geography and Social Studies Connection
Children can learn about cultures that make use of some of the examples or specimens noted above. Children locate them on a world map.

Students can draw maps of countries they will visit or have visited on their world food tour.

> The *National Geographic Picture Atlas of Our World* is an excellent resource. There is also a plastic map in the back of the book that is poster size and removable.
> *Where in the World is Carmen Sandiego?* videos and CD Roms are available at many public libraries.

Students can learn about how maps and various charts are made and they create their own maps.

Children can learn about the geographical and environmental conditions that result in the natural availability of different foods in different regions of the world, which in turn (along with cultural imagination) result in varying cuisines.

Students can learn about when foods are "in season" and why they are available locally during certain seasons.

Students can learn about different eating customs and learn to eat in ways they are not familiar with, e.g., some students have never experienced eating with chopsticks; some have never eaten a main course without using eating implements; some may not have used a fork and knife.

For references, see *From Hand to Mouth: or How We Invented Knives, Forks, Spoons and Chopsticks and the Manners to Go With Them* by James Cross Giblin (New York: Crowell, 1987). This book is "a history of the eating utensils and table manners of various cultures from the Stone Age to the present day."

See *Feeding Yourself* by Vicki Cobb, Illust by Marilyn Hafner (New York: Lippincott, 1989). This book "describes how knives, forks, spoons, and chopsticks came to be invented and how they are used today in eating."

While traveling the world, children can also learn how other children in the various countries of the world live now, including learning that some children are homeless and some do not have enough food to eat. For activities related to this concern, see "J: Caring for Others" in this curriculum.

Reading Connection

The teacher and/or students can read, and then discuss books that tell stories for children about food, diet, nutrition, and eating.

Suggestions for books the teacher can read to the class include:

Celebration! By Jane Resh Thomas, Illust. by Raul Colon (New York: Hyperion Books, 1997). This book "tells the story of grandmother, aunts, uncles, and cousins who get together for the annual family picnic in Maggie's backyard, complete with good food and family fun."

Sip, Slurp, Soup, Soup - Caldo, Caldo, Caldo by Diane Gonzales Bertrand, Illust. by Alex Pardo Delange (Arte Publico Press, 1997). This is a delightful bilingual picture book that tells a story in both English and Spanish of the creation of a delicious vegetable caldo/soup. The book includes a soup recipe.

How My Parents Learned to Eat by Ina R. Freidman, Illust. by Allen Say (Boston: Houghton Mifflin Co., 1984). This book tells the story of a Japanese woman and a US sailor who meet and eventually marry. Their adventures with each other's food and eating customs are explored. She learns to use a fork and knife; he learns to use chopsticks.

Writing Connection

Students can dictate or write stories related to their adventures with food. They also write about or draw pictures of their experience in their journal.

Students can, with guidance from the teacher, create a recipe that includes their favorite foods. They also search cookbooks to find vegetarian meals they would like to cook together. And each student can contribute to a class index file, entitled "My favorite vegetarian/healthy recipe."

Research Connection

Students search the school library and/or the internet for books on vegetarian cooking.

Students take an excursion to a local market, health food store, a salad bar, a farmer's market to learn about vegetarian foods.

Caring for Nature Connection

Students start and tend a compost heap with their vegetable peelings and leftovers.

> For a scientific experiment related to composting see, *Foodworks: Over 100 Science Activities and Fascinating Facts that Explore the Magic of Food* from the Ontario Science Centre, Illust. by Linda Hendry. (Reading, Mass.: Addison-Wesley Pub. Co., 1987.) p. 29.

Evaluation

See the discussion of partnership evaluation principles on pages 153 and 160.

Alternate and/or Additional Storylines

- History and use of herbs and spices in cooking
- And whatever else interests students and teachers.

(F) Popcorn: Let it Pop!

Children take a close look at "popcorn," the cultivated food of the indigenous peoples of North America. They do a series of activities related to popcorn, including popping and eating it. They learn that originally certain foods were only available in the places in which the plants grew or were cultivated. This section draws on the disciplines of botany, anthropology, and cooking.

Life-Long Learning Goals

- To know that popcorn was originally cultivated by the indigenous people of the Americas in a way that cooperated with nature;
- To understand the significance of corn in Native American and other cultures.
- To appreciate the multiple gifts that indigenous peoples have given to all the people of the world;
- To develop respect and tolerance for all people.

Introducing the Unit

We've learned about lots of different vegetarian foods. Now we'll look closely at one particular food that was cultivated by Native Americans, corn. It was a very important food in the history of the world. We already know that it's a staple of many people's diets today. We'll learn more about its significance now.

Activity One

Students pop popcorn, do a series of activities with it and of course, they eat it. In the process they learn about the significance of corn and where it comes from.

History and Geography Connection

The teacher reads students the following storybook as they learn about the history of corn cultivation and the variety of foods that come from corn.

> *Corn is Maize: The Gift of the Indians*, written and illust. by Aliki (New York: Thomas Y. Crowell, Co., 1976). As well as presenting the history of corn and foods made from corn, this book shows women (and men) planting and tending corn crops in the fields.

> Also see the children's storybook, *The Popcorn Book* by Tomie de Paola (New York: Holiday House, 1978).

> For more information on Native American history, especially as related to women; creation myths, cultural contributions, etc. see "Native Americans" in the Index,

p. 359 in *The Chalice and the Blade* and *Tomorrow's Children: A Blueprint for Partnership Education in the 21st Century* by Riane Eisler.

See also, *Women in American Indian Society* by Rayna Green (New York: Chelsea House, 1992). This book is intended for middle-school aged students but is a useful resource for teachers. It begins with the European contact with indigenous peoples and extends into modern times.

Students can learn about the travels of corn throughout history and across continents. They can plot the movement of corn on a map and/or draw their own map.

Social Studies Connection

Children learn about societal biases Native American children have had to deal with and obstacles they have successfully surmounted. Children also experience ways to be sensitive to others and how to overcome bias.

Three excellent books that present anti-bias curricula and have many suggestions for strategies that help children develop an awareness of stereotyping and help them learn to respect others are:

Unlearning "Indian" Stereotypes, A Teaching Unit for Elementary Teachers and Children's Librarians. Published by The Racism and Sexism Resource Center for Educators, a Division of the Council on Interracial Books for Children, 1981.

Anti-bias Curriculum: Tools for Empowering Young Children by Louise Derman-Sparks and the A.B.C. Task Force (Washington, D.C.: National Association for the Education of Young Children, 1989).

Open Minds to Equality: A Sourcebook of Learning Activities to Promote Race, Sex, Class, Land age Equity by Nancy Schniedewind and Ellen Davidson (Prentice-Hall, 1998).

Many books of this type are available from the "Teaching for Change" catalog, "a unique source for hundreds of books, videos, and posters for the K-12 classroom." This catalogue is sponsored by NECA (Network of Educators on the Americas), a non-profit organization that "promotes social and economic justice through public education." For information on NECA and their catalogue, see http://www.teachingforchange.org/

Also see *Rethinking Schools, An Urban Education Journal*, a grassroots newsjournal, published by Milwaukee public school teachers. www.rethinkingschools.org

Science Connection

How well corn pops depends, to a large extent, on how much moisture the kernels contain.

For an experiment related to this fact, see *Foodworks: Over 100 Science Activities and Fascinating Facts that Explore the Magic of Food* from the Ontario Science Centre, Illust. by Linda Hendry. (Reading, Mass.: Addison-Wesley Pub. Co., 1987) pp. 86-7.

Also see *Science Experiments You Can Eat* by Vicki Cobb, Illust. by Peter Lippman (Phila., PA: J.P. Lippincott, 1972) pp. 101-103.

Students learn about Native American science and engage in some experiments.

See *American Indian Science: A New Look at Old Cultures* by Fern G. Brown (New York: Twenty-First Century Books, 1997). Chapter one is on "Farming the Land."

Music Connection

Students can listen to some Native American music; music can be playing softly in the background during this whole unit.

For one music resource, see the CD, *Under the Green Corn Moon: Native American Lullabies*. (Boulder, Colo.: Silver Wave Records), p. 1997.

Also see recordings from the Smithsonian Institute available in many public libraries.

Music and Math Connection

See suggestions and resources above under, "Harvest and Planting Festivals: A Celebration."

Dance and Music Connection

See suggestions and resources above under, "Harvest and Planting Festivals: A Celebration."

Art Connection

Children can make corn dolls and wreaths with the husks.

Children can string popcorn on thread to be used as decorations around the room or on Christmas trees.

Children can learn how to make many other Native American arts.

Math Connection

Students can measure, via a measuring cup, the popcorn they will pop.

They can count the number of kernels before and after they pop to calculate a ratio.

A ratio can also be calculated by comparing the measurement of kernels with the measurement of popped corn.

The popped corn from different sources can also be compared to see if one type of kernel yields more popped corn.

Mythology Connection

Teachers retell stories and creation myths related to corn, which was often considered a sacred crop.

> See the web-site of Kathleen Jenks, Ph.D., www.mythinglinks.com, for a list of references on myths of indigenous peoples of the Americas.

> See also *Celebrating Nature: Rites and Ceremonies Around the World* by Elizabeth S. Helfman, Illust. by Carolyn Cather (New York: The Seabury Press, 1969), chapters 16 and 17 on Aztec and other North American myths and ceremonies related to maize and corn.

Caring for Nature Connection

Students engage in environmental activities inspired by Native American stories.

> See *Keepers of the Earth: Native American Stories and Environmental Activities for Children* by Michael J. Caduto and Joseph Bruchac (Golden, Colo.:Fulcrum, Inc., 1988).

Evaluation

See the discussion of partnership evaluation principles on pages 153 and 160.

Alternate and/or Additional Storylines

The sky's the limit! Use your imagination! Find out what students are most interested in. Draw on students' imaginations!

(G) The Continuing Story of Plants and Our Basic Human Needs

Children now engage in more dialogue about plants and what they give to the earth and to us; they discuss why we need plants for other reasons than for food. This brings us back to basic human needs: Plants provide shelter/housing (many houses are made from wood from trees); plants provide clothing (using cotton, flax, twine, jute); plants supply medicine to heal our bodies, fuel to heat and cool our homes, paper to write on; plants provide shade (especially appreciated on a hot day); the roots of plants prevent erosion of valuable topsoil; etc. Although the various ways in which plants contribute to our welfare are discussed, the focus is on how plants provide oxygen for us to breathe and plants' partnership role with us and other animals in the cycle of life. This section draws on many different disciplines in the sciences and social sciences, including the discipline of ecology.

Life-Long Learning Goals
- To understand the many uses of plants and the vital role that they play in the cycle of life;
- To know that without plants there would literally be no life on the earth and we could not survive.
- To develop an appreciation and respect for all that nature, in particular plant life, offers us;
- To learn that one's actions in the world do matter.

Introducing the Unit: Setting the Stage
You will remember that we learned that we need plants because they give us food which provides fuel or energy for our activities and they help us grow and stay healthy. Now we will learn where plants get their energy and how they participate in the cycle of life. All energy comes from the sun. The green leaves of plants convert solar energy into food for themselves and for human beings and other animals through the process of photosynthesis, which in addition to making energy available in the form of food, also converts carbon dioxide into the oxygen we need to breathe. Photosynthesis is vital to keep life going; without it there could be no life on earth.

Activity One

Children discuss the human needs for which trees and other plants provide and the many things that plants give us. The teacher eventually leads the discussion in the direction that allows students to explore the role that plants play in providing oxygen for us to breathe and their place in the cycle of life.

Meanwhile, students are busy building a mini-environment, an aquarium that contains water plants, fish, and snails which they will observe for scientific purposes and that they will care for. Students also explore the natural environments around them, searching for signs of cooperation and interaction in nature. Students observe signs of plants and animals working together in partnership in the cycle of life.

Reading Connection

The teacher reads the book, *Be a Friend to Trees* by Patricia Lauber, Illust., by Holly Keller (New York: HarperCollins, 1994). This is an excellent storybook that clearly explains the many uses of plants, including trees' role in the oxygen cycle. In simple terms, it elaborates on how the leaves of trees make oxygen as they are making food in the process of photosynthesis.

The teacher reads pp. 42-53 from the rhyming book, *The Berenstain Bears in the Bears' Nature Guide: A Nature Walk Through Bear Country* (New York: Random House, 1975). This is a wonderful resource for children. See "Actual Facts about the World of Plants," pp. 42-53.

Science Connection

To show that plants need light energy from the sun: Students can cover a few leaves on an indoor plant so they are not exposed to the sun. Students make predictions, and after several days, remove the covering and record observations. This is an indirect demonstration which shows that plants must have the sun's energy or they will die.

A good reference for teachers is *Photosynthesis* by Alvin Silverstein, Virginia Silverstein, Laura Silverstein Nunn (Brookfield, Conn.: Twenty-first Century Books, 1998).

Students can draw a poster of various food chains, webs, and pyramids to represent part of the cycle of life.

See *Chains, Webs & Pyramids: The Flow of Energy in Nature* by Laurence Pringle, Illust. by Jan Adkins (New York: Thomas Y. Crowell, 1975).

For more experimental ideas on ecosystems, life cycles, and interactions of life and environment, see *Environmental Experiments About Life (Science experiments for young people)* by Thomas R. Rybolt, Robert C. Mebane (Springfield, NJ: Enslow Publ., Inc., 1993).

Math Connection

Students can make a graphic organizer of the photosynthetic process and the energy chain. (See *Be a Friend to Trees* above.)

Precocious and/or interested students could figure out how much energy is lost as we go higher up the food energy chain.

Art Connection
Students can make light catcher mobiles.

Students can make bean bags, noodle jewelry, pomander balls, and other crafts which are derived from natural or plant products.

Art and Writing Connection
Students can create a diorama or a full scale museum that displays plants, animals, and human beings cooperating in various environments. Each display is accompanied by a written description.

Music and Movement Connection
Students sing the lead song, "The Circle of Life," from the Disney Studio movie, *The Lion King*.

Students give a performance of *The Lion King* or create their own musical production.

Students can listen to and sing along with Stan Slaughter's "In Tune With all Species" tape. Stan Slaughter has been described as the "eco-troubadour" of the earth. Included on this tape are "Little Blue Ball" and "Habitat," which are considered "two of the most popular environmental songs around." There is also a songbook with educational material for each song. Some songs are more appropriate for older children, while others are fine for younger children.

Caring for Self and Movement Connection
Children can learn various yoga asanas or exercises, many of which are named after plants and animals because, it is said, they represent what the original yoga masters observed in nature.

> See the children's book on yoga, *Be a Frog, a Bird, or a Tree* by Rachel Carr (New York: Harper Colophon Books, 1973). See also, *A Child's Garden of Yoga* by Baba Hari Dass (Santa Cruz, Calif.: Sri Rama Publ., Inc., 1980).

Evaluation

See the discussion of partnership evaluation principles on pages 153 and 160.

Alternate and/or Additional Storylines

- Architecture, building and lumber.
- Clothing, textile fibers and the History of Fashion.
- Erosion and how the roots of plants help to limit it.
- And whatever else interests students and teachers.

(H) Why We Need Clean Air

Children learn why we need clean air and engage in activities related to human respiration. This, in turn, leads to activities related to pollution with a focus on the causes and effects of, as well as, remedies for air pollution. This section weaves in knowledge from various social scientific and scientific disciplines including, the discipline of human biology.

Life-Long Learning Goals

- To understand a little about human respiration;

- To recognize the dangers of air pollution.

- To learn that pollution is not inevitable and that through human efforts the environment can be cleaned up;

- To appreciate that by acting together we can work to prevent future pollution.

Introducing the Unit: Setting the Stage

We've learned that plants provide oxygen for us to breathe. We've also learned a little about how plants breathe or exchange gases through their leaves, now we'll learn about how human beings breathe and why all living things, including plants, need clean air to breathe. We'll investigate the air in our community to see how clean it is and we'll learn about the dangers of air pollution and what we can do to stop it.

Activity One

Human Respiration: Students engage in movement activities as they learn to pay attention to their breathing. As they do so, they learn about the process of human respiration.

Science Connection

Begin the lesson by have students engage in some creative movement or exercise, starting slowly and then engaging in more vigorous exercise. Then, through questioning, have students recognize that they are breathing in more air when they exercise heavily. (When do you think you need more air/more oxygen, when you're resting or when you're running? You breathe harder when you run; you take in more air.) And have them realize that it is necessary to have clean air to breathe. (Clean air keeps us and other living things healthy.) Then, ask students, "What happens inside us when we breathe in and out?" (We breathe in fresh air/oxygen provided by plants; we breathe out stale air/carbon dioxide used by plants) to begin a preliminary discussion of human respiration.

Show students the sections "Breathing" and "Inside your lungs" from the picture-book, *Outside-In: A Lift the Flap Body Book* by Clare Smallman, Illust. by Edwina Riddell (New York: Barrons, no date noted). This clever book, as noted in the title is designed with flaps that cover pictures of the body as it normally appears "on the outside." When lifted, the flaps reveal various internal organs and systems.

Students can also engage in some deep breathing exercises, placing their hand(s) on their chests to feel their lungs expand and deflate as they inhale and exhale. (We breathe in fresh air with oxygen and breathe out stale air with carbon dioxide. Remind students that they learned that plants are essential for this process.)

> Another good resource for children about human respiration is *Magic School Bus Inside the Human Body* by Joanna Cole (Econo-Clad Books, 1999).

Caring for Self Connection

Students can learn some yogic deep breathing (and deep relaxation) exercises. Not only are deep breathing (and deep relaxation) good for the body, they are also a good way to calm and soothe the mind.

> See *A Child's Garden of Yoga* by Baba Hari Dass (Santa Cruz, Calif.: Sri Rama Publ., Inc., 1980, pp. 9 and 105).

Activity Two

Causes and effects of air pollution: Students don the hat of a scientist to investigate the causes and effects of air pollution. They monitor the air quality in their communities to see how clean it is. They also become artists who communicate their findings to a larger audience.

Introducing the Section

We'll now focus our attention on the air pollution created by humans (there is also pollution from natural sources such as sandstorms, gases and ash from volcanoes, etc.). We'll learn that nature can clean out some pollutants from our air (through wind, rain) but if there are too many pollutants in too large a concentration, nature cannot handle them; they upset the balance of nature. Pollution has many bad effects, not only on people, but on plants, animals, even inanimate objects, like buildings, works of art, clothing, etc.

Science Connection

Students can conduct interviews with joggers asking them if it is easier to breathe when they run near a roadway with lots of traffic or when they run farther away from traffic. They plot this information on a chart or graph. (Students learn that clean air keeps our bodies healthy. If the air we breathe is polluted, less oxygen is carried to our bodies. This causes us to breathe harder and to feel tired. It's not good to jog near a highly-traveled roadway.)

Students take a walk in the woods to look for lichens. Certain kinds of shrubby lichens are very sensitive to polluted air and can be used as a rough gauge or a clue to how polluted the air is in their community.

Students can conduct an experiment to determine the effect of air pollution on plants. They raise two plants from seeds, placing one plant in a polluted environment, such as outside near the school bus loading zone. Another plant is located in a non-polluted environment, such as inside the classroom. Students monitor and care for the plants for several weeks, making scientific observations and reports, noting differences in their condition and rates of growth in the different environments.

To ascertain particulate air pollution, students can conduct an experiment to answer the following questions: "How clean is the air I breathe? Where is the most air pollution in my community?" Students tape waxed paper to three, four or more small pieces of heavy cardboard. They then rub each piece with a small amount of petroleum jelly.

Next they place the cardboard squares in different locations around their community, leaving them for several days. They collect them, analyze them with a magnifying glass, and compare and record the results.

> The above experiment comes from the book, *Up the Science Ladder: Activity Based Ideas for Teaching Science to Primary Grades* by Lynn Molyneux, Illust. by Rosemary Park (Canandalgua, NY: Trellis Books, 1988), p. 26.

For an experiment that tries to determine if air pollution can harm clothing, see *Environmental Experiments about Air (Science experiments for young people)* by Thomas R. Rybolt and Robert C. Mebane (Springfield, NJ: Enslow Publ., Inc., 1993), pp. 60-64.

> For more experimental ideas related to air and air pollution, see the above book.

> A general reference for teachers on ecosystems, air pollution, and many other details relating to "our earth," see *Encyclopedia of our Earth* by John Clark, David Flint, Tony Hare, Keith Hare and Clint Twist, Illust. by Ron Haywark, Ian Moores, Alex Pang, Mike Saunders & Simon Tegg (NY: Aladdin Books, 1995).

Also see, *Earth Child 2000: Earth Science for Young Children: Games, Stories, Activities, and Experiments* by Kathryn Earth Child Sheehan, Mary Waidner (Council Oak Distribution, 1998).

Another great, easily accessible resource for teachers on environmental issues is the Environmental Research Foundation's *Rachel's Environmental & Health News* which is available in print form as well as via e-mail. The electronic version is available free of charge. To start your own free subscription, send e-mail to listserv@rachel.org with the words SUBSCRIBE RACHEL-WEEKLY YOUR NAME in the message. The Rachel newsletter is also available in Spanish. Back issues are available at the organization's web-site: http://www.rachel.org. The Environmental Research Foundation can also be reached at P.O. Box 5036, Annapolis, MD 21403; Phone (410) 263-1584; Fax (410) 263-8944; E-mail: erf@rachel.org.

Art Connection

Students draw "before and after" pollution pictures.

Students create a poster that gives examples of the visible and invisible causes of human-generated air pollution.

Students can create posters around the school and/or around town that teach about the dangers of pollution.

Reading Connection

The teacher reads and together, students and teacher discuss *The Lorax* by Dr. Seuss, Theodore Seuss Geisel (NY: Random House, 1971). This book tells the sad tale of environmental destruction but ends on a hopeful note. Those who care can and must make a difference. As the Lorax, the one who sounds the environmental warning states, "Unless someone like you cares a whole awful lot, nothing is going to get better, it's not!" This book is also available as an audio cassette and as a film. To order the 25 min. film contact the Distributor Population Reference Bureau, Inc., 202/639-8040. 1972.

The teacher reads and together, students and teacher discuss *The Wump World* by Bill Peet (Boston: Houghton Mifflin Co, 1970). "The Wump World is an unspoiled place until huge monsters bring hordes of tiny creatures from the planet Pollutus to turn the green meadows into a concrete jungle."

Two storybooks that provide scientific information include:

Where Does the Garbage Go? (Let's-Read-And-Find-Out Science, Stage 2) by Paul Showers, Illust. by Randy Chewing, Paul Chewning, Randy Chewning (HarperCollins Juvenile Books, 1994).

Who Will Clean the Air? by Thomas Biddle Perera & Wallace Orlowsky, Illust. by Richard Cuffari (New York: Coward, McCann & Geoghegan, Inc., 1971).

Drama Connection
Students can dramatize the actions of polluters as well as non-polluters.

Students can produce and perform their interpretation of *The Lorax* or *The Wump World* or they can write, produce, and perform their own play.

Music Connection
Students can sing along with Stan Slaughter's *Unintended Consequences* CD, Music to Care for the Environment. Titles include: "Household hazardous waste," "Half pint can of bright red paint," "Lead, bad actors," "Don't let the goo get you," "Teenager in wasteland," "What can I use instead?" "Storm drain stenciling," "Excuse me, sir, that's my acquifer," "We're all connected," and "Shoppin' for a better world." Some songs are more appropriate for older children, while others are fine for younger children.

Activity Three

Personal and Structural Ways to keep our air clean: Students engage in activities that demonstrate caring for the environment.

Caring for the Environment and Social Studies Connection
For environmental resources and for more information on "Our Living Planet" and "Caring for Life" see especially pp. 236-241 in *Tomorrow's Children: A Blueprint for Partnership Education in the 21st Century* by Riane Eisler.

Students recycle various recyclable objects.

Students monitor products used in their schools for their toxicity and make suggestions for alternatives if they discover problems, e.g., students assess whether the school uses cleaning products that are non-polluting, and if not, make recommendations for change.

Students monitor the air in their communities and report the results to local and state officials and the EPA.
Guided by the teacher, older students compare the air quality in different communities by conducting research on the internet. They learn that there can be a connection between pollution and social inequality. They become aware that poorer communities can be more polluted because of issues related to environmental injustice.

For more informationn on this issue, see The Center for Health, Environment and Justice (CHEJ) (formerly the Citizens Clearinghouse for Hazardous Waste (CCHW). The CHEJ was founded by Lois Gibbs, community leader at Love Canal. "CHEJ believes in environmental justice, the principle that people have the right to a clean and healthy environment regardless of their race or economic standing... CHEJ seeks to help local citizens and organizations come together and take an organized, unified stand in order to hold industry and government accountable and work toward a healthy, environmentally sustainable future." They can be reached at P.O. Box 6806 Falls Church, Virginia 22040 or on the internet at http://www.chej.org/.

Students send letters to companies that pollute the air, expressing their dismay and concerns, and suggesting remedies.

Children write letters to elected officials for help in acquiring the right to transform a local vacant lot into a garden or park or to secure the right to plant a tree in a public park.

Additional resources for teachers which show that kids can make a difference in protecting the environment include:

50 Simple Things Kids Can Do to Save the Earth by The Earth Works Group, Illust. by Michele Montez (Andrews and McMeel, 1990).

Recycle: A Handbook for Kids by Gail Gibbons (Boston: Little Brown & Co., 1992).

Earth Child 2000: Earth Science for Young Children: Games, Stories, Activities, and Experiments by Kathryn Sheehan, Mary Waidner (January 1998). The Dream Starter section in each chapter is a novel idea that can help children dream about the possibilities for a more partnership-oriented world.

Earth Book for Kids: Activities to Help Heal the Environment by Linda Schwartz, Illust. by Beverly Armstrong (October 1990). Although intended for children ages 9-12, teachers of younger students will find this a useful resource.

Evaluation

See the discussion of partnership evaluation principles on pages 153 and 160.

Alternate and/or Additional Storylines

The sky's the limit! Use your imagination! Find out what students are most interested in. Draw on students' imaginations!

(I) Rain Forests: Lungs of the Earth

Children discover the role that tropical rain forests play in producing essential oxygen for the creatures and organisms of the earth. They learn about foods that we regularly eat that come from the rain forests. They also learn about the remarkable variety of life forms in the rain forest and their significance to us. Children participate in projects related to the rain forest and engage in continuing activities centered on "caring for the environment." This unit integrates knowledge from many scientific disciplines.

For environmental resources and for more information on "Our Living Planet" and "Caring for Life"see especially pp. 236-241 in *Tomorrow's Children: A Blueprint for Partnership Education in the 21st Century* by Riane Eisler.

There are also many organizations on the internet that have web-sites that provide a wealth of information (including resources for teachers) on the rain forest and what we can do to protect it.

To begin, see the following web-sites:

- Rainforest Alliance at http://www.rainforest-alliance.org/.
  65 Bleecker Street, NY, NY 10012. 212-677-1900 (phone) or 212-677-2187 (fax)

- Rainforest Action Network at www.ran.org.

- Rainforest Information Centre, http://forests.org/ric/ (also has information on "Deep Ecology").

- All web-sites listed above provide links to additional sites.

Life-Long Learning Goals
- To understand the important role that the rainforest plays in the cycle of life;
- To learn to work with nature in a partnership way and become stewards of nature;
- To acquire the skills, dispositions, and intellectual and emotional tools to "Care for Life" while participating in actions to save the rainforest.

Introducing the Unit: Setting the Stage
We are going to continue learning about the cycle of life. Now we will explore the role that the rain forest plays in it. We already know how plants provide oxygen for us to breathe and why they are vital for the existence of all living things; we will now discover why the rainforest has been called "the lungs of the earth." We will learn that when rainforest trees are burned, instead of taking carbon dioxide from the environ-

ment, carbon dioxide is being released into the environment which several scientists think contributes to global warming. And we will come to understand the importance of preserving the rainforest as we take steps to care for it.

Activity One

The teacher and students create a rainforest environment as they take an expedition into the rainforest, recording their observations, insights, and feelings along the way. Sounds of the rainforest play gently in the background as they work on their creation.

> A selection of CDs that offer sounds from the rainforest include: *Sounds of Nature: Rainforest* by Chuck Plaisance, Suzanne Doucet; *A Month in the Brazilian Rainforest: Rain Forest - Sound Effects; Rainforest Suite* by Doug Hamer; *Birds in the Rainforest* by Sounds of The Earth.

Science Connection

To gain some sense of the rainforest environment, students grow two plants, one in tropical conditions and one in temperate conditions, and compare the rates of growth. Tropical conditions are created by placing one plant inside a transparent plastic bag and keeping it at a warm temperature. The other plant is grown in a cooler location without the plastic bag. After a week or more, compare the plants and record observations.

> The above experiment is included in the book, *Encyclopedia of Our Earth* by John Clark, David Flint, Tony Hare, Keith Hare, and Clint Twist, Illust. by Ron Haywark, Ian Moores, Alex Pang, Mike Saunders & Simon Tegg (NY: Aladdin Books, 1995), p.83. Also see pp. 82-89 on "Tropical Rainforests" and pp. 104-121 on "Rainforest Destruction."

> For many more experiments related to the rain forest see, *Exploring the Rain Forest: Science Activities for Kids* by Anthony D. Fredericks, Illust. by Shawn Berlute-Shea and Shawn Shea (Fulcrum Pub., 1996).

> For experiments related to global warming and the greenhouse effect, see *Environmental Experiments About Air (Science experiments for young people)* by T.R. Rybolt and R.C. Mebane (Springfield, NJ: Enslow Publ., Inc., 1993).

> For a good resource for children on rainforest plants see, *How Monkeys Make Chocolate: Foods and Medicines from the Rainforests* by Adrian Forsyth (Owl Communications, 1995).

Students learn about animals, people, and plants of the rainforest: See the extensive list of videos, books, and other resources available on these topics through the "Rainforest Alliance," noted above.

> Also see *The Remarkable Rainforest: An Active-learning Book for Kids* by Toni Albert (Trickle Creek Books, 1996).

Nutrition and Caring for Others Connection

Together students make and share a fruit salad made with fruits that they often eat that come from the rainforest, such as bananas, oranges, pineapples, avocados, etc.

Caring for Self and Movement Connection

Children can learn various yoga asanas or exercises, many of which are named after plants and animals because they represent what the original yoga masters observed in nature.

> See the children's book on yoga, *Be a Frog, a Bird, or a Tree* by Rachel Carr (New York: Harper Colophon Books, 1973). See also, *A Child's Garden of Yoga* by Baba Hari Dass (Santa Cruz, Calif.: Sri Rama Publ., Inc., 1980).

Reading Connection

The teacher can read books to students which they then discuss. There are many wonderful children's stories about the rainforest. To mention only a couple:

> *Amazon Diary: The Jungle Adventures of Alex Winters* by Hudson Talbott, Illust. by Mark Greenberg (1998). Alex details his adventures in the Amazon by means of his written and illustrated journal.

> *The Great Kapok Tree: A Tale of the Amazon Rain Forest* by Lynne Cherry (NY: Trumpet Club, 1993). A lumber jack falls asleep under a kapok tree only to dream of the animals and the young boy who approach him to plead for their home, the rainforest. This book is dedicated to Chico Mendes.

Art Connection

Students can paint a wall mural representing the variety of plants, animals, and human beings in the rain forests working in partnership with each other.

> Also, see *Crafts for Kids Who are Wild About Rainforests* by Kathy Ross, Illust. by Sharon Lane Holm (Millbrook Pr Trade, 1997).

Caring for the Environment Connection

Students grow a variety of houseplants to help purify the indoor air in their schools and homes, caring for each other and themselves as they care for the environment.

> See *How to Grow Fresh Air: 50 Houseplants that Purify Your Home or Office* by Dr. B.C. Wolverton (NY: Penguin Books, 1996).

> See Caring for the Environment resources listed above under "Why we Need Clean Air."

> See web-sites listed at the outset of this section for many more suggestions on what can be done to save the rainforest.

> Rainforest Alliance recommends the following actions (which students can participate in): Supporting companies that reduce rainforest destruction; choosing products that conserve energy; looking for products with minimal packaging; buying products that are made locally; reusing and recycling; letting people know about rainforest destruction; writing letters to elected officials; supporting groups that work to protect tropical forests; and using paper that is certified, or made from recycled products or that has been processed without chlorine.

Students can make their own recycled paper.

> For information on how to do this, see *50 Simple Things Kids Can do to Save the Earth* by The Earth Works Group, Illust. by Michele Montez (Andrews and McMeel, 1990), p. 153.

Evaluation

See the discussion of partnership evaluation principles on pages 153 and 160.

Alternate and/or Additional Storylines

The sky's the limit! Use your imagination! Find out what students are most interested in. Draw on students' imaginations!

(J) Caring for Others

Children participate in various activities associated with "Caring for others."

> For more information on "Caring for Life" see especially pp. 219-241 in *Tomorrow's Children: A Blueprint for Partnership Education in the 21st Century* by Riane Eisler.

Life-Long Learning Goals

- To students to acquire the skills, attitudes, and dispositions necessary to care for others;
- To provide them with the opportunity to learn how good it feels to care, to give, and to share with others.
- To understand the importance of caring for others in our human community.

Activity One

Students, with help from teachers, older students and parents, can help to conduct a food drive for organizations in their local community that collect and distribute food.

If such an organization does not exist, younger students can work with older students to form such an organization.

Children can get also get involved in a community garden project. "Official" community gardens were started by "Share Our Strength," one of the nation's leading anti-hunger organizations.

> For more information on community gardens, see *Garden Secrets! Garden Stories! Gardener Projects You Can Do!* by Michael J. Rosen and 41 Children's Book Authors and Illustrators (San Diego, Calif.: Harcourt, Brace & Co., 1998), pp. 62-3.

> For more information on "Share Our Strength," see their web-site at http://www.strength.org/.

Introducing the Unit

It is sad to know that some people in our communities and the world do not have enough to eat and even go hungry every day. But, working together, we can do something to begin to change this situation and we will.

> *Throughout this unit, there is discussion with students about the causes of hunger. Students learn, at a very basic level, that the reason most people do not have enough food has to do with structural causes; they learn that it is not individuals personal fault, e.g.,*

that they are too lazy to work. Students learn that there are not enough life-sustaining jobs in our society for everyone, but they learn that this situation is not inevitable, it can be changed.

Math Connection

As students collect food for the community food bank, they can categorize food into different food groups, labeling each box of food. They can count the different types of food they have collected and discuss whether lots of one kind of food results in a healthy diet.

Science Connection

To have students understand the importance of having enough food to eat, have students engage in some creative movement, jog in place, jog around the room or run around outside. Then, through questioning, have students recognize that they have used up energy. Ask students, "How do you replace that lost energy?" "How do you get energy for your activities?" The answer, of course, is through eating food or, more precisely, through digesting the food we eat. "You wouldn't have energy to run or do anything if you didn't eat and if you didn't have enough food to eat." This knowledge can help to connect students with other children's plights and give them some understanding of the importance of ending hunger in their communities and in the world.

Art Connection

Students can decorate the boxes of food in colorful ways.

Reading Connection

Students can read stories and/or discuss hunger in the world, especially stories focused on children. As they learn about hunger, teachers should help them to understand the structural causes of hunger.

> One resource the teacher can use for information on the structural causes of hunger is *Hunger: Examining Cause and Effect Relationships* by Neal Bernards (San Diego, Calif.: Greenhaven Press, 1994).

> Another valuable source that teachers can consult is "The Institute for Food and Development Policy" better known as "Food First." A wide array of resources are available from Food First, including books, reports, articles, films, electronic media, and curricula, plus interviews, lectures, workshops, and academic courses.
> See their web-site: http://foodfirst.org/.

> Food First "is a member-supported, nonprofit 'peoples' think tank and education-for-action center ... [whose] work highlights root causes and value-based solutions to hunger and poverty around the world, with a commitment to establishing food

as a fundamental human right…. The organization was founded in 1975 by Frances Moore Lappé and Joseph Collins, following the international success of the book, *Diet for a Small Planet*."

Writing and Art Connection
Students can write simple messages on the boxes or send "home-made" cards along with the packages of food. Messages can also be in the form of poetry.

Students write or dictate letters to their legislative representatives about helping to end hunger in the world.

Activity Two

Students can grow various kinds of potted plants from seeds for the purpose of giving the gift of their plant to another person. Once the plants are grown, students can give the plants to a person of their choosing. They can also deliver plants that they have grown to senior citizen homes.

Art Connection
Students can paint the pots before planting.

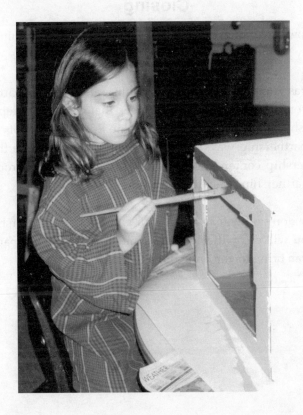

Writing Connection
Students can write simple messages on the boxes. Messages can also be in the form of poetry.
Music, Theatre, and Dance Connection
Students can develop a musical and/or theatrical performance which they present at the senior citizen's home when they deliver their plants. They can also invite guests who will be receiving the gift of their plants to a musical performance at school.

Evaluation

Children's demonstration of their caring for their plants and for other people is sufficient evaluation.

Alternate and/or Additional Storylines

The sky's the limit! Use your imagination! Find out what students are most interested in. Draw on students' imaginations!

Closing

I hope you now have some sense of what a Partnership curriculum means and of one systematic way to develop it.

As much fun as you have developing, teaching, and learning partnership curriculum (and I hope you have lots of fun!) remember, that curriculum represents only the content of Partnership Education. Since Partnership Education adopts a holistic or systemic approach, partnership ways of thinking and acting pervade the whole school through its partnership content or curriculum, its partnership process or teaching methods, and its partnership structure or learning community.

Finally, please don't hesitate to begin your journey with partnership curriculum. I am certain that you will enjoy the adventure and harmony that a partnership educational experience can bring to you and your students.

CHAPTER NINE

Music to Build Partnership

by Sarah Pirtle

Each song brings the listener into a unique experience. As we sing, "This Land is Your Land," we can see through the eyes of the songwriter Woody Guthrie the "sparkling sands of the diamond deserts." Or, joining in singing, "We Shall Overcome," we arrive in the vortex of our own passion for civil rights, and connect to the millions who have sung this song before us.

By recalling the feeling of singing around a campfire, we can get a sense of how music has been a basic source for connection throughout human history. Music involves interpersonal, kinesthetic, linguistic, and intrapersonal ways of knowing, as well as, musical intelligence. It links us to those singing with us and also opens ways of thinking, feeling, and sensing.

Music can focus, energize, inform, and inspire. Calm coherent music helps students concentrate. Songs with meaningful lyrics introduce new concepts or open conversations as music brings the subject matter closer. Studying the Underground Railroad becomes more vivid when we hear historical songs like "Follow the Drinking Gourd." Learning about Puerto Rico is enhanced when we include popular Puerto Rican songs or sing, "La Borinqueña" and learn of its significance as a national anthem. When we sing as a community, joyfully, open-hearted, we send unspoken messages: "You matter," and "We care about each other here."

Nick Page, author of *Music as a Way of Knowing*, says that, in fact, music charges the brain. He writes:

Of the five senses, the ears are the most active before birth.... Just as the umbilical cord is providing nutrients for the child to grow physically, the sounds provide needed resonance for the mind to grow. The ear has three purposes, not two. It is now believed that in addition to balance and hearing, the ear also serves as a charger of the brain.

The desire to learn is equated with the desire to listen. (Nick Page, *Music as a Way of Knowing*, p. 9, Los Angeles: The Galef Institute, 1995).

Yet whenever I train teachers in how to use music in their classroom, many express painful associations with music making. Teachers tell of times they were told not to sing, when they were belittled, when they were compared, or when they were pressured to perform skills beyond their reach until their personal connection to the music became eclipsed. They say that consequently, they are less inclined to incorporate music into their teaching today. This chapter is about reclaiming the power of learning through music and restoring the sense that music belongs to all of us.

Music, and all the expressive arts, are a primary avenue for building cooperation and experiencing community. When we don't use them this way, but use them to reinforce ranking or reify elites, we're cutting off a direct access to partnership.

When I was training teachers in Montana, several spoke about the pressure and hurt they experienced while playing in elementary school orchestras. Whether they were ranked first or last chair, they felt uncomfortable to sit in that structure, and questioned if that traditional format was helpful or necessary for elementary students. One teacher, Lyndsey Kaufmann, had an "a-ha" about the problem of being labeled, "last chair." We were standing in a closing circle at the end of our class, and the circle-shape had come to symbolize our new experiences of linking not ranking. Lyndsey looked around at the beaming faces of the people, representing a full spectrum of familiarity with music; there were those teachers who had never sung before as well as teachers who had taught others how to play instruments. In a flash of insight, she commented, "There is no last chair in a circle." This is the image to bring into our teaching — we can create a partnership format, a circle where skills are shared and no one will be placed on a bottom rung.[10]

Nick Page writes that music brings power. "Children are born with this power. When given the opportunity to shine with all their might through music and through the arts, children don't need the negative powers available in society. For cultures all around the planet, the expression of music is the expression of self. When an individual makes music, he or she is saying, *'This is my power. This is who I am. No one can take this from me.'* When a group sings, they become as powerful as stars, not a destructive hierarchical power where self-worth depends on being better than someone else, but a living power where self-worth depends on the interdependence of all" (Page, 1995, pp. 12-13).

In this chapter we look at how partnership structures bring back the joy of group singing and help students experience music as a place where the river of human life feels all the more palpable. We'll see nine lesson plans that introduce partnership content using song lyrics. Next, we'll look at a national organization that focuses upon music and partnership, the Children's Music Network, and hear about the songs of its members, ending with Ruth Pelham's engaging song, "Under One Sky."

Guidelines for Music and Partnership

1. Music belongs to all of us.

Talk together as a class about how to create a safe atmosphere for singing. Make agreements together, like, "We won't make fun of anyone's way of singing." And, "no one needs to apologize for their voice, including the teacher." Put up a sign in the room that says, "We are all are music makers."[11]

In other words the question is not — are you a music maker? The question is — how do you enjoy and participate in music?

2. Share music from many cultures and many musical styles.

Look for times in the day to put on listening music — when arriving, during writing, during art, during clean-up, while lining up. Broaden the students' listening experiences by sharing a wide variety of styles and cultures whether they be cajun music, Indian ragas, European classical, Armenian instrumentals, or contemporary music from the continent of Africa.

Be sure to share music from all the cultures represented in the classroom. Invite students or parents to bring in their music.

Envision all music makers and music teachers in partnership — piano teachers, members of Gospel Choirs, rock singers, folk singers, rap singers, Suzuki violin students, conga drum students — each making available the kind of music they love.

3. Make music together without comparing people.

Students don't have to hide their light for everyone to feel welcome in music. Encourage people to share their skills fully in singing, dancing, or playing instruments. Appreciating and receiving what one person offers does not imply that another person has a deficit. If we shift our attitude away from competition and jealousy, sharing our strengths means building the group and contributing, not detracting. Welcome strengths to be shown and shared.

This also involves not comparing ourselves to media stars. Here's a story to share with your class. A third grader wrote many songs, and she was excited when a songwriter came to her school as an artist in residence. The student brought in a song she'd written to share with the guest, but shrugged off the songwriter's praise. The girl said, "My Dad doesn't like my songs. He says I don't sound like the people on the radio." Talk about how the girl felt. What happens when we compare people? What might encourage this girl to keep on writing?

4. Involve students in leading songs and remembering tunes.

Seek out people in the class who are most comfortable with singing and encourage them to help sing. This takes the pressure off the teacher to be in charge of songleading. A teacher can present a song on a tape and ask for volunteers to memorize the tune. Then using song lyrics, these students can lead the class in singing the song.

5. Expect people to be able to write songs.

Set up a tape recorder in the classroom with a blank tape. Explain that this is available to use when someone invents a song and doesn't want to forget it. Songs can burst upon us suddenly, and then evaporate just as quickly as a dream if we don't have a means to "catch" them.

Researchers say that all people create songs at age two or three. All people are able to encapsulate their feelings and observations with a melody as part of growing and developing. Without cultural support, this ability withers and atrophies. If we supported early songwriting the way we support early speech and encouraged children to keep creating more songs, they would retain their songwriting ability.

Some children keep up frequent connection to this impulse to express with song. I met a six-year-old girl when she was picking blueberries with her mother. Knowing I was a songwriter, she told me that she was a songwriting, too. I sat down quietly in the grass with her, and she said she would share a song. It wasn't a song she'd created before. I watched as she allowed it to arise in her. We waited in silence. She would sing a little bit and then halt, listening for more and trusting that more words would thread themselves. Here is what she sang:

> In the hills at night
> the deer is chewing up the grass
> and the owls are making their home.
>
> The sun settles down in her new foundation
> getting all her things done,
> getting ready for the things to come.
>
> by Katie Ellison

I watched her birth expressive form out of nothingness. It was delicate and amorphous and powerful and specific all at the same time, this process of allowing words and melody to arrive. Birthing of nothing into something is not unlike the arising of animate life in our common story of cells begun in the oceans four billion years ago. When we use a partnership approach to the arts, we allow the surprise of finding inside how much we have to express.

<u>Nine Lesson Plans:</u> Song Lyrics that Teach Partnership

These lesson plans model ways to provide partnership messages through music. The activities explore the meaning of the words using partnership processes. The style of music is folk, the genre that is my home base. If folk is not an effective musical style to reach your students, look for general ideas in the lesson plans which can be extrapolated to other styles of music. Also, many of these songs can be used as poems, spoken or chanted rather than sung, or you can put them to a new tune.

Song Activity One: My Roots Go Down — Ecological awareness
Song Activity Two: The Colors of Earth — Human unity and diversity
Song Activity Three: Talk to Me — Conflict resolution
Song Activity Four: Sing About Us — Discussing diversity
Song Activity Five: The Cells Start Moving — Science studies
Song Activity Six: Seeds of Partnership — Prehistory
Song Activity Seven: Seed Savers — Ecological awareness
Song Activity Eight: The Mahogany Tree — The rainforest
Song Activity Nine: The Story of Julia Butterfly — Environmental activism

The first four songs are part of a collection of 46 songs that I developed for children ages three to nine in a book with a CD or cassette recording called *Linking Up: Using Music, Movement and Language Arts to Promote Caring, Cooperation and Communication.* (Educators for Social Responsibility, Cambridge, MA, 1998).

The next five songs show how to use music within your core curriculum of science or social studies to bring in partnership elements. Most of these nine songs are available on recordings:

- *Partnership Songs* has 20 songs for PreK-6th including "My Roots Go Down," "The Colors of Earth," and "The Mahogany Tree."

- *Green Flame* has 13 songs for grades 5 to adult including "Seeds of Partnership," "My Roots Go Down," and "Seed Savers."

- *Linking Up* has forty-six songs for preK-third grade including "Talk to Me," "Sing About Us," "The Colors of Earth," and "My Roots Go Down."

Contact: These recordings can be ordered through the Foundation for Educational Renewal, P.O. Box 328, Brandon, VT 05733 (800) 639-4122 or through the Discovery Center, 63 Main Street, Shelburne Falls, MA 01370, email discover@mtdata.com.

<u>Important Note to Teachers:</u>

These songs and others that you find are to be freely used. You don't need to get permission from the author. Permission is implied by the fact that it has been shared publicly. The copyright sign is a formality. This is true for any song you find in any book or hear on any recording — go ahead and use it. The only time you need to check with a songwriter is if you are creating a recording of the song that you will be selling; then you do contact the author. (Law requires either paying a small royalty, or securing their permission to waive the royalty).

Just as you would tell students the author of a poem or a book, introduce where the song comes from. Example: "We're going to learn a song called, 'World Citizen,' written by Stuart Stotts."

In your teaching you are encouraged to use songs, change words, expand them, and make them your own.

Song Activity One: My Roots Go Down

Children act out movements that connect them to nature.

Ages: 2 to adult

When to use: Cooperative movement game, whole language, or science studies

Language: English

Location: Side 2, Song 33

Source: Sarah Pirtle

Goals: • To create new words and movements
 • To collaborate with others
 • To bond with nature.

Procedure:

Preview the song "My Roots Go Down" to familiarize yourself with the music, the lyrics, and the pattern of the song.

Have the children stand with enough room to move in place without bumping into others. During this song children keep their feet anchored in place and swing their arms, as if their arms were the branches of a tree. During the chorus of the song,

encourage children to feel the earth under their feet. Notice whether children's movements indicate that they are feeling rooted and anchored, Ask the children, "Can you
feel your feet planted firmly on the ground?"

Have the children create different movements as they sing the chorus. For example,
suggest stomping.

Sing verses that connect children to animals, trees, and places in nature.
Some examples:

> *I am a willow swaying in a storm. (3x)*
> *My roots go down.*
> *I am a wildflower pushing through stones. (3x)*
> *My roots go down.*
> *I am a waterfall skipping home. (3x)*
> *My roots go down.*

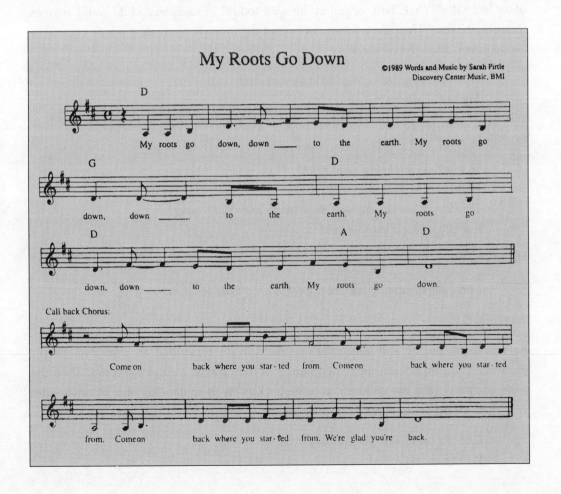

Chorus

My roots go down, down to the earth.
My roots go down, down to the earth.
My roots go down, down to the earth.
My roots go down.

Verse

I am a pine tree on a mountainside.
I am a pine tree on a mountainside.
I am a pine tree on a mountainside.
My roots go down.

Extensions: Children Invent New Words

Ask the children for a suggestion of an animal or something else in nature that they like a lot. Ask: "What shall we put in the song today?" Example: A child could answer, 'Jumping beans." Then the teacher can extend the thought to create a whole verse. The group jumps as everyone sings:

I am a jumping bean, jumping to the sun. (3x)
My roots go down.

Whenever possible, ask the children to expand upon their ideas and use their words to extend the verse. Example:

Teacher: *What do you want to be?*
Isabelle: *Dolphins.*
Teacher: *What do you want the dolphins to do in the song?*
Isabelle: *Dive into the waves.*

New Verse

I am a dolphin diving into the waves (3x) My roots go down.

Traveling Game

Review the recording and notice the variations in the lyrics that are provided. In this game the children act out their own verses as they travel around the room. Then the revised chorus calls the children to come back from their dancing and sit once more with their group on the floor or on their chairs:

Come on back where you started from. (3x)
We're glad you're back.

Plan the area that will be used for large movement. Use a scarf or rope to close off any areas from the room as "out of bounds." Clarify the boundaries of where the children can move. Set clear agreements. Examples: stay on the rug, or stay in the middle of our circle of chairs, or the rope closes off our block area so we won't dance in there.

Using the songwriting method described above, ask one child to decide what animal or other part of nature everyone will be as they dance.

Set agreements for safe group movement. Examples: remember to look out for each other, or no bumping.

Children dance and dramatize the story that has been created until the "call back" chorus of the song calls the group to go back to their original places.

> **Verse**
> *I am a deer running in the wind. (x3) and come on back.*
> **Chorus**
> *And come on back where you started from. (3x)*
> *we're glad you're back.*

Snapshot

Expanding on children's ideas, here's how the Eggs in the Nest game first got started. When I invited first graders in Point Reyes, California, to make the shape of a nest, to my surprise, one boy unexpectedly got inside the center of the nest and curled up very small. "I'm a rotten egg," he said. The class had been reading a chapter of *Charlotte's Web* that morning, where a rotten egg makes a big stink in the farmyard. Knowing that he often made disparaging comments about himself, I wanted to explore what would happen if I worked with the image and offered more possibilities. "Rotten?" I said. "It looks like there's a bird growing inside here." I led the group in singing new words: "This is the day the new bird is born." We watched as he gradually uncurled himself and came out of the shell as a newborn eagle. Then others took turns being eggs in the center and emerging.

Check on the agreements. Discuss if anyone bumped into anyone else. Make sure that all feel safe as they travel. On the recording this process is modeled:

> Ryan: *Let's go—I am a bear catching fish.*
> Peter: *But last time we did that somebody caught me.*
> Teacher: *What agreements could we make?*
> Ryan: *How about if we say that the people aren't the fish.*
> *We're all the bears and we have to pretend we see fish.*

Give other children a chance to create new verses. Add reminders or additions to the "story framework" that are necessary to ensure that all will feel safe.

Variation

Instead of all children dancing at once, pick four at a time to dance while the others sing. Singers clap, tap their legs, or drum on the floor to retain their interest.

Birds in Flight

Review the lyrics on the recording.

> *I am a bird flying through the sky. (3x)*
> *And come back to your nest.*

Make a nest by joining hands with your whole group or in small groups of three to eight people. Children ages five to eight enjoy inventing their own ways to link with each other, either standing or sitting (i.e., all hands in the center like spokes of a wheel or hands up high meeting in the middle like a roof).

To help children be aware of each member of their group, ask them to wave good-bye before they leave the nest. Children fly away from the nest as they dance, then return and form the nest shape again.

> Tip:
> Use the eggs in the nest game to bring a feeling of calm to your class. This game has a particular poignancy. As children have the chance to transition from being in an egg to pecking their way out and being greeted by friendly faces, a hush and expectancy comes over the game. Take time in the narration to help the children emerge slowly from their eggs.

Science Extension

Be an Eagle - Eagles are social birds and enjoy gathering together when they aren't raising their young ones. Explore what it would feel like to fly with the strength of the eagle. Imagine watching an eagle soaring above the plains. The bald eagle's broad wings stretch as far as seven feet. Think about the way an eagle can look from high above and spot tiny objects. Ask children to fly with the feeling of an eagle.

Eggs in the Nest

Ask for volunteers to pretend to be eggs curled up in the center of the nest. Those standing around them are the parents waiting for the babies to be born.

Tell the children, "This is the day the eggs are waking up. The baby birds inside the eggs feel warmth and they start to peck their way out of the shells. Their parents are waiting. They are so glad to see them come out of their eggs. When they are ready the parents teach them to fly."

Encourage those children playing the parent birds to help the babies fly around the space. Sing words that relate to the process.

Examples:

> *Show us your strong wings as you fly.*
> *We're happy to see you flying with us.*
> *The babies are learning to fly so far.*
> *Now come back to your nest.*

Cooperation in Small Groups

Divide the class into small groups of three to five children who will move together, sitting or standing, on each verse. Ask them to sit or stand together in a circle. Provide verses that lend themselves to collaboration:

- *We are whales swimming with our friends. (3x)*
  And come on back.
- *We are a stream with swirling ripples. (3x)*
  And come on back.
- *We are flowers opening to the light. (3x)*
  And come on back.
- *We are monkeys jumping through the vines. (3x)*
  And come on back.

After the children have collaborated on acting out verses you suggest, have them work in their small groups to develop their own dance using a verse that they make up. Invite each group to show their dance to the whole class.

Snapshot

Cooperative Songwriting - A classroom of second graders in Conway, Massachusetts, assembled in groups of three. For their science studies each individual had studied an animal she particularly liked. First, they each discussed the animal's habits, and then chose a phrase to form the verse of the song. Next, they created motions to go with their animals. Here is a verse from one of the small groups:

> *I'm a sidewinder snake sliding over the desert.*
> *I am a prairie dog popping from my hole.*
> *I am a lion prowling the savanna.*
> *My roots go down.*

All three children acted out all three animals,together, changing from snakes, to prairie dogs, to lions.

When experience with collaboration is limited, participation within the groups may be uneven. One child may dominate and not listen to the ideas others offer. Some may look away or distract others. If needed, guide your class step by step through the process of collaboration:

Step One: Provide a clear image in the verse, like "We are beavers building a new lodge."

Step Two: Ask each person on his own to create a movement that is the story framework the group selected.

Step Three: Number off (each child gets a number from 1 to 3, 4, or 5). One at a time have each child show her movements to the group. For example, to the words, "We are beavers building a new house," one person might decide to concentrate on tapping the mud, while another thinks of carrying branches. Let the children know that it is okay to pass.

Step Four: Say, "Put all the ideas together. Make sure to use at least one idea from each person."

Song Activity Two: The Colors of Earth

Children recognize their diversity and common connection to the each.

Ages: 3 and older

When to use: To complement language arts and social studies curricula

Language: English

Location: Side 1, Song 1

Source: Sarah Pirtle

Goals: • to recognize our basic unity and diversity

 • to initiate anti-bias discussions

Procedure:

1. Teach the chorus of the song to the children. Variation: Use American Sign Language.

2. Focus on the first verse of the song and facilitate a class discussion on the colors of our eyes. Ask: "How do you describe the color of your eyes? How is the color of your eyes mentioned in the song?" Clarify that the "topaz" is

a brown gemstone. "Is there a different way you'd describe the color of your eyes?" (For example, first graders have said "seaweed color" and "blueberry.") "Take a look at the eyes of the people next to you. How would you describe them?"

> **Tip:**
> Bring colors of the earth into the classroom for this song. Place a multi-colored cloth in the middle of the circle as you introduce the song. Add a bowl of sea shells, chestnuts, acorns, gem stones, and rocks. Each child then selects an item to hold as everyone sings together.

3. Focus on the second verse of the song and facilitate a class exploration of hands. Invite children to work in pairs to look for as many similarities and differences in their hands as they can find. Ask: "How are your hands the same? How are they different?" Discuss the discoveries children have made.

4. If you are playing an instrument to accompany the song, you may prefer to use easier chords than the ones listed in the transcription. The song is recorded and transcribed in the key of A flat. You can also sing it a half step lower in the key of G. Play these chords:

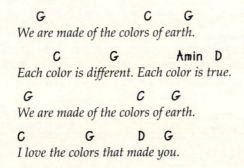

```
G                 C   G
We are made of the colors of earth.
      C       G         Amin D
Each color is different. Each color is true.
G                 C   G
We are made of the colors of earth.
C       G       D   G
I love the colors that made you.
```

Songwriter's note: *The seed for this song was planted when I heard an ecologist and poet from India named Vandana Shiva comment that if we look around at people we see that we all have the same colors as the earth.*

Snapshot

The Earth's Colors: Our Universal Paintbrush - second grade classroom teacher and educational consultant Barbara Rothenberg, from Fort River School in Amherst, Massachusetts, uses "The Colors of Earth" with her second-grade students every year. She teaches them how to interpret the lyrics in American Sign Language. Here is how she ties the song into her curriculum:

In discussing earth's colors the students become aware that these colors are seen by everyone, regardless of where one lives on our planet. There is a sense of a universal paintbrush. This song is a great tool to teach the concept of metaphor. My students explore which colors in nature describe their physical characteristics. We focus on the common frame of reference we all share. By celebrating the beauty of each, we celebrate the beauty of every human being. My students not only explore skin and eye color, but extend their comparisons to hair color, teeth, and lips. Their comparisons range from oyster shells and strawberries, to seal skin, sand dunes, and lily pads."

Barbara likes to use these additional verses that are recorded on my cassette, *The Wind is Telling Secrets.* To highlight the complexity of color, I call attention to the varieties of purples, including the deep purple in the skin of a peach.

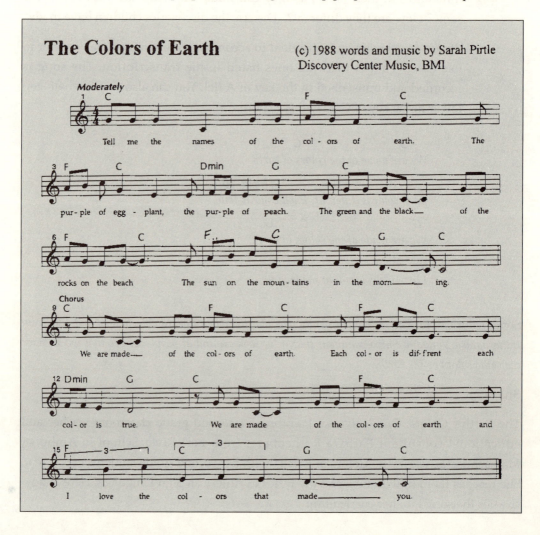

The Colors of Earth   (c) 1988 words and music by Sarah Pirtle
Discovery Center Music, BMI

1. *Tell me the names of the colors of earth.*
   The purple of eggplant, the purple of peach.
   The green and the black of the rocks on the beach.
   And the sun on the mountains in the morning.

2. *Earth that I love, do you know how I feel?*
   How much I love seashells? How much I love stones?
   When I walk barefoot through the fields all alone.
   I sing out a song to the morning.

Verse 2

When I look in the eyes of my friends,
I can see topaz, I can see sky.
The green and the gray of the sea
rolling by and the dazzling brown river in the morning

Chorus

Verse 3

When I look at the hands of my friends,
I can see chestnut, I can see corn.
The color of wheat fields and a dappled brown fawn,
And the rain-kissed black trees in the morning.

Chorus

Verse 4

Earth that I love, do you know how I feel?
How much I love seashells, how much I love stones?
When I walk barefoot through the fields all alone
I sing out a song to the morning.

Chorus

Extensions

Whole Language Songwriting

Option A - Write your own verse about eye color. List all the colors as the children describe their eyes. Make sure that everyone is included in the way they want to be included. Arrange the colors within the verse pattern. The lines do not have to rhyme.

Sample Pattern

    When I look in the eyes of my friends.
    I can see _____, I see _____,
    And _____ like _____, and _____ like _____
    I see _____ when I look at you.

Example

> *When I look in the eyes of my friends*
> *I can see seaweed, I see gray ocean.*
> *and brown like the tree trunks and blue*
> *like the waves, I see sparkles like cat's*
> *eyes when I look at you.*

Option B - Write your own verse about hands. Make a list of all the observations partners made (see #3 in the song activity) and craft the words into new verses.

Sample Pattern

> *When I look at the hands of my friends.*
> *I see _____ and _____,*
> *Some have _____ and _____*
> *And we have _____*

Example

> *When I look at the hands of my friends,*
> *I see long fingers and short fingers, too.*
> *Some have scars and we all have veins.*
> *And we have lines on our palms like*
> *tree branches.*

Art Activity

Materials: Multicultural crayon

Have pairs of children compare their hands. Ask the children to focus on all the details that emerge, such as lines, scars, freckles, and the shapes of their fingers. Then help children to pair up with a new partner and use these details to examine more differences and similarities between their hands.

Each child then traces his or her partner's hand on a sheet of drawing paper. Children decorate their own hands by drawing in as many details as they can. They can depict the back of their hand or their palm. Post the hands on a bulletin board with lyrics to the song or with their songwriting.

Literature Activity

Materials: *All the Colors of the Earth* by Sheila Hamonaka (New York: William Morrow, 1994)

Read *All the Colors of the Earth* to the children. Children ages three to nine enjoy the beautiful illustrations and works. Coincidentally, the song and the book relate to each other, although they were written independently. One of the many wonderful aspects of this book is that children who are biracial and children who are albino can find themselves in the illustrations.

Anti-Bias Activity

"The Colors of Earth" can help initiate discussions about bias and about ways to change bias to fairness. Share these messages with children: "It's not skin or hair color or any way that we look that creates the problem of discrimination. Discrimination happens when one group of people tries to say they are better and tries, unfairly, to claim more privileges. Who we are right now is beautiful. All eye colors are good eye colors. All skin colors are good skin colors. All kinds of hair are good."

Song Activity Three: Talk To Me

Grade level: PreK - 3rd

Overview: A song provides practice in choosing to talk out a problem instead of walking away or fighting. Use this song to teach these skills: how to share upset feelings constructively, and how to identify what would help next time. These lyrics work just as well if you say or chant them instead of singing.

Goals: To be able to say, "Talk to me."
To be able to say, "Next time … " and describe what you would like to have happen in the future.

Equipment: Two puppets.

Source: The first verse is from "¡Dilo! Talk To Me" written by Sarah Pirtle, Roberto Díaz, Luz Rodríguez, as recorded in *Linking Up!* The additional verses are by Sarah Pirtle.

Procedure:
1. Puppet demonstration:
Show a story with the puppets and tell it in such a way that the puppets can be either gender. Here's an illustration with a monkey and a turtle puppet.

Story: Monkey and Turtle were friends and played together at recess every day. One day they were playing ball. At first it was fun. Then Monkey kept missing the ball because there were bugs that kept biting Monkey's eyes. And Turtle began thinking so much about how high the ball could go that Turtle forgot to notice Monkey. Turtle threw the ball so high it was very hard to catch. Monkey got madder and madder and finally tossed the ball really hard. Hey! (show them turning their backs). Monkey thought — "I feel like fighting Turtle." Turtle thought, "I feel like running away and finding someone else to play with."

And then they remembered that they were friends. There had to be something they could do. And so this is what they said: (begin the chant and show them gradually begin to turn toward each other).

> *Talk to me. I know it's not easy.*
> *Talk to me. Don't give up now.*
> *Talk to me. It's really important.*
> *I want to be friends.*
>
> *Talk to me. What are you feeling?*
> *Talk to me. And I will listen.*
> *Talk to me. We'll figure this out.*
> *I want to be friends.*

Ask the students to supply words that Monkey and Turtle would say to each other. Show them sharing how they are feeling, explaining what the problem is, and expressing what they want to have happen next time.

Monkey: I feel so mad. The bugs keep biting my eyes and I can't see what I'm doing. I felt upset when you didn't notice that I was stopping to brush them out of my eyes and you kept throwing it higher than I could catch.

Turtle: I feel mad, too. When you threw the ball really hard, there was no way I could catch it. I guess I was really thinking a lot about throwing that ball as high as I could. Next time, I'll notice you more, and I'll stop if you need to stop.

Monkey: Next time I'll tell you what's going on for me, and I'll tell you when I'm angry instead of throwing the ball at you.

Turtle: Okay. Do you still want to play?

Monkey: Yeah. Let's play some place where there aren't so many bugs.

Turtle and Monkey: We're still friends.
Then end the puppet play with these words:

> *I hear you now. I see what's the problem.*
> *I hear you now. I know we can solve it.*
> *I hear you now. We'll make a new plan.*
> *I want to be friends.*

Note: Teachers can invent their own tune to these lyrics or chant the words instead of singing them.

Spanish words for first verse:

> *Dime. Yo sé que es difícil.*
> *Dime. No debes rendirte.*
> *Dime. Es muy importante.*
> *Yo quiero ser amigos. (o que conservemos nuestra amistad).*

2. Demonstration with teacher and a student: Use the song itself instead of the whole story. Start with backs turned in anger. Gradually turn toward each other to face each other and show your intention to talk it out. Repeat the song/chant above while doing motions. Ask the group to sing along on the repeating phrases, "Talk to me," "I want to be friends," and "I hear you now."

3. Partners form two lines facing each other. Clarify the goal: To feel what it's like to remember that you can talk to someone when you are having a problem. First, ask them to practice pantomiming throwing a ball to each other. Now ask them to decide what kind of problem they will pretend to have as they are playing ball. They can use the same story they saw the puppets do or they can invent their own story. Make it clear that the story will be done without actually touching each other or pretending to fight.

Curtain Up. Enter the story framework together. They play ball, then show the conflict. Ask them to turn their backs.

Begin the first two verses of the song. In the first verse, their backs are turned but they keep peeking around at each other. In the second verse, they face each other. Now stop the song and ask them to talk out the pretend conflict. End with the third verse. Ask them to choose a motion at the end to indicate they are friends now, such as shaking hands. Curtain down.

4. Post the words, sit and sing them or say them together so they become more familiar. Discuss what happens in the sequence. Ask if any partners want to share how they talked out their conflict. While the group reads or sings, they show everybody how they acted it out. As the song/chant stops, they replay the role play of what they said to each other.

5. Closure: Ask partners to sit together and tell each other something they enjoyed about working with the other person today.

<u>Song Activity Four:</u> "Sing About Us" — Exploring Our Diversity

Grade level: Pre-K - 6th

Goals: To discuss the diversity present in the room.
　　　　To look at many dimensions of diversity and expand thinking.
　　　　To set a positive direction: You don't have to be just like me to be my friend.

Source: "Sing About Us" by Sarah Pirtle (*Linking Up!* recording, Educators for Social
　　　　Responsibility).

Procedure:

1. Preparation: Decide how to use the lyrics provided. Think about whether to chant
　them as a poem, invent a tune, or learn the tune sung on the *Linking Up!* recording.

> *Chorus: Sing about us. Tell me again.*
> *You don't have to be just like me to be my friend, be my friend.*
> *You don't have to be just like me to be my friend.*

Variation: The phrase "sing about us" may be modified to "talk about us" so that the
activity can be done chanted or spoken and not just sung.

> *Poem: Talk about us. Tell me again.*
> *You don't have to be just like me to be my friend, be my friend.*
> *You don't have to be just like me to be my friend.*

2. Use this pattern to explore any dimension of diversity: Eye color, types of hair,
　favorite foods, heritage.
> *Some of my friends _____.*
> *Some of my friends _____.*
> *Some of my friends _____.*
> *You don't have to _____ to be my friend.*

Choose a dimension of diversity and ask students to list all the differences within that
dimension. Use the student's own words in the framework of the song. Notice that you
can fit either one or two items on each of the three lines in the pattern.

Diversity of eye color:

Some of my friends have brown eyes or blackish brownish.
Some of my friends have blue eyes or bluish greenish.
Some of my friends have green eyes or hazel eyes.
You don't have to look the way I look to be my friend.

Diversity of learning styles:

Some of my friends learn songs by reading the words.
Some of my friends learn songs by hearing the words.
Some of my friends learn songs by doing sign language.
You don't have to learn the way I learn to be my friend.

Diversity of favorite foods:

Some of my friends like to eat chili dogs.
Some of my friends like to eat corn fritters.
Some of my friends like to eat sushi.
You don't have to eat what I like to eat to be my friend.

Diversity of current concerns:

Some of my friends are thinking about lunch right now.
Some of my friends are thinking about their new bandaid.
Some of my friends are thinking about the wind outside.
You don't have to think the same as me to be my friend.

Diversity of heritage and ethnicity:

Some of my friends are Puerto Rican or Irish.
Some of my friends are Mohawk or French Canadian.
Some of my friends are Cambodian or European American.
You don't have to be just like me to be my friend.

Song Activity Five: The Cells Start Moving

Grade level: 2nd - 6th

Overview: Evolution of life on earth is taught with a song and timeline.

Source: New words by Sarah Pirtle to the traditional tune, "The Ants Go Marching."

1. Introduction: Explain that cells are the basic structure of independent life. They evolved from organic compounds. The first cells developed into food-producing cells and then to multi-celled animals. Convey the information that human beings are made of billions of cells. Say to students: "For a moment, hold this in your imagination and really try to feel this reality. Stand up for a minute. Wiggle like cells as you are thinking about this fact — we have billions of cells."

2. Make a yarn timeline to show evolving life on earth:

Prepare a 38 foot piece of string or yarn by marking segments. Ask students to help stretch it. Option: Put the string timeline into a hat and pull it out. (The originator of this timeline activity is unknown).

38 feet = 4.5 billion years ago. The timeline starts at the point when our sun began as interstellar gas clouds collapsed. The earth formed 4.45 billion years ago when swirling elements circled this newly-birthed sun.

4 feet and 2.6 inches from the beginning = 4 billion years ago water vapor condensed with the cooling of the earth to form seas. In the seas the first cells began and slowly began to evolve.

Now calculate from the other end of the string which marks the present:

8 feet and 5 inches from the present = 1 billion years ago. Evolution accelerates as cells learn to merge and retain two nuclei (meiotic sex). Now life can invent more varied genetic combinations.

5 feet from the present = jellyfish and flat worms begin.

10.7 inches from the present = dinosaurs appear 235 million years ago.

6.8 inches from the present = birds

1/4 inch from the present = first humans appear 2.6 million years ago

1/2,000 of an inch from present = Sumerian civilization 3,500 B.C.E.

3. Use this song as a way to "enter" the timeline. Give out the lyrics and sing together. Next, create movements to act out the song.

The Cells Start Moving

Tune: "The Ants Go Marching One by One"

Words: by Sarah Pirtle

> 1) *The cells start moving one by one, hurrah, hurrah.*
> *The cells start moving one by one, hurrah, hurrah.*

Lightning flashes on the sea, and simple cells start to be.
And we all keep dancing under the sun. What's yet to come?

Refrain: *Bom, bom, bom, bom. Bom, bom, bom, bom.*

2) *You can't fool a molecule, hurrah, hurrah.*
   You can't fool a molecule, hurrah, hurrah.
   We'll get genetic memory, and have more creativity.
   And we all keep dancing under the sun. What's yet to come?

3) *Jellyfish and worms come in, hurrah, hurrah.*
   Jellyfish and worms come in, hurrah, hurrah
   To get a backbone is our wish, so with a swish come the first fish.
   And we all keep dancing under the sun. What's yet to come?

4) *To leave the sea you know we oughta, hurrah, hurrah,*
   Find a way to carry water, hurrah, hurrah.
   The ferns and moss in a chain, keep water in their own membrane.
   And we all keep dancing under the sun. What's yet to come?

5) *Big and little start to soar, hurrah, hurrah.*
   The insects and the dinosaur, hurrah, hurrah.
   When the plants start to flower, the mammals can begin their hour.
   And gonna make a change heroic, hurrah, hurrah.
   We'll bring about the Ecozoic, hurrah, hurrah.
   The earth is teaching how to mend. New life awakes in us again,
   so we all keep dancing under the sun, cuz we're what's to come.

"Ecozoic Era" is a new term from Thomas Berry. (The Universe Story by Brian Swimme and Thomas Berry, Harper SanFrancisco, 1994). The Cenozoic Era has in effect ended because humans have caused species extinction, cut down rainforest, and devastated biodiversity. It is a mammoth event to begonna make a change heroic, hurrah, hurrah.

We'll bring about the Ecozoic, hurrah, hurrah.
The earth is teaching how to mend. New life awakes in us again,
so we all keep dancing under the sun, cuz <u>*we're*</u> *what's to come.*

"Ecozoic Era" is a new term from Thomas Berry. (The Universe Story by Brian Swimme and Thomas Berry, Harper SanFrancisco, 1994). The Cenozoic Era has in effect ended because humans have caused species extinction, cut down rainforest, and devastated biodiversity. It is a mammoth event to be part of a new era. We can join in creating an Ecozoic Era by becoming responsible for our actions.

<u>Song Activity Six:</u> The Seeds of Partnership Song

Grade level: 5th - 12th

Goals: To contribute information about prehistory to social studies units
       To enhance discussions about human nature, violence and nonviolence.

Source: Words and music by Sarah Pirtle, ©2000. On *Green Flame*, from Discovery
       Center Music, available from the Foundation for Educational Renewal.

Procedure:

1. Discuss: Have there been cultures that existed without making war on other groups?

2. Provide information about societies that related to each other by trading rather than
   by invasion or warfare. Add information on Neolithic societies using *The Chalice and
   the Blade, Tomorrow's Children*, or the summary found in Chapter Six in Activity 11
   called "What the Spirals Say." These relate the archeological interpretations of Marija
   Gimbutas. You can use a short timeline activity, "The Lost History of Peace," in
   Chapter Six as an introduction to the song.

3. As the class listens to the song, encourage them to allow the images to evoke pictures, like a movie in their mind. Explain that they will be asked to pick out one
   moment in the song that was most vivid for them.

Either read the lyrics as a poem, or play the song on the recording, *Green Flame*.

"Seeds of Partnership"
words and music by Sarah Pirtle © 2000

> *1. You and I were there when we beheld the gift of fire.*
> *The lightning lit the grass and set the burning.*
> *You and I were there when we chipped the grindstone round,*
> *we shaped the wheel and each hand helped its turning.*
>
> *Chorus: And when I worked with you, seeds were born anew,*
> *the earth wrapped us around, and the plants told what is true.*
> *We built the village homes, carved the snake's track into stone,*
> *And the seeds of partnership were planted.*
>
> *2. You and I lifted clay. We formed pots to hold the grain,*
> *baked in sun and blessed in rain, with spirals twining.*
> *You and I hand in hand as the longest dance began*
> *and the ground around us rang with circles winding.*

Chorus: The chalice of my heart holds the seeds of this dance.
Through centuries of winter I've held on to the chance,
that you will come with me, peace is deep in memory,
and the seeds of partnership be planted again.
Yes, I will come with you, we have not lost what we can do
and the seeds of partnership we're planting again.

3. The warriors came on horseback and they rode our village round.
They took us prisoner, trampled our pottery and tore our houses down.
But the lost times of peace are a vision that won't cease
and the seeds of partnership we carry again.

4. I go back to the cave where the carvings have been stored,
where the ancient prayers were poured with sacred singing.
You and I were there when the hallowed metal bowl,
that had kept our people whole, ceased its ringing.

Though the horsemen came and taught us to be afraid,
they taught us to kill, and changed the chalice for the blade.
We break this chain. We call out the Mother's name,
and the seeds of partnership are planted again.

For now it is winter, still I can feel the spring.
And with each new day I am learning
to plant these seeds again, turn enemy to friend.
that the seeds of partnership be planted.
There's a chalice in my heart, that is where the healing starts
and the seeds of partnership are planted again.

3. Discussion questions:
   What stays with you most from the song?
   Could you imagine yourself in any of these settings or time periods?
   What choices did a non-warring culture have when they were faced with warriors?

4. Writing: Ask students to "pick one moment that stands out for you in the panorama evoked by the song and place yourself there. Write about it imaginatively." Share with a partner.

5. Bring partnership into the present. What experiences of cooperation have you had this week?

<u>Song Activity Seven:</u> Seed Savers

Grade level: 5th-12th

Overview: Preservation of seeds and the loss of traditional agriculture practices are becoming a world wide concern. Use the song as a discussion starter for current events in social studies to make the complex issue easier to understand.

Goals: To apply concepts of partnership and domination to agriculture.
To understand the term, "economic violence."

Source: Words and music by Sarah Pirtle, © 2000. On *Green Flame*, from Discovery Center Music, available from the Foundation for Educational Renewal.

Procedure:

1. Background information: Through this song, we look at the issue of patenting hybrid seeds for monetary gain, unmindful of the effect on other people and on the earth. What is at stake is that a staple of partnership in the world is now being threatened for the first time. Plants produce seeds; farmers for the whole history of agriculture have collected seeds and saved them to plant for the next harvest. For economic gain, companies have found a way to intervene in this process and set themselves up as the source of seeds, at a price.

What is key to understand is that hybrid seeds don't produce crops with viable seeds that can be collected and planted the following year. There are many reasons why hybrid seeds are made, and some viewpoints say that hybrid seeds in and of themselves are not necessarily the problem; what matters is how they are being used. When hybridization is used to dominate the market or when the consequences of hybrids aren't examined, ultimately the whole world community is affected.

Jim Hightower, former Agricultural Commissioner of Texas, writes that corporations are "obtaining patents on indigenous plants that provide food, crops, medicine, income, and other needs of people impoverished regions around the globe." He explains for example, that a company called RiceTec Inc. has "grabbed 17 patents on Basmati rice, a variety that was bred over centuries by poor farmers in India" and when poor farmers plant rice "from saved seeds they must now pay the corporation a royalty." (quoted from Jim Hightower's syndicated column November 17, 2000 entitled, "Biopirates in search of the Plant Wealth.") Physicist Vandana Shiva, author of the book, *Biopiracy*, coined the term "biopiracy" to reveal that these corporations are stealing. These are examples of economic violence.

2. Read from the song lyrics as a poem or play the song on the recording, *Green Flame* by Sarah Pirtle

Seed Savers for Vandana Shiva (words and music by Sarah Pirtle © 2000)

> 1) *I hold a seed, black and small. I plant this seed. I plant for all.*
> *I plant for voices that make no sound.*
> *And it pushes through the briars, and it pushes through the stone.*
> *It's a gift from all people who planted it unknown. It can't be owned.*
> *It's for this our seed goes down. It's for this our seed goes down.*
> *Bridge: Who would place their flag upon a seed?*
> *Who would make this gift their colony?*
> *Who would patent it and just grow greed? This is global piracy.*

> *Chorus: Seed Savers, take back the commons.*
> *Send your seed down.*

> 2) *I hold a seed, flat and sharp. I plant this seed into the dark,*
> *not for the ones who want it bound.*
> *And it pushes through their tyranny. It pushes through their lies.*
> *It pushes through the threat to life their status can't disguise. We must stay wise.*
> *It's for this our seed goes down. It's for this our seed goes down.*

> *Down, down, down, down into the center, the red center of the earth.*
> *No, no, no. No you may not enter. This seed's our right since our birth.*

> *Who will refuse to buy their seed? Who will keep this life pulse guaranteed?*
> *Who will share this common treasury? This is our legacy.*

> *Chorus: Seed Savers, take back the commons.*
> *Send your seed down.*

> 3) *I hold a seed, rough and straight. I plant this seed, it's not too late,*
> *to save this force and pass it on.*
> *And it pushes for the children to know the fight we fight*
> *It passes on its courage, the grit, the hope, the might, oh, yes the might.*
> *It's for this our seed goes down.*

3. Discuss the images of domination in the song:
   - Planting a flag upon a seed
   - Making a seed a colony
   - Piracy

   Discuss the description of partnership in the song:
   - All the people who planted seeds are themselves nameless in history but they have contributed to an ongoing gift from generation to generation.
   - The people who are banding together to organize against biopiracy.

4. Seek out the core of the problem. For the whole history of agriculture, people worked with nature to develop seeds and followed a partnership practice of exhanging seed to improve it. Now this fundamental partnership practice is being supplanted. The groups listed below are working to help make people aware of the consequences of this alarming situation.

Ideas for further research:
   a. Vandana Shiva's group, Global Campaign Against Biopiracy, can be contacted through vshiva@giasd101.vsnl.net.in

   Vandana Shiva received the Right Livelihood Award, an alternative Noble Peace Prize, and has written more than ten books including *Biopiracy*.

   b. Seed Savers at www.seedsavers.org is a group in Iowa with 8000 members that saves heirloom garden seeds from extinction. They have 750,000 types of seeds.

   c. Seeds of Change at www.seedsofchange.com
   Seeds of Change is the first and only national company to offer exclusively 100% certified organic seeds. They are open-pollinated, which means the seeds are produced when plants are allowed to pollinate naturally through insects, wind, and water so that species can cross with one another. This leads to healthier soil and healthier food.

5. Seeds of Change provides this information:

   "What are GMOs? The term "GMO" refers to the genetic modification that has taken place in a plant's DNA to produce certain traits. It is an extremely new technology in plant breeding and has no historical place in plant breeding to date. Seeds of Change sells no "GMOs."

   "What is biodiversity? Simply put, biodiversity is the sum total of all the genetic variation in the world, plant, animal, insect, all organisms. This variation is crucial to the planet's ability to respond to the ever-changing environment. Nature uses this diversity as a fail-safe mechanism against extinction. Seeds of Change is devoted to maintaining plant biodiversity and promoting the use of sustainable, organic agricultural practices."

These concepts help students apply the concept of partnership to science. Discuss and define how partnership and domination practices are occurring today in respect to seed production and agricultural practices, allowing room for many viewpoints.

<u>Song Activity Eight:</u> The Mahogany Tree

Grade level: 1st - 12th

Goals: To enhance science units on protecting the rainforest
        To teach point of view in language arts

Source: Words and music by Sarah Pirtle, © 1990, on *Partnership Songs*, A Gentle Wind
        recording, available from the Foundation for Educational Renewal.

Procedure:

1. Provide this background information: The Selva Lacandona rainforest in eastern Chiapas, Mexico was the home of a small group of Lacandon Maya Indians until 1965, when logging roads bulldozed by timber companies opened the way for cattle-ranchers and peasant villagers, all backed by Mexican government policies. More than half of this rainforest was eradicated by 1987, and the intimate forest life of the native people was altered. The Lacandon Maya watch the mahogany tree to learn about the best time for planting crops. When the flowers drop from the mahogany tree, it signals the time to plant corn.

2. Read from the song lyrics as a poem or play the song on the recording, *Partnership Songs* or the recording, *Magical Earth*, by Sarah Pirtle.

   The Mahogany Tree
   (words and music by Sarah Pirtle, © 1990)

   Chorus: When you see, when you see the mahogany tree.
   Oh, tell me what do you see?
   When you see, when you see the mahogany tree
   in the rainforest of Mexico.

1. *"I see," said the farmer, "my calendar tree.*
Mahogany flowers speak to me.
When the blossoms fall and the petals are torn.
I know that it's time to plant the corn."

2. *"I see," said the great bird, "my butterfly tree.*
The food in her branches speaks to me.
I will feast on the moths that hide at the top
while the monkey howls and the raindrops drop."

3. *"I see," said the logger, "my money tree.*
The promise of lumber speaks to me.
This could bring a price at the company town.
Move the bulldozers in, and I'll cut it right down."

"And I see," said the banker, "my furniture tree.
The shine of the wood speaks to me.
On the forty-fourth floor this could make a fine desk.
Move the bulldozers in and I'll see to the rest."

4. *"Stop," said the child, "It's our grandmother tree.*
I've always known she can speak to me.
She lives in the Mayan memory
as a tree of life for my family."
Last chorus: Come around, come around the mahogany tree.
To cut her down, you'll have to pass by me.
I stand in a circle with my family.
Protect the rainforest of Mexico.
Protect the rainforest of Mexico.

3. Add sounds and pantomime to the song. Divide the class into small groups and assign each one a verse. Assemble instruments and have them devise sounds to match with the work. It's also fun to bring in kitchen utensils and other found objects that make interesting sounds and use these. Add pantomime to illustrate the actions.

4. Extension: The Children's Rainforest
Classes may want to contact The Children's Alliance for Protection of the Environment (CAPE) through Richard Fox, Route 1, Box 246B, Rixeyville, VA 22737. CAPE

has a project creating a Children's Rainforest and a native tree nursery in southern Costa Rica.

It is located on the Osa Peninsula, an area which contains the largest remaining rainforest on the Pacific side of Central America, critical for biodiversity and species preservation. The idea of the Children's Rainforest is that children in schools or clubs from any part of the world raise $100 to protect one acre. Other contributions help the nursery operation. In this project the rainforest is being protected by supporting fourteen families who live on 2,500 acres on the Osa Peninsula. The families are being trained in sustainable forestry and agricultural practices so that they have an alternative to clearcutting. Costa Rican children will also be linked to a Youth Center as part of the project.

Song Activity Nine: The Story of Julia Butterfly

Grade level: 4th-12th

Goal: To chronicle the story of an environmentalist

Procedure:

1. Introduce students to Julia Butterfly Hill who climbed up 180 feet into the branches of Luna, a thousand year old redwood tree, in December 1997 when she was twenty-four. The purpose of her action was to prevent Luna from being cut down by a logging corporation. Julia said:

> "I gave my word to this tree, the forest, and to all the people that my feet would not touch the ground until I had done everything in my power to make the world aware of this problem and to stop the destruction."

Julia lived in the tree without coming back down for two years to prevent the destruction of Luna. Teachers can use the song as a way to summarize her story. Go to the website www.lunatree.org/ to read her poetry and see a photo of the small platform where she lived.

After two years of risking her life, Julia, with the help of members of the US Steelworkers of America, Circle of Life Foundation, and other forest activists, successfully negotiated a permanent protection of Luna and a nearly three-acre buffer zone. However, a year after the signed agreement for Luna's safety was set up, an unknown person made a chainsaw cut two-thirds through the base of Luna. Arborists worked to secure Luna and her fate is not clear at this time. This song, however, is written from the stand-point of Julia at the end of her two years in Luna.

2. Present this as a poem, or engage students in creating their own melody. It's not currently available on a recording. Feel free to make any changes in the lyrics.

The Story of Julia Butterfly (words and music by Sarah Pirtle © 2001)

> 1. When I first met Luna, the tallest redwood on that hill,
> I put my arms around her. I said, "We'll save you with our will.
> The loggers plan to cut you down for their bosses' greed.
> You've been alive a thousand years. Your wisdom's what we need."
>
> Chorus: Sing it from the Spirit. Sing it in a poem.
> Sing it from the branches high up in Luna all alone.
> Sing it to the chainsaws. Sing it to the sky.
> We won't let Luna die, Julia Butterfly.
>
> 2. The first time that I climbed Luna, my arms nearly gave out.
> I tied the ropes and I slid the knots and I made it to the top.
> The platform's small as I can stretch. It holds water, tarps, and food.
> I sleep in the cold, I sleep in the rain, I sleep talking to the moon.
>
> 3.I've lived up here for two long years and I won't give up my ground.
> I've seen chain saws and helicopters, but they cannot scare me down.
> The winter storms have scraped my back and I've felt the freezing wind.
> I'll stay 'til the logging company says they won't come back again.
>
> 4. From this high place I send my voice by phone and radio,
> with the work of thousands on the ground we say Luna must not go.
> If the logging president could be in her branches, too
> He might see that she's alive and give respect the way I do.
>
> 5. The day's here that we worked for, a promise finally made
> Luna's safe. I can come down. It hits like a tidal wave.
> I rest upon my favorite branch with the sky so crystal clear,
> I weep now that I go back down. She says my wings are always here.

Last chorus: Sing it from the Spirit. Sing it in a poem.
Sing it for the ancient trees, you are not alone.
Sing it to the chainsaws. Sing it to the sky.
Fly, fly, fly, fly, Julia Butterfly.

3. To learn more about Julia, use the book, *The Legacy of Luna* by Julia Butterfly Hill, Harper, SanFrancisco, 2000. To contribute to the Luna Protection Fund, write Sanctuary Forest, PO Box 166, Whitethorn, CA 95589. Julia appeared on the "Today Show," after learning of the attack on Luna in November 2000, and shared these words:

"Luna is the greatest teacher and best friend I have ever had. I gave two years of my life to ensure that she could live and die naturally. But two years is nothing compared to the thousand years she has lived, providing shelter, moisture, and oxygen to forest inhabitants. It kills me that the last 3% of the ancient redwoods are being desecrated.... Words cannot express the deep sorrow that I am experiencing but I am as committed as ever to doing everything in my power to protect Luna and the remaining ancient forests."

This is an excerpt of the poem that she wrote:

I heard today …
Luna's been cut.
Two-thirds and maybe more.
Someone in their rage,
in their anger,
in their frustration
struck out at Luna
wanting to hurt Her …
wanting to hurt me
the way they must be hurting inside.
See …
what we do to the Earth
we do to each other.
And how we treat the Earth
is reflected in how we treat each other.
The pain I feel right now that threatens to rip me apart
is the pain I feel every time I see an ancient elder cut …

the pain I feel every time another species goes extinct ...
the pain I feel every time someone yells at a child ...
When do we begin to look at where this DIS-EASE begins?
In the disconnection from the sacred
In the disconnection from the heart ...

Julia Butterfly
Sunday, November 26, 2000

(Julia's poem appeared in "Luna: Tragedy Among the Ancient Redwoods," *Spirit of Change Magazine*, January/ February 2001)

Partnership Music Resource:
The Children's Music Network

Contact: The Children's Music Network, P.O. Box 1341, Evanston, IL 60204-1341.

Web Site: www.cmnonline.org

Classroom teachers can find songs for their students that talk about important themes through the Children's Music Network, known as CMN. The organization was founded in the 1980's specifically to increase contact and support among all the people who care about quality music for young people. CMN states, "We recognize children's music as a powerful means of encouraging cooperation, celebrating diversity, building self-esteem, promoting respect and responsibility for our environment, and cultivating an understanding of nonviolence and social justice."

The network links classroom teachers, music educators, full-time and part-time performers, professional and amateur songwriters, record producers, distributors, broadcasters, parents, grandparents, and children. It's a non-profit organization that has members across the United States and Canada. CMN connects people in search of meaningful music and features lyrics that are savvy about curricular and developmental issues. Through CMN teachers discover songs that fit their units of study — such as songs on endangered species, or about diverse families.

Often times teachers wonder why they haven't been aware of these resources before. Due to the way the music industry and distribution system is organized like a pyramid, the majority of educator songwriters and performers aren't readily visible. Dedicated performers who are also skillful teachers abound in this country and through CMN they connect and learn from each other's work. Looking through the lenses of the dominator paradigm of the music industry, children's performers would be seen as being in competition for sales and for fans, and being known would be equated with being valuable. The Children's Music Network operates within a partnership paradigm. Songwriters and performers not only interact in cooperation, but regard all people as generators of music and emphasize the community building aspect of music.

All ages come together through the CMN journal, *Pass It On!*, and through regional and national gatherings where workshops offer a chance to sample a wide variety of music providing a wide range of topics such as "Bilingual Music," "Songwriting with Students," "Environmental Music," "Songs for Older Elementary," and "Songs about Social Skills." In place of concerts that feature one star performer, at the CMN gatherings a partnership process is used. Every person who wants to perform is able to offer a song. To keep it egalitarian, names are put in a hat, and drawn at random to determine the order of presentation. For instance, at one CMN national gathering held in Los Angeles, the varied performers included six-year-old Madeline Brener who performed a parody that she had written of "Hush Little Baby;" Ruth Pelham who brings her Music Mobile to urban neighborhoods in Albany, Troy, and Schenectady; and the Hoose Family who presented a song that father and daughter, Phil and Hannah Hoose, wrote together called "Hey Little Ant."

The CMN Journal, *Pass It On!* has been used in graduate school courses for teachers because it provides new lesson plans as well as featured songs, and opens windows about a variety of ways to use music in the classroom. Gender equality in the lyrics of children's music was the theme of the Spring 2000 issue of *Pass It On!* Articles included, "Girls Voices Rising: Sending New Messages in Songs," and "A Remembrance of Malvina Reynolds." Back issues are available.

Educator and songwriter Tom Hunter from Bellingham, Washington, puts it this way in a song:

> *May the work we do, make the world we live in*
> *a little more worthy of our children.*
> *May the songs we sing, make the world we live in*
> *a little more worthy of our children.*

To find meaningful songs for the classroom, here is a list of educator/ songwriters and songleaders, each listed with one of their books, videos, or recordings. To locate these resources, order through any independent bookstore or children's toy store, look for a website, or contact the national office.

The number of CMN members who offer resources is actually much longer than this; these are just the CMN members who have led educational workshops at CMN National Gatherings. As you scan the list, there may be only a few names you recognize, but each has made significant contributions to learning through music. The power of partnership is that it creates broader lenses and more potential is available.

Peter and Ellen Allard -
   Sing Shalom: Songs for Jewish Holidays
Peter Alsop - When Kids Say Goodbye (video)
Lisa Atkinson - The Elephant in Aisle Four
Fran Avni - Happy Chanukah
Anne Leif Barlin - *Move and Be Moved* (book)
Marcia Berman - I'm Not Small
Bob Blue - What Matters (video)
Jacki Breger - Sing This Song
Kim and Jerry Brodey - Let's Help This Planet
Janice Buckner - Everybody's Special
Uncle Ruthie Buell - Take a Little Step

Sandy Byer - A Bedtime Story
Tim Cain - Tim and the Trees
Mimi Brodsky Chenfeld -
   Teaching in the Key of Life (book)
Dan Crow - Oops
Lydia Adams Davis - Gift of Story
Katherine Dines - Hunk-ta-Bunk-ta-Boo
Jan Dombrower - Get to Know Your Feelings
John Farrell - *Songs and Storytelling* (book)
Cathy Fink and Marcy Marxer -
   Pillow Full of Wishes
Fran Friedman - Songs for a Smile

Pearly Gates - Songs for a Healthy World
Jackson Gillman - Downeast Ballads
Red Grammer - Teaching Peace
Joanne Hammil - The World's Gonna Listen
Bill Harley - You're In Trouble
Monty Harper - Imagine That
Kim and Reggie Harris -
   Songs of the Underground Railway
Phil Hoose - *It's Our World, Too* (book)
Tom Hunter - Memories
Dave Kinnoin - The Earth's Birthday Sing-along
Bonnie Lockhart - Plum Pudding
Larry Long - Elders' Wisdom
Kate Munger - The Lullabye Tape
Ingrid Noyes - Earth Day, Every Day
Bruce O'Brien - Love is in the Middle
Jose-Luis Orozco - *De Colores* (book)
Caroline Parry - *Let's Celebrate*
   Canada's Special Days (book)
Suni Paz - Abecelebramos
Tom Pease - Daddy Starts to Dance

Ruth Pelham - Under One Sky
Sarah Pirtle - Two Hands Hold the Earth
Sue Ribaudo - Reach to the Sky
Sally Rogers - What Can One Little Person Do?
Betsy Rose - Motherlight
Nancy Schimmel - All in This Together
Ann Shapiro and Tom Callihan -
   Let's Clean Up Our Act
Pete Seeger - Abiyoyo
Patricia Shih - Big Ideas!
Nancy Silber - Dinosaurs,
   Dolphins and Dreams
Stuart Stotts - One Big Dance
Rachel Sumner - Sleepytime Lullabies
Barb Tilsen - Make a Circle Like the Sun
Ben Tousley - Lookin' For a Rainbow
Nancy Tucker - Glad That You Asked
Two of a Kind - Love Makes a Family
Elise Witt - Open the Window
Lesley Zak - Walk Dance Talk Sing
Patty Zeitlin - *A Song is a Rainbow* (book)

Teachers may be interested to find books based upon songs which can be skillful teaching tools. The colorful book, *Earthsong* (NY: Dutton, 1998), for instance, features Sally Rogers' song, "Over in the Endangered Meadow," illustrated by Melissa Bay Mathis. Sally did extensive research on endangered animals and ingeniously wove it into the traditional song, "Over in the Meadow." Rogers details facts about the Bengal tiger, black-footed ferret, gila monster, gray wolf, American crocodile, and other animals. See her web site: www.sallyrogers.com.

Spotlight

Hey Little Ant by Phil and Hannah Hoose (1998, Berkley: Tricycle Press) is a partnership resource for teachers that has become a runaway bestseller. The book shows an ant talking to a child who is about to crush it. In their dialogue, themes of empathy, bullying, and respect for all living beings are expressed in an engaging and non-didactic manner. We learn that both the child and the ant have families, and when the ant is accused of being a crook, it protests, but "one little chip could feed our town." The child is pressured by friends to squish the ant, and has to make a decision.

> *But all my friends squish ants each day,*
> *Squishing ants is a game we play.*
> *They're looking at me — they're listening, too.*
> *They all say I should squish you.*

The ant tells the child, "If you were me and I were you, what would you want me to do?"

One of the many valuable aspects of the book, is that it allows every reader to wrestle with that dilemma. The book ends not with a solution, but a question, and that question reverberates: "We leave that kid with the raised up shoe. What do you think that kid should do?"

Teachers encourage students to devise their own endings to the book by drawing or writing what they think should happen next. The story can also be used to launch discussions about classroom agreements that help every person feel seen and included, not left out or threatened like the ant.

Educators will find lesson plans that teachers have used to teach this book and a biography of the authors by contacting the web site at www.heylittleant.com.

Closing

The song that I sing most frequently in schools is "Under One Sky," by Ruth Pelham. It sings out about a fundamental concept. The chorus says:

> *We're all a family under one sky.*
> *We're a family under one sky.*

Like a seed traveling, the song plants this message in the minds and hearts of students.

For a recording of the song, contact: Ruth Pelham, Music Mobile, Inc. at P.O. Box 6024, Albany, NY 12206. A video of her work that was made for public television is also available. It's called, "Music Mobile: The Beat Of The Street."

"Under One Sky" has a "zipper format," used frequently by Ruth because she likes to empower children to express their own words. This means that the pattern of the song allows for new words to be zipped into its clear framework.

The verse presents eight phrases in a list which don't have to rhyme. Ruth likes to sing the first verse this way:

> *We're people. We're animals.*
> *We're flowers. And we're birds in flight.*
> *Yes, we're people. We're animals.*
> *We're flowers. And we're birds in flight.*

Another good starting verse is:

> *We're sisters. We're brothers.*
> *We're fathers. And we're mothers, too.*
> *We're teachers. We're neighbors.*
> *We're cousins. And we are friends.*

The song also invites movements.

> *We're hand clappers. We're toe tappers.*
> *We're knee slappers. And we pop our cheeks.*

Or, students can suggest eight activities that can be done seated using their hands, and then they pantomime them while they sing.

> *We hammer. We paint.*
> *We write letters. And we build with clay.*
> *We sew cloth. We do finger-weaving.*
> *We use puppets. And we speak in sign language.*

After suggesting eight activities that can be done standing, students stand up and pantomime while they sing.

> *We swim. We dance.*
> *We climb a rope. And we balance on one foot.*
> *We bounce a basketball. We do jumping jacks.*
> *We climb mountains. And we bike.*

Teachers have used the format for the verse a myriad of ways to create new verses about the things students are feeling, or things they are studying.

> *We're silly. We're angry.*
> *We're curious. And we're very sad.*
> *We're annoyed. We're confused.*
> *We're calm. And we're popping with joy.*

The song can be used to help students consolidate their learning in a subject area.

Teachers from the Belgrade, Montana area who I met while teaching for the Creative Arts in Learning Program of Lesley University collaborated on these versions:

The Digestive System

> *New chorus: It's all one system in our body,*
> *the digestive system in our body.*
>
> *There's the mouth. It chews the food.*
> *There's the salivary glands. They wet the food.*
> *There's the esophagus. It pushes it down.*
> *There's the stomach. It churns the food.*
>
> *There's the small intestine. It absorbs the nutrients.*
> *There's the large intestine. It removes the water.*
> *There's the rectum. It stores the waste.*
> *That's the digestive system. It's how we get our nutrients.*
>
> *by Jim Lubke, Tom Breitbach, and Brian Zimmer*

The Polar Regions

> *New chorus: We all are critters in the polar regions.*
> *We're critters in the polar region.*
>
> *We're pudgy penguins. We don't fly.*
> *We're powerful polar bears. We eat seals.*
> *We're chomping caribou. We run away.*
> *And we're silly seals. We lay on rocks.*
>   by Kristi Crawford, Amy Severance, Jonna Whitman

New versions of "Under One Sky" can also be written to describe the Dewey Decimal System. Each line helps students remember what the numbers in the decimal system stands for, such as: "We are the 900's. You'll find history, We are the 920's. You'll find group biographies." Teachers and librarians Kathy Derby, Barb Oriet, Rebecca Pike, and Joan Schritz developed this idea. Here's one of their verses.

> *We are the 600's. Applied Science.*
> *We are the 700's. Arts and Recreation.*
> *We are the 800's. Literature.*
> *We know what to do for fun and games.*
> *In the 600's, there's Pets and Motors.*
> *In the 700's, there's Sports and Drawing.*
> *In the 800's, there's Plays and Poetry.*
> *We have what you need for fun and games.*

Other teachers use the song with language arts assignments. The verse can chronicle favorite activities or describe summer vacation: "We went to Puffer's Pond. Jumped off the rope swing." Still other versions can detail the wetlands, describe the features of planets in astronomy, list the class rules, or describe all the community workers in a city. Teachers continually find more ways to use the zipper song format of the song to help students integrate their understanding of the subject matter.

"Under One Sky" is a reminder of the intended generosity of music. Songs are meant to be extended, elaborated, and developed to fit any feeling or experience that asks to be shared. May music bring the spirit of shared creativity to lift your classroom and help you feel that music-making rightly belongs to all of us.

CHAPTER TEN

The Conscience of the Earth: Weaving the Theme of Evolution Using the Expressive Arts

by Sarah Pirtle

It was only eighty years ago that astronomers themselves held a vastly different picture of the universe than we do today. "At the beginning of the 1920's," writes John Gribbin in his book *In the Beginning*, "astronomers were only just beginning to comprehend that the stars we see in the sky represent only a tiny fraction of the Universe. With the aid of new telescopes, they discovered that the entire Milky Way system, which is made up of perhaps a hundred billion stars, each more or less like our Sun, is just one island in space, a galaxy" (Gribbin, 1993, p. 3). Today we are in a period of exponential growth of a different type — we grow in understanding our impact on the planet and our responsibility as a species for our actions. The tools we need are different than a more powerful telescope. We need perspective on who humans are on earth, and a way to guide our species from a deep moral core.

A wedding of science and art together helps impart new understanding. Students are active creators of knowledge. Integrating the expressive arts into science reinforces that learning involves directly touching the world and exploring it, not just passively receiving facts. *Tomorrow's Children* encourages us to develop curricula that "show not only intellectually but also experientially, that partnership relations are possible." (p. 14). The expressive arts — whether drawing, poetry, singing, painting, dancing, storytelling, creative dramatics or songwriting — provide direct participation in understanding the fundamental interconnection of life forms.

This means we can take the material that we are teaching in science and expand it three ways: (1) Include the expressive arts to involve our senses and engage multiple intelligences; (2) treat the learning process as a process of collaboration and discovery; and (3) weave the thread that we are part of the continual growth and development of the earth and this carries with it social responsibility.

As a starting point, help students realize that each concept and vocabulary word studied comes from a common treasury of knowledge. This treasury is made of discoveries that unseen people made and passed along. For instance, during a unit on clouds and weather, as we learn to identify the forms of clouds we are joining with people from time immemorial who studied the clouds and learned from them how the weather is moving and changing. If technical words like nimbostratus and altostatus are only dry terms that students ingest for a test, then the meat of learning is lost, but if we join the study of clouds with all of our senses, learning is expanded.

Here's an assignment: Draw the clouds three times this week. Each time make a prediction about what weather that cloud shape signals. Record what the actual weather was the next day. Now take all the drawings in the class on a given day and compare them to pictures in the science book until there is a consensus about what type of clouds you have seen. Perhaps you saw wispy cirrus "mares-tails." Scientists have found that cirrus clouds announce a storm or warm front in the next one to three days. Did this happen? For further assignments write poems about clouds, feel the texture of cotton and form it into a collage, or do movement exploration in pairs, waving hands like clouds.[12]

Ralph Waldo Emerson said, "The Sky is the Daily Bread of the Eyes." Another level of study is to look at clouds with a poet's way of knowing. How do the changing forms in the sky echo changing emotions, changing intentions, changing substances of thought? On each of the three days, draw not only the clouds in the sky, but also draw a symbolic representation of your inner weather inventing a cloud form to describe it. As a class, create words and pictures to describe the various states of inner weather.

The teachers that I've met in the Creative Arts in Learning Program of Lesley University report that storytelling, creative dramatics, music, art, poetry, or movement activities embedded within a unit exponentially increase their students' comprehension of the curriculum. A social studies unit can be summarized through songwriting; students take the facts they have learned and craft verses of a song. Students studying a period of history can enter it by learning its poems, hearing its styles of music, and painting as its painters did. Movement activities can facilitate a deeper understanding of a science unit than rote memorization; actually becoming the parts of the ear and moving the way they function becomes a memorable lesson as shown in Activity 17, "A Pantomime of How the Ear Hears," in Chapter Six. The arts within a partnership paradigm employ multiple intelligences, engage students in partnership processes, involve young people in creating partnership narratives, and support cultural transformation theory by making partnership models tangible.

As we engage students in actively exploring the world, this discovery process has an even larger meaning. One of the key messages for learners is that all of us are important to the story of the earth. This poem conveys it:

> In all the universe, in all time, you are the only you.
> Never before have molecules come together exactly like you.
> Never again will your footsteps be repeated upon the earth.
> Your strength is the strength someone can count on.
> Your thoughts are the thoughts that can make the difference.
> Your life is a life that can move the whole world toward the good.
> Dare to be the person you're meant to be!
>   by Barbara Loots
>   (Ambassador Greeting Cards, Wildwood Press, Canada)

This is what we can and need to tell students. Through everything else we are teaching, we can tell them that they matter to us and ultimately they matter to the world. And through the ups and downs of the day — the lunch room getting too loud, a lost sweater, unexpected interruptions, the sudden blast of a fire drill in the midst of a moment of concentration — that message continues. They are not a nuisance, not one more cog in a learning machine, not someone to be written off; they are to be cherished. Our teaching of science and social studies can be done in such a way that we awaken the wonders of the earth and the wonder of each individual life.

Rachel Carson is a scientist who passionately shared her sense of wonder. She also shouldered responsibility in caring for the earth. Jeannine Atkins describes the life of Rachel Carson in her book, *Girls Who Looked Under Rocks: The Lives of Six Pioneering Naturalists* (Nevada City, CA: Dawn Publications, 2000):

One strand of seaweed might hold thousands of microscopic creatures, as well as periwinkles, starfish and crabs hiding from sea gulls. Rachel always wondered how each life survived. What did it depend on? (p. 36).

In studying the people behind the facts that we learn, students can also see that the quiet thoughts and realizations of one person, and their courageous decisions, ripple out and touch many. Atkins writes:

Rachel's quiet, contented life was interrupted in 1957 by a letter from a friend. Many robins had died, her friend said, after the land near her house was sprayed to kill mosquitoes. Rachel stared at this letter the way she had gazed at the fossils she had found when she was young. Then, she had been amazed at how the earth had changed over millions of years. Now, she realized that humans could change the earth in only a few years…. Five years later in 1962 *Silent Spring* was published (ibid.).[13]

When students learn about the feelings and decisions of people who are part of developing the knowledge they study, then they can more easily visualize themselves as adults sharing responsibility for the world. Science lessons that provide information about the partnership perspective on human nature help students perceive that they are themselves a valuable part of the earth's story.

Here are some guidelines for developing your own partnership lesson plans using the expressive arts:

- **Structure activities so that students can make discoveries.**
  Is the assignment an invitation that directs the learner to explore?
  Can they investigate the subject matter directly and personally?
  Does the activity help them experience learning as a process,
  as an ever-expanding and ever-continuing journey?

- **Provide opportunities for students to express themselves.**
  Is the activity an open-ended activity where they can become
  acquainted with their individual artistic voice?
  Have we allowed for multiple responses and not one right answer
  students have to seek?
  Are we holding them in a partnership learning environment where
  people will respect each other?
  Recognizing that some learners need more structure and guidance,
  have we helped provide stability?

- **Give them a broad view of learning.**
  How can you include the lives of the women and men who
  developed this knowledge?
  How can you inspire them to feel that are partners in expanding
  social evolution?

Riane Eisler's work directs us to align ourselves with "the life generating and nurturing powers of the universe" (*The Chalice and the Blade*, p. xvii). What is transformational about the expressive arts — when used for linking and not ranking — is they help learners find and develop their own creative powers. The arts provide direct experiences of our uniqueness. They also provide a direct experience of being interconnected in community.

The Earth's Story

We are intrinsically part of all humans, part of the earth, part of the universe. At the same time, we are unique individual life forms who will never be again.

This is who we all are. We are encoded to create. When we participate in the arts in a partnership process, we are directly part of human evolution. We are born into intricate human bodies that have ears and eyes and hands and the power of a beating heart, while at the same time we have threads that connect us to a vaster but invisible self. In the one-celled organisms that arose four billion years ago, there were at the same time the latent seeds of the jellyfish and dinosaurs and human beings who would come after. So, we too hold the seeds of what is evolving through us. The green place in us is the name I like to give the place that carries those seeds. Our green voice is our expression of it into the world.

As we encourage exploratory expressive art, we help students maintain this green voice. This is the place inside them that directly connects to wholeness, to unity, to imagination, to wonder. In a sense, we could say that partnership knowledge isn't conveyed or added on because it is inherent; it is right there to be rediscovered. As we watch the absorption of a student creating a fresh drawing of a sunset or writing a poem, the joy in their art-making says that at this moment they feel linked to the whole.

Many people in the modern age find meaning in traditional religious stories of Creation, and their spirituality adds an important dimension to Partnership Education. Still, for a large number of modern people, the old stories no longer stir the soul, and the search for new meaning is imperative. Theologian Thomas Berry talks about our need for perspective to see the wonder of who we are. He says we need a New Story to help us find our place. In the Introduction to his book, *The Dream of the Earth* (Sierra Club, 1988), he writes:

"For peoples, generally, their story of the universe and the human role in the universe is their primary source of intelligibility and value. Only through this story of how the universe came to be in the beginning and how it came to be as it is does a person come to appreciate the meaning of life or to derive the psychic energy needed to deal effectively with those crisis moments that occur in the life of the individual and in the life of the society.... The deepest crises experienced by any society are those moments of change when the story becomes inadequate for meeting the survival demands of a present situation" (p. xi).

These four activities show ways to address what Thomas Berry calls, the New Story. They follow the vertical threads of Eisler's Partnership Curriculum Loom described in *Tomorrow's Children*. This means that they weave through science, social studies, and language arts activities, knowledge about the history of the earth and human potential.

Evolution and Human Potential:
Exploring with Music, Movement, and Drawing

Activity One: the Birth of the Earth

Grade level: 3rd - 12th

Goals: To gain a deeper understanding of the scientific story of how
the earth was created.

To use movement to bond with distant and mysterious events to
which we are essentially connected.

To awaken a sense of being a part of the earth by involving
kinesthetic learning.

1. Scientific information: Ask students to use pastels or draw while they hear this
description. They can focus upon whatever parts stand out for them. It may be helpful to read the sequence twice. Afterward, share drawings and discuss what they
depicted.

The earth formed from interstellar dust that consolidated 4.6 billion years ago. The
fiery ball of earth gradually cooled. Molten lava became rock and water from the
rain clouds collected, forming the seas.

"The third planet from the sun, our own earth, came into being.… The ground then
was rock and crystal beneath which burned tremendous fires. Heavier matter like
iron sank to the center, the lighter elements floated to the surface forming a granite
crust. Continuous volcanic activity brought up a rich supply of minerals, and lifted
up chains of mountains.

Then, about 4 billion years ago, when the temperature fell below the boiling point of
water, it began to rain. Hot rain slowly dissolved the rocks upon which it fell and the
seas became a thin salty soup containing the basic ingredients necessary for life.

Finally, a bolt of lightning fertilized this molecular soup and an adventure into biology began. The first cell was born. You were there. I was there. For every cell in our
bodies is descended in an unbroken chain from that event. Through this cell, our
common ancestor, we are related to every plant and animal on the earth" (from
"Evolutionary Remembering"by John Seed and Pat Fleming, *Thinking Like A
Mountain*, pp. 46-47 (New Society Publishers, Philadelphia, 1988).

2. Students move together to express the story of the creation of the earth.

Background information: Tell students that throughout time people have used circle dances to help experience important knowledge directly as a community. According to a circle dance teacher from Touchstone Farm in Easthampton, Massachusetts named Shaker, many villages in Neolithic or New Stone Age times kept certain long dances ongoing day and night. By learning the dances, a child would in a sense step into a circle where their ancestors once danced. In the case of "Issos," a traditional Greek seed-planting dance that is said to be 7000 years old, the dance speaks of the renewal of the earth while at the same time assuring people that we live within a circle of life, embraced by the earth throughout our youth, maturity, and old age. Today we can invent new dances and songs that encode outlooks and information we value.

3. Practice the Chant

Read out loud together this chant that will be basis for the movement. Make sure to contrast speeds. Some sections are marked to be read rhymically, and some slower.

Rhythmic:
The birth of the earth. (da, da, da)
The birth of the earth. (da, da, da)
Sun, sun, like a drum.
Sun, sun, like a drum.

Slower:
The moon in the sky circles the earth.
The moon in the sky circles the earth.

Rhythmic:
Zap, zap, the fire is born.
volcanoes rise like a musical horn.
Zap, zap, the fire is born.
volcanoes rise like a musical horn.

Slower:
Let the dust swirl and make the clouds. Cloud, cloud, cloud.
Let the clouds fill and make the rain. Rain, rain, rain.

Faster:
We are the clouds and we make the rain. (cha, cha, cha)
The ocean rolls to rise again. (cha, cha)
We are the clouds and we make the rain. (cha, cha, cha)
The ocean rolls to rise again. (cha, cha)

Slowest:

Cool, cool down. Cool, cool down.
Rocks hold your firey knowing.
What will come from all of this? Where are we going?

I feel the slosh of the sea inside me. Slosh, slosh.
I feel the slosh of the sea inside me. Slosh, slosh.
And I fling to the moon and curl back in the sea.
And I fling to the moon and curl back in the sea.
I feel the tides inside me.

4. Chant Accompanies the Movement

This movement sequence allows students to try out elements of the earth's history.

The repeated phrases help each group stay coordinated together. The words give structure to the movement exploration.

Get into positions for the movement.

Divide into four groups:

a) The readers of the chant.
b) The majority of the group who create the central circle.
c) A small group in the center who are the volcanoes.
d) A group of 3 or 4 outside the central circle who join hands
    and represent the moon.

To form the central circle, keep a lot of space between each person. Establish that all movement will be without touching others. Tell them, "Keep their feet planted in your own space."

The Birth of the Earth

Step One: Molten lava

Say to the central circle: "In the beginning you represent the sun steadily shining. Find flicking movements with your hands that express the feeling of extending the rays of the sun."

The birth of the earth. (da, da, da)
The birth of the earth. (da, da, da)
Sun, sun, like a drum.
Sun, sun, like a drum.

Step Two: The Moon is Formed

Say to the 3-4 students who are the Moon: "Make your own smaller circle outside the central circle to represent the moon. Rotate and spin around the circle."

The moon in the sky circles the earth.
The moon in the sky circles the earth.

Step Three: Inner circle starts to dance as volcanoes

Say to the Inner circle: "You are the molten lava exploding without touching other movers. Find movements to show this, while you keep your feet planted and watch out for the people behind you."

Zap, zap, the fire is born.
Volcanoes rise like a musical horn.
Zap, zap, the fire is born.
Volcanoes rise like a musical horn.

Step Four: The Seas — The outer circle becomes the clouds of rain

Say to the central circle: "With your palms outstretched, receive the flying debris from the volcanoes. As you move, feel all the particles in your own body. Now you become clouds."

Let the dust swirl and make the clouds. Cloud, cloud, cloud.

Say: "As you get denser, you condense into rain. Imagine you are sending the rain onto the lava."

Let the clouds fill and make the rain. Rain, rain, rain.

Say: "Make the motions of the sea forming. Without touching people in the inner circle who are the volcanoes, show with your body that you have become the ocean."
Repeating chant:

We are the clouds and we make the rain. (cha, cha, cha)
The ocean rolls to rise again. (cha, cha)

Say to the central circle: "The volcanoes are cooling into mountains.

Freeze into rock. Practice suddenly freezing into a shape."

Cool, cool down. Cool, cool down.
Rocks hold your firey knowing.
What will come from all of this? Where are we going?

Step Five: The Moon and the Tides.

Now the ocean of the outer circle becomes more aware of the circling moon.

Teacher instructions: "Sense the slosh of the water in your own body. While keeping your feet in place, respond to the pull of the moon. Watch where it circles and fling yourself toward it and then curl back again."

> *Chant:*
> *I feel the slosh of the sea inside me. Slosh, slosh.*
> *I feel the slosh of the sea inside me. Slosh, slosh.*
> *And I fling to the moon and curl back in the sea.*
> *And I fling to the moon and curl back in the sea.*
> *I feel the tides inside me.*

5. Repeat

Rotate roles and repeat this same sequence. Ask the people in the center (volcanoes, mountains) to pick new movers to take their place. Ask the three to four people on the outside who have been the moon to pick four new people to take their place. Note: I find that groups enjoy doing the sequence three or four times.

Resource:

The Touchstone Farm website provides information about workshops and recordings on circle dancing. See www.sacredcircles.com or write Touchstone Farm and Yoga Center, 132 West Street, Easthampton, MA 01027. Their CD called *The Long Dance: Volume One* includes the Neolithic planting dance, "Issos."

Activity Two: the First Cells

Grade level: 1st-5th

Goals: To experience the wonder of life beginning.

Procedure:

1. Share pictures from science books to show what single-celled and simple-cell life forms look like. Bring students into the mystery of life beginning in the ocean. "How did something start from nothing? How did the first cells feel?" At first there was not moving self-guided life. Then chemicals became organic life. Lightning hitting the ocean helped cause animate life to begin.

Explain: "We will do an exploration two ways — with moving and with art. Find out what helps you imagine this moment in the history of our world. Which art form helps you investigate this with your senses? Go to the place inside yourself that could be called your green place. When we are in this green place, we can feel things in our imagination. It's like going into a cave with our own lantern."

2. Start the movement exploration seated. "You are water, and now you are more than water. You are a cell of life." Ask people to move fluidly in the shape of a cell. Sit with enough space between each person so that they can wiggle flexibly without touching. "Connect your arms with your hands pressed together and move like the shape of a cell." Next, move standing. Then move in space. Play a recording of instrumental music that will be evocative.

Afterward, use art to go into this exploration in more depth. Set up art supplies so that students can explore this time when life was born with chalk, markers, or paint. "How do you want to draw the first life being born?"

Leave time for students to share what they have done.

Option: Return to dancing and moving as these first cells. Take turns having five students improvising sounds with drums and rhythm instruments while others move.

3. Writing: Each student creates a page of writing that helps them enter in their imagination the beginning of life. Emphasize that they are exploring a mystery. Sample sentence starter: I am there when life began and _____. Add drawings as an option.

Resources:

• *The Field Guide to Prehistoric Life* by David Lambut and the Diagram Group (Facts on File, 1994). This book has wonderful illustrations. Note: It also lists the work of a paleotologist named Mary Anning (1799-1847) who found the first British pterosaur and the first complete ichthyosaur and plesiosaur.

• *On the Day You Were Born* by Debra Frasier (Harcourt Brace, 1991). Science and poetry combine to look at the history and mystery of the earth.

• Song Activity Four, "The Cells Start Moving," from Chapter Nine.

• *The Universe Story* by Brian Swimme and Thomas Berry (Harper San Francisco, 1994).

<u>Activity Three</u>: Our Own Active Place in Social Evolution

Grade level: Various activities here can be modified for grades 3 - 12.

Goals: To help students feel the wonder of their essential uniqueness.
　　　　To convey the interconnection of life.
　　　　To examine the repeating theme of change.

Overview: Choose one or several of the following. They do not need to be used in
　　　　sequence.

Choice 1: **Drawing: Our Nuturesphere**

This activity involves groups of students drawing within interconnected circles. It is described earlier in Chapter Six, "Partnership Education: A Place to Begin:"Activity One.

Choice 2. **Partner Activity on Uniqueness in Nature**

Engage students in reflecting upon the fact that each life form creates a way of being alive that no other form has. This is true of every life form — pine tree, dinosaur, porcupine. Each body provides a special way to experience being alive.

If this part of nature could talk:

Provide a basket of natural objects to explore — shells, nuts, gemstones, rocks. Make sure that there are more than enough objects for each person to have a different one. Again form pairs. Each partner chooses one thing from the basket. They study it and silently write about what that life form has experienced, listing the places it's been.

Now they switch and write about the object their partner was holding. Lastly, meet together and share your writing. Working in partnership create a combined list of observations for each object. Choose one or both objects and create a story to tell the class about what this object would say if it could speak. Notice how you were you able to think of more things by sharing ideas. Discuss the roles you'll take as you share your story — will you both speak? Will you take turns holding the objects?

Choice 3. **Humans Changing**

What makes humans unique is that we can learn and change.

Partner Interviews on Change: As you talk in pairs, search together for your answers to these questions and make lists.

- How have each of you changed physically?
- What new skills have you learned?

- What behaviors have you changed?
- Is there anything about your family that has changed?
- What beliefs of yours have changed?

Come back together and share lists as a whole class.

Songwriting Extension: Help students craft their words into a song. Pick a familiar tune for your pattern, or use the pattern below and invent a tune for it.

> *Song: The Changes in Our Lives*
>
> *Some of us wear braces to change our teeth.*
> *Changes in our lives.*
> *Some get glasses to give our eyes relief.*
> *Changes in our lives.*
>
> *When a new baby comes to a family.*
> *Changes in our lives.*
> *We might change our room or get less sleep.*
> *Changes in our lives.*
>
> *Families change when there is a divorce.*
> *Changes in our lives.*
> *It's harder when you travel back and forth.*
> *Changes in our lives.*
>
> *A cousin of ours died of cancer.*
> *Changes in our lives.*
> *It was too late to treat her, though she looked for an answer.*
> *Changes in our lives.*
>
> *We have a new teacher in the fall.*
> *Changes in our lives.*
> *Over the summer we grow tall.*
> *Changes in our lives.*
>
>   *by Joy O'Leary's fourth grade class,*
>   *Park Street School, Springfield, Vermont*

Choice 4. **Partner Activity on Uniqueness of Individual People**

Each person has their own way of being, feeling, expressing, knowing. Explain, "You can do what no other person who lived can do because you are unique from any human being who has ever lived before. When you think about this, what aspects of yourself do you think of?"

a. Partners explore hands:

"We'll test out if our hands are different." Pair up students and ask them to look for similarities and differences with their hands. Look for size of fingers, shape of nails, scars, or lines on their palms that might resemble letters like W, X, or M. (Note: The activity for the song, "The Colors of Earth," in Chapter Nine can be used to extend this exploration.)

b. Partners explore with drawing: Sit with your partner, not facing but back to back, each with paper, a surface to draw upon, and pencils or markers. Fold the paper in half so that you'll be able to do two drawings on it. Take turns — one person names something to draw from nature. Example: sunrise, willow tree, volcano. Both draw it in their own unique way on one side of the paper. Then the second person suggests a part of nature to draw and both draw it their own way on the other half of the paper. Now turn back towards each other and enjoy each other's drawings. Take turns saying something you notice and appreciate about the other person's way of drawing. Discuss ways in which the other person depicted the choice differently than you might have.

Choice 5. **Evolution Book**

Illustrate a sentence of celebration of who you are, as someone taking part in the story of human growth.

Option A: Read the poem "In All the Universe" by Barbara Loots at the beginning of this chapter. Ask students to use a phrase from the poem, or create their own words related to the poem.

Option B: Provide suggestions and let students write their own or select a phrase. Here are suggestions.

I am the eyes of the universe, seeing as no one saw before.
In my heart I grow new seeds for the world.
I give the world my own way of seeing and thinking and feeling and being.

Option C: Share this paraphrase of the words of physicist Brian Swimme.

I am the creative flame of this awesome universe.

Share with students what Brian Swimme says about our place in evolution by reading his words or paraphrasing them and adding your own feelings:

As we lie in bed each morning, we awake to the fire that created all the stars. Our principal moral act is to cherish this fire, the source of our transformation, our selves, our society, our species, our planet. In each moment, we face this cosmic responsibility: To shape and discharge this fire in a manner worthy of its numinous origins. We cherish it by developing conscience in our use of it: Are we tending this fire, revering it? Are we creating something beautiful for our planetary home? This is the central fire of the self, the central fire of the entire cosmos: It must not be wasted on trivialities or revenge, or resentment, or despair. We have the power to forge cosmic fire. What can compare with such a destiny? p. 169 - 170 The *Universe is a Green Dragon* by Brian Swimme (Bear and Company, Santa Fe, NM, 1984).

It's a lifetime task, this asking of ourselves, "What do you want to do with your own cosmic fire?"

Choice 6. **Big Questions Activity**

In whatever way is appropriate for your class, talk about this time on planet earth when we are trying to learn how to work together as partners cherishing the earth and each other, and not be engulfed by violence or domination.

One framework for this discussion is to describe domination as a spell: We are under a spell and we are trying to awaken. What is this spell? What is it that you can do to help bring our species away from violence to partnership?

Individual writing:

Ask students to create a story about how people did awaken from the spell of violence without using violence. If this is difficult, ask them to picture one place or scene in the future that takes place in a world without constant wars, where the preponderance of violence has shifted, and social justice and nonviolent communication create a secure foundation. Describe that one scene.

Extension: Group Storytelling

This is a high-level cooperation activity. Using cooperative learning strategies, provide the amount of structure and guidance needed at each stage to help groups collaborate.

   a. Sharing writing in Small Groups: Involve students in groups of two, three, or four. Each person reads their writing to the others.

   If needed, break the task down into smaller tasks — pick numbers for the order in which you'll read, take turns looking at the speaker and listening, paraphrase what you heard.

b. Reflection: Next, talk about what is similar about the stories. Talk about what is different about the stories.

c. Collaboration: Discuss ways to weave together some aspect of each vision to create one short scene that includes some element from each person's contribution. Make a list together of characters you could have in that scene. Each person in the small groups takes a turn telling what character they want to be. Work together until everyone is able to select a character that will work for them.

d. Presentation: Decide if you want to tell or show a section of your story. Give each person the chance to select the character they want to portray.

Activity Four: The Conscience of the Earth

Grade level: grades 6 - 12

Overview: This will require at least two to three classroom periods to help students process and integrate this information.

Goals: To awaken students to the ecological problems facing the world today.
To engage students in addressing the ecological crisis as an evolutionary choice-point.
To understand the concept of "re-inventing" the human in the Ecozoic Era.

Procedure:

Part One: Looking at the Problem

1. Present to students a current health report of our earth. Notice the framing of the situation as an "evolutionary" choice. The source of the information is Worldwatch Institute, P.O.Box 879, Oxon Hill, MD 20797. 800-555-2028. Here are excerpts from the press release for the State of the World 2001:

> Global Environment Reaches Dangerous Crossroads
>
> Global environmental trends have reached a dangerous crossroads as the new century begins, according to State of the World 2001, which was released today by the Worldwatch Institute, a Washington-based research organization. Signs of accelerated ecological decline have coincided with a loss of political momentum on environmental issues, as evidenced by the recent breakdown of global climate talks. This failure calls into question whether the world will be able to turn these trends around before the economy suffers irreversible damage.

New scientific evidence indicates that many global ecosystems are reaching dangerous thresholds that raise the stakes for policymakers. The Arctic ice cap has already thinned by 42 percent, and 27 percent of the world's coral reefs have been lost, suggesting that some of the planet's key ecological systems are in decline, say the Institute's researchers. Environmental degradation is also leading to more severe natural disasters, which have cost the world $608 billion over the last decade-as much as in the previous four decades combined.

With many life support systems at risk of long-term damage, the choice before today's political leaders is historic, even evolutionary, in nature: Whether to move forward rapidly to build a sustainable economy or to risk allowing the expansion in human numbers, the increase in greenhouse gas emissions, and the loss of natural systems to undermine the economy.

"Governments squandered an historic opportunity to reverse environmental decline during the prosperity of the 1990s," said Christopher Flavin, President of the Institute and co-author of the report. "If in the current climate of political and economic uncertainty, political leaders were to roll back environmental laws or fail to complete key international agreements, decades of progress could unravel."

Unless fossil fuel use slows dramatically, the Earth's temperature could rise to as high as 6 degrees above the 1990 level by 2100, according to the latest climate models. Such an increase could lead to acute water shortages, declining food production, and the proliferation of deadly diseases such as malaria and dengue fever.

One sign of ecological decline described in this year's *State of the World* is the risk of extinction that hangs over dozens of species of frogs and other amphibians around the globe, due to pressures that range from deforestation to ozone depletion. Co-author Ashley Mattoon describes amphibians as "an important bioindicator—a sort of barometer of Earth's health—more sensitive to environmental stress than other organisms."

Some of the other facts shared in the report:

Pesticides: In the United States in the 1990s, nearly 60 percent of wells sampled in agricultural areas contained synthetic pesticides.

Pollution and Resource Use

Global Warming: The transportation sector is the fastest-growing source of carbon emissions. Road traffic, which accounted for 58 percent of worldwide transportation carbon emissions in 1990, claimed 73 percent by 1997.

Transportation: The United States uses more than one third of the world's transport energy.

Groundwater Pollution: Sixty percent of the most hazardous liquid waste in the United States — 34 billion liters of solvents, heavy metals, and radioactive materials-is injected into deep aquifers via thousands of "injection wells."

2. One of the fundamental concepts of Partnership Education is that cultural transformation can occur through concerted and coordinated conscious effort. Focus on this statement from the press release:

"Mobilizing the worldwide response needed to bring destructive environmental trends under control is a daunting task," said co-author Gary Gardner. "But people have surmounted great challenges before, from the abolition of slavery in the 19th century, to the enfranchisement of women in the early twentieth. Change can move quickly from impossible to inevitable."

3. The press release lists early signs of progress that have emerged in the past year:

- In December, negotiators from 122 countries agreed to a historic legally binding treaty that will severely restrict 12 persistent organic pollutants.

- Iceland launched a pioneering effort to harness its geothermal and hydropower to produce hydrogen, which will be used to fuel its automobiles and fishing boats-an effort that is attracting investments from major oil and car companies.

- Organic farming, which avoids the use of synthetic fertilizers and pesticides, has surged to a worldwide annual market of $22 billion-and may get a further boost from strict organic farming standards issued by the U.S. government in December.

- Technology — Fuel Cell Cars: DaimlerChrysler is devoting $1.5 billion to fuel cell development, and plans to produce and sell 100,000 fuel cell cars by 2004.

- Industry is one key to environmental progress. Last year, Ford Motor Company Chairman, William Ford, questioned the long-term future of both the internal combustion engine and the personal automobile, as his company stepped up its efforts to develop new transportation technologies. At the same time, three oil companies announced that they are moving "beyond petroleum" to a broader portfolio of energy investments.

With oil, natural gas, and electricity prices all rising simultaneously during the past year, the world has had a timely reminder that over-dependence on geographically concentrated fossil fuels is a recipe for economic instability. In many regions, renewable energy is now the most economical and inflation-proof energy source available, and can be installed much faster than the three-year minimum for a natural gas-fired power plant.

4. In another section of the report, emphasis was placed on the role that the United States can play. These paragraphs are also from the press release:

> Co-authors Hilary French and Lisa Mastny noted that failure to enforce many existing international environmental agreements is hampering progress on many fronts. State of the World 2001 calls for stronger enforcement of treaties, and for increased North-South cooperation, particularly among the environmentally and economically influential E9 countries: China, India, the United States, Indonesia, Brazil, Russia, Japan, South Africa, and the European Union. "Globalization must go beyond commercial relationships to embrace strengthened political and civil-society ties between diverse nations if we are to avoid a shared catastrophe," according to the report.
>
> One example of the potential influence of the E9 countries is the effort to slow climate change. These nine nations account for nearly three-quarters of global greenhouse gas emissions. A collective commitment by the E9 to new energy systems could have a dramatic impact on energy markets and reduce the rate of global warming.
>
> Flavin said, "The U.S. has the world's largest economy and its environmental impact is second to none, so the signal it sends is crucial."
>
> Amid the December 1999 breakdown in global trade talks and the collapse of climate negotiations a year later, it is clear that the world is still searching for consensus on how to forge an environmentally sustainable economy. If the U.S. retreats to a more defensive view of global environmental threats, it would create a leadership vacuum. "The question now is one of leadership," Flavin said. "Will the United States help lead the world to a sustainable economy in the twenty-first century-as it led the way through global crises in the last century? Or will it be left to other countries to show the way to a sustainable economy in the new millennium?"

5. Digest the information above using partnership processes. Ask students to break into pairs and paraphrase to each other what stays with them from this report. Ask

them to tell each other — What are the problems that the earth faces according to Worldwatch Institute?

6. Brainstorm a list of all the emotions that come up upon hearing this information. Use the brainstorm to enter a period of sharing feelings about this crisis. It is through sharing our own personal response — whether it be despair, anger, denial, sorrow, apathy — that we can pass through to a new place together.

Part Two: Summoning courage

1. Facing these facts is a tremendous challenge for people of every age. Thomas Berry, in his book *The Dream of the Earth*, says that it requires a "re-inventing" of what it means to be human. Share these concepts with students:

> Berry describes the uniqueness of our time period in a new way. He says that up until now the earth directed itself instinctively. Now the earth is "entering a phase of conscious decision through its human expression." This is the "ultimate daring venture for the earth." The earth is "confiding its destiny to human decision, (and making) the bestowal upon the human community of the power of life and death over its basic life systems" (Berry, 1988, p. 19). We have moved from instinct to consciousness, but a deeper consciousness is required.

He says that the way out of our dilemma is to embrace the reality of the earth as a living organism, a reality which has been shown scientifically by Lynn Margulis and James Lovelock. If we take in the reality that the earth is alive, we realize that we are part of the earth and that gives us a place inside from which we can mobilize. He writes, "This reenchantment with the earth as a living reality is the condition for our rescue of the earth from its impending destruction that we are imposing upon it. To carry this (reenchantment) out effectively, we must now, in a sense, reinvent the human as species within the community of life species. Our sense of reality and of value must consciously shift from an anthropocentric to a biocentric norm of reference.... We can recognize ourselves not simply as a human community, but as genetically related to the entire community of living beings, since all species are descended from a single origin" (Berry, 1988, p. 21).

2. Use the expressive arts to help students digest and grapple with what it means to be part of re-inventing the human. Some of these choices will be too much of a stretch for the group. Find one you can modify that will work for your class.

• Play instrumental music that creates a mood of reflection. Ask people to move their hands slowly while they watch their fingers move, and at the same time think to themselves, "I am the earth moving through these fingers." Do stream of consciousness writing beginning with the phrase, "I am the earth."

• During the weekend, ask students to stand by themselves outside, reflecting on, "I am the earth seeing through me." Journal on this experience.

• In the 1980's ecologists developed a format called "The Council of All Beings" which allowed people to speak on behalf of the earth. This method is detailed in the book, *Thinking Like A Mountain* (New Society Publishers, Philadelphia, 1988). Participants choose a life form that particularly calls to them and write or speak the voice of that part of the earth — be it elephant, or topsoil, or water, or frog. A special setting is created for sharing these voices in a circle so that there is a sense of leaving ordinary life for a moment and entering sacred time to hear the earth speak from all its forms.

• Conversation with Gaia: Do a simultaneous role play, with students working in pairs, facing each other in two lines. Everyone takes part in their own conversation, unaware of what other pairs in line are saying. People in one line take one role, while everyone in the other line has the other.

One role is to speak as "Gaia," the earth. The other role is to speak on behalf of the human species. Prescript it so that Gaia isn't wrathful and vengeful. Instead, Gaia is an infinitely wise elder, either female or male. But Gaia has no lips to talk or hands to move or legs to walk. Gaia depends upon humans to take action. What does Gaia say and ask? What does the Human say and ask? Afterward discuss: What did you discover? Look for pairs who will volunteer to replay their role play while the others listen.

- Have this same conversation with art. Each student has their own piece of paper and two pens or markers. Instead of trying to draw representationally, work with line and form expressively in a more doodle-like manner. One hand makes marks to represent Gaia talking, and the other hand makes marks to represent Human talking. After exploring with art, use words to catch what you have discovered.

- Work with this question: "If I really believed that I am part of the earth and everything I do matters to the earth, what would I do?" A variation of this is, "If money and time were no object how would I coordinate with others to act on behalf of the earth? What is one step in this direction?" Questions like these are used within a national network called Interhelp to gain perspective (Interhelp, PO Box 61, Delmar, NY 12054). Students can either address these questions through writing or by having conversations in pairs or small groups.

3. Look for an action that the class can take together on behalf of the earth. Contact the Earth Day Network at www.earthday.net. In their eight-page guide for teachers called "Waterways" there are dozens of activity ideas.

- Adopt the slogan, "Earth Day, Every Day," and include a weekly or monthly Earth Watch time where news and concerns about the earth are shared.

- Actions related to the songs, "Seed Savers," and "The Mahogany Tree" about the rainforest can be found in Chapter Nine, "Music to Build Partnership."

- Study the interrelationship of Julia Butterfly Hill and the thousand year old tree, Luna.

    Julia sat on a small platform for two years to protect Luna from being cut down, and in her poetry expresses her growing consciousness of her role as a human. Look at the website at www.lunatree.org and see Activity Nine in Chapter Nine.

How to Create an Extended Unit

There are other expressive arts activities in this book for grades 3rd - 12th that can be used in combination with the ones above to create a month-long unit. Here is a sequence:

    1. We replay the birth of the earth: 4.6 to 4 billion years.
       Use Activity One: "The Birth of the Earth" in this chapter.

2. We explore the first cells.
   Use Activity Two: "The First Cells" in this chapter.

3. We feel the development of organic life.
   Look in Chapter 9, "Music to Build Partnership" for Song Activity Four: The Cells Start Moving.

4. We meet early humans in the Paleolithic Period of human life.
   Look in Chapter 6, Partnership Education: A Place to Begin," for Activity Fourteen, "The Paleolithic Period of Human Life." This uses creative dramatics, art, and writing.

5. We explore partnership-based societies.
   Look in Chapter 6, Partnership Education: A Place to Begin," for Activity Eleven, "What the Spirals Say," and Activity Twelve, "Entering a Partnership Village in Neolithic Times."

6. We discover that we're part of ongoing evolution.
   Use Activity Three: "Our Own Active Place in Evolution" in this chapter.

7. We share responsibility for the earth.
   Use Activity Four: "The Conscience of the Earth" in this chapter.

Writing Option: Select any of the activities above and help students create pages of writing or drawing on each topic to compile a book that spans human history.

Closing

"Who am I?" and "How am I responsible?" are matters essential to Partnership Education. These large questions become grounded through experiences in exploratory arts.

We meet the whole child when we help students rebond with nature. We meet the emotional self. Upset and trauma affect how we treat the earth, as well as how we treat ourselves, and how we treat the people around us. When children are working hard to deal with painful feelings, opening them to the earth is not a simple matter. Recently, as I took a walk around my neighborhood, I saw closehand a poignant and upsetting expression. An eleven-year-old boy, who I'd never talked to before but knew had gone through hard changes in his family, was hitting a maple tree with a heavy stick. I overheard him say to his friend, "I hate Mother Nature." I felt shock, and I also felt his pain. Hating Mother Nature is at core an expression of dis-ease with self, of inner upset becoming contorted and ricocheting without healing release. I wish I had gone over to him, put my arm around his shoulder, and said, "I'm so sorry."

Being able to be close to the earth involves being able to feel. "What we're doing is teaching aesthetic," says Jack Borden, co-author of *For Spacious Skies*. "It's the opposite of anaesthetic. We are teaching feeling." A rich resource of people crisscross this country who are dedicated to helping students rebond with the earth. They're teachers, they run nature centers, they work at camps, take photographs, and write books.[14] Through their work they help rekindle a spark of wonder inside that leads to reawakening awareness.

Opening to the earth is part of this journey, whether it requires coming out of anaesthetic, encountering new questions and activities, or finding a teacher who is interested in hearing our deepest feelings. The arts have a tremendous potential in this work. **The expressive arts help children locate themselves within nature, within the creative life-generating force of the universe.** They help us ask:

- Who am I? What is my creative voice and how does it come forward? What are my gifts? Where am I drawn when I'm in touch with my center?

- Who are humans? What is the deepest nature of the human within the story of the cosmos?

- How can I be responsible to my unique gifts? How can I respect my contributions?

- How am I responsible to the universe? What is my role in this unfolding story?

CHAPTER 11

The Connections Curriculum at Nova High School

by Bobbi Morrison

Context

I have been involved in teaching at Nova High School since 1974. The course I prepared on systems led me to the work of Riane Eisler in the 1990's. After the principal of our school, Elaine Packard, contacted Eisler, Nova began an ongoing relationship with Partnership Education. For more information on Nova, see the article in the next section, "Partnership Structure at Nova School."

During the 1999-2000 school year I was part of a group of science and history teachers who created a multidisciplinary course called "Connections" that dealt with Eisler's theories. What follows are my units on cosmology, myth, and systems theory and cultural transformation. Both the information conveyed in my lectures as well as specific assignments are detailed.

These focus questions show the link between the study of myths and an understanding of partnership. Students examine:

1. How do myths validate or perpetuate the values of a culture?

2. How do myths function as a transition from partnership to domination?

3. How do certain myths reflect relationships of women and men?

4. What values within a given myth are similar to partnership values?

5. What is the lens that this myth is told through?

Cosmology and Creation Myth Unit

Grade level: 9th-12th

Overview: Myths from seven different cultures were studied: Sumerian, Babylonian, Minoan, Hebrew, Egyptian, Hopi, and Chinese.

Important Concepts to Cover in a Lecture Format

- A creation myth is a narrative that describes the original ordering of the universe. It tells how order and existence were established. The word "cosmogony" derives from two Greek words: *kosmos* meaning order and *genesis* meaning birth. In other words this is the story of the original ordering of the world.

- Myth itself has an analogous meaning to a culture that a dream has to an individual. According to William Irwin Thompson, myth is the "mirror opposite of history. Myth is not the story of the ego of a civilization, but the story of the soul." Creation myths are archetypal patterns that show how the culture works with the continuing threat of disorder and chaos to bring Some-thing out of No-thing.

- There are five basic structures of creation stories: emergence from chaos or nothingness, emergence from a cosmic egg, creation when world parents separated, creation caused by the earth diving, emergence from other worlds through several stages.

- Several archetypal or recurring characters appear in creation myths. One is the creator or creatrix. One is a trickster. Another is a searcher (the first man and first woman) who leaves one dimension and brings creation to our time or space. Lastly, is a flood character, a hero/heroine searching for a new beginning after a catastrophe such as a flood. Here are the seven myths:

1. Minoan: Although representing a society that existed from 3000-1500 BCE (Before Common Era), the Legend of the Minotaur was told 1000 years later from a perspective of a culture much changed from the original one.

2. Sumerian: Agricultural community in the Bronze Age (3500-1250 BCE). Sumer's myth of the creation of Nammu and An-Ki, the central Goddess of Inanna, and the story of the sacrifice of the son-lover.

3. Egyptian: The creation story of Isis as the Great Mother Goddess.

4. Babylonian: The Iron Age, begun in 1250 BCE, spawns the Babylonian creation myth Enuma Elish, which was unearthed from tablets in 1848 CE (Common

Era). The myth dates from 1750 BCE when Hammurabi ruled Babylonia and was used to establish the ruled of Marduk.

5. Hebrew: The Creation Myth of Genesis is in fact made up of two somewhat distinct myths. Genesis I contains the version composed probably as late as the fifth century BCE; Genesis II is a much earlier text, perhaps as early as 950 BCE. The difference to be particularly noted is how the myth describes the creation of the first humans. The story of the first humans in both of the Genesis versions continues to affect relationships between men and women, nature and our vision of the spiritual.

6. Hopi: The dominance of Spider Woman, the female creative principle, befits a culture that remains to this day matrilineal. The Hopi creation myth uses many familiar motifs; the creation by thought and song is quite unique. One motif is the story of people emerging gradually, as in childbirth. At each stage they grow in knowledge and ability and only when finally born are they bathed by the light of the sun god's power, Tawa, ready now for proper social ordering.

7. Chinese: There are several creation myths from China. One tells of the cosmic egg. The primary sources for these are popular legend and a third century literary text entitled San-wu li-chi. In this myth called Phan Ku, we find several elements: Creation from a primal cosmic egg, the separation of heaven and earth, and the ordering principle, yin-yang. The more philosophical creation myths are from 200 BCE, beginning with chaos, and from Lao Tzu's *Tao Te Ching* from the sixth century BCE.

Model Presentation

Present the Minoan myth of Theseus and the Minotaur to model the process of analyzing a myth. Use *The Myth of the Goddess: Evolution of an Image* by Ann Baring and Jules Cashford (London: Penguin Books. 1993, pages 137-139). Then compare it with the version in Riane Eisler, *Sacred Pleasure* (San Francisco: Harper Collins. 1996, pages 128-130).

This myth, re-created by the Greeks a thousand years after the downfall of Crete, may describe the collision of two different cultures. On the one hand we have the partnership societies of the Neolithic where a female divinity represented the organizing values. On the other hand we have the invasion of the Mycenean and Dorian cultures with male gods reigning supreme in the figure of Zeus. The male-dominated cultures rose in supremacy, just as the male gods ascended. The myth evolved to account for those invasions. The story line on the surface pictures the heroic tale of Theseus who outwits the curse on this city, slays the monster Minotaur in the dark labyrinth, and wins freedom for his country.

Throughout the tale, signs of the old goddess partnership religion abound. Ariadne bestows on Theseus the thread of woman's intuition to unravel that will guide his conscious mind out of the labyrinth leading to the source and give him a way back to safety. Theseus, the questing consciousness, must journey into the unknown to seek treasures of the heart. But here the story is very different. Still, the image of the labyrinth is linked to the palace where sacred ancient rites, now altered, were once performed. The recurrent imagery of the sacred bull as part of the goddess sacred marriage reflects the journey of male and female to achieve harmony and fertility of the Minoan world. But in this story, the bull is demonized, as Eisler points out, a reversal of earlier myths. (See Eisler, *Sacred Pleasure*, chapter 7).

Cooperative Learning Structure

The class is divided into six groups to study a culture's myth and present it to the whole group. These are the instructions that students receive:

Step 1. Study the Myth

> Each group should read the myth and clarify the main story line of the myth. Look for significant symbols and characters that make up this myth and take note of clues in the story that would signal that culture's understanding of the cosmos, the ordering of the world.

Step 2. Plan a Presentation of the Myth

> Each group is responsible for relaying the story of this myth to the larger group. You may decide to have a narrator with different people taking on roles either by acting, using symbolic figures or using body movement. The group can also decide to divide the story up into parts with members taking a section of the story to tell and illustrate that section with an image. Each group should decide on music that your group feels lends itself to the telling of this tale or decide on a certain beat that is heard throughout the storytelling to help draw the listener into the tale. You should use at least two other modalities besides language such as role playing, image making, movement, and music.

Step 3. Analysis of the Myth

> After telling the tale, your group should be prepared to analyze the myth, answering the following questions:

> 1. How does the story reveal that culture's vision of the original ordering of existence?

2. What does the myth say about that culture's relationship to nature?

3. What does the myth say about that culture's relationship to the spirit world?

4. What does the myth say about that culture's view of the two sexes or the essential relationship between what we think of as the masculine and feminine modes of being? If there are gods/goddesses, what is the nature of their power or their domain of power?

5. What does the myth say about that culture's relationship with birth and death?

6. What does the myth say about that culture's perspective of power relationships: Is it gylanic or androcratic or is there a blending or subtle shift of relationships that indicate a change happening in that society?

Partnership process during the presentation of the myths:

Each student has two grids where they record categories of information about each presentation: On one they note information they receive to summarize the major points of each group's analysis of their myth, and on the other chart, they evaluate the presentation and write down feedback for the group.

Cross-Cultural Myth Grid

Myth Group	Dominant Imagery	Relation to Nature	Spirit World	Male/ Female	Ranking or Linking
Minoan					
Sumerian					
Babylonian					
Egyptian					
Hebrew					
Hopi					
Chinese					

Myth and Symbols Unit

Grade level: 9th-12th

Important Information to Cover in a Lecture Format

As historian Robert Artigiani says, "History is how a society explains itself to itself." It is understandable how the new order had to re-vision history and either left out, ignored, transformed or re-created the story. And consequently we are just re-covering this history and we are also discovering how the mythic tales of these societies were also either repressed, the symbols absorbed and re-interpreted, or they were just demeaned or demonized.

We don't have the myths from the partnership cultures to study, but we have the language of symbols on pottery and shrines to indicate meaning. For instance, doubled spirals meant rebirth or renewal according to scholars who have studied the repetition of images across cultures. The myths we have come from later cultures organized around domination rather than partnership. In the myths of the Greek Mycenaean or Hebraic pastoralists we can see how the patriarchal religions re-created stories to demonize the snake as malevolent or a trickster or an ominous creature. Similarly stories of the female goddess become transformed from the original progenitor of the universe to a consort of the main male deity Zeus. In Babylonia, the creatrix mother is raped by her son deity Enki to form the universe.

Activities

- Look at the symbol of the snake and collect myths in which the snake appears. According to Marija Gimbutas, "Representations of snakes are known since the Upper Paleolithic and continue in the Mesolithic and Neolithic.... The shrines in which images of the ... Snake Goddess appear go back to about 6000 BCE or earlier" (*The Language of the Goddess*, Harper-Collins 1991, p. 123, p. 132). The snake was once considered a powerful transformative image of nature's cycles and symbol of the feminine goddess. Now contrast the Hebrew myth describing the snake as temptor of Eve, and the Greek myth of Medusa and Perseus. If snakes symbolize the earlier partnership cultures, what is the coded message of blaming the snake for the downfall of humans, or heroic slaying of the snake?

- Examine the Greek myths of the birth of Athena. The earliest appearance of Athena is in Crete where she is identified with the snake. Although Athena is a much older deity than Zeus, her story was retold to say that she had no mother but was born from the head of Zeus. What is the coded message of changing the female deity in this way?

• Choose symbols such as bird, water, snake, spider, fish, butterfly, pig, cow or bull and look for them in myth and in ancient art. Choose one symbol from ancient art, draw it, and create a poem about its meaning.[15]

Myth and Connections Unit

Grade level: 9th-12th

Overview: As we look through the lens of mythology, the common threads — or meta-structures — that run through our human existence are revealed. Students look at three macro-thinkers and how they work with myth: Joseph Campbell, Carl Jung, and Riane Eisler. After examining a myth, they write their own using archetypes that speak to current issues related to partnership and domination.

Important Information to Cover in a Lecture Format

Joseph Campbell believed that through identifying with a myth and the archetypal element at its core, our lives could open up and inward to reveal life as a rich symphony of experiences. The archetypes are there to guide us through the situations of our life and when we are in harmony with the form, then we are following a deeper level of self-fulfillment.

Explain three concepts from the Swiss psychoanalyst Carl Jung (1875-1961) who greatly influenced Campbell: The collective unconscious, archetypes, and individuation. Jung described the collective unconscious as an inborn predisposition to certain feelings, perceptions, and behaviors that are not dependent on the individual, but are instead something we inherit as a kind of unique human genetic memory. The collective unconscious is a reservoir of unconscious forms with which we are born. These forms are identifiable as archetypes. Archetypes are prototypes or first models in our unconscious such as rebirth, a wise old person, a trickster, or a giant. Joseph Campbell identified a repeated motif in myths and legends that he called the Hero's Journey that features the hero archetype. Mythology is born from the archetypes and speaks directly to our lives metaphorically.

Eisler, by contrast, asks us to look at archetypes and other symbols in their cultural context. She contrasts dominator and partnership archetypes and symbols, pointing out that although the basic human questions myths often seek to answer are the same, the answers are radically different in the context of dominator or partnership social structures. The collective unconscious is not genetically but culturally transmitted.

Myths of the hero's journey carrying a sword and rescuing the heroine are dominator myths. Myths where women and men have equal power and magic rather than violence transforms our partnership myths.

From Marx and Freud, to Normal O. Brown and Spengler, and now Riane Eisler, the message is that something's gone awry and we, human beings, should and can correct it. Eisler's unique contribution is pointing to our human encoding for partnership, and showing that by returning to our partnership archetypes, we are able to be guided back to partnership relationships within society. (See the summary of Eisler's work in the Systems unit below.)

There is some similarity between Jung's microcosmic view of balance within the individual and Eisler's cultural transformation theory which has a macrocosmic view. But Eisler questions Jung's archetypes of masculinity and femininity, pointing out that they are hardly universal, that ideas of what is feminine and masculine have varied greatly from place to place and time to time. For example, while in 19th century Europe and America, femininity was associated with physical delicacy and feebleness, during the same period in some African societies femininity was associated with a woman's capacity to carry heavy loads of water and wood for her family and to perform other tasks that require great physical strength. Moreover, archetypes change, as we can see today, when many men are changing fathering archetypes to be more like those once only associated with mothering, and archetypes of female helplessness are being challenged by many women.

Lesson Plan for Myth Reading

We turn to myths as essential in communicating insights for personal and societal change. Therefore, we will first read a myth, analyze it, and then attempt to create a myth for a new worldwide story that models our present situation.

Assignment: Read *The Sword and The Grail* retold by Constance Hieatt (Thomas Y. Cromwell: New York 1972). Also read pages 60-63 of *The Partnership Way* by Riane Eisler and David Loye (Revised Second Edition. Brandon, Vermont: Holistic Education Press, 1998) on Partnership and Dominator Heroes and Heroines.

Objective: How does the Parsifal story embody the hero's achieving balance of what we have been taught to think of as the masculine and feminine? How is this individual's individuation process affected by and in turn affect the society? How would this process of individuation be different in a more partnership-oriented social context?

Class Day 1

Step 1 Divide the class up into four parts and have each section re-tell the Parsifal tale out loud.

Step 2 Have the class brainstorm their qualities of what makes a hero/heroine and actions. Review the elements of Campbell's mono myth and have the students compare Eisler's ideas, as well as their own ideas, with Campbell's.

In its most elemental form the mono-myth, as Campbell described it, is this: Separation-initiation-return. In the case of the hero's journey it can be fleshed out in this form (See diagram on p. 263 in *Hero with a Thousand Faces*).

The Call to Adventure - the unexpected call to action

Supernatural Aid - the helper figure that prepares the hero in some way for the trials to come

The Threshold - the point in the story where the hero stands poised to enter a mysterious world

The Trials - the tasks and ordeals the hero must endure

The Return - having completed the trial, the hero brings back a boon to the original departed society

Note the differences and similarities.

What parts of the story can be identified as the forms for the Hero's Journey?

If Jung's assumptions that the purpose of human life is to move towards wholeness and not perfection as formally implicated in Western spiritual doctrine, how does the story of Parsifal illustrate that insight? According to Jungians, "The movement toward wholeness is a formidable task, for it always involves us in a paradox. What has been excluded from the Christian Trinity is the dark, feminine element in life. We are moving towards a quaternion view that includes the feminine" (pp. 62-63, Robert Johnson, *He: Understanding of Male Psychology*). But Eisler rejects the stereotypes of the feminine as the dark and the male as the light. She points out that Jungian stereotypes of masculinity and femininity are colored by assumptions appropriate for a system that sees the male as superior to the female and hence often portrays woman and the "feminine" as dangerous to man or conversely, over-idealizes woman as the embodiment of caring and compassion, but only if she is a "good" rather than "evil" woman.

Seen from this perspective, the Parsifal myth is the story of an insensitive man with a sword becoming a somewhat more sensitive man and caring human being by embracing some characteristics stereotypically associated with women in dominator thinking. But at the same time, the story idealizes violence as "masculine" and heroic. Moreover, the hero's mother is portrayed as giving him bad advice — a reflection of the rejection of the wisdom of the mother in dominator mythology, where the wise elders are almost invariably male and old women are often evil witches.

Still, the Parsifal story supports Riane Eisler's view of the importance of re-gaining the dignity and status of the feminine in our culture so as to re-gain the balance, creativity, and health of our planet. In what way(s) does the Parsifal myth offer patterns of behavior that might help restore this balance? How does the Parsifal story of the unconscious, inexperienced, and insensitive boy becoming a man who accesses his "feminine" side work for our age? What does it really mean to balance our "masculine" and "feminine" sides?

Assignment:

Many other stories, fairy tales, and myths that you know illustrate the heroic journey from a dominator perspective where individuation is seen as integrating what Jungians call the shadow or anima/animus? For example how does the heroine/hero — Joan of Arc, Luke Skywalker from *Star Wars*, the Hobbit from Tolkien's trilogy *Lord of the Rings*, or Harry Potter in his adventures — illustrate her/his heroic individualization according to this script?

Study the opera of Richard Wagner's *Parsifal* and analyze his rendering with Christian de Troyes' Perceval version (See Appendix from R. Johnson's book, *He*) and re-write the story in a play form that reflects more partnership themes.

Write your own myth for our planet's age. Consider:

• What archetypal situations are compelling for you?

• Will you have a hero/heroine or will the central action revolve around group effort?

• If you choose a single main character, how does she or he reflect Campbell's "universal myth" model or Eisler's "cultural myth" model?

• You might want to consider these thematic elements in writing your effective worldwide myth/story: Natural awe/sacredness of the world, bringing together traditional enemies, stereotypes of masculinity and femininity, powerful visual elements, family/community, space element as exploration or pioneering, peace versus security, sustainability versus momentary glitz, bringing back more gylanic ethos as true love, pedagogical element of acceptance of differences, driving force for evolutionary growth.

Consider also what elements make a good story:

- Plot: The story must contain adventure, moral challenge, rescue, discoveries, prophecies, travels, lesson, spiritual elixirs, larger-than-life supernatural element. You can begin the story in the middle of the action and flashback to the past or start off by invoking the Muse.

- Characters: Common ones have included mentors, sidekicks, monsters, villains, magical beings, healers, traitors, tricksters, and cowards. Can you think of others?

- Setting: Myths are timeless and set in forests, swamps, mountains, caves, sacred groves of trees, oceans, castles, cottages, lakes, cities, the beginning of time or future planets.

- Sound of language: Consider the mythic sound which usually reflects the setting and occasionally is formal rather than "spoken" or slang, but not necessarily, and is different depending on the time and place.

Assignment Thoughts

While imagining the inner workings of your tales, remember to include the broader thematic points of this creative process. We are hoping to incorporate elements of the various macro-thinkers we have been studying: Jung's ideas (individuation, archetypal symbols, the shadow aspects of your heroine/hero's journey), Campbell's stages of the "mono myth," and Eisler's "cultural myths" and her cultural transformation theory. Keep in mind partnership with the earth, that is, linking with the wisdom of nature, animal powers, more humane relations. Consider broader societal partnerships linked to an individual's own inner ability to expand his/her consciousness and to reflect through his/her self those acts of a truly heroic nature, acts that are spontaneously generated from love of compassion and clarity.[16]

Systems Theory and Cultural Transformation

Grade level: 9th-12th

Lecture Presentation

Understanding systems helps us understand what behaviors maintain partnership. Introduce to students the systems way of looking at the world. These are the basic principles:

- All living beings are connected.

- Environment is an integral part of any living system.

- Beings are defined by the environment in which they interact.

- A system is more than its individual parts.

- A system iterates itself throughout.

- There are two kinds of systems — closed and open.

A closed system is characterized by lack of self-regulation and will become increasingly disorganized as input is not regenerative. An open system exhibits the ability to self-regulate with new input. Open systems exhibit the following characteristics:

Purpose: Open systems are organized in a meaningful way to produce output for a particular goal.

Equifinality: This means that the final state of the open system can be reached by different paths independent of the original input.

Morphogenesis: Open systems have the ability to add new structures or capabilities in the drive for self-actualization.

Homeostasis: Open systems are self-regulating to restore the system's equilibrium or integrity. Systems of human interactions are also rooted in these same systems' principles. When certain people in a human system are cut off from having feedback into the system, imbalance results. In a dominator system, women's views, views of people of color, and others who are marginalized are left out. A partnership system is a system structured for feedback from all community members.

Next, explain to students how a system shifts. Eisler summarizes this process: "Mathematicians studying the dynamics of systems processes speak of what they term attractors. Roughly analogous to magnets, these may be "point" or "static" attractors, which govern the dynamics of systems in equilibrium; "periodic" attractors, which govern cyclical or oscillatory movements; and "chaotic" or "strange" attractors, which are characteristic or far-from-equilibrium or dis-equilibrium, states. Chaotic or strange attractors may sometimes, with relative rapidity and unpredictability, become the nuclei for the build up of a whole new system. If the system is stable, the new functioning represented by these fluctuations will not survive. But if these 'innovators' multiply fast enough, the whole system may adopt a new mode of functioning. In other words if the fluctuations exceed what Prigogine and Stenger call a "nucleation threshold," they will spread to the whole system. As these initially small fluctuations are amplified, critical "bifurcation points," in effect, paths to possible system transformations, open up." (p. 136, *The Chalice and the Blade*.)

Clarify the phrase, "bifurcation points" to describe these amplified fluctuations. In Eisler's Cultural Transformation Theory, human societies are looked at from a systems perspective. Bifurcation points in human societies have influenced an entire web of relationships. Through the lens of cultural transformation, there are two basic models of human systems: (1) a dominator or androcratic model in which hierarchies of domination are backed up by force as one group is ranked over another, and (2) the partnership or gylanic model where linking and hierarchies of actualization lead to a more peaceful ecologically balanced society. Notably, in the dominator model one half of humanity — men — are ranked over half of humanity — women.

Partnership educator, Sarah Pirtle, explains it this way: "What we see is not a victory of men so much as a victory of domination. The problem of sexism in a dominator structure then is not a problem of men against women. It's a systemic structural problem. Structuring domination in reference to gender hurts both men and women; they are no longer in an open system. What is significant about the times of partnership is that all members of a community are inter-related in an open system. Domination took the differences among the community members and used them as a basis for imbalance rather than using them as a basis for interconnection."

Eisler illuminates new archaeological digs and re-interpretations of former ones. According to Eisler, during the Neolithic or New Stone Age in places such as the Balkans, in Mediterranean islands such as Crete and Malta; in Çatal Hüyük, in Turkey; and other Old Europe sites, as well as in Indus River Valley Dravidian cities, and pre-Shang dynastic communities of China, there was a more egalitarian view of the sexes with social structures based on the partnership model. These societies were organized around a partnership-basic spirituality where a Goddess/Creatrix was viewed as the all-giving Mother. This Mother Goddess didn't maintain a reverse hierarchy favoring women. Rather, she was seen as a mother who loved equally all her children. The arts of these societies evinced values more in harmony with nature's cycles, and non-violent technologies (plumbing, farm, trade tools) were developed. War is not glorified and trade and more equal distribution of wealth existed as noted by burial sites and houses unearthed. Minoan Crete in 3500 BCE exemplifies a culmination of social and technological advancement.

Eisler's Cultural Transformation Theory thus "proposes that the original direction in the mainstream of our cultural evolution was toward a partnership, but that, following a period of chaos and almost total cultural disruption, there occurred a fundamental shift" (Eisler, p. xvii in *The Chalice and the Blade*). This way of life was overcome by a series of "chaotic" attractors at the time — invasion of the Kurgans or Indo-European mounted horsemen, and ecological crises such as tidal waves and earthquakes — that came together to weaken the system and create a social "bifurcation" point after which the societies shifted to an androcratic system. (For a look at this cultural transformation in China, see Min Yiayin, editor in chief, *The Chalice and the Blade in Chinese History*, Beijing: China Social Sciences Publishing House, 1995, which is available from the Center for Partnership Studies in both English and Chinese.)

Activities: Three options for exploring this material.[17]

The Cultural Transformation Theory also posits that we can affect a social reorganization today toward partnership through systems transformations. Students can examine: What are the bifurcation points today? What innovations and fluctuations are currently challenging the dominator systems? What trends and events reinforce the dominator system? What partnership and dominator influences do they see in current media? How does this affect relationships between women and men?

Ask small groups to create a skit that shows four stages of a human system:

A. First show an open system characterized by clear feedback mechanisms and respect for differences.

B. Next show this open system being closed down either by a take-over by certain elements asserting dominance, or by outside forces restructuring it for dominance.

C. Tell a myth that has been put forth about why the dominator system is better and is the way things always have been.

D. Show the beginning of the restoration of the healthy functioning of the open system.

For example, during the second phase, interfering beings could say, "What would be a great way to mess with this system? Aha! Let's take the most fundamental human difference and use it to separate people instead of connecting them." Symbols used in the well-functioning open system are now reversed.

E. Create a myth about why the partnership system is better and is the way things once were and can again be.

Make a schematic diagram of an open system and of a closed system. Now think of social situations in history or from your life. Pick one group or situation that illustrates an open system and one that illustrates a closed system. Diagram these. Share what you have done with a partner and explain the meaning of your drawings and how they relate to the dominator and partnership models.

CHAPTER 12

Speaking Our Peace: Teaching the Language of Partnership

by Lethea F. Erz

> "In trying to shift from a dominator to a partnership way of thinking and living, a major obstacle is our language. How can we think and live as partners if the words in our heads keep reinforcing dominator stereotypes? Words have a powerful effect on how we think and act.... Today, as the equal value and equal rights of all people are increasingly asserted, changes in language are also being recognized as important steps toward the creation of a just society."
>
> Riane Eisler and David Loye,
> "The Language of Partnership," *The Partnership Way*

The Challenge of Language

It's not just what you say, it's how you say it.

"Saying is believing," I say, and believe! Language both shapes and reflects consciousness, revealing a culture's deepest beliefs and values. It's very hard to talk about concepts for which we have no vocabulary. And the words we do have affect how we think about the people, ideas, and phenomena those words describe.

If we hope to create a truly new paradigm based on partnership thinking, it's vital that we be aware of the underlying messages in the very words and metaphors we use to express our thoughts. If we don't, our good intentions may be undermined by the language we use to state them.

Discussing Language

In our attempts to teach about partnership, the language we use can either support our vision or subvert it. The following activities create awareness of many ways, subtle and not, in which English contains and perpetuates concepts, beliefs, and stereo-types based on a dominator way of life. They also help students participate in the discovery and creation of partnership-oriented alternatives.

Even if we agree that language is vitally important and that English is seriously flawed for expressing a partnership worldview, it's the only language many Americans know — and most other major world languages reflect similarly patriarchal worldviews. And, like it or not, our consciousness has been profoundly influenced by the language of our childhood. So what can we do about it, to bring about change and to help future generations grow up using language that is more consistent with partnership values?

The first thing is to recognize the challenge we face, and to be extremely patient with ourselves, and with others. We have all been conditioned by our language, and old expressions often "pop out" regardless of our conscious desire to change. Once our awareness of dominator language has been expanded, we may find ourselves standing aghast, in shock at something we've just said. It might have been an expression we've used unthinkingly for years, but suddenly its underlying sexism or racism or ageism or heterocentrism sounds loud in our ears.

The last thing we need is to be so careful of our language that we become tongue-tied and inarticulate, monitoring our every utterance in advance. Besides, even when we wish to replace a dominator-oriented word or phrase, English vocabulary may not contain the words we are seeking.

One step is to practice really *listening* to ourselves and to others, observing the hidden messages in the words and expressions we use, *without* projecting shame or blame when we find our partnership intentions undermined by dominator language. Another step is to engage in respectful dialogue about the language we use, clarifying *all* levels of meaning, and exploring together how to create more partnership-oriented ways of speaking.

The sixteen activities that follow provide the basis for a sequence of language arts lessons that help students examine language from a partnership perspective. Each activity is offered as an example, to be expanded, simplified, or adapted in creating a lesson plan to fit the time available and the age and abilities of the students. The content is sequenced from simpler to more complex, so teachers of younger students may use only the first several activities, while teachers of older students may use them all and create additional assignments that deepen students' interactions with the material.

This chapter is based on my article, "Speaking Our Peace: Teaching the Language of Partnership," which is excerpted from my doctoral dissertation on Gylanic

(Partnership) Communication.[19] To receive an e-mail copy of the original article, contact Lethea Erz at Letheafay@aol.com.

Activity One: Who Is Included?[20]

Note: This lesson establishes three important themes that run through all the activities that follow. First, students learn that we can engage in the fun of investigating problematic language *without blame or judgment*. They become aware of the importance of being conscious of the way our language reflects and affects our thinking. Finally, students learn that language change is continual and that we can all be part of it.

A. The unit begins with a tone of exploration and tolerance: "We are starting by looking at a mistake in language use that was made by a famous anthropologist. We'll catch the difference between what his words implied and what he meant to say."

Ask students to read and think about this sentence:

"All the people departed the next morning, leaving the women and children behind in the deserted village."

Ask students to discuss the implications of the sentence. Who are implicitly considered "people" in this statement, and who are not?

The source of the quote is a famous anthropologist named Claude Levi-Strauss. We can imagine him explaining, "I didn't mean to imply that women and children aren't people." Yet his word choice is in many ways an historical marker showing unconscious bias in research during this time period. The mistake may reveal an unexamined assumption; in his studies of that village he may have unconsciously thought what the men did was more significant than what the women and children did. Our choice of language can reveal our thoughts, beliefs, and values, even if we are not conscious of them.

We study language in this way not to blame anyone for their errors in thinking and speaking. We study to understand and to grow in our ability to speak accurately and inclusively.

B. Looking again at the sentence by Levi-Strauss, this way of thinking is termed "androcentric." "Androcentric" means "treating male experience and perceptions as the norm while ignoring or trivializing female experience." This does *not* mean that most men believe women and women's experiences are unimportant; it is simply an unconscious way of thinking that results from a long-established dominator social organization. Many of the activities that follow will help students to identify androcentric language and to replace it with usage that more accurately includes all people.

Activity Two: Gender Assumptions and Stereotypes

A. This lesson begins with a riddle:

> A boy is hit by a car while out walking with his father. In the emergency room, the surgeon on duty takes one look at the boy, gasps "My son!" and passes out in shock. How can this be? Have students try to guess the solution.

> The riddle "stumps" people only because of the androcentric cultural assumption that the surgeon is male. If people did not unconsciously think in stereotypical terms (e.g., "all surgeons are male" or "all families consist of a mother and a father"), they would easily think of several solutions.

> One solution to the riddle is that the surgeon is the boy's mother. Another is that the surgeon is the boy's stepfather. A third possibility is that the surgeon is the boy's other father in a same-sex partnership.

> Here are other words to consider. Ask students what sex is automatically assumed when they hear "housekeeper," "lawyer," or "president"? These assumptions are based on stereotypes, not on people's actual abilities. But stereotypes can limit what people are willing to try to become, and that's why it's important to be aware of them and change them.

B. Non-stereotyped words: What sex is assumed when you hear the word, "waiter?" Some restaurants have changed the word "waiter" to server, waitperson or waitron. Discuss the options that you like. Ask students to think of other roles that are stereo-typically associated with one sex or the other, and to suggest more neutral words to describe them.

Activity Three: Male-generic Pronouns, Nouns, and Verbs

A. **Pronouns**

Write the following sentences on the board:

> Each voter should place her ballot in the ballot box.
> Would anyone who wants a cookie raise her hand?

Ask students to discuss whom these sentences seem to be talking about (females). Ask if they think men or boys would feel included if they heard these sentences, and if not, ask if they think this is fair.

Next, write the same sentences using male pronouns and ask students if girls or women would feel included in these sentences. If not, is this fair?

A "male-generic" or "generic masculine" pronoun is a pronoun that is used when the sex of the actual person being referred to is not known, or when speaking about people in general. In *theory*, according to old-fashioned rules of grammar, this includes females as well as males, but in *reality* most people don't hear it that way (as the previous discussion probably made clear).

Ask for student ideas on alternatives that are more-inclusive, and write them up on the board. Apply the same questions about these alternatives: Would females and males both feel included?

If the following examples have not already been mentioned, now write them up and discuss them:

> Each voter should place her or his ballot in the ballot box. Or "her/his" ballot. Or "their" ballot. Or "your" ballot.
> Will anyone who wants a cookie raise their hand? Or "your" hand. Etc.

Discuss all the inclusive alternatives written on the board. What are the advantages or disadvantages of each form? If anyone objects that "she or he" is awkward, ask if it is any more awkward than "one or more," which is often used.

If someone says that "their" should only be used as a plural, explain that it is no different from using "you/your/yours" for both singular and plural. Also explain that singular "they/them/their" was commonly used and considered proper until 1850, when the British Parliament passed an act prescribing the use of male pronouns when gender was not specified. If appropriate, discuss the possible power motivations for such an act. Emphasize that English is a living language and we have every right to change it to make it more fair and inclusive.

B. Nouns

Discuss the phrase, "Peace on earth, good will to men." Do girls feel included?

"Male-generic" or "generic masculine" are phrases that describe the way the noun "men" is used in this sentence. What is another, more-inclusive, way to convey the meaning behind, "Peace on earth, good will to men?" (Examples: "to all," or "to people".)

Another example of a male-generic noun is the word "mankind." What more inclusive words could be substituted for "mankind?"

When male-generic words are questioned, the way they have been justified is the argument that they are meant to include women. To see if that reasoning makes sense, try a reversal. How would it feel to say, "Peace on earth, good will to women" and claim that the word "women" includes all people? Would men feel included?

When groups including both women and men are addressed as "you guys," this is androcentric language. One possible inclusive alternative is "you gaians" — because Gaia means Mother Earth, and both women and men, girls and boys, are her children!

Have students brainstorm ways, in the last few decades, that some male-generic nouns have been replaced with neutral terms. Examples: fireman/firefighter, mailman/postal worker or mail carrier, committee chairman/committee chair.

Brainstorm some male-generic nouns that are still in common usage. Examples "manpower," "manhole," and "Men working" signs. Have students brainstorm possible inclusive alternatives.

C. **Gender-Generic Verbs**
Brainstorm alternatives to such usages as:
"We need someone to *man* the cash register," or "I'll man the front desk while you man the phones," or "She mothers that kitten like it was a baby."

Discuss the message in such language — that certain jobs can (and, by implication, should) only be done by members of one sex or the other. In a world where both women and men work inside and outside the home, it's important that language acknowledge that *any* person can do *any* task.

D. **Other Male-Generic Terms**
Imagine exclaiming "Oh girl!" when you're excited. Or "Woman, that's really cool!" when you admire something. Why do you think male words are commonly used in these cases? What are some possible alternatives that would be more inclusive?

Male-generic pronouns, nouns, and verbs reveal the history of our language and our culture. They could be called historical markers. Embedded in these words is their source. In the cultures that shaped modern English, certain privileged men were in the dominant position. Men controlled writing, printing, and the "rules" of language. Now this is changing, and we can help language "catch up" with changes in society.

In today's world, although many adult women have learned to think of ourselves as included, male-generic language still serves the purpose of teaching people that it's ok for women to be invisible and secondary to men. Inclusive language implies that both women and men are important enough to mention, and that any job can be done by either sex.

<u>Activity Four:</u> Gender Labeling, or What Linguists Call "Marking"

What sex do you instantly think of when you hear "executive" or "poet" or "nurse?"

Now let's look at the terms "female executive," "female poet" or "male nurse"? These nouns have been labeled, or "marked." Think about this: How often would the nouns be marked in the reverse: "male executive," "male poet," or "female nurse." Why do you think they wouldn't be marked in the latter case?

The markings are provided to contradict stereotypical assumptions, yet at the same time the markings themselves *reinforce* the stereotypes. Labeling an occupation by sex reveals how language usage can perpetuate gender stereotypes and assumptions.

Likewise, when a woman is routinely labeled a "feminist author" while non-feminist men are *never* marked as "androcentric" (or "sexist" or "patriarchal") authors, one can guess what dominator society considers "usual" and "normal" or "unusual" and "aberrant."

Example: Here's a sentence with unequal marking: "In my literature class, we read works by novelist Norman Mailer, poet Robert Bly, Jewish feminist novelist Starhawk, and black lesbian poet Audre Lorde." What does this imply about which sex, race, or religion poets and novelists are "expected" to be?

Here's the same sentence with equal marking: "In my literature class, we read works by white sexist novelist Norman Mailer, white androcentric poet Robert Bly, Jewish feminist novelist Starhawk, and black lesbian poet Audre Lorde." Which parts sound strange or silly, and which sound "ordinary"?

Now here's the same sentence with no marking except equal identification by profession: "In my literature class, we read works by novelists Starhawk and Norman Mailer and poets Audre Lorde and Robert Bly."

As an assignment, students can be asked to bring in examples of unequally-marked writing and to rewrite them with equal or no marking.

Activity Five: Language and Racism

A. Using the same nouns from the previous activity, what assumption is made about the *race* of the person being referred to when you read: "executive," "lawyer," "president." Maybe you never thought about it before.

B. Language marking reveals which group is dominant, whether it is a particular sex or race. Which series of words, below, are seen more frequently than the other series?

- white executive, white lawyer, white president

- Latina executive, Asian lawyer, African American president

In general, any group that is *not* marked is assumed to be the norm. When a group is marked by race or sex, as in "black executive" or "woman doctor," it is assumed that they are *exceptions* to the norm.

C. Adjectives and racial assumptions: Partnership includes eliminating racism as well as sexism and other "isms. We'll look now at how adjectives create metaphors that conjure up vivid images and opinions in our minds.

Even when used without conscious racist intent, such terms as "black-hearted villain" or "deep dark secret," contrasted with "white knight" or "innocent white lie," contribute to fear and demonization of dark-skinned people. It's important to examine and replace language that implies something evil about "darkness" or "blackness."

Brainstorm a list of words and phrases that use "black" and "dark" to talk about something considered negative. Ask students to suggest other terms for these meanings that do not include "black" or "dark," e.g., "different-colored sheep" (which does not suggest there is anything *wrong* with being different).

D. Discuss that the very word "race" is itself a social construct, which means people made it up — it's not a distinct category in nature. Human beings are really one race. We couldn't share blood or intermarry if that weren't the case. The invention of the word "race" was part of inventing "racism." "Race" separated people of different cultures, heritages, and ethnicities into categories so that one group — white-skinned Europeans and European Americans — were dominant.

E. Historical perspective on color and norms: It's also important to consider that in many ancient cultures, black was celebrated as the color of the rich fertile earth, while the *white* color of bones was feared because it was associated with death.

Activity Six: Reversals

In the classroom, there are several techniques which can help learners explore and expand their awareness of dominator and partnership images, metaphors, assumptions, stereotypes, and concepts such as we've discussed here:

"Reversals" have great humor and shock value, often highlighting areas of dominator usage that might otherwise remain unconscious. Some examples:

- Think of a joke that makes fun of a group of people, such as "blondes" or people of Polish descent. Now tell the same joke but put another category of people — such as African Americans or "white men" — in place of the group that is being targeted. What do you notice? If the substitution seems outrageous but the original doesn't, that is an indication of how certain prejudices come to be tolerated as "normal," when they really shouldn't be.

- Change the order in mixed-gender pairings — "she or he," "women and men," "wives and husbands," "girls and boys." How does it feel — does it sound natural or weird? This is a test of habitual androcentric speech patterns: If the change sounds strange, it's because we are used to thinking the male "should" come first. If we want to help make our culture more equal, so that everything male is not thought to "come first," one way we can promote more equality is to put female nouns and pronouns first when we are speaking of both sexes.

- Substitute female nouns and pronouns for male-generic language when reading a text aloud, and notice the reactions of the listeners. Do the same with common clichés (e.g., "No woman is an island") and ask if the men in the group feel included. Discuss people's responses to the reversals.

- Change the sex of someone being described in a news story or piece of fiction, leaving all other descriptive words the same. See if the scenario would still sound "natural," or if it would sound ridiculous or disorienting. This is a good way to spot non-parallel vocabulary or usage, as well as gender stereotypes.

- Look for labeling, or "marking," in news articles. Substitute "Black" or "Asian" or "Native American" or "Jew" for "woman" or "lesbian/gay/bisexual" or "old person" or "fat person" in news articles or other discussions of rights or responsibilities or characteristics of certain groups. If the statement sounds outrageous with the substitution, there's probably some prejudice present in the original.

<u>Activity Seven:</u> Sticks and Stones and Gender Stereotypes

A. Take the sentence, "Sharon was called a tomboy." Write a description of Sharon and share your writing. Now take the sentence, "He called Louis a sissy." Make up a story about this event, and share it.

The saying goes, "Sticks and stones may break my bones, but words can never hurt me." Can words hurt? What messages does Louis get when he is called a "sissy?" What messages does Sharon get when she is called a tomboy?

Using what you wrote, examine what it means in the culture of your school to be so-called "masculine" or so-called "feminine." Is it more positive for a girl to be labeled a "like a boy" than it is for a boy to be labeled "like a girl?"

Do names like "sissy" imply that it is *good* to be female or like a woman or girl? Does "tomboy" suggest that it is better to be male or like a man or boy? Do such names suggest that if someone has qualities associated with the other sex, they are not a "normal" girl or boy?

Ask students to consider the following "proverb": "Sticks and stones may break my bones, but words can break my heart." Ask how many students have been hurt by words? How many are willing to stop calling each other names, because they know how much it hurts?

B. Make a list of qualities that anyone can have: assertive, nurturing, athletic, studious, gentle, creative — have students brainstorm others.

Discuss whether any female or male can have any of these qualities, and be described as attractively "feminine" if female, or attractively "masculine" if male.

3. Ask students to consider that maybe the words "masculine" and "feminine" are fossils of an androcentric past — concepts whose time has gone.

The adjectives "feminine" and "masculine" describe society's definitions of *gender*, even though they are often *claimed* to describe qualities "natural" to one sex or the other. These words have enormous power to affect people's self-image and self-esteem. To describe a man as "un-masculine" or a woman as "un-feminine" cuts to the very core of her or his identity as a person.

Discuss the way that words also have tremendous power to limit people's possibilities in life. If "feminine" and "masculine" are believed to be exclusive and opposite categories, what is a girl to do whose interests are identified with "masculine" pursuits? What happens to a boy whose personality is closer to the stereotype of "feminine"?

Reflection: Children learn early the painful consequences of being labeled "tomboy" or "sissy." If they persist in expressing all parts of themselves, they pay the price of non-conformity; if they try to root out their "unnatural" qualities, they pay the price of self-denial. Either way, their human wholeness is lost.

Many girls, "complimented" as "masculine" or called "tomboys" for being athletic, assertive, or creative have felt like "abnormal" or "unnatural" *females*, as a result. As adults they often speak of feeling they had to choose between being their whole selves, or being "feminine." And, because nearly everything associated with femaleness has been devalued in most modern societies, boys never want to be called "feminine" and will do almost anything to hide or eradicate traits or behaviors that cause them to be labeled that way.

Of course, the terms "feminine" and "masculine" — and the stereotypes associated with them — are not going to vanish overnight. While working to change our language about gender, we can acknowledge society's past use of gender stereotypes by saying "so-called feminine" or "stereotypically masculine," and by enclosing these words in " " when we write.

And we can encourage each other, and our children, to express all parts of themselves, regardless of the language used to label them. We can tell them: If anyone ever says to you 'Women aren't like that' or 'Men don't do that' — and yet you *are* a woman and you *are* like that, or you're a man and you *do* do it — don't question *yourself*, question them and their gender stereotypes! And go on being a whole human being.

Activity Eight: Examining Books and Media

A. Collect texts, newspapers, magazines, and library books. Examine them for the following:

- Relative numbers of people of color and whites, girls and boys, men and women represented. Presence or absence of people of different sizes, lifestyles, classes, sexual preferences, religions, and physical capabilities.

- Stereotypical presentation of gender roles, occupations, traits, and behaviors. Stereotyped images of race, age, religion, size, or class.

- Instances of violence, and the attitudes presented toward violence. Is violence by males treated as "normal" or "just human nature."

- Instances of domination or partnership.

B. Select one of these sources and journal about instances of dominator language or any form of stereotyping. Refer also to television shows or movies on video.

C. Find and re-write passages of text (or time-worn proverbs, expressions, and "sayings") so that they do not contain stereotyping. Think of partnership-oriented alternative language.

Activity Nine: What's in a Name?

A. Have students brainstorm a list of last names that have "son" or "man" in them: e.g., Johnson, Bateman.

Discuss: Why do English surnames frequently contain male terms embedded in them, but they never contain "daughter" or "woman."

B. Explain the historical reason. For most of the last 5,000 years in many cultures, ancestry was traced through the father. Women and children were considered property of the man.

In contrast, the earlier partnership-oriented cultures of the Neolithic period traced ancestry through the mother's line; archaeological evidence indicates these cultures were matrilineal.

In most western cultures, until very recently, most married women have given up their surnames and taken their husband's surname, losing their original identity. This custom not only perpetuates the idea that the husband owns his wife, but it also makes a person's maternal ancestry very difficult to trace.

C. Names that simply add a diminutive "feminine" ending to a male name (such as Paula, Jackie, Stephanie, Roberta, Josephine, Geraldine, Claudia) similarly reinforce the male as standard and the female as "added on" or *derived from* the male. How many male names do you know that have a female name as a root?

D. Names given babies also reflect stereotypes about gender — how many boys are named after sweets (Candy), flowers (Rose), and virtues (Faith)?

Activity Ten: Male as "Norm" and Female as "Other" or "Derivative" (Added-on)

Ask students to think about the words, "poet" and "poetess." What sex is associated with each word? If a "poet" is defined as "a person who writes poetry" and a "poetess" is "a woman who writes poetry," the implication is that a "real poet" is male.

When maleness is the implied "norm," anything female is compared to what is male, and often treated as less important. Terms like "actress," "sculptress," "aviatrix," "stewardess," "comedienne," and "ballerina" are "derivatives" of neutral words ("actor," "sculptor," "aviator," etc.) which originally meant simply "a person who acts/ sculpts/flies etc." By adding the endings, or "diminutive suffixes," maleness is treated as the neutral "norm" and women who pursue those activities seem to be imitators of the "real" (male) thing.

This is similar to deriving girls' names from boys' names (see Activity Eight). The shorter male name (e.g., "George" is considered to be the "base" from which the "female version," "Georgina," is derived, or added on.

Activity Eleven: Non-parallel Gendered Words and Meanings

Sometimes androcentrism or sexism can be detected when words used for one sex have different values and meanings than similar words used for the other sex, or when a word exists to describe a member of one sex, but there is no word with a similar meaning for members of the other sex. Ask students to consider the following examples:

A. Often, words associated with maleness have lofty, important meanings, while words associated with femaleness imply inferiority or pathology. For example, contrast "seminal" ideas with "hysterical" ideas; both adjectives come from the human reproductive system, but what a difference in meaning between the male and the female!

"Seminal" and "hysterical" are examples of "parallel" words with non-parallel meanings. Another example: "master" (a person of great competency) and "mistress" (a man's illicit paramour).

B. Sometimes there are gender-associated words that have no parallels for the other sex. For example, try to think of a female equivalent of "emasculated" or "virile." Or a parallel word for "feisty" or "dainty" that would apply to a man. What terms derived from female genitals are parallel in solemnity and importance to "testimony" or "testament" (derived from *testes*)? Imagine a woman writing her "last will and ovariment."

C. Animal names are often used to describe males and females in non-parallel ways. Those applied to women are often degrading or sexualized: Heifer, filly, chick, dog, shrew, pig, sow, beaver, old crow, bunny, bitch, bat, fox, cold fish, hen, vixen, cat, kitten (usually paired with "sex"); while those applied to men frequently reflect power, virility and cunning: Buck, bull, stag, stallion, wolf.

D. Another non-parallel use of gendered language can still be found on bathroom doors in public places. If the sign on the door says "Men" it identifies its users by biological sex; if it says "Ladies" its occupants are defined by gender role. "Men" and "Women" are parallel terms, as are "Ladies" and "Gentlemen." "Wife and husband" are parallel; "man and wife" are not.

E. "Miss" and "Mrs." are traditional female "courtesy titles" that have no parallel male term. The title "Ms." has been adopted by many women since the 1970's as a parallel for "Mr." since neither "Mr." nor "Ms." provides information about an individual's marital status.

Activity Twelve: Either/or Language, Comparisons, and Ranking

The purpose of this lesson is to help students recognize and change language and thought patterns that promote the kind of intolerance and narrow-minded judgmentalism that often lead to verbal conflict and physical violence.

Evaluation and judgment are important human capacities that are also necessary for partnership — how else could we determine whether a particular action promotes domination or partnership, for example? However, when *human beings* (rather than their actions) are judged as *right* or *wrong* based on their differences, there is great potential for conflict as all parties struggle to dominate or avoid being dominated by others.

Language which honors diverse cultures and perspectives, and which goes beyond "either-or" to "both-and" thinking, can contribute to partnership and peace by decreas ing the need for one party or culture or practice to be "right" and all others to be "wrong" (and therefore prohibited or controlled). This is not to approve a relativistic "anything goes" philosophy (which can actually perpetuate domination); it is to suggest that many common English speech habits which compare and rank people according to their differences are counterproductive, if tolerance and partnership are our goals.

A. "Either/or," or "dualistic" thinking and speaking: English speakers often talk in pairs, and speak as if differences were opposites, even when they're not. Students might consider the beliefs hidden in the following examples:

- "Everything is black or white with them."
- "You're either for us or against us."
- "There are two sides to every question."
- "Are you a man or not?"
- "America — love it or leave it!"
- "On the one hand … on the other hand.… "
- "Members of the opposite sex.…"

Questions to discuss: What creative possibilities do such sayings (and beliefs) exclude? How might this dualistic, either-or way of thinking and speaking make it hard to consider other possibilities or solutions to challenges? How might cooperative partnership — for example, between individual fulfillment and community service — be made difficult by each language?

B. Comparison and ranking: Part of the problem with dualistic, either-or thinking is that differences are rarely equated with *equality*. One part of any pair is usually valued more than the other, especially if the two are considered to be *opposites*, as they so often are.

This comparison of value leads to hierarchical thinking, where one part of a pair is ranked above the other. The structure of English is such that whatever is mentioned first is traditionally considered the more important or valuable of the pair, as in "right or wrong," "good or bad," "boys and girls," "winners and losers," "'haves' and 'have nots,'" "rich and poor." To test this, try saying these pairs in reverse and notice how strange and "unnatural" they sound.

In each of the following common pairs of apparent "opposites," the first word is frequently used to mean "better" (of greater value or importance) and the second "worse" (of lesser value), often in a moral as well as literal sense: Higher/lower, superior/inferior, above/below, heaven/earth, mind/body, spirit/flesh, spiritual/physical, spiritual/carnal, mental/physical, divine/earthly, God/"man," man/woman, dominant/subordinate.

The English language is filled with words that compare and judge: "Some/more/most," "good/better/best," "bad/worse/worst." Common comparative suffixes — "-er" and "-ier," "-est," and "-iest" - make it easy to compare and rank people, things, and events.

This tendency to compare, judge, and rank promotes competition, and an attitude that every difference of opinion or desire must mean one "side" is right and the other wrong, or one must win and the other lose. The assumption is that whomever is judged "good" or whoever "wins" has the right to dominate the "loser" or whomever is judged "bad." It is easy to see how this way of thinking leads to more competition, judgmentalism, conflict, violence, and domination.

Partnership, in contrast, appreciates differences and treats them as equally valid and valuable, as long as nobody is dominated or harmed. It seeks resolutions to conflicts where everyone gets their needs met, and nobody has to "lose." But the English language makes it hard to speak of "both-and" instead of "either-or." It takes a conscious effort to change this way of speaking, but it can be done.

Ask students to think of their own ways of speaking, and to find quotes from the news and entertainment media, which exemplify the points just made. Discuss more partnership-oriented ways of speaking about the same issues.

C. Dualism, gender, and hierarchy: English speakers often base their language choices on the "structural metaphor" of "up is good, down is bad." A structural metaphor is an association between two things, which is rarely explicitly stated and often unconscious, but which affects many word choices and meanings that people use in their everyday speech and thinking. Some examples of language based on "up is good, down is bad" include:

- The words "superior" (above, or over) meaning "better" and "inferior" (below, or under) meaning "worse."

- The association of "heaven" with "high" and "hell" with "low."

- "Peak experiences" are considered good, while "depression" is bad, both emotionally and economically.

- In athletic competitions, scores are announced as winners over losers.

- Even the words "domination" and "submission" imply that whomever is on top has power *over* whomever is on the bottom ("sub").

- Ask students to think of other examples.

Even the most well-meaning partnership advocates often unwittingly perpetuate the language of hierarchy and dualism on which domination depends. Expressions like "higher consciousness" or "higher power" pervade the speech of many wise and thoughtful people. But the unintended implication in such language is to associate the "good" with the "higher" (or "spiritual" or "godlike" or "male") — and the "bad" with the "lower" (or "carnal" or "earthly" or "female"). This way of thinking and speaking subtly validates male domination of women, since what is "lower" is often considered dangerous and in need of control (as humans believe they have the right to control "lower" animals).

There do exist other semantic scales that could be used to describe quality comparisons when they are needed: depth (deeper/shallower), breadth (wider/narrower), volume (more/less), content (fuller/emptier), degree (greater/lesser), distance (nearer/farther). None of the other scales contains metaphoric associations with the religious dualisms of good and evil, and none of them is regularly used in contexts implying moral judgment. Thus, they are useful for creating alternatives to common expressions which reinforce ranking (for example, "deeper wisdom" rather than "higher wisdom").

D. The impact of dualism, comparison, and ranking on violence: Many peace advocates point out that much, if not all, violence and warfare comes about because people judge *themselves* to be right and judge anyone who looks, acts, or believes differently to be wrong and must therefore be controlled or dominated. In such a dualistic, either-or framework, people are almost compelled to compete to dominate each other, so they will not *be* dominated.

Most acts of violence are preceded by verbal violence — judgments, arguments, name-calling, condemnations, threats, and ultimatums. If we learn to speak less judgmentally and comparatively, and to speak of non-oppressive differences as equally valuable, we may thus learn to *think* of them that way. Thus, by "speaking our peace" through acceptance, tolerance, and non-judgmentalism, we may contribute to more equality and partnership on all levels, from personal to racial to international relationships.

<u>Activity Thirteen:</u> Competition and "Battlespeak," or Problems/Conflicts as Warfare

Ask students to discuss the difference in mental imagery between these phrases: "fighting drugs" and "healing addictions." Now look at these contrasts: "war on crime" and "transforming violence." Which language deals with problems in a peaceful, partnership-oriented way? Which evokes images of conflict, competition, winning and losing, and domination?

A major goal of partnership is moving from "either-or" thinking to "both-and" conflict resolution. Yet many of our everyday expressions perpetuate the dualism of "either-or." These include metaphors of combat and warfare, which philosopher Susan Sontag calls "battlespeak."

Such language promotes domination: It implies that one side must win and the other lose, and also that violence is an acceptable way of dealing with challenges. In addition, it creates disturbing, conflictual mental images and emotional associations which we may not be consciously aware of, but which can subtly affect our health and our expectations of how the world works.

A related structural metaphor in contemporary American English usage is the idea that "argument is war" or "disagreement is war." While people don't often use these explicit words, the following commonly-used sentences are based on them:

> "Your claims are *indefensible.*
>
> She *attacked* every weak point in my argument.
>
> His criticisms were *right on target.*
>
> I *demolished* her argument.
>
> I've never *won* an argument with him.
>
> You disagree? Okay, *shoot*!
>
> If you use that *strategy,* she'll *wipe you out.*
>
> He *shot down* all of my arguments."

These statements would make no sense if the underlying metaphor of "argument is war" were not implicitly understood and agreed upon by both speaker and listener.

Rather than using language of mastery, control, domination, opposition, or violent competition, we *could* use metaphors of birth, growth, creation, harmony, construction, transformation, journeying, healing, helping, loving, nurturing, cooperation, and connection — all of which implant much healthier images in the unconscious mind.

Sexism, racism, and other forms of inequality and oppression stem from conflict, with the winners dominating the losers. People are divided into groups labeled "us" and "other." Changes in language can emphasize partnership. If a partnership world is to be free of violence, war, and destructive competition, we must be able to envision a peaceful world in our language. Instead of "fighting" and "defeating" and "winning" we might attempt "healing" social ills, "negotiating with" our opponents, or "resolving" our problems.

Activity Fourteen: "Other" Sex, Not "Opposite" Sex

A. Discuss the distinction between "sex" and "gender." These terms are often confused and misused as interchangeable.

- "Sex" is physical and biological.

- "Gender" describes qualities of personality, character traits, interests, skills, and behaviors, all of which are defined by a culture as being either "feminine" or "masculine." While, in any given society, certain of these may appear more frequently in members of one sex or the other, virtually all *can* belong to both women *and* men.

- While *sex* is biological, *gender* is "constructed" — defined by society. One is biologically identified as female or male, and this doesn't vary between cultures. But what it *means* to be "a man" or "a woman" — the territory of *gender* — varies greatly from culture to culture, and from era to era.

Although women and men are *complementary halves* of the human race, in whom 97% of DNA is identical, dominator language persists in labeling them as "opposite" sexes. Since our species would quickly become extinct if men and women didn't contribute equally to the reproductive process, it might be more accurate (and less conflict-inspiring) to speak of "the *other* sex" rather than "the opposite sex."

B. Heterocentric language: Language that describes romantic love only between women and men may not intentionally promote homophobia, but it is "heterocentric" — it implies that heterosexual coupling is "normal" and that same-sex unions either don't exist or are aberrant.

Looking again at the riddle about the surgeon whose son arrived in the emergency room, we see that people who think the only possible solution is that the surgeon is the boy's *mother* are engaging in heterocentrist thinking.

The word "partner," in place of "husband" or "wife," is a term that can apply equally to other-sex *and* same-sex committed relationships.

C. Writers and comedians often refer to "the war of the sexes." How might it affect young people to grow up hearing this phrase? What assumptions are passed on through that use of language? What kind of power structure is maintained? Ask students to explore subsitute phrases using partnership language. For instance, we might speak instead of "the dance of the sexes."

Activity Fifteen: Transforming Language Toward Partnership

The challenge of dominator language: Discuss this quote from language scholar Jackie Young: "It is our culture and communication system that constructs — and constricts — our reality, and if the male culture controls that system then our reality is created and shaped (constricted) by male perceptions." Ask how what we think about women and men and the possibility of partnership is shaped (constructed) and limited (constricted) by such language habits as male-generic language, marking, parallel and non-parallel terms and meanings, comparisons and ranking, "battlespeak," and referring to women and men as "opposite" sexes.

The following are some ideas for changing how we use language, so that we do not reinforce domination-oriented ideas, assumptions, and beliefs. In each case, it will be helpful to give examples and ask students to come up with more. When domination-oriented language or usage are identified, encourage students to cooperate to co-create partnership-oriented alternatives.

A. Reclaiming old words: Although it is difficult and takes much time, some people find it worthwhile to attempt to redefine or reclaim existing words to which dominator culture has attached negative or derogatory values. "Witch" and "crone" are two such words for which women are reclaiming their original meanings of "healer" and "wise older woman," respectively.

B. Inventing new words: English is a living language, and we are perfectly free to make up new words, "from scratch" or by creative combining, as long as their meaning is clear.

The adjectives "sexist," "racist," "ageist," and "homophobic" are relatively recent inventions of the English language, created to describe attitudes of inequality which once were taken for granted as "natural." A "sexist" attitude implies that one sex is better than the other, "racism" infers superior and inferior races, and so on.

To even speak of "partnership" itself — in a way that recognizes the centrality of the female/male relationship to *all* forms of social organization — requires the invention of new words. Riane Eisler coined the term "gylany" to describe equal *linking* between men and women, rather than the hierarchical *ranking* of patriarchal domination; it combines parts of the Greek words for woman and men and linking. While "partnership" is used throughout this paper because of its familiarity to most people, it has the disadvantage of having many other meanings (business partnership, for example). "Gylany" is a more percise, but less familiar term. Perhaps if it is used enough it will enter common usage, but in the meantime "partnership" gets the basic idea across, with less explanation. This is an example of the kind of trade-off that is often necessary in our efforts to change language and consciousness.

C. Word play: Often it's possible to find less-common but still perfectly-serviceable words right in the English language. Using these words in place of commonly-used terms and expressions can create surprise in the listener, which in turn prompts them to listen more closely to the meaning of what we've actually *said*, and to contrast it with the meanings of the words we *didn't* say (but they expected).

If there isn't a readily-available alternative to androcentric or sexist or racist or ageist language, it's sometimes possible to playfully invent a word or expression whose meaning is perfectly clear and which calls attention to the problems inherent in the words *not* used. We can describe a partnership-oriented inclusive record of human experience as *"ourstory"* — a combination of *"history"* and *"herstory"* and *"theirstory."* Or one might speak of finding a bunch of "senior singles" (replacing "old maids" to describe unpopped kernels) in the bottom of the popcorn bowl. Such words, like "foremother" or "waitperson" may eventually find their way into general use; "Ms." has already done so.

D. Adding words from other languages: Adopting and adapting words from other languages is a process that English has used for centuries. Often other languages contain simple and elegant words which express complex concepts that English has not developed vocabulary for. Some examples: "yoni" — a Sanskrit word for the vulva which means "gate to the source"; "namaste" — a Tibetan greeting which translates approximately as "the divinity in me recognizes and salutes the divinity in you"; and "shalom" — a Hebrew word used in greeting and parting, which means "peace be with you." The Hawaiian word "aloha" is particularly useful for greetings and farewells, for it combines the meanings of love, welcoming, hello, and goodbye. "Shalomaloha" is a salutation I coined to express a wish for peace and love.

E. Reshaping language to reshape perception: In a partnership-oriented language, surely we would have more than one four-letter word ("love") to describe such varied forms of affection as romantic passion, long-standing friendship, the devotion of a long-partnered couple, the feeling of parent for child, the reverence of child for parent, the attachment of people and pets, enthusiasm for skiing, or a taste for vanilla ice cream!

What does it say about our culture that we have no single word for sexual intercourse that is neither clinical, violent, or taboo, yet we have so many different and graphic words to describe conflict and killing? Why are our most "obscene" oaths and expletives so often words for female sex organs or violent acts of dominator sex?

F. Non-verbal language: In addition to spoken and written language, it's important to pay attention to non-verbal communications — the "language" of behaviors such as eye contact, paying attention, changing the subject, interrupting, questioning, body movements, tone of voice, and "holding the floor" longest in conversation. In a partnership-oriented society, these behaviors would be evidenced fairly equally among women and men, and among people of different ages, races, or appearance. When they are not, it's likely that dominator dynamics are at work.

In teaching communication skills, it's helpful to have students evaluate whether any given conversational technique contributes to equally-participatory, respectful, and mutually-cooperative dialogue, or whether it fosters domination by certain individuals and silencing or muting of others. In paired or group discussions, attention to the *dynamics* of conversation is as important as attention to the words used. Teachers can ask students to partner with them, in assuring that nobody dominates discussion, and that all voices are heard and respected.

Activity Sixteen: Advocating for Partnership in Deed and Word

A. Speaking up, being response-able: Ask students to brainstorm ways to intervene when they hear language used for put-downs or in other domination-oriented ways.

As teachers and responsible individuals of any age, how do we respond when we hear jokes that ridicule or denigrate people who belong to diverse groups (women,

people of color, people of certain religious or ethnic backgrounds, lesbians/
gays/bisexual/transgendered people, old people, differently-abled people, large-
bodied people, people who don't fit the "mainstream" definition of beauty)? What
do we do when our students or peers make stereotypical pronouncements about
people from these diverse groups? Do we discuss the consequences of such language in a way that expands people's consciousness *without* shaming them, or do
we shrug and let it pass, saying to ourselves "it's only words"?

Ask each student to describe how they would prefer to be made aware of any domination-oriented language they might unconsciously use. In this way, students are
likely to observe that it is kinder and more effective to call attention to inappropriate language in a friendly, sympathetic way than to accuse another person of being
sexist or racist (which is in its own way a dominator approach). If we assume that
the other person is well-meaning and would never intentionally say cruel, biased,
or prejudiced things, we are more likely to get a positive response, even if they do
hold dominator beliefs and intentions.

B. Writing assignment: A letter advocating change

Although we need to be patient and tolerant of ourselves and other *individuals* as
we work to change language, we need to make our standards known to public figures, institutions, and communications media. It's especially important to work for
non-discriminatory, non-stereotyped, non-dominator language in textbooks, news
and entertainment media, and public pronouncements of celebrities. Our individual
efforts to change consciousness through language change are important, but social
transformation will really accelerate only when change comes to the media whose
words and images reach great masses of people of all ages.

Ask students to write a letter to a publisher or broadcaster that describes a language-
related problem they've observed and asks for specific changes. Ask them to be sure
to write their letter in partnership-oriented language and to explain their reasons.

Conclusion: The Challenge of Change

As educators advocating for partnership, we may find ourselves asking our students to develop skills we are ourselves still new and unpracticed in. For example, in
the process of "teaching what we would learn," do we teach our students to speak the
language of emotions, to make "I" statements to describe their feelings, to disagree with
respect, to negotiate their differences without resorting to insult, ostracism, or force? A
language and pedagogy of partnership would provide for all these lessons. But how
many of us have learned these skills? Perhaps one of our first acts of partnership will be
to become co-learners and co-creators, with our students, of a partnership language.

The English language has been shaped by and reflects the values of those who have held power in western dominator cultures for the past 5,000 years. Poet Adrienne Rich, expresses our dilemma as partnership educators, in her statement: "This is the oppressor's language, yet I need it to talk to you."

Another poet, Audre Lorde, sounded a seemingly pessimistic note when she stated: "The master's tools will never dismantle the master's house. They may allow us temporarily to beat him at his own game, but they will never allow us to bring about genuine change."

But what if we don't *try* to "beat him at his own game?" What if we step out of the paradigm of competition, of winning and losing, and co-create a new language that expresses a completely different vision of relationship — a vision of peace, partnership, equality, and celebration of difference?

In linguist Suzette Haden Elgin's visionary novel, *Native Tongue*, women create their own language to express female perceptions and concerns which are not represented in their patriarchal culture's common language. It eventually causes completely unforeseen changes in consciousness, which affect every aspect of their lives. Trying to understand how this could have happened, one of the characters plaintively asks: "How can you plan for a new reality when you don't have the remotest idea what it would be like?" The answer is, of course, that you can't — no science exists that can predict a new-paradigm world from within the old one.

So perhaps we can't completely predict what far-ranging effects a language of partnership might have on our individual consciousness or on our society. But we *can* see how the language and culture of domination and violence reinforce each other, and how continuing to speak in these terms can only bring us more of the same.

And we can ask: What might children be like who've learned to speak in terms of cooperation instead of competition, of creating and nurturing and healing instead of fighting and defeating and dominating? We can try presenting them with words and pictures (and experiences) of peace and pleasure and partnership, of art and music and dance, of love and sharing and caring — and we can watch what happens.

If we can even *begin* to imagine a non-hierarchical, cooperative, nature-honoring world which respects and celebrates all life's diversity — and if we can educate our children with words and images and metaphors that describe this vision, perhaps our children will be the ones to bring our vision to life!

A Few Common Words and Phrases, and Some Partnership Alternatives

Note: These are only a few possible alternatives, to use or not according to your personal preference, and to inspire classroom creativity in developing further partnership-oriented language. Please share any ideas you come up with by e-mail (Letheafay@aol.com), so that I can pass them on to other people who "speak partnership."

Domination-oriented	*Partnership-oriented*
Consciousness-*raising*	Consciousness-*expansion*
Deadline or *Target* date	Goal
Dear Sir or Madam	*Greetings*
Fellow man	*Human kin*
Fight crime or injustice	*Heal* crime or injustice
High technology	*Advanced* technology
Higher consciousness	*Deeper* consciousness
Higher value	*Greater* value
Highly-developed	*Well*-developed
Man the office	*Staff* the office
Mankind	*Humankind*
Man-made	*Mind-made, or human-made*
Master (as noun)	*Head, Expert, Leader*
Master (as verb)	*Develop expertise or competence*
Miss or *Mrs.*	*Ms.*
Opposite sex	*Other* sex
No-man's land	*No-one's* land
Rule of thumb	*Guideline*
Spearhead an effort	*Initiate* an effort
War of the sexes	*Dance of the sexes*
War on drugs, poverty, etc.	*Effort to heal* addictions, poverty
Win-win solution (reinforces competition)	*Grow-grow* resolution
You *guys* (for both women and men)	You *gaias* or You *gaians* (for both)
Kill 2 birds with one stone	*Hatch 2 birds from one egg* or *Feed 2 birds with one hand*

Recommended Reading

Cameron, Julia, ed. (1990). *The Feminist Critique of Language: A Reader*. London: Routledge.

Daly, Mary, in cahoots with Jane Caputi (1987). *Websters' First New Intergalactic Wickedary of the English Language*. Boston: Beacon Press.

Elgin, Suzette Haden (1993). *Genderspeak; Men, Women, and the Gentle Art of Verbal Self-Defense*. New York: John Wiley & Sons.

Hardman, M. J. (1993). "Derivational Thinking, or, Why is Equality So Difficult?" pp. 250-263 in *Seeking Understanding of Communication, Language and Gender*, edited by C. A. Valentine: CyberSpace Publishing.

Hardman, M.J. (1996). "The Sexist Circuits of English." *The Humanist*: pp. 25-32.

Hardman, M.J. (1998). "Metaphorical Alternatives to Violence — Report From a Workshop." *Women and Language v. 21 no. 2 (Fall '98)* p. 43-6 v.21: pp. 43-6.

Hardman, M. J. (1999). "Why We Should Say 'Women and Men' Until It Doesn't Matter Any More." *Women & Language* 22: pp. 1-2.

Hedley, Jane. "Surviving to Speak new Language: Mary Daly and Adrienne Rich." *Hypatia* vol. 7, no. 2 (Spring 1992).

Kramarae, Cheris and Paula A. Treichler, eds. (1992). *Amazons, Bluestockings and Crones; A Feminist Dictionary*. London: Pandora.

Lakoff, George (1987). *Women, Fire, and Dangerous Things; What Categories Reveal About the Mind*. Chicago: University of Chicago Press.

Lakoff, George, and Mark Johnson (1980). *Metaphors We Live By*. Chicago: University of Chicago Press.

Lakoff, Robin Tolmach (1990). *Talking Power; The Politics of Language*. BasicBooks.

Mills, Jane (1989). *Womanwords; A Dictionary of Words About Women*. New York: Macmillan.

Musgrave, Kate. "Eve Names Names: Feminist Neology and How to Do It." In *Women and Language* Vol.XV, No.1, pp. 27-31.

Olds, Linda E. (1992). *Metaphors of Interrelatedness: Toward a Systems Theory of Psychology*. Albany, NY: SUNY Press.

Penelope, Julia (1990). *Speaking Freely; Unlearning the Lies of the Fathers' Tongues*. New York: Teachers College Press.

Rosenberg, Marshall B. (1999). *Nonviolent Communication: A Language of Compassion*. Del Mar, CA: PuddleDancer Press.

Schaffner, Christina and Anita L. Wenden, eds. (1995). *Language and Peace.*, vol. 6, Edited by S. P. Reyna and R. E. Downs. Amsterdam: Harwood Academic Publishers.

Spender, Dale (1980). *Man Made Language*. London: Pandora.

Tannen, Deborah (1990). *You Just Don't Understand; Women and Men in Conversation*. New York: Ballantine.

Tannen, Deborah (1994). *Gender and Discourse*. New York: Oxford University Press.

Tannen, Deborah. (1998). *The Argument Culture: Moving from Debate to Dialogue*. New York: Random House.

CHAPTER 13

The Wisdom of the Elders: Curriculum Resources for Unlearning Sexism

by Sarah Pirtle

Middle School students sit riveted at an assembly as they hear speeches from the suffragist movement portrayed on stage. Fathers stop by for breakfast at an elementary school in a monthly "Donuts for Dads" program. A video brings the topic of date rape into a high school and allows much-needed discussion to occur with a trusted school counselor. These and a multitude of programs and resources developed by educators, community organizers, and many others are helping to change sexism in the United States.

According to early childhood experts Louise Derman-Sparks and the Anti-Bias Curriculum Task Force, children as young as two or three-years-old show that they have ingested the gender messages of society. Hungry to be part of the world, children pick up the social cues presented. They notice in social interactions how men are deferred to and command roles of authority. They notice on television when women who dress and talk certain ways receive the most praise and attention. They take heed if teachers respond to students differently, reinforcing prettiness in girls and activity in boys.

To counter the programming of sexism, adults need to step in and take the traditional cultural role of elders. Through anti-bias, gender equity, and other movements in education, educators can guide and support healthy development, and help young people reject the conscription of sexism to take part in creating partnership culture. This chapter takes the viewpoint that we are called to actively contribute to the unlearning of sexism.

Working for Change

Here are websites where you can meet some of the organizations that are engaged in this important work and see the partnership changes moving through this country.

This first group of websites connects teachers to media resources, lesson plans, and training:

- **The Center for Research on Women**, Wellesley College

  www.researchonwomen.com

  The Center's work includes the Project on Bullying and Sexual Harassment founded by Nan Stein, author of *Bullyproof*, and the new Project on Teasing and Bullying which offer curriculum and teacher training.

- **Media Education Foundation**

  www.mediaed.org

  "Date Rape Backlash" is the video referred to above. MEF has eleven videos on Media, Gender and Culture including "Tough Guise," "Reviving Ophelia," "Recovering Bodies," and "Dreamworlds: Desire/Sex/Power in Music Videos." MEF also offers "Tomorrow's Children," a video on Partnership Education which includes an interview with Riane Eisler and footage from Nova School.

- **New Moon Magazine for Girls**

  www.newmoon.org

  This website tells how to order *New Moon Magazine*, where "we listen to girls and women and celebrate their power." Many resources are available, including the New Moon Network for Adults who Care About Girls. Girls ages 8 to 14 can apply to be a member of the editorial board of the magazine by sending a letter telling why they are interested. The board brainstorms themes and suggests articles.

- **Myra Sadker Advocates for Gender Equity**

  www.sadker.org

  This is a website based on Myra and David Sadker's work. Helpful lesson plans under "Gender Equity Activities for Teachers," are available. Also there are ideas for how to participate in Myra Sadker Day. Anecdotes from the essay, "Profiles in Fairness," which details the Sadker's partnership can be used in class discussions, such as their experience sharing time during a television interview.

- **The National Coalition for Sex Equity in Education**

  www.ncsee.org

  Announcements, news about the annual conference, information about the newsletter, and a full bibliography and list of resources are available at this site.

- **The National Women's History Project**

  www.nwhp.org

  At this website teachers can learn about performers who can come to the school and portray famous women in history such as Sacagawea, Sojourner Truth, or Eleanor Roosevelt. Other sections of the site include, "History Quiz," "Teachers Lounge," "Students Center," and "Intimate Portraits." Free catalogs can also be ordered.

- **Teen Voices**

  www.teenvoices.com

  "Put down that lipstick and let go of the need-a-guy attitude! You don't need them when you have Teen Voices, an intelligent alternative to the fashion/boy-crazy publications. Dedicated to inspiring and publishing the unrecognized voices of teen women the world over since 1990."

This next group of web sites support feminism, women's studies, and alliances of women for social change.

- **Ms. Magazine**

  www.msmagazine.com

  The Ms. Foundation sponsors a national day devoted to girls, Take Our Daughters to Work Day.

  "*Ms.* was the first U.S. magazine to feature prominent American women demanding the repeal of laws that criminalized abortion. To explain and advocate for the ERA. The first to rate presidential candidates on women's issues. The first to put domestic violence and sexual harassment on the cover of a women's magazine, to feature feminist protest of pornography, to commission and feature a national study on date rape, and to blow the whistle on the undue influence of advertising on magazine journalism. *Ms.* was the first national magazine to make feminist voices audible, feminist journalism tenable, and a feminist worldview available to the public." The web site includes book reviews and selections from the magazine.

- **National Women's Studies Association**

  www.nwsa.org

  The National Women's Studies Association (NWSA) was founded in 1977 to further the development of Women's Studies throughout the world at every educational level and in every setting. The site includes pages on caucuses such as "Jewish women," task forces such as "Anti-white supremacy," and interest groups such as "Medieval and Early Modern Women."

- **National Organization for Women (NOW)**

  www.now.org or web site 63.111.42.146

  NOW is the largest organization of feminist activists in the U.S. with 550 chapters in all 50 states. Since its founding in 1966, NOW's goal has been to take action to bring about equality for all women through electoral and lobbying work and lawsuits. NOW also founded hot lines and shelters for battered women and lobbied for government funding of programs aimed at stopping violence against women, winning passage of a new ground-breaking federal law in 1996. Sexual harassment was one of the key issues that has motivated students across the country to form high school chapters of NOW.

- **Women's Action for New Directions (WAND)**

  www.wand.org

  WAND is a grassroots organization with members in all fifty states, and an e-mail alert network focusing on empowering women to act politically to reduce militarism and violence and redirect excessive military resources toward human and environmental needs. It was founded by Dr. Helen Caldicott in the early 1980's.

- **Women's International League for Peace and Freedom (WILPF)**

  www.wilpf.org

  The Women's International League for Peace and Freedom was founded in 1915 during World War I, with Jane Addams as its first president. WILPF works to achieve through peaceful means world disarmament, full rights for women, racial and economic justice, an end to all forms of violence, and to establish those political, social, and psychological conditions which can assure peace, freedom, and justice for all. The web site includes selected readings, and information about WILPF's campaigns to challenge corporate power, dismantle the war economy, and work for racial justice. Committees work on a range of issues such as the death penalty, the Middle East, Cuba/Latin America, and drug policy.

These websites help students encounter organizations that affirm and support men, deconstruct sexism, and develop male identity that is pro-male and pro-feminist.

- **Men Against Domestic Violence: MADV**
  www. silcom.com/~paladin/madv/
  The site includes articles such as, "What can men do to help stop domestic violence?'

- **Men for Change: A Pro-feminist Organization**
  www.chebucto.ns.ca/CommunitySupport/Men4Change
  Men for Change "formed in the aftermath of the tragic killing of women engineering students in Montreal in 1989 by a man who singled out his victims because they were a bunch of feminists." Men for Change developed "Healthy Relationships: A Violence Prevention Curriculum" for Junior High students.

- **MensNet**
  www.inforweb.magi.com/~mensnet/
  This Canadian network links men working in a variety of ways against sexism, patriarchy, and homophobia, who are opposed to the many forms of violence. It has an extensive library section with articles and discussion papers.

- **Men's Resource Center (MRC)**
  www.mrc-wma.com
  MRC in Amherst, Massachusetts offers support group, youth education programs, batterer treatment, and many types of training and consultation and is a model for other groups nationwide. Teachers can request a copy of MRC's magazine, *Voice Male* on supporting men and challenging violence, which has been published quarterly for sixteen years. The "Donuts for Dads" program mentioned above was created by William Farkas at MRC. The American Men's Studies Association doesn't have a website, but they can be contacted through Sam Femiano at MRC.

- **Mentors in Violence Prevention**
  www.jacksonkatz.com
  MVP's primary mission "is to empower men who are not abusive to women to confront men who are." The Media Education Project's video, "Tough Guise," documents this work. Using MVP Playback scenarios, men practice responding

constructively to situations where they as bystanders can intervene. Jackson Katz, the founder of MVP, trains sports coaches to teach their team members to be anti-sexist, as well as other work with businesses, fraternities, and the military. He also majored in sports in college and minored in Women's Studies. Teachers can download a biography of Jackson at this website and present him as a role model for students.

- **The National Men's Resource Center**
  www.menstuff.org
  The National Men's Resource Center "believes that positive change in male roles and relationships is possible." Since 1985, their role has been to end isolation by creating a directory that now lists 2600+ men's services and publications committed to a positive change in male roles and relationships. They support the development of Men's Studies programs on college campuses and provide non-hazing programs for fraternities as well.

- **Real Men, an anti-sexist men's group in the Boston area.**
  www.cs.utk.edu/~bartley/other/
  At this site, schools can download a description of Real Men, or click "10things" and copy a one page handout called, "Ten Things Men Can Do to End Sexism and Male Violence Against Women.," written by Harvard Anti-Sexist Men.

How Sexism Operates

No previous generation to our knowledge has made the intention to transform sexism. Partnership Education tells young people that they have a choice. As educators we need to understand why such a decision isn't easy, why it is difficult to step out of the force-field of sexism.

Gender equity pioneers Myra and David Sadker authored the classic *Failing at Fairness: How our Schools Cheat Girls*. In it page after page of anecdotes combined with two decades of research document their assertion that "gender bias makes it impossible for girls to receive an education equal to that given to boys." They write, "Today's schoolgirls face subtle and insidious gender lessons, micro-inequities that appear seemingly insignificant when looked at individually but that have a powerful cumulative affect." (1994, p. ix.)

After Myra's death, David and his colleagues have continued their gender equity work. David Sadker reports in 2001, "Myra and I thought ... you do research, you find bias, and Americans will want to change it. That's what this country is all about.

Wrong. There are people who find this very threatening, who want the traditional female role to be well established, who are conservative and who are willing to spend money. They are using smear methods and they are well organized. They are tying into a national ennui, an attitude of 'Oh, that's not a problem anymore.' I even had school principals say, 'Title IX is not in effect any more.' There's this notion that equity is not a real issue.... I can go into most classes today, do my coding, my objective counting of how many times a teacher calls on boys and girls, and see the same results I saw fifteen years ago. The bias in our culture is so pervasive that we don't even recognize it." (Myra Sadker Advocates for Gender Equity website.)

If gender-equity could be achieved simply by adding more stories of women scientists, mathematicians, and historical leaders into the curriculum, it would be a simpler matter. But the point is not just that what has been left out but why it has been left out. Sexism is a matter of power and changing sexism means changing well entrenched power-over mechanisms. Unlearning sexism is not simply a process of adding on new behaviors. Unlearning sexism requires going through a change in consciousness and responsibility, and this can feel like an earthquake.

I remember working with a group of middle school-age girls over the course of the week talking about the adult world. As the group felt safer, questions erupted — "But why do men hurt women? I don't understand!" "My mother works at a battered women's shelter. Why does it happen that a man would want to hit a woman?"

Sexism, like other oppressions, replicates itself not unlike a virus. Stepping into the shoes of young people, one can see why "feminism" is a label shunned by many students. One of the developmental tasks of a young woman or man is becoming part of the adult community. The dominator culture clearly says, "real men aren't feminists," and "real men don't like women who are feminists." The subliminal message is, if you want our acceptance you better not identify with this. Since taking on the mantle of adulthood or becoming a "real man" or "real woman" appears to require taking on dominant attitudes about gender, young people are in an excruciating bind.

Sexism like other oppressions is learned. It's not a fact of biology. It is culturally taught within the culture as if it were a required curriculum. What is learned can be unlearned, but support is needed for the shift.

One belief to unlearn is the belief that changing sexism would hurt men and boys or be at their expense. Riane Eisler writes that a myth or misperception about partnership is that it would mean women are going to take over. If we think only inside the "dominator box," all we can conceive of is forms of domination. This mindset warns if patriarchy is altered, then the reverse of the seesaw would result. In reality both females and males are hurt by sexism and both benefit by social reconstruction.

Here are vocabulary terms commonly used to describe how oppression operates. An encounter with sexism can be:

- direct (e.g., verbal and/or physical abuse)
- indirect (e.g., absence from history books)

Sexism is promulgated in three main forms:

- individual: Personal attitudes, beliefs and behaviors.
- institutional: Social policies, laws, and regulations whose purpose is to maintain economic and social advantage.
- cultural: Social beliefs and customs that promote the assumption of superiority.

J. M. Jones articulated three types in discussing racism in 1972: They have been generalized by many educators to describe all forms of oppression. Individual, institutional, and cultural sexism are all inter-twined.

Individual sexism includes a wide range of behaviors. Direct abuse that students experience includes demeaning jokes, verbal slurs, sexual harassment in school halls, and date rape. Indirect abuse includes media messages that the most important thing about a girl or woman is her appearance and not her values and how she lives her life. When year after year the school curriculum doesn't fully acknowledge the importance and the realities of women's experiences and contributions, this distortion takes a heavy toll.

At the time that *Ms. Magazine* started in 1970, "a woman earned less than 60 cents for every dollar a man earned. Married women could not get credit in their own names. Terms like "sexual harassment" and "date rape" had not yet entered the public vocabulary. Job discrimination on the basis of gender was legal in most instances … and magazines for women generally doled out advice about saving marriages, raising babies, or saving face — literally, by using the right cosmetics." Today women earn 76 cents for every dollar earned by men, and nearly 75% of women earn less than $30,000 a year. A majority of women can't afford to retire because they don't have pensions to support them. (Ms. web site.)

One of the ways that oppression continues unchecked is that, covertly or overtly, it is backed by the threat of physical, economic or psychological harm. The fact that every woman is a potential target of rape gives sexual harassment added impact. Once rape was invented as part of the arsenal of domination, rape traveled down through the ages. It was only in 1997 that rape was declared a war crime under the Geneva

Convention. Both men and women, each in different ways, are victims of the culture of violence. For women, the backdrop of violence reinforces economic dependence, stifled voices, diminished respect, and constricted opportunities.

Archeological evidence infers that violence targeting women may have been unthinkable in Neolithic times before the invasions of the Indo-European nomadic groups. It suggests that women and men were both centrally involved in decision-making in a partnership structure. Yet institutional sexism is in place by the time of ancient Greece, celebrated by historians as a time of democracy. Women could not vote or engage in transactions worth more than a grain of barley. It was only in 1920 that women were allowed to vote in the United States. The Nineteenth Amendment is referred to as "giving women" the right to vote. Women in China gained the right to vote in 1974.

At the same time cultural beliefs about women reinforce institutional sexism. Here are examples from history. These quotes were gathered by the Guerrilla Girls who overturn sexism in the art world.

"There is a good principle, which created order, light, and man, and an evil principle, which created chaos, darkness, and women."

Pythagoras, 6th century BCE

"Girls begin to talk and to stand on their feet sooner than boys because weeds grow more quickly than good crops."

Martin Luther, 1533 CE

"The souls of women are so small, that some believe they have none at all."

Samuel Butler, 1605 CE

"Every women would prefer to be a man just as every deformed wretch would prefer to be whole and fair, and every idiot and fool would be learned and wise."

Torquato Tasso, 1573 CE

In standard textbooks, the story of the world is told with massive omission of women's lives. In American History units, rarely is this spoken of, and unconsciously the message comes across that it is only men who have done and still do the important things in the world. Looking at the creation of the U.S. Constitution, few teachers invite students to discuss the kind of incomplete democracy that was created: "Have you noticed that only the minority, those who are white men of certain economic means, could vote?" Educational sexism also manifests in institutional, cultural, and individual forms.

A searing personal way that sexism hurts girls and young women in schools is when they encounter classmates who denigrate or harass them. In the Young Feminists section of the NOW web site, a writer asks, "Has this happened to you?... You're tired of taking the long route to class to avoid the staircase landing where guys hang out and make lewd comments. You notice your own posture in the showcase reflection — you're creeping around as though you're trying to hide."

Too often in schools there are individual boys who dole out sexist behavior. And too often adults don't step in. One all too familiar response is to ignore the behavior and label it as unchangeable and inevitable: "Boys will be boys." Another response in the case above could be to place monitors at that stairway. But this is a temporary solution that doesn't get at the root cause. The violators would seek another avenue and another location. A more complete response is to face that sexism is a social disease, and require that the people who are trapped in it have help unlearning it. Instead of requiring that the girls and young women who are targeted must adjust, it is the boys and young men who are doing the harming that need to engage in social learning, face why they target girls, take responsibility and relearn new behavior. As a society we are just beginning to picture what a commitment to changing sexism would require.

Developing a Positive Gender Identity

As educators accept the mantle of elders, we break the silence about oppression and ask our culture to mature. In dialoguing about this with an educator friend from Wisconsin, Stuart Stotts, he commented, "Being an elder isn't about being wise and knowing all the answers. Being an elder is about understanding how to engage deeply in the process." Let's look inside the maelstrom of moving free of sexism.

Here is an intellectual framework for this change:
• Starting point — a person is not aware of sexism, and not grappling with it.
• Events happen that cause the person to be conscious of sexism.
• A choice emerges:
   To go through the earthquake of facing the reality of sexism and learn how not to participate in it.
   Or, to return to the norms and values of sexism.
• If sexism is rejected, further steps of awareness include growing to see that each human struggle for justice is interconnected and contributing to this work.

The challenge is to develop a positive identity independent of sexism when we live within a society where sexism is the norm. This involves resolving conflicting dynamics: To be able to say, "Sexism exists," and at the same time to be able to develop a positive identity as a female or a male which isn't coercively formed by the way sexism pre-scribes what is is to be female and what it is to be male.

One important model of identity development in the face of oppression is found in the research of Janet Helms and William Cross on racial identity development. Cross (1971, 1978, 1991) describes the process of forming a positive identity for a person grow-ing up African American in US culture: Racism is ingested and experienced, and in order to form a positive identity with one's own personal power, internalized Racism needs to be ejected.

They describe how a White person also ingests racism but from a different van-tage point. Helms (1990, 1991) discusses stages of White racial identity development. The first stage is characterized as being unaware of socialization and unaware of white privilege: "I don't have a racial identity. I'm normal" and "racism is not my concern." Next, a White person goes through the disintegration of letting in the reality of racism and then either chooses to reject participation in racism or rejects the messengers talk-ing about racism. This latter choice can feel like it reestablishes equilibrium, but it is at the expense of blocking out the social reality of racism. Many Whites don't pass through the earthquake stage of personally facing the reality of racism.

Gender Identity for Boys and Men

Citing the research of Helms, Beverly Tatum writes, "the evolution of a positive White racial identity ... (involves) both the abandonment of racism and the develop-ment of a non-racist White identity." (Tatum, 1992, p. 13). To create a positive White identity without participating in individual racism involves actively recognizing and opposing institutional and cultural racism.

Let's extrapolate from this model to look at sexism. A positive male identity involves the abandonment of sexist behaviors and the development of a non-sexist male identity. Sexism tells men the lie that, to feel valued, you need to construct an identity that is around "not being female." The transformative model of Cross and Helms shows how a positive nonsexist male identity can be developed while actively abandoning sexism. This involves re-examining what we have been taught is "real" masculinity. Conventional gender stereotypes equate domination with masculinity and being dominated with femininity. This programming says that masculinity means superiority. Femininity indicates inferiority. And anything associated with women or "femininity" is considered less important and valuable. This programming comes up for re-examination if the earthquake stage is entered.

For men, without finding personal support, it is difficult to look at the reality of sexism as a force that is molding them, and giving false promises while hurting them as well. According to Helms this shift involves traversing dissonance. She cites the work of Festinger (1957), who "theorized that when two or more of a person's cognitions (e.g., beliefs or feelings about oneself) are in conflict, an uncomfortable psychological state that he calls 'dissonance' likely results. He suggests that when dissonance is present, a person will not only attempt to reduce it, but will also take steps to avoid situations and information that are likely to increase it ... then it seems plausible that the same sorts of strategies used to reduce dissonance in general may also be used to reduce race-related dissonance."

There are two basic ways people deal with dissonance. One strategy is to avoid or deny the new information. This reaction can lead to avoiding contact with the reality of sexism by withdrawing, or denying that the information is true, and returning to the old sexist attitudes and beliefs with renewed fervor. As Tatum writes, "the bliss of ignorance or lack of awareness is replaced by discomfort of guilt, shame, and sometimes anger" (Tatum, 1991).

Social pressure to accept the status quo becomes too strong. Males may feel that the weight of sexism asks them to "give up their self" and try to restore that old self back who didn't encounter sexism. Growth stops. Often, anger is transferred to the victims of the oppression, projecting that they, not sexism itself, are causing this discomfort.

But there is another way to deal with dissonance. Dissonance can open the door to personal growth. The disintegration of old beliefs by being confronted with new information can be a time of healthy personal growth and reintegration in a new more conscious form. It can be a time of inquiry, of making a new choice, asking, "What can I do?"

Instead of building a positive male identity that is dependent upon sexism, dependent on showing, "I'm not feminine," boys and men learn to develop a positive identity by becoming autonomous from sexism. Eisler comments:

> We need to look at the way males are taught to avoid "feminine" traits such as sensitivity, empathy, and caring, as when boys are called wimps for being "too soft" of "feminine." This puts boys and men in a position where they have to deny part of their humanity to be "real men." While they are told to be kind and caring, this goes against what they are also taught about their very identity. There is an evolution of a positive male identity as we leave behind sexist assumptions. Boys can then evaluate traits stereotypically associated with masculinity and choose to still identify with positive ones such as assertiveness, accomplishment of goals, and logic, at the same time that they recognize that these are human traits that girls and women can also have. Conversely, sensitivity, empathy, and caring can be redefined as human traits boys and men also have. Girls can do the same, choosing a positive "feminine" identity that is not equated with subservience and helplessness, but with those traits that help both women and men live fulfilling lives.

At further stages of identity development, according to this model, a boy or man integrates the reality that "sexism exists," and holds the realization, "I'm not bad because I'm male," while at the same time adding to it responsibility for helping to change the situation. Just as white people work against racism and heterosexual people work against homophobia, just as owning class people work against poverty and able-bodied people support disability rights, males work on behalf of humanity to transform sexism.

Here are the kinds of questions that can assist boys and young men in developing a pro-male, anti-sexist identity:

- What does this song/book/movie say about what it means to be male?
- What does this song/book/movie say about what it means to be female?
- Do I agree with these messages? What do they imply?
- Is the social situation I'm in structured to be fair to girls and women?
- Is this joke/behavior/event I'm hearing or witnessing mistreating girls and women?
- What is my responsibility in a social setting when I notice something unfair happening to a girl or woman?
- What do the girls and women I know have to say to me about their experiences of sexism?
- What support do I want from the men I know as I define myself?
- How can I support other boys and men in my life as we affirm ourselves as male in the way we define male?
- If I felt free of anyone else's expectations, what are my dreams for myself?

Gender Identity for Girls and Women

For girls the process of forming a positive feminine identity proceeds along a parallel but different route. When girls and women begin to recognize the reality of sexism, these are the dynamics they are called to integrate in developing a positive identity independent of sexism. One voice says, "I am female and I am valuable and powerful and equal," and the other voice says, "Sexism exists. People in positions of power and authority who matter to me still live and act and think as if I am not valuable and powerful and equal." Intertwining the two realities, a girl tries to make sense of, "I am valuable and will treat myself as valuable although sexism exists."

At the first stage of identity development, sexism is background noise. A girl or young woman is not conscious of the sexism that she is ingesting. She wants to be accepted in the culture as it exists, and she particularly wants acceptance by males.

If a joke that targets girls and women comes up in the classroom, in the hall, in the cafeteria, it may be a girl who indicates quickly, "That joke doesn't bother me." This is part of living in an environment that says, "Don't be seen as a feminist." Sexism exists, but it is more painful to acknowledge it. It threatens that necessary feeling of belonging. It's safer to ally with the ones who say, "It's no big deal. Why does it bother you?" and remain one of the group. At this stage, a female student listening to the joke couldn't speak up and assert from a solitary position, "This joke may seem like a small thing to you, but it's one of the eroding daily reminders that women are in a secondary position not only throughout the world but right here in our school."

Then an encounter with sexism disrupts denial, and the reality of sexism must be faced. An event or series of events, direct or indirect, forces a girl or young woman to acknowledge the personal impact of sexism. Helms writes, "During the Pre-encounter stage, the person expends considerable mental energy in rationalizing such occurrences and/or pretending they have no implications," (Helms, 1990, p. 24).

Evidence of sexism may have been presented previously by a teacher, but until a girl or young woman is ready to digest this information, she may need to push it aside. This is because to grapple truly with sexism and positive identity is to enter that earthquake stage. This earthquake stage may be ignited by a put-down, "you're a dumb blonde," or by exclusion by other girls on the basis of appearance and fashion. The event might be sexual harassment in the hall, or date rape. It might not have happened to her but to a friend. Something from the reality of sexism breaks the bubble that a positive identity can be maintained by denying that noise of sexism. It becomes a roar that can't be ignored, and a tumble of thoughts and feelings follow.

At the next stage, she seeks out sources that affirm her as female, and surrounds herself with women in her life or in books or media that affirm her identity as herself, not as a woman defined by sexist society. When we end denial, feelings are aroused. There may be anger, maybe rage at betrayal, or fury that, "Violence against women should have been stopped before this."

Now she actively seeks out opportunities to explore aspects of her own history and culture as a woman. Anger at the dominant culture gives fuel to energize self-development without getting stuck. As she says, "no" to sexism, she feels herself moving to build what she wants and take charge of her life.

When we look at these stages of development, we see why young people negotiating shaky steps into adulthood would denigrate feminism. It is difficult to go through the earthquake. For both females and males in our schools to develop a positive gender identity, a process is needed where the earthquake stage is entered with help from adults and peers who have aligned with partnership.

New Moon Magazine speaks to this need for support and explicitly helps readers leave the box of sexism. It says, "Other publications portray a 'perfect girl' for readers to measure themselves against. By contrast, *New Moon* challenges stereotypes by accepting girls as they are, listening to them, and celebrating their diverse experiences and dreams."

The founder of the National Young Girls Coalition, Andrea Johnson does work all over the country providing help for girls. In her book *Girls Speak Out: Finding Your True Self* (NY: Scholastic Press, 1997) she describes how she helps girls recognize their own voices, develop their self esteem and take control over their lives. Johnson taught school for thirty years and then left the classroom to devote herself full-time to leading girls ages 9 to 14 through a process of support, new information, and conversation. She was one of the first teachers in the country who helped stop sexual harassment by a male teacher in her school.

During one of the activities Johnson leads, she brings reproductions of ancient artifacts into the sessions: The Cretan Snake Goddess, the Willendorf Goddess, Kuan Yin, an image of a dreaming woman from Malta, a wooden statue from Africa. Girls hold the artifacts, make up a name for them, and write what they feel the figure is saying. Here are examples of what girls express as they give voice to the images:

A Spiritual Woman by Kila, age 10

"Once upon a time I was a spiritual woman. I was also faithful to my people. I was hurt when people made fun of my spiritual life…. In my country, angels walk with women and watch over men." (Johnson, 1995, p. 52.)

My Lost Girl by Lizard, age 11

"I am a young girl of long ago. I live in a time when no one had heard of sexism. Men and women are equal in everything they do. I can express my feelings in any way I want to. If I am really excited they do not tell me to calm down. I'm trapped inside a young girl of today. I cannot let out my feelings. No one even knows I exist. I feel like I am dead. For only dead people should not be free…. Don't keep me trapped. Only here for the public's eye, not for myself. Let me dance and play in the wind and rain…. I am myself, not another person's property, so I'll let my feelings out so much, and really cry and laugh and do anything that I want to do." (ibid, p. 43.)

Here are the kinds of questions that can support girls and young women in developing a feminist, anti-sexist identity:

- What does this song/book/movie say about women?
  Is this true for me? Do I want to model myself on this image?
- What is going on as I hear or watch or experience this joke/behavior/event? How am I feeling?
- If this joke/behavior/event is unfair, what role do I want to take in intervening? Is there support I could use?

- What is this song/book/movie saying about how men and women interact? Is anyone getting harmed? Are both respected?
- What are the qualities I respect in the girls and women I know?
- What are the qualities I respect in the boys and men I know?
- What do my friends have to say about sexism they experience?
- What support do I want from the women I know as I define myself?
- How can I support other girls and women in my life as we affirm ourselves as female in the way we define female?
- If I felt free of anyone else's expectations, what are my dreams for myself?

The earthquake, then, is a passage where hidden feelings of fear, sorrow, or pain erupt, and also a time where longing, hope, and the joy of new possibilities push through. The walls of old social patterns, like walls of an old prison, are opened. What has been familiar is now seen as confining and ensnaring. As the earthquake erupts, new closeness and connections break into our lives that could not have been dreamed of from our old vantage point. The earthquake signals real change is taking place, and from that new nourishing life will come.

Implications for Teaching

How can we support students in our classrooms with this process? How do we help them develop their self-affirming nonsexist selves? How do we face sexism together, females and males, and experience the dizzying disintegration of the former social constructs without turning away from the challenge of change?

Create an Atmosphere Where All Students Can Seek Their True voices

The process of growth depends upon finding people who will listen. It also depends upon people asking new questions to help you encounter lost parts of your own self.

<u>Activity One:</u> Giving Voice

Grade level: 3rd - 12th

1. Inspired by the work of Andrea Johnson (*Girls Speak Out*) collect artifacts, photos of artifacts, comic books, postcards, and advertisements that portray women and men in a myriad of ways.

2. Ask each student to select one that calls to them and have them write what that person or statue is secretly saying. You may want to read sections of the writings by girls in the chapter in her book, "In Our Image," to give a sense of possibility.

3. Add other questions to ask this figure. For instance:

   Has anyone ever talked to you before?

   What do you believe about women?

   What do you believe about men?

   Do you have a message for people in the world?

   What is your picture of the way women and men interact?

Create an Atmosphere of Learning Where There Is No Blame

Give a clear description of the problem. Here's how I like to articulate it to groups of students: "The problem of sexism is that it acts like a virus and wants to 'enslave' each generation into passing on its tenets, lies, and practices. Sexism doesn't mean that either men or women are bad or at fault, but changing sexism will involve both men and women in being part of the change. The problem is that in the construction of sexism a basic human difference is grossly misused and distorted in service of power-over."

By studying how the virus of sexism operates, students gain tools for taking it apart and forming healthy relationships and social structures. We need to talk about why change in gender construction is very threatening, and help students sort out the messages that interfere with change.

Activity Two: Media Watch

Grade level: 1st- 12th

Procedure:

1. Invite all members of the class to look for examples that they see of sexism. Bring in ads, copies of magazines, or describe a scene in a rock video. Invite people to look for subtle examples as well as blatant ones. You can use as a model, the section "No Comment" in the back of *Ms. Magazine* which shows examples of sexism sent in by readers. In the February/March 2001 issue, for example, an ad was reprinted from *Bicyling* magazine that shows a woman on the roof of a jeep looking as if she were a deer brought back from a hunt.

2. Use this opportunity to have an experience of talking about sexism in a manner that feels safe and informal. Make sure everyone can ask questions, disagree, and have

their voice. Set a tone of exploration: "Tell us why this feels sexist to you." Allow for humor and keep a relaxed tone so that conversation can increase.

3. Unpack messages. Example: When a commentator labels a woman's voice as "shrill," this signals that she has left the box of acceptable behavior for a woman. We can reinterpret what seems like a casual adjective as in fact a reprimand. It's code for saying that her words are threatening and culturally she is being asked to "be quiet."

Activity Three: Role Models

Grade level: 4th - 12th

Procedure:

1. Study two biographies of people who dedicated their lives to changing sexsim: Myra Sadker and Jackson Katz. Their lives model how a person can engage others in becoming accountable for change.

See each person as valuable.

Continually reinforce for students that each one of them matters and the choices they make will touch lives. In a dominator culture, the phenomenon of fame can actually push students away from feeling they can be part of important activity or give them false standards. When we ask students what they want to be when they grow up, often they exhibit cultural bias — in essence, "I want to be whatever will make me rich and famous." In a pyramid of fame, only a few people can achieve that stamp of approval. Study significant people in a way that includes all students and enhances humanity.

Activity Four: We're Part of History

Grade level: 1st - 12th

1. Share this quote from Dorothy West: "There is no life that doesn't contribute to history."

2. Explain how to study people from within a partnership perspective. From a dominator viewpoint, some people are famous and significant and as we elevate some, we imply that others are insignificant. From a partnership perspective, we study what is possible so that we can use the opportunity of our own life to make contributions in our own ways. Bring in books that reveal hidden women such as *Multicultural Women of Science, Girls and Young Women Inventing, Outrageous Women of the Renaissance, 100 Women Who Shaped History*. These are described in the National Women's History Project catalog.

Activity Five: Interconnected Struggles

Grade level: 5th - 12th

1. Study the formation of the Women's International League for Peace and Freedom to exemplify that caring for one part of the world means caring for the whole. Here is information from their web site:

> On April 28, 1915, a unique group of women met in an International Congress in The Hague, Netherlands to protest against World War I, then raging in Europe, to suggest ways to end it and to prevent war in the future. The organizers of the Congress were prominent women in the International Suffrage Alliance, who saw the connection between their struggle for equal rights and the struggle for peace. WILPF's foremothers rejected the theory that war was inevitable and defied all obstacles to their plan to meet together in wartime. They assembled more than 1,000 women from warring and neutral nations to work out a plan to end WWI and lay the basis for a permanent peace. Out of this meeting the Women's International League for Peace and Freedom was born. WILPF's first International President was Jane Addams, founder of Hull House in Chicago and the first U.S. woman to win the Nobel Peace Prize.
>
> It was the wisdom of the founding foremothers in 1915 that peace is not rooted only in treaties between great powers or a turning away of weapons alone, but can only flourish when it is also planted in the soil of justice, freedom, non-violence, opportunity, and equality for all. They understood, and WILPF still organizes in the understanding, that all the problems that lead countries to domestic and international violence are all connected and all need to be solved in order to achieve sustainable peace.
>
> This remarkable vision still guides us today as we face the challenges of the twenty-first century. In today's context this means
>
> • the equality of all people in a world free of sexism, racism, classism, and homophobia;
>
> • the guarantee of fundamental human rights including the right to sustainable development;
>
> • an end to all forms of violence: rape, battering, exploitation, intervention and war;
>
> • the transfer of world resources from military to human needs, leading to economic justice within and among nations, and world disarmament and peaceful resolution of international conflicts via the United Nations.

2. Discuss this process: The same group of people who worked together for the rights of women were led to broaden their concerns. They wanted to end all forms of domination, and not just end the aspect that personally impacted them the most.

3. Ask students to work in small groups to create a diagram or picture of interconnected social struggles.

Make it Clear that Sexism Hurts Males As Well As Females

As the Sadkers express it, "Sexism is not a 'girls only' issue. It is a two-edged sword: Sexism injures girls, but it harms boys as well." Discuss: How does it benefit both girls and boys to end sexism?

<u>Activity Six:</u> Changing Male Culture

Grade level: 5th - 12th

Procedure:

1. Help students meet men who are supporting boys and young men. Explain that society programs males into constricting roles that harm them. Men are in effect threatened that if they don't go along with the programming of toughness, they will be physically harmed and/or socially outcast. Changing male culture doesn't only involve changing how males treat females; it means helping men change how they treat and regard themselves.

2. Talk about how these messages come into our lives. Create a safe atmosphere to name movies, ads, or personal events. Keep the emphasis on the inherent goodness of men. In any topic that is challenging and charged, jokes can erupt that are potentially hurtful. Help the class not make statements that denigrate men.

3. If possible, bring in a speaker from your community. Or, go to the Men for Change website. Copy for students, "The Group," which contains this paragraph and use it for discussion:

"It's not only that men have used violence to maintain power and control over women, children, and other men. Men have learned to think of power as our ability to dominate and control the world, the people around us, and our own unruly emotions...we learn that to be a man means having some sort of power and control. Most men are not violent, but most of us feel we have to perform and be on top at least somewhere in our lives.

Michael Kaufman, Cracking the Armour

Also share an anecdote described in the Men for Change website under the section, "Personal growth." It tells of a male student ganged up on by other men who is left unsupported by a male teacher. Discuss how this relates to the problem of sexism and how sexism hurts males as well as females.

Embrace Complexity: Accountability with Mutual Respect

Unlearning sexism asks us to analyze different perspectives and reflect upon multiple and contradictory points of view. It's about growing and learning.

It's difficult to carve out new thoughts in direct opposition to the dominant culture, and a person passes through many different stages as we have examined. Make it clear that unlearning sexism is not about being PC, politically correct. This term comes from the old dominator paradigm. It is another silencer. When a person goes through a growth in consciousness, at times they may hold a new position tightly while they are first arriving there. Helping each other move to other stages means all sides and all positions need to make room for full dialogue.

In the 1980's Rush Limbaugh invented the term "feminazi" as an insult and as a tactic. As one person commented in reaction, "but feminists don't try to kill people to further their cause." Accusations like this purposefully arrest discussion and freeze growth. Our role is to help students go through the uncomfortable process of change in consciousness. If phrases like "PC" or "feminazi" come up, unpack together what underlies them, and redirect attention to sincere growth.

When I reflect upon the anti-racist and anti-oppression trainers that I've met over the past two decades, I think of people of deep insight, complex understanding, and compassionate hearts. Teachers can help students encounter people who are involved in gender equity and pro-feminism through written materials, videos, and visits to the classroom.

In our traumatized culture many people haven't experienced a compassionate request to examine their behavior and change. They expect blame and shame and are ready to defend against it. Owning a mistake can be threatening. Unlearning sexism is not about, "I caught you doing something wrong." It's about accountability with compassion.

Activity Seven: Complicating our Thinking — Messages in Popular Music

Grade level: 4th - 12th

Procedure:

1. Listen to a range of music from the fifties and sixties sung by women and by men. What messages about gender relationships are in the songs? How do they affect the listener?

Listen to songs with overt messages. Examples: "Johnny Get Angry," and "Judy's Turn to Cry" sung by Lesley Gore. "Under My Thumb," and "Stupid Girl" by the Rolling Stones. "Run For Your Life" by the Beatles. "He Hit Me and It Felt Like a Kiss" by the Ronettes.

Many students have heard the swaggering golden oldie by Dion called "The Wanderer." This song gives only a one-dimensional view of Dion and what he values. On a radio interview, Dion commented that he wrote the song about a sailor he knew whose life he saw as sad. "It's about a guy who is stuck in a shallow lifestyle." (NPR, "Terry Gross Show", January 1, 2000). But the song comes across as if it describes a lifestyle to emulate. Mention or play the song, discuss its message, and then add the complexity of Dion's recent comment. A lesser known song by Dion is called "Born to Cry."

Create names for categories of different types of love songs from any era.

Example: "I want to make you mine" songs.

2. Brainstorm songs where women and men share their feelings. Look at the range of feelings that are expressed: Sorrow, hurt, anger, and joy. Are some emotions expressed more than others? Are some emotions expressed more by women? By men?

3. Discuss the lyrics of more current songs and what they prescribe for relationships between women and men.

- Look for songs that give questionable or negative messages. Example: Britney Spears sings the line, "Baby hit me one more time," in the song "One More Time." Amazon.com says about the recording that contains that lyric, "Britney's songs have a strange submissive twist … a desperate need to keep a boy by her side."

- Instead of blaming or denigrating her, describe and examine the message that she is conveying to her audience.

- Present this statement for students to discuss: "A singer is responsible for examining the message that they pass along."

Look for songs that directly aim to give new messages.
Examples: "Song for the Man," by the Beastie Boys, "Woman is the N— of the World," by John Lesson on "Once Upon a Dream."

4. Seek out examples of feminist music by women and men.
Sources: Olivia Records - Chris Williamson, Meg Christian, and Redwood Records - Holly Near.

The lyrics for the following songs are in *Rise Up Singing* edited by Peter Blood-Patterson, Sing Out! Corporation, 1988.
Songs: "The Ballad of Erica Levine" by Bob Blue, "I'm Gonna Be an Engineer" by Peggy Seeger, "Still Ain't Satisfied" and "Who Were the Witches" by Bonnie Lockhart, "Truck Driving Woman" by Si Kahn, "Everything Possible" by Fred Small, "No Hole in My Head" by Malvina Reynolds, "There was a Young Woman" by Meredith Tax, "Let the Woman in You Come Through" by Peter Alsop, "John Wayne Image" and "Changing as I Go" by Bruce and Peter Kokopehl and Scott Glascock, "For a Change" and "Goodbye John Wayne" by Geof Morgan.

The Ballad of Erica Levine
When Erica Levine was seven and a half,
Up to her door came Jason Metcalf,
And he said, "Will you marry me, Erica Levine?"
And Erica Levine said, "What do you mean?"
"Well, my father and my mother say a fellow ought to marry,
And my father said his brother, who is my Uncle Larry
Never married, and he said Uncle Larry is a dope,
So will you marry me?" Said Erica, "Nope.
My piano teacher's smart, and she never had to marry,
And your father may be right about your Uncle Larry,

But not being married isn't what made him a dope.
Don't ask me again, 'cause my answer's 'Nope!'"

When Erica Levine was seventeen,
She went to the prom with Joel Bernstein,
And they danced by the light of a sparkling bobby-sock,
'Cause the theme of the prom was the history of rock.
And after the prom, Joel kissed her at the door,
And he said, "Do you know what that kiss was for?"
And she said, "No, I don't, but you kiss just fine,"
And he said, "What it means is that you are mine."
And she said, "No, I'm not!" And she rushed inside,
And on the way home Joel Bernstein cried,
And she cried, too, and wrote a letter to Ms.,
Saying, "This much I know: I'm mine, not his."

When Erica Levine was twenty-three,
Her lover said, "Erica, marry me.
This relationship is answering a basic need,
And I'd like to have it legally guaranteed.
For without your precious love, I would surely die,
So why don't we make it legal?" Said Erica, "Why?
Basic needs, at your age, should be met by you.
I'm your lover, not your mother. Let's be careful what you do.
If ever I should marry, I will marry to grow,
Not for tradition, or possession, or protection. No.
I love you, but your needs are a very different issue."
Then he cried, and Erica handed him a tissue.

When Erica was thirty, she was talking with Lou,
Discussing and deciding what they wanted to do.
"When we marry, should we move into your place or mine?
Yours is rent-controlled, but mine's on the Green Line."
And they argued, and they talked, and they finally didn't care,
And they joined a small cooperative near Central Square.
Their wedding was a simple one. They wanted it that way.
And they thought a lot about the things that they would choose to say.
"I will live with you, and love you, but I'll never call you mine."
Then the judge pronounced them married, and everyone had wine.
And a happy-ever-after life was not the kind they got,
But they tended to be happy more often than not.

by Bob Blue, from *Their Way*[20]

Visions of New Partnership Curriculum

Dominator culture has tried to take the movement for the liberation of women and skew it to mean that women get to be dominators, too. The other side of the coin is not that women are "allowed" to be more like men. Men are "allowed" to be more like women.

We learn from women how to care, how to empathize, how to connect, and how to be concerned for the whole. Despite the weight of sexism, women have persevered in developing crucial ways of knowing and feeling and living that are called "women's ways." These are human values that women have developed on behalf of all of us. These basic human skills are not fully seen or studied or valued. When we see women's liberation as a partnership movement, new layers are revealed.

Partnership educator Dierdre Bucciarelli says that teaching students to uncover sexism is crucially important but it is not sufficient to move towards a partnership society. Here is her voice:

> Once we uncover the sexism, what do we do? And what are women's contributions? By women's contributions I do not simply mean recovering "lost women," e.g., women scientists, artists, philosophers, mathematicians. Although this is important, it will only take us so far, and if not done properly can even be misleading. We cannot, as Charlotte Bunch put it, simply "add women and stir." In other words, we cannot add them to typical disciplinary categories without distorting women's experience. For example, history is divided into periods of time that students study. But, these very periods (or categories of thought) are based on male experience of the world. Take "The Enlightenment" and "The 'Renaissance" as examples. Feminist historians have noted that typically in the study of history, these are "not treated as male-centered term(s): They are presented as gender-neutral". To be more specific in terms of the Renaissance, some feminists claim that "women...may not have had a Renaissance in Europe during the same time or in the same way as (some) men did" and if we want to determine whether women had a "renaissance," we first have to reconceptualize this notion according to female categories of experience rather than use traditional disciplinary categories that are unconsciously disguised as gender-neutral (Minnich, *Transforming Knowledge*, p. 88).

I think there is, conversely, not enough emphasis on uncovering systematic sexism in the curriculum. Part of uncovering sexism in the curriculum, as I see it, is to help students (and teachers) understand that we are talking about something much more profound than finding the "lost women." We are talking about systematic sexism in the disciplines, in the very categories of thought that students are typically expected to use. "...work by and about women is not just missing from the academic curriculum; it is to a remarkable extent incompatible with it" (Ibid., p. 31). In women's experience through history, the world has not been classified so much into discrete "disciplines" but perceived and acted upon organically through what Nel Noddings has called "domains of caring." An education that approaches knowledge through such domains is quite different from an education divided into intellectual categories.

Finding lost women and documenting that women were discriminated against and excluded from the public realm as is typically done in schools (as important and necessary as that is) "leaves untouched some other critically important questions. What were women who led the lives prescribed for them doing in the past? What were those lives like? What do we all, women and men, need to learn from as well as about them?" In order to answer these questions, we need to "undo the established centrality of men" (Minnich, pp. 27-28).

Women's contributions, which have often occurred in domains of caring and nurturance (whether in the public or private realms), are excluded from disciplinary study because the disciplines are centered on male experience of the world (actually the experience of rich, white, Euro-centric males). "Valuable" experience is traditional "male" experience in this framework. Unless the disciplines are revised to include women's experiences and knowledge, and unless disciplinary study brings women's experiences from "margin to center" (a term from bell hooks), we will continue to repeat old mistakes and we will not help our students to unlearn sexism.

As students become more versed in identifying sexism, engage students in describing and designing what kind of curriculum would be more inclusive. By leaving women out of history, we have left out the actions that are part of the human values that have been falsely prescribed only to women. Take a social studies unit and work together as a class to ask new questions like these and invent more questions of your own:

• What would we have to study about this time period to make sure that we included all the people involved?

• What is commonly taught about this event? What new vantage points can we discover?

• If we shift what is valued, what are other ways we would study this event? Who took care of insuring the long-term sustenance of this society and how did they do this?

• Does this historic event celebrate actions that hurt women or people of color without noticing this?

- How can we look at mistakes of the past in such a context that our emphasis is on learning from them and setting new directions?

- How did people care for each other and their community during the challenges they faced? What does this say for us today?

Epilogue: A Personal Vision of the Wise Elders

When Bobbi Morrison teaches partnership content to high school students at The Nova Project, she talks about archetypes. As I try to become anchored in partnership ways of knowing, I look to an archetype of wise elders. I picture them in a cave.

At first we see the Women in the Cave. Here are Hypatia and Hildegard von Bingen and Hatshepsut watching us and fervently supporting our efforts. And Harriet Tubman and Mary McLeod Bethune and Marija Gimbutas and Eleanor Roosevelt. And further back, way, way back, there are the women whose names we don't know, who sat in circles upon circles, governing villages and holding their communities together. I see through their eyes and feel in my bones what it is like to live from the place where they live.

The "war between the sexes" is real and it is also a misnomer. War implies adversaries contributing to the ongoing violence in similar ways. Sexism itself is the real adversary. Both males and females can choose to be conscientious objectors. Partnership Education wants to offer an entranceway to a place of truce, and from there a place where the war is declared over. Furthermore, we seek a place that is safe enough to stand back and look at the war that was and know it will not return. This is the work of lifetimes that is built upon our own steps.

Once upon a time the earth had no living cells. It was a soup of water and volcanic rock and storm. The scientists say lightning bolts ignited life; lightning made the oceans rich in organic molecules and life began. The ancient Egyptians believed that the way people grow when they are ready to grow to the next level is that they are sent a lightning bolt. Facing the reality of the full weight of sexism, is like being struck by lightning. We zig zag from one state to another - the safety of denial, then the wrenching knowledge of violence and betrayal — and integrate this, lit up by the lightning, until what is reached is a place of inward shining and strength.

I sense the women in the cave. And I sense another circle. The wise men. They have watched it all. They have seen the witch burnings, the gang rapes by soldiers throughout recorded history, the rapes in Bosnia. And they are weeping. In both circles women and men are weeping. Do they sit together now? Or are they sometimes together and sometimes apart? They are calling to us. What is it they want us to know and to do?

I hear the voices of a conversation that happens in another room. The wisest parts of us are speaking. Women and girls sit in one half of this circle, and men and boys sit in one half. These are the conscientious objectors in the war of the sexes, deftly refusing the subtle invitations that promise acceptance.

A large golden ring is placed in the center of the circle, and it crosses in front of their hearts. It is the ring of their new intention.

What do they tell each other? What do they promise?

Do they say, we don't want this to continue. Do they say no one sitting here will be blamed, but we now are all accountable for change. It isn't bad to be a girl, or boy, or woman, or man. We have inherited a structure that is hurting us all. Together bravely we will change it. Despite what humans in the past have done, we will work in our actions and in our hearts to transform inwardly and from there outwardly. We will not wear the old false dazzling clothes that have been made for us. Sexism asks us to pass on its ways, but we won't. We have a choice and we won't participate. We want to end the war of the sexes together. We want to end people warring against each other in any form and truly learn to care for the whole.

And they drink in these words. They take them into the cave of their hearts. They believe what they hear, and believing, this new intention ripples along their spines and brings them to a new place.

This would be a beginning. This would be the next step. This would open a new journey, entering the earthquake, but not alone. Their voices call me, call us, to bring hearts and minds together to forge a new path.

PART THREE

PARTNERSHIP STRUCTURE

Introduction to Part Three, Partnership Structure

Partnership structure refers to *where* learning and teaching occur. It represents the type of learning environment or culture that we craft. It also involves the context in which we teach, such as the underlying structure for decision-making that interlaces the classroom and the school. A partnership environment is one that models and promotes caring, considerate, and democratic relations between and among all members of the school community.

In Chapter 14, Dave Ketter, Bobbi Morrison, and Elaine Packard describe the structure in place in their public high school in Seattle, Washington. Nova School, which began in 1969, bases its community structure on a systems approach. Students and staff together created an ingenious model for feedback, discussion, decision-making, and coordination which has stood the test of time.

In Chapter 15, Ruthmary Powers uses her extensive experience in education to show how to change school culture. She helps readers examine hierarchical roles, look at the classroom environment, involve parents, and be prepared for predictable challenges. Together, the authors illustrate this basic concept: a partnership structure has a clear leadership structure while insuring that all members of the school community are treated as important contributing partners.

CHAPTER 14

Partnership Structure at Nova School

by Dave Ketter, Bobbi Morrison, Elaine Packard, and Sarah Pirtle[21]

The Nova Project, an alternative high school in the Seattle Public School District, has been a place of learning where students have had real substantive power for over thirty years. From the very start, it was student-led. In 1969 a group of 26 students representing 12 Seattle High Schools worked together to plan, organize, and carry out the necessary fact-finding to develop a proposal for the school board to create an alternative approach to high school. Their ideas were adopted by the Seattle School Board in February of 1971. The school was launched and Nova began its first steps.

Developing Partnership Structure

When the school opened, it was piloted by 54 students who were selected by lottery, and a faculty member chosen by a committee that included students. Inspired by the School Without Walls model exemplified by the Philadelphia Parkway Project, the whole city was the classroom. Originally its hub, or planning space, was located downtown in a store-front, then the school moved to the fifth floor of the Seattle downtown YWCA. These headquarters provided an office and limited space for classes. A variety of locales hosted other classes based on student interests.

From the beginning The Nova Project had a commitment to democratic process. Consensus was used in decision-making, and at first decisions were made at weekly all-school meetings. Faculty selection occurred through a student-staff committee. Courses determined by student interests were planned and evaluated through written contracts. Student-chosen staff coordinators created a personal link to a mentor. All these features, with some elaborations, are still in place today.

In 1973, due to a philosophical split, Nova spawned a sister school named Summit. New staff were selected including three people who are still part of The Nova Project: Elaine Packard who is principal, Bobbi Morrison, and Gregg Onewein. In 1975 the school district experienced a double school levy failure. As a result, Nova moved out of its rented space in the YMCA into a temporary location in an elementary school. Persevering without furniture or even chalk, the school met in a public park adjacent to the school during the first two months of the school year to start the hard work of restructuring. A group of staff and students forged new ways of making decisions to replace the all-school meetings which had proved unwieldy.[22]

As Nova coalesced and went through reform, reassessment, and growth, an ingenious and carefully constructed method of decentralization was designed. To replace the general meeting, students and staff developed committees as a focus for consensus decision-making. The Systems Management Committee (SMC) was added to oversee the entire structure and to form new committees as needed, providing a way to adapt to changes in the school. This proved to be such a strong and flexible democratic structure that it was able to continue into the present. Nova is a place where students don't just hear about democracy and choice; they practice them.

Nova's Mission

Today Nova has 250 students at grade levels 9 through 12. The Nova Project has been located in the Horace Mann Building in the central area of Seattle since 1975. Self-determination and freedom continue to be hallmarks of the school. Nova states: "The mission of Nova Alternative High School is to be a democratically governed learning community of broadly educated, creative and independent critical thinkers who work collaboratively and demonstrate a high degree of individual and social responsibility. Nova provides a strong academic program, interdisciplinary curriculum, interest and project-based learning, small group and independent study, team teaching, teachers as advisers, student/staff governance and decision-making, and community building activities."

The community of students ranges from the academically capable who have been un-stimulated in other settings to those with personal or social at-risk factors. Schedules are flexibly designed to meet the needs of each student. Staff are seen as partners in learning who collaborate with students, facilitating learning, challenging, encouraging, and assisting students in finding resources within themselves and the school, and in the greater community to further their education. Credit is given for courses within the school as well as internships, service learning, and coursework conducted away from school. Program offerings include communication arts (literature, writing and poetry), thematic social studies, world languages, all levels of mathematics and science, drama, environmental and outdoor education, desktop publishing, internships, social justice activism, computer graphics and multi-media workstations, student-designed courses, and a vocational horticulture project that includes organic gardening and a greenhouse. Students follow state requirements for language arts, math, history, and science, while creating an individualized learning plan. Interest-based learning can take a student in many directions including environmental activism, video production, boat building, and desktop publishing and computer graphics.

The Nova learning model is summarized by four C's: Coordinating, committees, community, and contracts. Next, we'll look at how each of these four C's foster partnership.

C for Coordinating

Coordinators and COOR Groups

A basic structural feature of Nova from its beginning has been the relationship between each student Coordinatee and her/his staff Coordinator. The structure requires that each student build a partnership relationship with a staff member. When a person decides to come to Nova and is accepted, the very first step is to choose a Coordinator from among the staff of twelve. A new student has five days to form this new relationship. The Coordinator explains to them directly the school agreements which have been made by the students and staff of the whole community, and the new student signs a contract with his/her Coordinator personally. The students who wrote the Nova Handbook describe the relationship this way:

"This is your chance to get what you want and need from Nova.... Not only will this person help you academically, but they can also be someone with whom you can discuss nonacademic problems and goals. Your coordinator is there to be an advocate for you — a resource for information and guidance. They will go over your past academic records with you and help you figure out how many credits (and in what areas) you still need in order to graduate. They will sit down with you regularly (how often is up to the two of you but at least once a month) to go over your contracts and help you get clear on what still needs to be done to complete them. They will enter all of your credits on your official transcript. They will write you recommendations for colleges, jobs, and internships. They will be your parents within this school."

The bond is so important that a student without a Coordinator for five days has to leave Nova. Both parties are considered to have equal responsibility, and there is complete choice in both directions; either the Coordinator or the Coordinatee can refuse the relationship at any time. The handbook gives this advice to any student who is thinking of switching Coordinators, "Think carefully about your decision, and if possible discuss your feelings with your current Coordinator. Perhaps they will be willing to make some changes that will satisfy you. Also, your Coordinator may have put a lot of work into working with you — getting to know you and how to help you succeed — so that it might not be in your best interest to switch because of, say, one thing you're unhappy about. However, if you do decide to switch, please also be sensitive to your Coordinator's feelings. They may be sad to lose you, so be honest, but kind about it."

The handbook also describes what it means to the student to keep their own half of the bargain: Show up for meeting on time, come to COOR Group, and follow through on what you say you're going to do. Communicating together and developing this crucial relationship are part of building partnership skills.

As Nova has grown, the way of working with a Coordinator has grown. In the past students met alone with Coordinators. But once the size increased there was a need for smaller communities to help offset the problems of growth and to prevent cliques from forming. These concerns were brought to the SMC and discussed, resulting in the formation of COOR Groups. These are weekly advisory groups with all the students who have the same Coordinator congregating together. They range in size from 10 to 35 people. COOR Group is a place to socialize and meet others. It functions as a communications hub helping students stay connected to the broader school community. School issues are discussed and input is given to SMC. COOR Groups also do community service and school service, as well as have times of fun and celebration like weekend outings or bowling trips.

There is a requirement in the Seattle School District to do service learning. This interface with the community can occur not only through classes, but also through COOR Group. COOR Groups have selected many different activities: Tutoring students at the Islamic School across the street; collecting food, clothing, blankets, and money for an urban encampment of homeless people called Tent City; making lunches for a teenage shelter; and a trip to Mt. Rainier which resulted in a commitment to an ongoing tree planting project in the city. One COOR Group organized a joint poetry reading with the homeless that was held at the school.

Several community service projects initiated by a COOR Group have touched Nova as a whole, and they show the way that a spark travels and inspires the community in a very organic way. One COOR Group decided to make comfort blankets for seriously ill and traumatized children through the national Linus Project. Knitting and crocheting were taught at an overnight gathering as a kick-off for the project. Students and teachers knit and crocheted colorful afghan squares which were sewn together to complete the blankets. Another COOR Group organized a big Thanksgiving meal where every COOR Group made a part of the vegetarian feast — pies, salads, vegetables, bread — and it was then shared with guests including state legislators and children from the neighboring Islamic school. This year, when the Islamic students arrived, they rushed into the arms of their Nova tutors.

C for Committees

Coordinated Decision-Making

In the Systems course co-taught by Joe Szwaja, Dave Ketter, and Bobbi Morrison, students learn that a well-functioning open system has clear feedback mechanisms and clear methods of coordinating change and making new adaptations. Within the school students actively participate in a living, changing, open system through the committee structure.

Governance is provided by committees which are open to all at any point during the school year. Each person — student and staff — has one vote. As the handbook explains, committees "have created a place for teachers, students, parents, and the principal to have equal voice, voting power, and responsibility." For instance, Elaine Packard, the principal, doesn't use a veto, and her vote is no more powerful than anyone else's vote. At noontime an hour is deliberately set aside for committees, illustrating that they are equally important as a learning experience. To underscore this, participation in committees is credit-bearing like a class.

Each committee takes on different goals, rules, and responsibilities. Each has its own voting method and the right to make its own process. One method is called, "consensus minus one." This means that two votes against will vote an issue down and indicate that consensus, which usually can be blocked with just one vote, hasn't been reached.

The main committee at Nova is the Systems Management Committee, or SMC, which is a highlight of the school. Within SMC students seriously participate in difficult decision-making in many realms. SMC meets once a week. To make sure that all members of the community, student and staff alike, are able to attend, it is held when no other events or committees are scheduled.

Since SMC decisions are made by consensus, or actually by "consensus minus one," it's important that everyone who is present for the vote understands all the facets of that particular issue. Most topics take three to five meetings before there is a decision. This means that it would be counterproductive for someone to walk in at the middle of the final phases of the discussion, make a snap decision without having heard all the underlying complexities, and vote against the consensus that had been evolving. For this reason, in order to vote at a meeting, a person needs to have attended three consecutive meetings of the SMC. This practice insures that voters are informed voters. If a person who has been attending regularly suddenly misses one meeting, he/she doesn't necessarily lose the right to vote. When the student returns the next week, she/he gives a reason for the absence, and participants vote as to whether it is legitimate, by being asked, "Is anyone opposed to this excuse?"

Over the decades of SMC, various methods have been passed along which insure well-functioning meetings. Each week a facilitator is chosen who is usually a student. The facilitator follows specific methods for running the meeting and for making the agenda. One method for coordinating the discussion is name taking; when many hands are up to speak to an issue, the names are taken down in order, and the next speaker is called upon in turn. These methods are passed along according to an oral tradition which has not yet been written down. In fact, it could be said that Nova operates like a tribe where wisdom is held by practicing and teaching customs to each new generation by example.

Last year the custom of consensus was slightly modified. On issues that kept resurfacing and needed to be resolved, SMC decided it was wise to shift from "consensus minus one" to a super majority of two-thirds. The new practice is that if an issue makes it to the floor four times, on the fourth time, the group can ask, "Is this an issue we want to have go to a super majority?"

Nova committees meet at lunchtime, most weekly, some monthly, some as needed. No more than three committees are scheduled on the same day to encourage broad participation. In addition to the SMC, the committees are:

• Student Leading Against Mediocrity (SLAM)

This committee wrote the student handbook. SLAM is the only committee with no voting procedures or membership rules. It is essentially a ways and means committee which brainstorms and carries out ideas, often from SMC, that help the community. It conducts surveys, brings proposals to other committees, and coordinates activities which will build community at Nova.

• Tech

The Technology Committee has jurisdiction over the computer labs. It originally was set-up to handle $70,000 given from the Seattle School District specifically for the labs. Now it manages the computer room, keeping it useful and stable. One of the questions it addresses is whether computer games are allowed to be played at school. Another issue is to maintain updated Mac's and IBM's to respect student interest in both types. It provides a place to use the Internet, check e-mail, create a web-site, or use Photoshop.

• Public Relations (PR)

The PR Committee puts out a newsletter periodically which is also a literary magazine. It shows what Nova is like, and includes poetry and graphics. The members of the committee decide what should be in the newsletter, write, produce it, and do the layout. They also approve public art in the Nova community. The PR committee is in charge of organizing two orientation meetings for interested families, community members, and potential students to give an introduction to Nova.

• Budget

Oversight of the school budget is done by students and staff together. Money received from the school district, fundraising, and other sources, is allocated by the Budget Committee. Any community member is allowed to bring proposals for expenses to the committee. Proposed expenses could include funding a workshop leader from the community, purchase of supplies, or big ticket items like a van or a computer. They weigh the needs of the school together. Like the SMC, participants have to establish voting membership.

• NIB

The Nova Interview Body consists of students responsible for interviewing potential students. A student must have been a Nova student for at least three months before being trained to interview prospective students. The committee meets monthly except during peak interview periods when it may meet as often as weekly. People who are interested in becoming a Nova student must visit for a whole day; they have four interviews one-to-one with four different members of NIB, and three more interviews, each with one of the COOR Staff Coordinators. They must also attend an entire committee meeting.

• Yearbook

As the handbook describes, "It starts off with students who say, 'I want to have a better yearbook than last year.'" Photography, layout, and design, and negotiations with printers are all part of the work.

- **Recruitment**

  The goal of the committee is to recruit new students through presentations at schools, Parent Teacher School Associations, and community groups.

- **The Environment Committee**

  Newly formed in the spring of 2000, this committee was initiated by Joe Szwaja's COOR group and Connections class. It deals with ecological sustainability at Nova itself. This includes recycling, reducing energy use and solid waste, water use, and composting systems at the school. A goal for the future is local field trips and week-long adventures.

- **Educational Reform**

  The Education Reform Committee looks at Nova in its overall delivery of education and addresses new ideas in education. Recently established in June 2000, it illustrates another function of SMC — to notice the need for new committees and create them. The committee is responsible for doing research into the field of education and school reform and is designed to analyze the school as a system, determine the best process for changing the system, and implement it.

- **Hiring**

  The Hiring Committee meets on an ad-hoc basis. It does a review of current teachers who have been at Nova just a year or two, and is in charge of making recommendations for the hiring of new staff.

During the fall of the year 2000 about 15 students and half of the staff regularly attended SMC meetings. Two issues which surfaced during this period help give a window into democracy at Nova. One issue revolved around the COOR Groups. Getting credit for committee participation signals their importance. Students in one COOR Group suggested that attendance at their weekly COOR Group meetings should also lead to academic credit, to indicate that these groups are central to being active in the community. A healthy round of discussion followed. Other COOR Groups were against credit because they felt that participation should be something you do because you value it. During a five-month discussion among students and staff, this issue came to SMC three times, and the SMC decided the fairest procedure would be to survey the whole school rather than make the decision by themselves.

Another central issue for SMC arose during the school year 2000-2001 as part of the adjustments to Nova's growth. Looking at The Nova Project as an open system, the recent increase in size of eighty new students asks a lot of flexibility and adaptability from the community. One way growth has affected the school is that it's harder for the community to hold students accountable for the behavior agreements they've signed. SMC discussed whether an Accountability Committee should be formed to set up consequences when the school agreements aren't kept and to articulate any other standards that need to be spelled out. We'll look at these issues more in the next section on community.

In summary, Nova's SMC structure allows the school to respond to changing times, hear problems that come to the surface, and be flexible in devising responses. Although to an onlooker, Nova's method of decision-making may seem slow and cumbersome, once a decision is made through SMC, people know that it is solid. Also, they know that if it doesn't work, the consequences will be discussed and evaluated through the SMC.

C for Community

Issues of Responsibility

The handbook puts it succinctly: "Community is very important at Nova. For as long as Nova has been a school we have had a community where people can feel safe and welcome."

Accountability for behavior at Nova has always been a personal matter, encouraged through relationships rather than relying per se on the making of rules. Nova believes that a person maintains responsible behavior by feeling connected to the community and knowing that her or his behavior has an impact on everyone. A key issue in any high school is responsibility: Being on time for class, showing up for drama rehearsal, getting assignments done on time. New methods for enforcing and encouraging responsibility are being developed and discussed through the SMC.

Some issues such as drug use or physical fights would never come before an Accountability Committee. These are serious legal matters that will remain with the adults at the school. It's significant to look at how the breaking of the agreement for no drugs in school is handled. The drug policy is that for a first offense, the student must meet with the whole staff and also meet with a drug counselor. In addition, they are assigned community service, such as twenty hours of washing dishes, to make amends to the community because the drug use as school is breaking the contract they make with their Coordinator. Here is what the handbook says:

Illegal Substance Policy

It is against school policy to use, deal or be under the influence of illegal drugs or alcohol on school property. Engaging in these activities is a violation of the Nova learning community. Violation of this policy will result in the following consequences:

1) Accused student must meet with the staff to investigate the accusation.

2) Parents/guardians will be informed if student has violated the policy.

3) Student must do 20 hours of school service within one month of the violation.

4) Student must attend drug/alcohol assessment within the one week of the violation and agree to follow through with the assessment recommendations.

5) Your coordinator will drop you if you fail to follow through with these consequences. Student will be subject to suspension for a second offense.

Nova has relied upon the strength of the Coordinatee's relationship with their Coordinator, but this has been affected by the growth of the school. Occurrences that have always been handled as teachable moments by staff — such as a student trashing the lounge, or one community member being rude to another — can now happen out of the public eye. Interpersonal conflicts of all forms — student-staff, staff-staff, or student-student — need clearer means of resolution. It's harder to have face-to-face contact with each person and this means that the former ways of dealing with accountability personally and directly aren't working as well. Breaking agreements is a serious matter because community is taken seriously.

The handbook advises:

1. Do not do things that compromise the integrity of the school and its community, such as stealing, doing graffiti, or otherwise defacing the school.

2. When you see other people doing things like that PLEASE do something about it. You can either intervene yourself or go get a teacher. If you can find a way to tell the person to stop in a way that doesn't offend them, it can end up having a wonderful effect on the community.

3. We also train students to be peer mediators. Mediation is a good way to resolve conflicts confidentially and peacefully. If you are interested in being a peer mediator, speak with Elaine.

4. Meet new people. This helps the community because it reduces the "cliques" and when everyone knows each other it cuts down on destructive behavior.

5. Help around the school. Clean up your dishes or messes that you leave behind. Do garden work. There are so many things that you can do at Nova that are fun and that contribute to the community.

One way to measure the community feeling at Nova is through the yearly Seattle School District student climate surveys. The Nova results are significantly higher than District averages on issues of community, as well as, on issues of learning. In the areas of safety, fairness, good relationships among students, leadership, student involvement, and friendliness of students, the scores are high.

Elaine Packard informally interviewed students recently on the question of responsibility and found remarkably similar responses. In essence, they said what students even fifteen years ago said: The hardest part and the best part of being at Nova is that you have to follow through on what you say you will do. Students receive the consequences of how they handle their choices. They get important feedback that wouldn't happen if learning were set up using a punishment model. Even problems and failures give important input; they learn from what doesn't work, as well as, what does. It is the freedom at Nova that helps develop responsibility so that the structure that is fostered is an internal structure that will serve them life-long.

Students felt that they even have choice about how much external structure they have. They said, "If you want more structure — like having deadlines — you can ask for it." Students also observed, "Teachers don't bug you here." But teachers do intervene. Rather than using a laissez-faire approach, staff have, what Packard calls "agency." Staff are agents of growth and change without taking over control. They set a common agreement about what is acceptable, make reasonable expectations, remind students, and coach them about following the agreements. But the consequences rest with the students. This means that staff are dealing with a dynamic and delicate balance between giving enough structure and enough freedom. Their aim is to turn over responsibility on issues which are within the students' range to accomplish. This means that students have to know their reason and purpose for being at Nova and take charge of their power to learn.

There are several consequences of this freedom and choice for students. They frequently fall behind on learning credits. They may choose to make up credits in the eleventh and twelfth grades by attending community college where classes are both free and worth double high school credit. Those student "elders" spend less time at Nova, and this results in a loss of student leadership, involvement, and presence at school. Other students may take more than four years to graduate. In either case, this student freedom and choice places more demands on the teachers to track student progress and develop strategies for students to complete course requirements in a timely manner. These are issues that are constantly discussed and debated at Nova.

C for Contracts

Learning Options

Students choose their schedule, their curriculum, and how they go about getting credits. Classes tend to be small because of the variety of learning options. The way that grades and credits operate at Nova is the opposite of traditional high schools where the grade varies but full credit is given for any level of work performance. The structure of grading and credits is set up to encourage responsibility. At Nova the only grade given is a "pass" based on 100% completion of work at an 80% mastery, and the amount of credit is based on the amount of work completed. While a student at a traditional school might receive a D and full credit for doing half the work, at Nova doing half the work as long as it is at 80% mastery equals half the credits. This makes credit harder to get at Nova, and therefore, the consequences of one's actions are more directly felt. Another detail of the system is that honors and advanced placement credit are available as well.

The hardworking staff of twelve includes six teachers new in the last year, and three teachers with ten or more years of experience. The principal has been at Nova nearly from its beginning, and one teacher brings 26 years of Nova experience. Two teachers have been recognized for their teaching excellence in *Who's Who Among America's Teachers 2000*. One teacher was the United Nations Association of Seattle Human Rights award winner in 1999 for working on human rights for East Timor. Mark Perry is the author of *Walking the Color Line: The Art and Practice of Anti-Racist Teaching* (New York: Teachers College Press, 2000).

Partnership structure in the way classes operate is in evidence. Classes are democratically run. Students have choice in their projects, and some teachers seek student feedback using periodic check-ins. Policies and expectations within a class are negotiated; teachers bring a rough draft of the semester plan to the first class and discuss issues of attendance, assignments, and projects. In fact, one teacher creates a class charter with students that details behavior agreements up front. All students make learning contracts which define what they need to do and they describe what they want to learn. They state both their academic and personal goals for the learning experience.

There is a productive dynamic tension at work here. On the one hand, students are honored as individuals who make their own independent decisions. On the other hand, adults give their knowledge and perspective as adult mentors who help hold them responsible for important learning experiences.

Contracts are used to set intentions for learning. The Nova Credit Contract applies to classes offered within the school. For every course, the student answers on the front of the contract, "Why are you taking this course and what do you intend to learn?" The facilitator provides a brief course description and explains the basis upon which credit will be earned. For evaluation, on the back of the contract both the student and facilitator have two types of entries.

> Student: Comment on what you learned and how you learned it and the quality of your work.

> Facilitator: List specific activities involved in this course.

> Student: Comment on the quality of the facilitator's help, such as class organization, quality of assignments, useful and timely feedback, attitude toward students, effective use of class time, instructional style, and mastery of subject.

> Facilitator: Comment on quality of student participation, such as mastery of subject, initiative, motivation, attitude, study skills, and preparation.

Within classes, if something isn't working for a student, they have the right to go to the teacher and have it modified to meet their needs. Adjustments are then worked out together. Instead of a student privately feeling "I don't like this class," at Nova, students are encouraged to answer "What would you like to see different about it?"

Staff-led courses aren't the only learning options. A second type of contract is called the alternative learning experience or ALE which is used for Independent study or Field study. For instance, a person in the community can be a resource for learning how to write a novel, taking music lessons or studying martial arts. On this contract, the facilitator or coordinator (if it is a field study) describes the learning activities the student is expected to successfully complete, as well as, how learning will be demonstrated. This section establishes requirements for documentation of hours, or a plan for doing journaling or making a presentation.

In addition, students can propose and teach a course with teachers signing the contract and providing teacher supervision. Students have led courses on African drumming, ultimate Frisbee, and a study of revolutions. In January 2001, the second semester will begin with four days of student-led intensives. These won't be for credit, but they will help build community.

During the 2000-2001 school year, Nova students were interns at architectural firms, legal firms, and local hospitals. They also did internships with the Chief Operating Officer of the Seattle School district, the Northwest Puppetry Theater, Jack Straw Studios (an alternative radio station), The Independent Media Center, Child Haven, and a literary house called Hugo House. In the past midwives, veterinarians, and glass blowers have worked with Nova interns.

These practices of personalized learning enhance academic development. Nova students receive outstanding scores on standardized achievement tests, and consistently high scores on all standardized test indicators, including Washington Assessment of Student Learning and Direct Writing Assessment. In the 1999-2000 school year, Nova had the highest SAT verbals and second highest SAT math scores of all Seattle's public high schools.

Although many students who come to Nova often are not considering further education after high school, Nova is quite successful at directing its graduates to higher education, with a majority going on to four-year colleges as diverse as Antioch, Barnard, Dartmouth, Evergreen State College, Friends World, Smith, Stanford, Swarthmore, Tufts, the University of Chicago, the University of Michigan, Wellesley, Wesleyan, and Whitman. Other students have gone directly into starting their own businesses, becoming an artist and creating an art studio, traveling or doing other forms of job training such as being a veterinarian assistant. It's part of the relationship with the Coordinator to articulate what your future goals are and to explore "What will you need to do now to go to the next part of your life?"

Nova staff contacted the Center for Partnership Studies in 1998 to establish a more formalized connection between the two groups. The Connections class at Nova draws upon Riane Eisler's work, and in turn, the teaching practices of staff are helping to build and inform Partnership Education.

The Four C's All Together

Nova's partnership structure allows it to be a learning, growing, changing community. Nova has adapted ingeniously as its numbers have increased five times from the size of the original student body. Nova relies upon democratic processes to explore and address needs and formulate solutions using consensus. The result is that students graduate from Nova with partnership experiences rarely possible in most high schools in the United States and are ready to contribute methods of partnership to any setting where they participate.

To contact Nova:

The Nova Project
2410 E. Cherry Street
Seattle, Washington 98122

Telephone: (206) 726-6730
Fax: (206) 726-6731

Internet address: www.novaproj.org

CHAPTER 15

Partnership Structure

by Ruthmary Powers

Structure is about the interrelationships of parts to a whole. It is not always easy to see how things go together or why. In the past thirty-five years, I have had many opportunities to see educational structure from many aspects. As a student, teacher, administrator, superintendent, and, forever, a learner, I have had the good fortune of working with many different cultures and all ages of students from kindergarten through college to adult. Many of the questions in this chapter come directly from my own experience in one or more of these roles. This chapter, as with my own life, does not contain all the answers. I continue to be challenged by how to create partnership structures on many levels. Working toward this end, however, is a worthwhile endeavor. One important ingredient in the process is a sense of humor. Being able to laugh and see the incongruities and foibles of daily life help keep a perspective about the goals you are trying to achieve. As you read on, keep in mind that creating partnership educational structures should be enjoyable as well as challenging.

The last several decades have seen a continual cry for the "restructuring" of the educational process. However, it is not always evident that the new structures being proposed will bring about any fundamental change in teaching practices or the learning environment. Any genuine "restructuring" of educational institutions ought to address the hierarchy of roles, the dynamics of power, the quality of the educational environment, and the maintenance of rules and procedures that determine the atmosphere in which teaching and learning take place. A careful look at educational structure raises serious questions about who makes decisions about curriculum, instruction, and a school's professional culture — and how these decisions come to be made and implemented.

Partnership Education, a vision of educational transformation based on Riane Eisler's pioneering studies of cultural evolution, includes a thorough analysis of educational structure. In the Prologue of *Tomorrow's Children*, Eisler explains that "partnership structure is about where learning and teaching take place; what kind of *learning environment* we construct if we follow the partnership model."(Eisler, 2000, xvi.) Partnership structure has to be present in any move toward partnership-oriented learning communities. In partnership structure, the interrelationship of the people, the content, and the process must be consonant with the principles of partnership as outlined in *Tomorrow' Children*.

Creating a community of learning based on partnership requires looking at all aspects of the systems now in place. (A review of the concepts involved in systemic change is appropriate. The work of Peter Senge as cited in the bibliography would be a good place to begin this review.) The restructuring work includes addressing understandings of concepts that have held sway in the current system. An example of this is in the concept of hierarchy. Eisler *(The Chalice and the Blade*, pp. 105-106) states,

> [In dominator systems, the] term hierarchy refers to systems of human ranking based on force or threat of force. These domination hierarchies are very different from a second type of hierarchy, which I propose be called hierarchies of actualization. These are the familiar hierarchies of systems within systems, for examples, of molecules, cells, and organs of the body: a progression toward a higher, more evolved, and more complex level of function. By contrast, as we may see all around us, domination hierarchies characteristically inhibit the actualization of higher functions, not only in the overall social system, but also in the individual human.

When beginning a movement toward educational systemic change, reflection on passages such as this help to deepen the understanding and commitment of those involved in the process. A dialogic process helps to expand and clarify the concepts on both a personal and group level. Partnership structural change is a group process. It cannot happen if only one individual has this as a goal.

Initially anyone can begin gathering others to work toward partnership restructuring. However, for the partnership to progress, there needs to be support from each of the school components: Teachers, administrators, staff members, and parents. The ideal group to begin the planning process would include someone from each of these areas of school life.

A word here about leadership: Leadership is critical in creating a partnership structure. As stated above, it is a leadership of actualization rather than domination. Leadership resides in each member of the group. The shared personal power involved in partnership creates the synergy for transformation. Each member of the group has her or his own "role" as well. That is why job descriptions and role clarifications are extremely important in the beginning of this process. An equally important aspect of the role clarification is that of personal talents and skills. If one of the group members is particularly blessed with the gift of organization, be he or she maintenance or principal, that person can be called forth to use this talent in the process. Redefining *hierarchy, leadership* and *power, personal and group*, is well worth the time it might take to do this. As the group matures, redefinitions may occur. Keep in mind that this is a process so that redefining and change are to be expected, especially in a systemic change movement. Shared vision around these issues will be most helpful in developing the other aspects of school life toward partnership organization.

It is vital that a school's administrator or principal be fully supportive of a partnership restructuring process. However all involved will benefit by becoming steeped in the partnership literature. Key titles include *The Chalice and the Blade, Tomorrow's Children, Sacred Pleasure,* and *The Partnership Way*—all by Riane Eisler. These books describe the underlying principles for making a shift away from an unconscious dominator approach toward a conscious implementation of partnership ideals.

Once the organization has decided to work toward developing a partnership-oriented structure, here are some steps that must be included in making this change in the educational school program:

1. Take enough time to make a plan.

2. Read the material on partnership education carefully.

3. Gather a group of like-minded interested people.

Including parents at the outset is important to consider. They should be allies of the process, as well as, have a critical eye as to how this might or could affect their children.

Begin outlining the plan with regular meetings where as stated above, job descriptions, schedules, and curriculum changes that are required in moving toward partnership are determined. Tools to use in implementing these are outlined by Eisler (*Tomorrow's Children*, pp. 242) to serve as a foundation for your process:

1. Use the partnership and dominator models as analytical tools.

2. Show the interaction between broadening your personal choices and developing a partnership cultural and social organization.

3. Develop a way to teach for partnership literacies and competencies.

4. Create a democratic and nurturing learning environment through partnership process.

This group should meet at least once a week. Assignments and homework can be determined and agreed to by the group. For individuals who commit to working toward a partnership educational restructuring must be prepared for the process. The planning can be done over a semester or summer or several months to begin this preparatory step. Attempting to do this in the midst of a school year would be like designing the airplane while flying it.

However, we know that most of life is not ideal, and in the event that these changes are being made in the middle of a school year, the whole staff must be involved. This includes those who hold hourly positions as well as salaried, the maintenance, secretarial, food service staffs, and aides. The group that has been meeting includes the others by giving an overview of the project thus far. The whole faculty and staff then decide on some short-term goals that can be accomplished during the school year. Working through the goals may take more than one meeting, but agreement on one or two goals is essential in beginning the process. Probably not all will commit to the reading and study necessary, but where possible, staff members could commit to forming study groups to digest Eisler's work.

Changing the School Culture

This is the beginning. Once there is a group committed to looking at some short term goals, planning for the future can begin. One of the first things that will probably need to be changed is the culture of the school. The emphasis to be made here is that a partnership culture must be consciously constructed through stories, images, and symbols. The influence of the dominator paradigm on our non-rational and subconscious level has been constructed over millennia. Therefore, a conscious effort will be necessary to create a school culture aligned with partnership values and vision.

School culture is created in the newsletters, the publications, and the kind of recognition that is given to those in the learning community.

> Whose pictures line the walls? What fills the trophy case? Partnership values will be present in both the content and presentation of material. What is the school known for? What symbols are displayed? Who/what are the mascots? How is this consonant with a partnership structure?

What type of language is used to describe who the school says it is? Is it all based on competition or ranking? What stories do faculty members, students, parents tell about the school? What makes the staff proud? What do the parents expect, especially from the sports teams? Are the arts, musical, literary events as highly touted? What kind of art is displayed in the classrooms? A friend of mine visited her daughter's classroom where the pictures displayed were of the U.S. Presidents. What message does this send to the girls, children of other races, boys in the class?A school can change its culture consciously by the way it describes itself. Here is another reflection/action tool that can be employed by the group to further the individual and communal understanding of "moving toward partnership." It is important that each group member acknowledges both their individual, experiential connection to domination and partnership, as well as the societal influences that hold all of us captive. Therefore, this tool should move on from reflection to understanding to action.

Movement From Persons as Other-Determined toward Persons as Self-Determined

Who is invisible? Who is not named? Who is spoken about rather than spoken to? When decisions are made, who is consulted? Who makes the final decision? Where is there delegation concerning decision-making?

Movement from Exclusion toward Inclusion

How are individuals and groups included in the daily and extraordinary work? What system is used to check on who's been left out? Is there a process to check? What does the staffing look like? What symbols, images, quotes are displayed in the school environment? How can it be made more inclusive? What is the feeling about inclusive language? Is it used? Is it insisted upon?

Movement from Ethnocentricity toward Cultural Puralism

Do individuals or the group make statements like: "I'd (we'd) be happy to have more _____, if only they would _____." Who provides diversity on the staff? Is there an active seeking out of those who may be "different"? How are differences seen as growth and learning opportunities?

Movement from Triumphalism and Condescension toward Collaboration and Mutuality

What is the attitude toward authority? Power? Does the group or individuals in the group have "all the answers"? Are there concerns that individuals and groups are incapable of making decisions for themselves? Does the group try to find ways that they are "different" or "superior" to those with whom they work, teach? How does the group understand collaboration? Mutuality? (See the section on hegemony and privilege later in text.)

Movement from Win-Lose Mentality to a Win-Win Mentality

Is there a competitive streak in the group or group members? Is it acknowledged and dealt with? What kind of language is used concerning dispute situation? What is considered to be successful negotiation?

Movement from Isolation toward Connection

Who is isolated? How does the group know about those who are isolated? What plans or processes are in place to insure connectedness? How do members of the staff feel? Do those employed feel a part of the school community? If someone says they feel isolated, what kind of emotions does that raise in the group or individuals? What kind of reactions are seen?

Movement from Bewilderment and Confusion to Defining Core Values

Where does the group or the staff in general feel vague and confused? What kinds of emotions are regularly displayed at staff meetings, parent gatherings, etc. How does the group respond when anger, frustration, resentment or rage is displayed? Is there blaming, dismissing, anger in return? Do the goals created for moving toward partnership include an assessment tool in the light of "negative" responses? When goals and values are defined, how does the group acknowledge and celebrate this?

Other Areas to Consider

Context: What is the educational environment like? What stands out that is helpful to partnership or hinders partnership? Assessing the building itself is important here. What is the physical arrangement of the building? Does it support or impede partnership?

Climate: What elements, qualities, and characteristics need to be present to create an environment which fosters partnership? How are the classrooms arranged? What kind of work is displayed, etc? Emotional climate is also important — what kind of daily "spirit" can be found in the school? Is it one of joyful learning? How can this be created?

Productivity: How is success measured? What kind of assessments are used to determine movements toward partnership? What kind of "testing" is considered consonant with partnership values? Rather than "grading" are there processes implemented to support teachers and students assessing each student's process in learning? How does the staff and school measure its success? How is that celebrated?

Each of these sections is connected to every other aspect of the school life. In beginning to develop partnership structure, the physical environment needs to be considered, as do the classrooms, as does access to nature. Harmony and flow are important in the school environment. This may be easier than changing internal structures but can present a challenge nonetheless. Partnership process is organic. It is an understanding of how people and our planet actually function. It is attuned to the natural life forces and rhythms within us. Connecting the students with nature is essential to a community of learning that emphasizes a partnership ecological consciousness. To become conscious of these connections is a first step toward change.

Changing Hierarchical Roles

Eisler makes it clear that a partnership social organization does not do away with leadership. As mentioned previously in this chapter, each person has personal power that can be used in a relational way to empower others rather than dominate them. In a school setting there are those whose roles define them as "leaders." This includes teachers and administrators. Administrators, in exercising their responsibility to lead, need to determine how they use their power and authority. Their commitment to helping to create a partnership community of learning will be evaluated by the way they exercise this authority. Anyone who has been an administrator knows there are times when the "buck" stops with *them*. However, there are many instances where that is not true and the dialogue can be opened to include others in the decision-making process. How decisions are made and who is consulted when making a decision should be examined in the movement toward partnership.

A "working paper" by Peggy McIntosh on "white privilege" (1988) helps to expose the hegemony in our everyday actions and assumptions. In this paper she connects many of our assumptions around race and gender and then reflects them back to the reader. They range from simple to profound unconscious beliefs that we hold because they have been supported by the dominator system in which we live. For example, she writes,

I can, if I wish, arrange to be in the company of people of my race most of the time.

If I should need to move, I can be pretty sure of renting or purchasing
housing in an area that I can afford and in which I would want to live.

When I am told about our national heritage or about "civilization"
I am shown that people of my color made it what it is.

The entire working paper contains many more assumptions. The extent of the assumptions actually reaches beyond race and gender. The aspects of life that each individual or group takes for granted without deeper exploration tend to support and hold in place the unconscious dominator model. What does the group feel "entitled to?" Has anyone in the group made a statement like, "Well, I would never do ... " About what does the group (or individual in the group) tend to feel superior. Have the members of the group experienced "powerlessness?" Are they able to translate that into their actions that may, in turn, create that feeling in others? The hegemonic aspects in our society have kept the dominator system in place because we do not even understand them as privilege. Partnership leaders are called to a continual examination of the cultural assumptions that individuals and groups make about power.

Power is a main characteristic of discipline in a learning community. Although discipline and punishment are not the same our societal norms often connect the two. Therefore, a close examination of the discipline code of the school must be made. Does it support partnership relationships, calling students to responsibility for their actions, and an understanding of consequences for decisions? How are students and teachers being empowered to become self-determined and responsible for their own actions?

Students, parents, teachers — the whole learning community is interested in fairness. Codes can be developed in a participative manner. What are some ways these codes can be built in a fair and equitable manner? Each school community must develop this for itself. And, it will not happen all at once. When a school community finds that the "discipline" is being handed over to one person, this is not partnership. Threats and punishment need to be replaced with some clear consequences to actions that students and teachers alike know and understand.

In determining aspects of school policy, those responsible (administration, administrative team, school board, etc.) should get as much input as possible. Even if the input is contradictory, clarity around who has been consulted and the reasons for decisions show that a partnership process has been followed.

In working toward partnership continually expand the circle of inclusion. As an administrator when I had particularly knotty issues, I would ask the faculty to give me their best thinking on it. Usually, they could come up with a solution I never considered. It also made them much more willing to be involved in helping to solve the problem.

Leaders should not be afraid to admit that they have made a mistake, nor be afraid to change their mind. This does not mean being wishy-washy, but when faced with a better solution or more inclusion partnership possibility, go for it. Pride and ego do not work well in trying to implement partnership structure. Those involved in working toward a partnership social organization need to model this behavior for others. In this way, everyone in the community of learning is a leader and a follower.

Reflection must necessarily precede action. Small movements toward partnership should be acknowledged and celebrated. The process may be difficult, but it should have elements of joy and fun or it will be too discouraging. Building a community of learning demands honest conversation. In a course I was teaching at a college level on diversity, the cohort of instructors met regularly to discuss where each of us drew our "line" on diversity. Being able to discuss freely the difficulties to implementation, the frustrations encountered, and emerging issues will help each understand the other at a level where support and challenge can be freely offered.

Changing the Classroom Environment

Partnership structure throughout the school will necessarily demand a change in each classroom. Teachers need to look at their classroom environment to make sure it reflects a partnership structure. How are the desks or tables arranged? Is the environment friendly and welcoming to each student who enters? Are both genders and all the cultural and racial diversity of your class reflected there? Who plans the environment? Have you or do you include students in cooperating with you to create the classroom environment best suited to their learning styles? Displaying students' work is also very important — everyone's work — not just the "best." If there is not enough space, how do you rotate your displays so that at some point everyone finds herself or himself highlighted? In one school a teacher had the students draw dates and on that day, the student was highlighted as student of the day. Another way is to use birthdays and have a short presentation from the student about herself/himself on that day.

The daily schedule will also have to reflect partnership structure. The schedule may at first pose a particular problem since most teachers, administrators, and school districts (to say nothing of the parents) are used to the familiar period designation for structuring the "school day." How time is proportioned may be one of the most significant pieces and possibly most difficult decision to be made by those working toward a partnership structure.

1. Are classes broken up into discrete pieces of information?

2. What schedule would better suit a partnership community of learning?

3. Who makes the schedule?

4. Is this something that the faculty does?

5. If so, how can you best design your day for integration?

Working with others is essential in a partnership structure. Much depends on the size of the faculty, but having one or several partner teachers would be a great benefit.

Responsibility for research necessary to have a gender, racial, and culturally balanced curriculum could be shared. Help in the classroom will also be necessary. There will need to be smaller classes and more aides so that every child is included in the educational process. If the school district does not have enough money to provide this, partners or other members from the community-at-large can be incorporated as volunteers. Building partnership relationships with parents and the larger community will enhance classroom learning. Volunteers must also be fully acquainted and comfortable with partnership principles. Where volunteers are inserted into a classroom structure without the proper preparation, problems and conflict will ensue. A good summer project might be to train a cadre of volunteers for the fall.

Parents in Partnership Communities of Learning

Parents, as partners in the learning process, are absolutely essential to a productive program. Involving parents at the planning level is important as noted earlier. Communicating with parents in a regular, positive, systematic way also helps lessen the fears and anxieties parents may feel. Informed parents — those who feel valued — will be the best public relations the school can have. Parental involvement must be an integral part of the school's movement toward a partnership social organization.

Including the Community-at-Large

In beginning the partnership restructuring process, an in depth research study should be done of the strengths of the community in which the school is located. What possibilities for learning are situated there?

1. Are there museums, libraries, parks, conservatories, hospitals near by?

2. Is the school situated near public transportation?

3. What cultural opportunities are available for the students?

4. Are there service-learning opportunities: Nursing homes, food kitchens, day care centers?

5. What businesses are located in the community? Have they been interviewed about how they would like to work with the school?

6. What about local churches, synagogues, mosques? Are there programs that would be beneficial to them and the school?

7. Walk the neighborhood — are there possibilities for connecting with those who live in the area either as volunteers or as recipients of service-learning program?

In every case, there are opportunities for expanding the learning environment. The challenge is to find them. This need not be the sole work of the faculty. Keeping the safety of the student always at the forefront, there are times when the students themselves are the school's ambassadors of partnership to the larger community.

As the partnership mentality takes hold, the staff, students, and parents will continually offer other ways to extend the school into the community and vice-versa. In developing the partnership model the limits are primarily the imagination and creativity we bring to the situation.

Challenges to Creating
Partnership Learning Communities

There are many challenges to creating partnership structures. The first, I believe to be the most critical, is assuming that it will be easy or that it will fall into place without a struggle. Not all will agree that partnership schools are the best and most important way to restructure education.

The second very serious challenge is recognizing the need to create a new "system." The systems approach to developing a new worldview is imperative if the new worldview is not to be co-opted by the old dominator paradigm. We are totally

imbued with the dominator system. We have had at least five thousand years of dominator oppression ruling our minds, our hearts, our social, and political organizations. To assume that schools can be created that demonstrate a partnership model of social organization is to deny the years of dominator hegemony that has been our heritage. I do not mean to state that it is hopeless, no, far from it. What I do mean is that it will not be accomplished easily or quickly. Small movements toward partnership must be acknowledged and celebrated. Dominator backsliding must be acknowledged and accepted, but not allowed to cause loss of heart in this very important movement.

Senge and his partners in the work, *The Dance of Change*, (1999) outline ten challenges they have found in trying to create learning (partnership) organizations. These challenges are as true for education as they are for the corporate world. These challenges will not sound strange. They are familiar stumbling blocks whenever profound change is being attempted. They are:

1. Not enough time — profound change takes TIME.

2. Not enough help — need for mentoring and coaching.

3. Not relevant — how does this make a difference to me?

4. Walking the talk — are we who we say we are?

5. Fear and Anxiety — when we do this what will happen?

6. Assessment and Measurement — how we will evaluate?

7. True Believers and Non-Believers — create opposition
   rather than community, in-groups and our-groups. They're not like us.

8. Governance — who's in charge? How are things managed?

9. Diffusion — have we gotten too far a field?

10. Strategies and Purpose — continually move toward
    a more partnership environment. Not losing focus.

Deeper levels of structural challenges are described in *The Fifth Discipline Field Book*. Senge and his colleagues give case studies of groups working together to form learning communities. I advise those involved in developing the partnership learning communities to have these resources readily available. They help all of us realize that the human condition will be present in all group and change processes.

There are many resources available to help in this change process. Some are cited in this chapter, some can be found in the bibliography, and others will be found as the process evolves.

We are called to transform ourselves as we transform society. A dualistic mentality will continually sabotage a movement toward partnership. This means that in each situation, the group must seek for the both/and rather than the either/or. The assessments as they are made need to be based on movements toward partnership rather than an all or nothing approach to change. In many cases the infrastructure will not support the partnership mentality. That is why each aspect of change has both an inner and outer landscape. Most difficult to determine will be the unconscious mental attitudes that undermine the restructuring movement with "we can't," "we should," and "we've always done it like this." Nothing is insignificant in creating a partnership structure. Simple, subtle steps move the process forward. Social movements often happen at the margins and are created by not losing hope. Take time to celebrate and enjoy the partnership moments when they occur.

Riane Eisler's words in *Tomorrow's Children* give passion and meaning to a quest for Partnership Education.

> At the core of partnership education is learning, both intellectually and experientially, that the partnership and dominator models are two underlying alternatives for human relations. Relations based on fear, violence, and domination are a possibility. However what distinguishes us as a species is not our cruelty or violence but our enormous capacity for caring and creativity. Constructing relations and institutions that more closely approximate the partnership model helps us to actualize these capacities (Eisler, p. 10).

This alternative, partnership, is the best gift we offer our children, the planet and the future. It is also the best gift we can nurture in one another and ourselves.

Recommended Reading

Bedford, T. & Kinnear, P. (1993). *Internationalizing the Curriculum.* Tokyo: Japan. Council of International Schools.

Best, R. (1983). *We've All Got Scars: What Boys and Girls Learn in Elementary School.* Bloomington, IN: Indiana University Press.

Bowers, C.A. (1995). *Educating for an Ecologically Sustainable Culture: Rethinking Moral Education, Creativity, Intelligence, and Other Modern Orthodoxies.* Albany: SUNY Press.

Brislin, R., Cushner, K., Cherrie, C., & Yong, M. (1986). *Intercultural Interaction: A Practical Guide.* Newbury Park: Sage Publishers.

Caine, G. & Caine, R.N. (1991). *Making Connections: Teaching and The Human Brain.* Alexandria, VA: Association for Supervision and Curriculum Development.

Eisler, R. (1987). *The Chalice and The Blade.* San Francisco: Harper & Row Publishing Company.

Eisler, R. & Loye, D. (1990). *The Partnership Way*. San Francisco: HarperSanFrancisco.

Eisler, R. (2000). *Tomorrow's Children: A Blueprint for Partnership Education in the 21st Century*. Boulder CO: Westview Press.

Freire, P. (1970). *The Pedagogy of the Oppressed*. New York: Continuum Publishing Company.

Gibbs, J. (1994). *Tribes: A New Way of Learning Together*. Santa Rosa, CA: Center Source Publications.

Gilligan, C. (1982). *In a Different Voice: Psychological Theory and Women's Development*. Cambridge, MA: Harvard University Press.

Hitt, W. D. (1998). *The Global Citizen*. Columbus, OH: Battelle Press.

Kohn, A. (1992). *No Contest: The Case Against Competition*. New York: Houghton Mifflin Company.

Kriesberg, S. (1992). *Transforming Power: Domination, Empowerment and Education*. Albany, NY: SUNY Press.

Law, Eric H.F. (2000). *Inclusion: Making Room for Grace*. St. Louis, MO: Chalice Press.

McIntosh, P. (1988). *White Privilege and Male Privilege: A Personal Account of Coming to See Correspondences Through Work in Women's Studies*. (Working Paper 189). Wellesley, MA: Wellesley College Center for Research on Women.

Noddings, N. (1984). *Caring: A Feminine Approach to Ethics and Moral Education*. Los Angeles, CA: University of California Press.

Powers, R. (1994). *Pathways to Partnership: Partnership Possibilities for Transforming the Education Restructuring Movement*. Unpublished.

Senge, P. (1990). *The Fifth Discipline: The Art and Practice of the Learning Organization*. New York: Doubleday.

Senge, P., Kleiner, A., Roberts, C., Ross, R., Smith, B. (1992). *The Fifth Discipline Fieldbook: Strategies and Tools for Building a Learning Organization*. New York: Doubleday.

Senge, P., Kleiner, A., Roberts, C., Ross, R., Roth, G., Smith, B. (1999). *The Dance of Change: The Challenge of Sustaining Momentum in Learning Organizations*. New York: Doubleday.

Wheatley, M., (1999). *Leadership and The New Science*. San Francisco, CA: Berrett-Koehler Publishing Company.

Your Next Steps
With Partnership Education[23]

The Partnership Education Program (PEP) of the Center for Partnership Studies (CPS) warmly encourages individuals to be involved in Partnership Education. We suggest several avenues that you can use to be connected and help further this work.

Practice: Embrace Partnership Education in your classroom and in your school.

Share successful ideas: Send information about your experiences teaching Partnership Education.

Participate in outreach: Help spread the word about Partnership Education among other educators.

Here Are Specific Actions You Can Take

To Stay Connected

Contact PEP to be on the mailing list. You will receive copies of the newsletter and periodic mailings as they are developed.

> The Partnership Education Program
> Del Jones, Director
> *cpsdel@aol.com*
> (520) 546-0176
> P.O. Box 30538 Tucson, Arizona, 85751

Join the International Partnership Network (IPN) at the same address, and receive their newsletter.

Visit the website at www.partnershipway.org to learn about opportunities to network and connect with others. You can submit a message in the contact section. Periodically check the web site for updates on activities and new materials.

To Develop Teaching Units

PEP encourages each person to develop her or his partnership work and keep PEP informed. Through networking we can hear about each others practices and further the process of developing Partnership Education.

- Select an activity described in *Tomorrow's Children* or in this book. Test it and send a short description that describes what modifications you may have made, and your evaluation.

- Create a new activity with partnership content.

  For example: Lead a classroom unit on prehistory. Work with the class to create a school assembly presentation that shares the information with the whole school.

- Share your teaching experiences with PEP. Email a short description to let us know about your involvement. Informal communication is fine.

We also encourage more detailed descriptions of successful activities. Use any of these questions as guides in writing:

- What curricular content or standards were your focus?
- What goals did you set for the unit / activity / lesson?
- What processes did you use and why?
- How did you use and integrate student input?
- How did you evaluate student learning?
- What helped the activity to work?
- What might you do differently?

Articles about successful activities and partnership practices, as well as interesting anecdotes will be published on the web site and in the newsletter. Check the web site for information about how to submit your writing for publication.

If there are exemplary student drawings or essays which would help other educators learn how to lead your activity, send copies of student work with your submission. Include a signed permission form for each student that states permission to share the work with other educators.

To Identify Resources

- Locate books, songs, and videos that further partnership education and send their name, a brief description, and contact information to PEP. Remember: It doesn't have to use the word *partnership* to be about Partnership Education.

- Create books, songs or videos that further the goals of Partnership Education.

- Check the webpage at www.partnershipway.org for a list of resources and resource links.

To Investigate Partnership Practices

Set up a *Tomorrow's Children* study group.

- Develop a question that matters to you. Choose an issue germane to Partnership Education that relates to your classroom goals or relates to information and perceptions you would like to impart. Share your question with the office. Ask that it be listed on the web site to search for others who are also investigating this area.

  Example: How do I help ninth graders understand the impact of racism and develop a unit studying the partnership of people of color and European Americans to change individual, cultural, and institutional racism?

  - Study the formats for self-assessment found in the appendix and choose one method of self-assessment to promote dialogue within your school.

  - Design an Action Research Plan related to Partnership Education.

  Scott Forbes, the Program Director of the Action Research for Holistic Education Program describes the process this way. Contact EnCompass for more information at scott@encompass~nlr.org.

    A. Pose a question about your own practice.

    B. Plan an action or intervention that will help you answer your question.

    C. Gather data that shows the consequences of your action or intervention.

    D. Analyze the data.

    E. Engage in some structured reflection. This will produce another question.

  From this process your practice will evolve and develop.

  - Learn more about partnership by reading *The Chalice and the Blade* by Riane Eisler.

To Share with Colleagues

The Partnership Education Program provides brochures, articles, and other appropriate handouts that describe Partnership Education. To help guide those who are interested in creating a school or program model, a Partnership Education framework is available on the web at <www.partnershipway.org>.

Within Your School

- Place Partnership Education on the agenda of your staff meeting. Request to have 10 minutes to talk. Bring a copy of *Tomorrow's Children* and *Partnership Education in Action* to share. You have our permission to photocopy Ron Miller's article at the beginning of this book, "An Overview of Riane Eisler's *Tomorrow's Children*." Articles from the website can also be downloaded, photocopied, and distributed.

- Arrange with PEP to have a PEP consultant provide an introductory workshop for your staff, or work in conjunction with PEP to learn how to lead the workshop yourself.

- Give a copy of *Tomorrow's Children* to your school library. Put a notice in your school newsletter to inform parents and staff about this resource.

- Show the video "Tomorrow's Children: Partnership Education in Action, with Riane Eisler," produced by the Media Education Foundation. This dynamic new video combines an interview with author Riane Eisler on the theory of partnership education with classroom scenes of partnership education in practice. Included is commentary by school principals, teachers, and students at the secondary-level Nova School in Seattle, as well as comments and lively elementary classroom exercises with singer, writer, educator Sarah Pirtle. Educators, parents, and those preparing to be teachers, will all benefit from this stimulating, illustrated discussion of how education can prepare our children for partnership as citizens and move us all toward a more peaceful and just world.

Approximate length: 45 minutes

Available September 2001

Prices: For classroom use and public performance: $275 for Colleges and Universities; $150 for High Schools, Non-Profit Organizations, and Public

Libraries; $39 for Individual Home Use Only. Add $7 for shipping and handling. Free Previews are available for institutional purchasers. All sales are final. To Order: Call Media Education Foundation at 1 (800) 897-0089 or e-mail mediaed@mediaed.org. For more information and study guide go to <www.mediaed.org>.

With Other Educators

• Notify PEP about educational conferences that you did or will attend. Give contact information about PEP to the conference coordinator and suggest that they have a workshop or exhibit table on Partnership Education at the conference next year.

• Organize a Partnership Education workshop in your region for teachers and other educators from many different schools. PEP can arrange for presenters.

• Learn how to be a presenter of a Partnership Education workshop. Watch the website and newsletters for announcements of professional development opportunities for facilitators.

To Participate in the PEP Community

A broad network of individuals interested in Partnership Education is being developed which includes educators, parents, administrators, school board members, educational consultants, and students. The Partnership Education Program works within a partnership model itself. We recognize the potential of each person in this community to make contributions to Partnership Education, and one of our goals is to create avenues such as the website, the newsletter, and PEP gatherings, where these contributions can be seen and encouraged.

Here are guidelines we advocate.

At workshops, trainings, and meetings of Partnership Educators:

We respect each person's discoveries of how to develop partnership.

We function within democratic processes.

We use clear leadership structures and share leadership.

We grow in our expertise in using nonviolent communication with each other.

We grow in our ability to be anti-racist, anti-sexist, and anti-bias in our teaching and in our lives.

We discover and define partnership together.

— Sarah Pirtle and Dierdre Bucciarelli

We welcome you into this network.

Self-Assessment Tools

Here are three different methods of assessing your school with respect to Partnership Education. In keeping with the basic tenets of partnership, we recognize that each school will want to ascertain which type of tool will be most effective for their school environment. The methods that follow can be used in a variety of settings: During staff meetings, for staff development days, by a committee, by a school board, or for individual reflection by teachers.

Method One: Discussion of Partnership Goals

Create a handout with the following information and invite participants to respond.[24] Ask for discussion on these points: Are these your goals for your classroom/school?

This is the vision of Partnership Education described in Riane Eisler's book, *Tomorrow's Children*. Education has three main goals:

1. To help children grow into healthy, caring, competent, self-realized adults.

2. To help them develop the knowledge and skills that will see them through this time of environmental, economic, and social upheavals.

3. To equip young people to create for themselves a sustainable future in which human beings and our natural habitat are truly valued and chronic violence and injustice are no longer seen as "just the way things are."

For goals in which you are in agreement:

• What practical challenges would need to be confronted to move toward this goal?

• What are specific action steps that you, the staff, or community could do that address this goal?

This vision of education is grounded upon the belief that people learn and live best when they come together as partners. The vision is also centered on the belief that teachers can confront the practical challenges inherent in educational change.

Method Two: Self Assessment Survey

Items in this survey are adapted from the analysis and recommendations in the book *Tomorrow's Children: A Blueprint for Partnership Education in the 21st Century* by Riane Eisler (Westview Press, 2000). All references and quotations noted below are from this book.

Purpose of the Survey

The purpose of the **Partnership Education Self-Assessment Survey (PE-SAS)** is to provide teachers, other educators, and interested individuals with a tool that they can use to assess the level or extent of Partnership Education that currently exists in their schools, academic departments, classes or grade levels. We recognize that no school will exemplify the partnership ideal perfectly. This is simply a way to identify areas of your program where you are already practicing elements of Partnership Education, as well as areas in which you hope to strengthen your application of partnership principles.

Who Can Use this Survey

Anyone interested in creating a more partnership-oriented school can use this survey. It can be used by individual teachers, parents, administrators, as well as, students and parents to evaluate the level of Partnership Education in their individual classes or schools. It can also be used by groups of such individuals working together. Finally, it can be used in collaboration with others in a community or town as an instrument to assess the overall level of Partnership Education in a school district as a whole.

How To Use the Survey

Conduct an informal survey or field study of your school as you look through the lens of the Partnership framework, elaborated below. Use the rating system to determine to what extent your school uses Partnership processes, content, and structures. Discuss results and how to encourage improvements.

Rating System

1   Always   2   Frequently   3   Sometimes   4   Rarely   5   Never

Informal Scoring

As you reflect upon your answers, notice whether your scores are primarily in the 1-3 range, 2-4 range, or 4-5 range. Do particular areas — instruction, curriculum, or school environment — have similar scores? Method Three suggests an alternative way of working with the questions to set up a conversation about "how" or "when" the various areas are met.

More Comprehensive Assessment:

Circle numbers. Add up for each section as indicated. Divide by the number of questions to obtain an average score for each section. This will provide a more formal result for circulation among assessment group participants, as well as, presentation to administrators, et cetera. It also provides a way of comparing and discussing possibly differing levels for process, content, and structure.

Survey Questions

Survey questions are categorized according to the three core Partnership Education elements that were presented in the Introduction to this book.

For a more thorough understanding of these elements, see *Tomorrow's Children: A Blueprint for Partnership Education in the 21st Century* by Riane Eisler. You may also want to refer to *The Chalice and the Blade: Our History, Our Future* by Riane Eisler, the book that the core ideas in *Tomorrow's Children* derive from.

Partnership Education
Self-Assessment Survey
by Dierdre Bucciarelli

Please use the following Rating Scale for all questions:

    1   Always   2 Frequently   3 Sometimes   4 Rarely   5 Never

Partnership Process (Instruction)

1. Do students have the opportunity to play an active role in contributing to the design of at least some aspects or some sections of the curriculum?

    1   Always   2 Frequently   3 Sometimes   4 Rarely   5 Never

2. Do students have the opportunity to work cooperatively on joint projects?

    1   Always   2 Frequently   3 Sometimes   4 Rarely   5 Never

3. Do students actively engage in all phases of their learning?

    1   Always   2 Frequently   3 Sometimes   4 Rarely   5 Never

4. Do students share their interests, skills, and ideas with other students?

    1   Always   2 Frequently   3 Sometimes   4 Rarely   5 Never

5. Do students help each other learn through peer mentoring processes, cooperative learning groups or other appropriate strategies?

    1   Always   2 Frequently   3 Sometimes   4 Rarely   5 Never

6. Do students have opportunities to acquire the skills and self-confidence they need to become competent human beings and life-long learners?

    1   Always   2 Frequently   3 Sometimes   4 Rarely   5 Never

7. Do teachers work as mentors and facilitators alongside the students?

    1   Always   2 Frequently   3 Sometimes   4 Rarely   5 Never

8. Do teachers enthusiastically share their knowledge with students and invite them to become learning partners along with them?

    1   Always   2 Frequently   3 Sometimes   4 Rarely   5 Never

9. Do teachers motivate students by connecting with their interests, experience, and knowledge?

    1   Always   2   Frequently   3   Sometimes   4   Rarely   5   Never

10. Do teachers nourish and value the unique learning styles, multiple intelligences, and cultures of each child?

    1   Always   2   Frequently   3   Sometimes   4   Rarely   5   Never

11. Do teachers encourage and help students explore topics and domains that excite them - even if in previous classes they were seen as not capable of such exploration?

    1   Always   2   Frequently   3   Sometimes   4   Rarely   5   Never

12. Do teachers allow students to work on self-directed projects which help support them in their quest for learning?

    1   Always   2   Frequently   3   Sometimes   4   Rarely   5   Never

13. Do teachers help the class to democratically develop joint purposes and common interests that will engage all learners?

    1   Always   2   Frequently   3   Sometimes   4   Rarely   5   Never

14. Do teachers support students' efforts and development in diverse domains of human growth?

    1   Always   2   Frequently   3   Sometimes   4   Rarely   5   Never

15. Do teachers work together with their colleagues modeling partnership processes through co-teaching and team-teaching?

    1   Always   2   Frequently   3   Sometimes   4   Rarely   5   Never

---

Total All Points: _____ Divide by 15 to Determine Average: _____

Circle the Result Below to Record

1   Always   2   Frequently   3   Sometimes   4   Rarely   5   Never

Partnership Content (Curriculum)

16. Do teachers take students' purposes or reasons for learning a particular subject matter into account when planning the curriculum?

    1   Always   2   Frequently   3   Sometimes   4   Rarely   5   Never

17. Do teachers use students' interests as the starting point for the design of the curriculum?

    1   Always   2   Frequently   3   Sometimes   4   Rarely   5   Never

18. Do teachers value the knowledge that students bring to school by integrating it into the curriculum?

    1   Always   2   Frequently   3   Sometimes   4   Rarely   5   Never

19. Do teachers help students make connections between school knowledge and their real lives?

    1   Always   2   Frequently   3   Sometimes   4   Rarely   5   Never

20. Do teachers use the partnership-dominator continuum (See pp. 4-13) as an analytic lens to help students learn to recognize these configurations both in school and in their everyday lives?

    1   Always   2   Frequently   3   Sometimes   4   Rarely   5   Never

21. Do students learn the value and feasibility of creating a partnership way of life?

    1   Always   2   Frequently   3   Sometimes   4   Rarely   5   Never

22. Do students learn about the interconnectedness of all forms of life and the importance of creating and maintaining a sustainable environment?

    1   Always   2   Frequently   3   Sometimes   4   Rarely   5   Never

23. Do students learn how to care for the natural world?

    1   Always   2   Frequently   3   Sometimes   4   Rarely   5   Never

24. Do students have opportunities to engage in caring practices that promote caring for other human beings and for the natural world?

    1   Always   2   Frequently   3   Sometimes   4   Rarely   5   Never

25. Is the curriculum in all curricular areas solidly anchored in partnership values, content, and images?

    1 Always 2 Frequently 3 Sometimes 4 Rarely 5 Never

26. Is the entire school curriculum informed by gender-balance and multiculturalism?

    1 Always 2 Frequently 3 Sometimes 4 Rarely 5 Never

27. Does the curriculum allow students to connect to the community by examining local issues and problems through a partnership lens?

    1 Always 2 Frequently 3 Sometimes 4 Rarely 5 Never

28. Are the views, experiences, and knowledge of different cultural and ethnic groups a core part of the curriculum?

    1 Always 2 Frequently 3 Sometimes 4 Rarely 5 Never

29. Are the views, experiences, and knowledge of both the female and male halves of humanity a core part of the curriculum?

    1 Always 2 Frequently 3 Sometimes 4 Rarely 5 Never

30. Does the curriculum highlight the contributions of peaceful societies and call attention to advances in aesthetics and partnership ways of relating rather than commending male violence and focusing on conquest, war, and technical advances?

    1 Always 2 Frequently 3 Sometimes 4 Rarely 5 Never

31. Is the curriculum organized in a way that takes advantage of interdisciplinary issues and thematic content?

    1 Always 2 Frequently 3 Sometimes 4 Rarely 5 Never

Total All Points: _____ Divide by 16 to Determine Average: _____

Circle the Result Below to Record

1 Always 2 Frequently 3 Sometimes 4 Rarely 5 Never

Partnership Structure (School Environment)

32. Do teachers have the time to get to know and understand students as people with diverse and unique needs and purposes?

    1   Always   2   Frequently   3   Sometimes   4   Rarely   5   Never

33. Do teachers care for all their students and do they express their care in a way that the students would recognize?

    1   Always   2   Frequently   3   Sometimes   4   Rarely   5   Never

34. Do teachers have the resources they need to support the overall development of all students?

    1   Always   2   Frequently   3   Sometimes   4   Rarely   5   Never

35. If students discover dominator patterns in their schools or local communities, are they provided with the tools and support they need to take action to bring about positive change?

    1   Always   2   Frequently   3   Sometimes   4   Rarely   5   Never

36. Do students have the responsibility for determining at least some of the school rules and for making sure that they are promoted?

    1   Always   2   Frequently   3   Sometimes   4   Rarely   5   Never

37. Does the school function as a learning community where all adults and students in the school regularly learn from each other and share their enthusiasm for learning?

    1   Always   2   Frequently   3   Sometimes   4   Rarely   5   Never

38. Do school structures enable teachers, administrators, and other staff to model caring behavior and attitudes towards students?

    1   Always   2   Frequently   3   Sometimes   4   Rarely   5   Never

39. Is the environment or culture of the school generally democratic?

    1   Always   2   Frequently   3   Sometimes   4   Rarely   5   Never

40. Are decisions made in a partnership way?

    1   Always   2   Frequently   3   Sometimes   4   Rarely   5   Never

41. Is community action modeled for students by teachers, administrators, and other school staff?

    1   Always   2   Frequently   3   Sometimes   4   Rarely   5   Never

42. Is the school environment one where students learn to appreciate and celebrate each other's differences and unique gifts on a regular basis?

    1 Always 2 Frequently 3 Sometimes 4 Rarely 5 Never

43. Are the voices of all parties in the educational community represented in educational and policy decisions through interactive discussions?

    1 Always 2 Frequently 3 Sometimes 4 Rarely 5 Never

44. Is the school organized so that it takes advantage of the knowledge and skills of all its members?

    1 Always 2 Frequently 3 Sometimes 4 Rarely 5 Never

45. Do school structures solicit and encourage active involvement and participation of parents and community members in the life of the school?

    1 Always 2 Frequently 3 Sometimes 4 Rarely 5 Never

46. Are community resources available to support teachers and parents in helping children develop and learn to lead meaningful lives?

    1 Always 2 Frequently 3 Sometimes 4 Rarely 5 Never

47. Is the school organized so that accountability flows in two directions (i.e., does accountability flow not only from the bottom-up but also from the top-down)?

    1 Always 2 Frequently 3 Sometimes 4 Rarely 5 Never

48. Is there a professionally-recognized high teacher to student ratio and small class sizes?

    1 Always 2 Frequently 3 Sometimes 4 Rarely 5 Never

49. When conflict arises, are constructive methods used that allow all parties (whether students, staff or parents) to express feelings, listen to one another, brainstorm solutions, and choose a plan together that addresses the issue or problem?

    1 Always 2 Frequently 3 Sometimes 4 Rarely 5 Never

Total All Points: _____ Divide by 18 to Determine Average: _____

Circle the Result Below to Record

1 Always 2 Frequently 3 Sometimes 4 Rarely 5 Never

Summary Of Current Averages For

_____
(name of school)

_____
(class, grade level, etc.)

Partnership Process Score   =   _____

Partnership Content Score   =   _____

Partnership Structure Score   =   _____

Method Three:
Using Assessment Questions for Dialogue

Take the questions listed in the "Self Assessment Survey" above, but work with them in a different manner.

Select questions and reframe to say "how do" or "when do" rather than "do." For instance, "How do teachers use students' interests as the starting point for the design of the curriculum?" and "When do teachers work together with their colleagues modeling partnership processes through co-teaching and team-teaching?"

Other Variations:

- Ask teachers to pick one question that represents a key area where they would like to grow in their own teaching. Meet in small groups of two or three. Each speaker takes a turn thinking out loud about this issue and formulating one concrete next step (not too large) that would promote development in this area.

- Look as a staff at school-wide change. Each teacher works alone first to identify three questions that represent for them the most important areas of growth for the year. Lists are put together. The three questions that are noted the most then become the topics for discussion. Before examining them as a whole staff, first divide into three groups, with each person picking the topic most germane for them. Small groups discuss, and make recommendations, and then bring these suggestions to the whole staff as they reconvene.

APPENDIX B

Glossary of Partnership Terms[25]

BCE	Before Common Era (used in lieu of BC)
Androcentric	Treating male experience and perceptions as the norm while ignoring or trivializing female experience
CE	Common Era (used in lieu of AD)
Centers of Care	Where a person focuses or expresses one's care, or how a person extends one's caring. The term comes from Nel Noddings who delineates that care can be focused upon "care for self, for intimate others, for associates and acquaintances, for distant others, for animals, for plants, and the physical environment, for objects and instruments, and for ideas." Noddings writes that "today the curriculum is organized almost entirely around the last center, ideas," TC p. 18.
Competencies of Caring	Nel Noddings develops this term in her book, *The Challenge to Care in Schools* (New York: Teachers College Press, 1992), TC p. 29.
Counterfeit Culture	A culture where what is portrayed as having worth does not provide fundamental nourishment and support, TC p. 6.
Cultivation of Conation	Development of the will to act, TC p.14; conative learning — education that cultivates our capacity to act, TC p. 136, 142-143.
Dimensions of Diversity	Indicates that every aspect of difference is important and needs to be recognized (heritage, learning styles, economic class, and spiritual or religious beliefs, are some examples of the more than 50 different dimensions that could be identified)
Empathic Cooperation	Working together for a common purpose with mutual regard, TC p. 12.

Gylanic	A term describing linking that was created by Eisler to indicate that "the female and male halves of humanity are linked rather than ranked" based upon "gyne(woman) and andros (man) linked by the letter l for lyen (to resolve) or lyo (to set free)", TC p. 302.
Gylany	The resolution of our problems through the freeing of both halves of humanity from the stultifying and distorting rigidity of roles imposed by the domination hierarchies inherent in androcratic ("man ruled") systems.
Hierarchies of Actualization	A structure based on "power to (creative power, the power to help, and to nurture others) as well as power with (the collective power to accomplish things together)" rather than power over. Such a structure is characterized by accountability flowing in both directions, TC p. 21, 91, 313.
Nurturesphere	The realm of caring and nurturing, a term coined by Bruce Novak to express that we are primarily caring, teaching, nurturant beings. "Nurturesphere" is related to theologian Teilhard de Chardin's term, "noos-sphere," but extends de Chardin's perception.
Other-Regarding	Actions of mutual aid, mutual respect and cooperation, a term used by Nel Noddings, TC Foreword, p. x.
Partnership Intelligence	Skill and capacity for partnership, potential for expressing partnership awareness; a term from Rob Koegel ("Healing the Wounds of Masculinity: A Crucial Role for Educators," *Holistic Education Review* 7: 42-49), TC p. 14.
Pattern Recognition Skills	Critical faculties for discerning patterns, as applied to patterns of domination and partnership, TC p. 33.
Spiritual Courage	Putting love into action, even when it means going against established dominator norms. Eisler, TC p. 82.

Endnotes

Chapter One

1. Founded by teachers in 1981, the Northeast Foundation for Children fosters safe, challenging and joyful classrooms and schools for Kindergarten through 8th Grades. NEFC does this by promoting and developing the principles and practices of *The Responsive Classroom* approach to learning and teaching. For more information, call (800) 360-6332 or visit www.responsiveclassroom.org

2. Dishon, Dee, and Wilson O'Leary, Pat. *A Guidebook for Cooperative Learning.* Holmes Beach, Florida: Learning Publication, Inc. 1984. (p. 4-5)

3. Pirtle, Sarah, "Poost Siegda/ May There Always Be Sunshine." recorded on *Two Hands Hold the Earth.* A Gentle Wind, 1984.

4. Forest, Liana, and Graves, Ted. The first four elements from "Basic Elements of Cooperative Learning." *What is Cooperative Learning?* Cooperative College of California, 1987. The fifth element was added by Dishon and O'Leary.

5. Pirtle, Sarah. *Discovery Time for Cooperation and Conflict Resolution.* Nyack, NY: Children's Creative Response to Conflict. 1998.

6. Graves, Nan, and Graves, Ted. *Creating a Cooperative Learning Environment,* Cooperative College of California, 1988, (p. 410).

7. Sapon-Shevin, Mara, and Schniedewind, Nancy. "If Cooperative Learning's the Answer, What are the Questions?" Unpublished article, (pp. 26-27).

8. Einstein's words appear in a letter to a friend, as quoted in *America Without Violence* by Michael Nagler Covelo, CA: Island Press, 1982. (p. 11).

Chapter Three

9. This approach to education grew out of my experiences teaching college and university classes in Toronto. From those experiments in the classroom, I came to develop Partnership Learning, a collection of approaches to teaching that are now used in a variety of settings, mostly to teach adults in college, university or professional development situations. For more information on Partnership Learning or Teacher-Guided Professional Development research, contact Jim Knight, The University of Kansas Center for Research on Learning, 1122 West Campus Road, Lawrence KS 66049 (e-mail jknight@ku.edu).

Chapter Nine

10. Here is a resource for graduate study which teaches a partnership approach to the expressive arts. The Creative Arts in Learning Division of Lesley University offers four Masters of Education programs. One of these, the Curriculum and Instruction Program with a specialization in Creative Arts in Learning, is offered through more than 38 off-campus sites. Hands on experiences with the creative principles involved in music, poetry, storytelling, movement, the visual arts, and drama open up methods of using the expressive arts in any classroom. Contact: Creative Arts in Learning, Lesley University, 29 Everett St, Cambridge, MA 02138. Website: www.lesley.edu.

11. For more insights on creating safety for group singing, see Chapter Two by Mara Sapon-Shevin, "Building a Safe Community for Learning." Her newest book is *Because We Can Change the World: A Practical Guide to Building Cooperative, Inclusive Classroom Communities*, by Mara Sapon-Shevin (Allyn & Bacon, 1999). This remarkable resource combines theory and practice, using clear anecdotes to show how a classroom becomes a strong community. Forty-two songs are included that illustrate the contribution of music.

Chapter Ten

12. For extensive information on studying the sky, get "For Spacious Skies," a program featured in *Time Magazine* for its inspirational impact. A video and an activity guide by C. Whitney Ward and Jack Borden are available from For Spacious Skies, P.O. Box 191, Lexington, MA 02173. Jack Borden believes that one way to help students come home to themselves and locate themselves in the world is to help them relate to the sky.

13. Dawn Publications, who published Atkins book, *Girls Who Looked Under Rocks*, has a whole line of books dedicated to inspiring in children a deeper understanding and appreciation for all life on earth. Dawn Publications can be contacted on the website ww.dawnpub.com or by calling 1-800-545-7475. They also publish the classic nature awareness guidebook, *Sharing Nature with Children* by Joseph Cornell.

14. Eagle Eye Institute in Somerville, Massachusetts, provides opportunities for urban youth to learn about the environment. Founded by Anthony Sanchez, Eagle Eye is a pioneer in providing hands-on exploratory learning on the environment and career bridging to natural resource fields for urban people with an emphasis on underserved youth. Contact www.eagleeyeinstitute.org/ or eeaglei@aol.com. Their programs include Rainbow Stewards which educates youth about the value of urban trees while conducting a city tree survey, as well as Learn About Water and Learn About Agriculture.

Chapter Eleven

15. *The Language of the Goddess* by Marija Gimbutas, HarperCollins, 1991.

Lady of the Beasts: Ancient Images of the Goddess and Her Sacred Animals, by Buffie Johnson, Harper, San Francisco, 1988.

The Woman's Encyclopedia of Myths and Secrets by Barbara Walker, Harper, San Francisco, 1983.16

16. Honors Readings:

Riane Eisler, *Sacred Pleasure: Sex, Myth, and the Politics of the Body*, San Francisco: Harper Collins, 1996; Demaris Wehr, *Jung and Feminism*, Boston: Beacon, 1987.

Robert Johnson. *He: Understanding Male Psychology*, Harper & Row Publishers: New York. 1977.

Emma Jung and Marie-Louise von Franz. *The Grail Legend*. Sigo Press: Boston.1986.

Richard Wagner's opera *Parsifal*

Demaris Wehr, *Jung and Feminism*, Boston: Beacon, 1987

17. These activities were created by Sarah Pirtle

Chapter Twelve

18. To learn more about my complete curriculum design for a semester-length (15 week) graduate course, you can e-mail me directly or contact me through the Center for Partnership Studies. This curriculum, *Speaking Our Peace: Communicating Partnership in Deed and Word — A Curriculum for Teacher Education* uses original stories, music, and ritual along with interactive, experiential pedagogy to model collaborative structure and process and encourage learners to integrate its content with their personal and professional lives. It includes a contextual essay describing the larger field of gylanic (partnership) studies as well as elements of partnership-oriented pedagogy and communication, both verbal and non-verbal.

19. Sarah Pirtle contributed to this activity and to design of the activities in this chapter.

Chapter Thirteen

20. Order from Catharine Haver, 34 Bay Road, Belchertown, MA 01007.

Chapter Fourteen

21. This article was written using a partnership format. Nova staff Elaine Packard, Dave Ketter, and Bobbi Morrison gave extensive phone interviews and actively revised text while Sarah Pirtle coordinated and provided an outsider's perspective and appreciation.

22. Michael Wiater, David Taylor, and Mark Kabush were also essential to this transformation. Many students provided important ideas including Martha Magraw who contributed insights from her experiences as a Quaker.

Closing

23. Sarah Pirtle, Dierdre Bucciarelli, Maureen Cain, Riane Eisler, Del Jones, and Carol Massanari contributed to this chapter.

Appendix

24. Partnership Goals by Jim Knight, the University of Kansas Center for Research on Learning.

25. The page numbers indicate where the term is used in *Tomorrow's Children* (TC).